ADOLESCENT SPIRITUALITY

ADOLESCENT SPIRITUALITY

*Pastoral Ministry
for High School
and College Youth*

Charles M. Shelton

CROSSROAD · NEW YORK

1989

The Crossroad Publishing Company
370 Lexington Avenue, New York, N.Y. 10017

Copyright © 1983 Charles M. Shelton, S.J.

Printed in the United States of America

Library of Congress Cataloging-in-Publication Data

Shelton, Charles M.
    Adolescent spirituality : pastoral ministry for high school and
college youth / Charles M. Shelton.
        p.   cm.
    Reprint. Originally published : Chicago : Loyola University Press,
c 1983.
    Bibliography: p.
    Includes index.
    ISBN 0-8245-0917-X
    1. Youth—Religious life.   2. Church work with youth.   3. Church
work with youth—Catholic Church.   4. Catholic Church—Clergy.
I. Title.
BV4531.2.S53   1989
253.5'088055—dc19   88-31685
                                                            CIP

Contents

Preface

One of the most exciting happenings in the church today is the ministry to high school and college youth. Over the past seven years, through the ministries of teaching and counseling, I have been fortunate to have had contact with numerous adolescents at both the secondary-school level and the college-undergraduate level. The adolescents I have come to know through these ministries have challenged me to examine and reflect upon my own questions, attitudes, and beliefs concerning the meaning of faith in my own life. They have motivated me to attempt to understand, in a stark way, what Jesus invites us to do in his invitation to "come, follow me" (Mk 10:21).

In reflecting on Jesus' call, I have come to realize that the acceptance of Jesus' invitation requires two things. The first is the capacity and willingness to give myself to this call in a total way. This means that I must allow Jesus' call to touch the cognitive, emotional, moral, and faith dimensions of my life. The second requirement, I have realized, arises out of my own need to understand this call's beckoning as I have experienced it in my own life situation.

When we are ministering to adolescents, both of these points are crucial. As young people attempt to answer the call of Jesus, they are highly influenced by both personal, developmental issues and their own individual life situations. These two perspectives highlight in a bold way the Catholic theological principle that grace builds on nature. When we consider the adolescent's "nature," we must be particularly sensitive to both the young person's developmental self and his or her particular life situation. Thus, the main thesis of this book is that the adolescent's response to Jesus' call is inextricably tied to the beckoning of grace as it is experienced at his or her own developmental level and in the context of his or her own life experience. Especially during adolescence, developmental issues must be examined in order to make Jesus' call a clear and conscious reality. The adult's presence in the adolescent's life can exercise a pivotal role in helping the adolescent to respond to Jesus' invitation to "come, follow me."

In my own pastoral work I have been struck by the important need for materials that would offer insights, understanding, and practical suggestions to foster or enhance the spiritual growth of adolescents. During my search for such material, I often discovered books on spirituality and spiritual growth, but I found little mention of the adolescent experience. Although numerous books on the adolescent's psychological growth were available, little was done to link this development to spirituality. Whenever I did manage to discover such books, I would find that these books lacked the insights and strategies so necessary for ministering to today's youth in their high school and college years.

It is with a view to this pastoral need that I have written this book. It is not meant to be a theological work, although it incorporates the wisdom of theological writing—especially recent thinking in spirituality, moral theology, and pastoral theology. At the same time, this book is not meant to be an examination of developmental psychology, although it incorporates a developmental perspective of adolescence. Finally, it is not a counseling handbook, although it does provide the adult with suggestions, observations, and techniques that are intended to facilitate the adolescent's fuller, richer response to Jesus' call.

It is a *pastoral* book, above all. It is written for adults who relate to adolescents in various roles, whether as teachers, religious, administrators, student personnel, campus ministers, youth ministers, or counselors; indeed, this book is meant for all adults who are concerned with the spiritual life of youth today. In writing this book I have been sympathetic to the words of theologian Monica Hellwig, who has said: "Anything in theology that does not authentically serve the pastoral needs of ordinary priests and ordinary believers is as trivial and dishonest as the money changers in the temple." This book is an attempt to speak to both the adolescent who is experiencing this ordinariness, as well as the adult who is attempting to aid the adolescent in answering Jesus' call.

In writing a pastoral theology for adolescents, I have emphasized three perspectives. First, I have borrowed from the thought and insights of the sixteenth-century Jesuit saint, Ignatius of Loyola. Through a profound book known as the *Spiritual Exercises*, this remarkable man has greatly influenced the lives of countless men and women. Through the experience of his *Exercises*, we are drawn closer to the consoling presence of Our Lord's love and grace, and we find within this experience the strength to respond more openly to him in the context of everyday decisions and actions. In aiding the spiritual journey towards God, Ignatius popularized methods of prayer, discernment, and the "examen." When they seem helpful, these insights are described and utilized in developing a pastoral theology for adolescents.

The second source I have incorporated is the developmental perspective of psychology. The contributions of such theorists as Jean Piaget and Erik Erikson have recently been joined by the developmental perspectives of Lawrence Kohlberg and James Fowler. In the pages that follow, I have paid close attention to the insights of these developmental thinkers.

The third aspect of this book is the practical nature and pastoral emphasis that I have attempted to stress for a pastoral ministry to youth. I hope that the many practical suggestions I have offered in the following pages will stimulate the reader to develop other strategies and techniques for youth ministry.

In writing this book, I fast became aware of the many realities that touch the lives of today's youth. No doubt, some readers might criticize my work for not dealing in detail with such adolescent issues as parental divorce, drug and alcohol abuse, or problems of "select" groups of adolescents, such as runaways, cult followers, emotionally disturbed teens, and so forth. It is not my intent to slight such audiences, but all books must have limits, and this one is no exception. I believe that many of the approaches and techniques presented herein can profitably be used with such troubled adolescents. And, most certainly, any adults who are interested in these adolescent issues should use the many notes to each chapter for further study while, at the same time, using the book itself as a base line for ministering to adolescents.

What is more, in the process of writing this book, I also came to understand how indebted I am to others for their advice and support.

First, I would like to thank Dr. Harry Hoewischer, S.J., and Dr. Martha Ashmore, members of the psychology department at Regis College, Denver, Colorado. Their insightful comments and helpful observations did much to clarify the issues and concerns I have addressed in the following pages. In addition, I would like to thank the following for their help, encouragement, and support during the past three years: Frank Adams, S.J., Pat Arnold, S.J., Mike Barber, S.J., Francis Baur, O.F.M., Jack Boyle, S.J., Joe Brown, S.J., Mike Buckley, S.J., Daryl Cornish, S.J., John Costello, S.J., Bob Dailey, S.J., Pat Earl, S.J., Mike Engh, S.J., Toinette Eugene, P.B.V.M., John Fava, S.J., Anthony Forte, S.J., Helen Garvey, S.N.J.M., Don Gelpi, S.J., Joe Gibino, S.J., John Golenski, S.J., Ken Gregorio, S.J., Jim Harbaugh, S.J., Barbara Hazard, S.N.J.M., Frank Houdek, S.J., John Keating, S.J., Pete Klink, S.J., Dan McGann, Pat Madigan, S.J., Mike Mahon, S.J., Annmarie Mitchell, Phil Nemec, Kenan Osborne, O.F.M., Steve Potter, John Ridgway, S.J., Tom Rochford, S.J., Steve Ryan, S.J., Phil Schmitz, S.J., Steve Seaman, S.J., Mike Sheeran, S.J., Dennis Simms, S.J., Andy Sotelo, S.J., Bill Spohn, S.J., Phil Steele, S.J., Tom Steele, S.J., Bill Udick, S.J., Bill Verbryke, S.J., Don Vettese, S.J., and Terry Walsh, S.J.

I also wish to thank my brother Jesuits at both the Regis Jesuit Community (Regis Jesuit High School and Regis College, Denver, Colorado) and the Jesuit Community at the Jesuit School of Theology, Berkeley, California. Their encouragement and support is something I simply could not have done without.

Finally, and in a special way, I wish to thank all the young people who have been part of my life during these past few years. Not only have they been my students, but, in many ways, they have been some of my best teachers. It is to them that I dedicate this book in the hope that their lives and the lives of all young people might be a living witness to the God who loves us so.

Charles M. Shelton, S.J.
May, 1983

CHAPTER ONE

Adolescents and
Their Spirituality
An Overview

There is an appointed time for everything,
and a time for every affair under the heavens:
A time to be born, and a time to die;
a time to plant, and a time to uproot a plant.

Ecclesiastes 3:1–2

Every stage of human development—childhood, adolescence, adulthood—is an "appointed time," and each life stage is a "time" when developmental issues influence our response to the invitation of Jesus to "come, follow me" (Mk 10:21).

The "appointed time," which is currently under increasing scrutiny and stress, is the stage of adolescence. The writer of Ecclesiastes says that God "has made everything appropriate to its time" (Eccl 3:11). Adolescence reflects this view, inasmuch as during this developmental period youth seek to question, understand, and confirm the deepening search for ultimate meaning. Through the adolescent passage, youth come to discover what following the call of Jesus really means for their own lives, and it is through this growing self-discovery that the adolescent builds a foundation for future Christian adulthood.

Adolescence: A Definition

When discussing a spirituality for adolescents, it is helpful to begin with what we do and do not know about this period of human development. One important finding is that there is actually a great lack of knowledge regarding the adolescent experience. Not only in the area of spirituality, but also in the area of psychological research dealing with adolescence, there is more that we do not know than there is that we do know about this perplexing age group. Most studies on youth focus on selected groups, such as college students or disturbed adolescents. Only recently have researchers undertaken

1

more intensive, longitudinal studies that, over time, measure growth through the high school and college years. Thus, one researcher notes: "In addition to being sketchy, our knowledge of adolescence remains confusing and controversial."[1] This lack of knowledge is especially noticeable with regard to youth's religious experience, because "we know nothing, essentially, about normal religious experience in the young."[2]

It is also important to examine what the term "adolescence" actually means. A definition of adolescence might concentrate on chronological age, intellectual development, social behavior, or physiological growth. To include all these facets of human development, the American Psychiatric Association's *Psychiatric Glossary* defines this period as follows: Adolescence is "a chronological period beginning with the physical and emotional processes leading to sexual and psychosocial maturity and ending at an ill-defined time when the individual achieves independence and social productivity. The period is associated with rapid physical, psychological, and social changes."[3] This definition enjoys several advantages, inasmuch as it situates adolescence in a time frame and also emphasizes the emotional, social, and physiological changes that are taking place during these developing years.

In addition, this definition allows us to incorporate in our discussion not only the freshman in secondary school, but also the senior in college, inasmuch as both are on the path to "maturity." Behaviorally, this definition is appropriate because this developmental stage is marked by great variety and disparity in behaviors. Given the appropriate situation, a high school sophomore, for example, might at times show more maturity than a college undergraduate. Furthermore, this definition awakens us to the fact that adolescence is not an insignificant amount of time in the lives of persons in our society. Often this developmental period can exist for ten years or more. In this book, then, "adolescence" refers to a developmental period that begins with puberty and stretches through the secondary and undergraduate college years.

Because this definition incorporates a prolonged developmental period, it is helpful to place adolescent experiences in a developmental perspective. Many health professionals, such as Harvard psychiatrist Armand Nicholi, speak of various "stages" in the adolescent years.[4] Nicholi has determined that adolescence consists of

2

three stages. The first stage, called "early adolescence," is most commonly identified with puberty. During this early stage, adolescents are preoccupied with their physical selves. On an intellectual level, adolescents in this stage are developing the capacity for reflection, critical thinking, and creative thought. They begin to think more abstractly, and "questions of meaning and destiny may cause him [or her] to think seriously about philosophical and religious issues."[5] During this stage of development, the adolescent is subject to erratic emotional expressions. At the same time, personal relationships take on more significance, becoming buffers against anxiety and helping to create a supportive network for sharing fears and doubts.

The second stage, known as "middle adolescence," is generally viewed as the years from age 15 to 18. This stage is most usually associated with the secondary school years. During this middle stage, the adolescent experiences a deepening understanding of a sexual self. At the same time, the adolescent struggles with parental separation in order to achieve personal identity. This critical juncture sometimes creates lonely, confusing, if not isolating experiences for youth. The adolescent assuages these emotional states through deeper, more involved relationships with peers, identification with various causes, and infatuation or deeper relationships with friends, members of the opposite sex, and adults. Adolescents now look outward, seeking emotional involvement in relationships with significant others.

In the final stage, or "late adolescence," youth are preoccupied with college choices, undergraduate studies, career decisions, and marriage. Adolescent concerns are increasingly focused on roles and duties that prepare them for entrance into the adult world. It is at this stage that issues of identity and intimacy are often acute for the adolescent.

In his study of male development, psychologist Daniel Levinson speaks of late adolescence as "Early Adult Transition." Late adolescents encounter two tasks as they venture into the adult world: they experience the need to terminate adolescence and the need to accept the tasks of young adulthood.[6] For the former task, the adolescent needs to separate, alter, or terminate existing relationships, while attempting to redefine the self. For the latter task, on the other hand, the adolescent undertakes exploratory, tentative commitments to the adult world. In the following pages, we will usually concentrate on the middle and late adolescent stages, because these are the stages most associated with the secondary school and undergraduate college years.

During the past two decades, the behaviors and lifestyles of youth have spawned a variety of stereotypic impressions, which have proven unfounded upon closer examination. A common theme in popular literature, for example, portrays the adolescent as confused, troubled, and frustrated. Although this theme of turbulence is popular, when we examine the research we find that this commonplace assumption is questionable. No one denies that youth undergo various degrees of stress, or that some adolescents are severely impaired in their ability to cope with their environment. Nonetheless, most adolescents are capable of adequate adjustment to the stresses of this developmental period.

Psychologist John Conger, a leading authority on adolescence, says: "It appears that the stresses adolescence imposes on the individual, particularly in our culture, do not, for the great majority, lead to the high degree of emotional turmoil, violent mood swings, and threatened loss of control suggested by some clinical theorists."[7] Psychologist Joseph Adelson concurs with Conger's assessment, noting that "adolescents, as a whole, are *not* in turmoil, *not* deeply disturbed, *not* at the mercy of their impulses, *not* resistant to parental values, *not* politically active or rebellious."[8] Of course, there are numerous experiences of frustration, questioning, and doubt that all adolescents periodically undergo, but we can say with assurance that most youth are resilient to the stresses and strains associated with this developmental period.

This notion of adolescent resilience is important in our ministry to adolescents. Perception of the "normalcy" of the adolescent experience enlarges the adult's perspective and provides a context in which to minister to the needs of each adolescent. One need not "expect" a particular adolescent to experience great crises or constant turmoil. A much more productive pastoral viewpoint visualizes the adolescent as predisposed to numerous feelings that are, at times, *acutely felt*. With time and understanding, the vast majority of youth withstand the everyday disturbances and problems that are so much a part of this developmental period.

Adolescent Attitudes

A knowledge of adolescent attitudes and values provides a grounding for ministering to the spiritual needs of each adolescent. In a paper presented at the National Symposium on Catholic Youth Ministry in the '80s, Catholic University sociologist Dean Hoge cautioned against an uncritical acceptance of research on youth concerns. He also noted that, when compared to adult attitudes, adolescent attitudes are more "volatile" and subject to "short-run environmental influences."[9]

The need for a critical examination of youth's concerns is warranted when one considers the common misperceptions many people have of present-day adolescents. A commonly held assumption, for example, is that youth today are more traditional than their counterparts of ten years ago. There no longer exists a confrontive, radical youth. Instead, youth today have ushered in a wave of neo-conservative thinking, shedding the ideas and values of the sixties and seventies, and opting for more traditional values and standards of behavior. As noted, it was a popular (although false) assumption a decade ago that most young people were anti-institutional and wanted nothing to do with the adult world.[10] Ironically, by the late seventies, the popular assumption was exactly the opposite. With the disappearance of both campus unrest and the almost daily headlines that detailed the latest confrontations, many adults had come to view adolescents as returning to many of the values and attitudes of the late fifties and early sixties.

When we examine the evidence, however, we find that this assumption, too, remains unfounded. Although surveys do show a weakening of the confrontive, antagonistic attitudes of the late sixties and early seventies, it is unrealistic to view the adolescent of the eighties as favorably inclined to the ready-made answers or institutional securities of two decades ago. "What does appear to be happening," observes John Conger, "is the development of a more pragmatic approach to life."[11] In other words, youth now seem to have opted for something in between. Young people today have adopted some of society's expectations but they still pursue their own private goals and desires. One extended survey of college youth, for example, finds that young people value a career, but believe that a job must offer them meaning and self-fulfillment. Youth today reject violence and place great value on education. Yet, there does exist a new sexual morality among the young, a trend any adult ministering to adolescents needs to be aware of and understand.[12]

Other studies show the variable nature of adolescent interests but note youth's acceptance of commonly held values such as love, fulfillment, and friendship. A recent study of the collge graduating class of 1983 finds students rating work, marriage, family life, strong friendships, and the discovering of the purpose and meaning in life as extremely important goals. Students also appear to express a great deal of optimism about their own future lives.[13] In an annual poll of college freshmen, a study conducted jointly by UCLA and the American Council on Education finds the major objectives of freshmen include the following: becoming an authority in their field, helping others who are experiencing difficulty, being financially well off, and raising a family.[14]

Studies of adolescents' religious attitudes and practices are also revealing. Adolescents overwhelmingly express religious needs and find personal value in religious commitment. What adolescents often find difficult, however, is their relationship with the institutional church.[15]

Echoing this view, psychologist John Conger writes: "There is also some indication that today's adolescents are placing more emphasis than previous generations on personal rather than institutionalized religion. This is consistent with the greater stress among adolescents generally on personal values and relationships and on individual moral standards, with less relevance on traditional social beliefs and institutions."[16]

Hilmar Wagner nicely sums up this phenomenon when she asserts that "youth have always tended to reject institutionalized religion during adolescence."[17]

These statements are supported by surveys assessing the religious practice of adolescents. Adolescents do "distance" themselves from institutional forms of religious behavior.[18] In particular, the college years confirm the decline in religious observance among late adolescents.[19]

This disaffection can continue through the ensuing years of young adulthood. Religious researcher Bruno Manno notes that, through their twenties and early thirties, young adults might distance themselves from the church.[20] In doing this, says Manno, the young adult's life is lived out in one of "five distancing stories." In the "alienation" story, the young adult combines some level of religious association with only minimal religious practice. By definition, "un-churchedness" assumes there exists no religious affiliation and only rare church attendance (less than yearly). In the "dissatisfaction" story, young adults are religiously associated but dissatisfied with the local parish. In "disidentification," young adults leave the religious denomination; whereas in "voluntarism," they affiliate with the religious denomination but refuse to accept many church teachings.

Noted pollster George Gallup provides an insightful overview of adolescent religious behavior. In an address before the National Family Life Conference, sponsored by the Department of Education of the U.S. Catholic Conference, Gallup noted that youth are very concerned about meaning and prize human friendship. He stated that young people (1) tend to be more tolerant than their elders toward persons of different races, religions, and backgrounds; (2) continue to be remarkably service-oriented in their occupational choices, with many seeking careers in medicine, teaching, social work and other "helping" professions; and (3) are a particularly religious segment of the population. Although they tend to be "turned off" by organized religion, their levels of religious belief and practice are as high or higher than those of their elders.[21]

In one of his strongest statements, Gallup reports: "It is important to establish religious values with children before they go off to college, because we have found in surveys tht the college years have a very pronounced secularizing effect on youth. With each succeeding grade, students become less religious, at least in traditional terms. While it could certainly be argued that the college years represented a period of healthy introspection and questioning, it is important to give youth values which they can come back to in later life, if they choose to do so."[22]

Gallup urges that strong support be given to family life because of its centrality in youth's development. He also finds that two encouraging areas for ministering to adolescents' spiritual development are Bible study groups and youth retreats.[23] Both of these activities are highly popular among youth today and obviously need fostering in youth ministry programs.

7

Other research has concentrated on the difference between adolescents who practice their faith and those who do not. Compared with their peers of a decade ago, for example, adolescents who currently attend the Eucharist are more likely to attend for reasons of worship rather than because of pressure from an exterior cause, such as parental authority.[24] This finding augurs well for a deepening understanding of faith among religious-practicing youth. Finally, a large survey of practicing Catholic adolescents found that those who attend mass show a significant difference in the value they give to personal religious belief and prayer, and display less feelings of alienation than their nonchurch-going peers.[25]

Adolescent Spirituality

The essential question remaining is as follows: What is the role of spirituality for today's youth? Before addressing this question, however, it will be helpful to explore the meaning and significance of the term "spirituality." Essentially, spirituality is concerned with personal response to and growth in the Lord. Concretely, this response to God's call takes place in the context of prayer and one's efforts to proclaim the Kingdom of God through service to one's brothers and sisters. Spirituality is linked to prayer, worship, and service to the faith community. In the midst of society, every Christian is uniquely called to live out and proclaim the saving power of the life, death, and resurrection of Jesus Christ through meaningful ministerial service.[26]

Although adolescence reflects a developmental age in which there is usually a decline in traditional religious beliefs and practices, most young people do search for deeper answers and meanings for their lives. Adolescents place great importance on a relationship with God. Perhaps, as religious educator James DiGiacomo remarks, for adolescents "God may not be well but he is certainly alive."[27] Essentially, many adolescents believe their own relationship with Jesus Christ need not be tied to more traditional religious behaviors and beliefs. This stress on relationships is not limited to a personal relationship with Jesus Christ, however. Instead, today's adolescents thrive on personal relationships and the meaning that these relationships give to their own lives.

Adolescent spirituality assumes the task of addressing these important issues in the adolescent's life.[28] At the same time, adults must seek ways to encourage the adolescent's growing exploration of personal attitudes, values, and interests so that youth will be able to respond openly and totally to Jesus' call to "come, follow me."

First of all, then, we can begin our description of adolescent spirituality with Pope John Paul II's historic visit to the United States and his talks with young people. In his homily in Boston, the Pope was speaking primarily to youth, when he said: "I extend—in the name of Christ—the call, the invitation, the plea, 'Come and follow me!'"[29] In his speech to youth in Madison Square Garden, the Pope said: "When you wonder about the mystery of yourself, look to Christ who gives you the meaning of life. When you wonder what it means to be a mature person, look to Christ who is the fullness of humanity."[30]

A foundation for an adolescent spirituality emerges from the Pope's address to youth. First, there is Christ, who is the center of life. A spirituality for adolescents is, then, first and above all *Christ-centered.* It focuses on the personal, loving invitation given the adolescent to "come, follow me"—to walk the path of Jesus, while increasingly realizing what journeying with Jesus really means. At this crucial age, youth need to focus on this Christ centered relationship, inasmuch as adolescence "is a time, finally, when the call of Jesus can become personal and the demands of religion very real."[31]

A spirituality for adolescents might be viewed in a triangular fashion. Foremost in this triangle is Jesus, who invites and beckons the adolescent to follow him. Second, there is the adult, whose role to witness in a distinctive way to Jesus' grace and love is inseparable from personal strengths and weaknesses. Finally, there is the adolescent, whose life encompasses a unique set of experiences and whose search "for truth and the deepest meaning of existence"[32] is the future of our world.

A second characteristic of an adolescent spirituality is its *relational* aspect. As noted earlier, the adolescent's relationship with Christ is first. On the other hand, human relationships also enter the adolescent's experience for spiritual growth, and this growth "is concerned with ultimate meanings and values, but it is incarnated in human encounters and circumstances."[33] As survey findings indicate, the adolescent finds relationships to be of critical importance. Relationships with family, peers, teachers, and others take on new meanings, as the young person attempts to integrate these others into a growing self-identity. A goal of adolescent spirituality, then, is the examination of these relationships, so that the adolescent's personal experience of Jesus might be realized more fully in family bonds, friendship ties, and relationships with the opposite sex.

As a third aspect of his or her spirituality, the adolescent adopts certain values, ideas, and strategies for *future living.* Developmentally the adolescent grows more outward. Even though the future is by no means secure, adolescents are willing to explore and to attempt answers to life's questions. The adolescent begins to forge a mature identity that is made personally meaningful in the context of his or her current developmental level. Adolescent spirituality speaks to this present life in the context of the adolescent's future growth possibilities. In the adolescent's future plans, career goals, and deepening relationships, a spirituality for adolescents asks how these experiences encourage, in a yet-to-be future, the adolescent's response to Jesus' call.

The fourth aspect of adolescent spirituality is its sensitivity to the need for a *developmental perspective* as youth undergo diverse intellectual, physical, and emotional changes. The writings of Lawrence Kohlberg and James Fowler have recently broadened this developmental perspective to include both moral and faith dimensions. A spirituality for adolescents needs to make use of these developmental insights in order to enhance the adult's understanding of the adolescent's understanding of his or her own spiritual growth. An adolescent spirituality seeks to touch all aspects of the adolescent's life in order that the young person might realize more and more that responding to Jesus' call means laboring for God's Kingdom. Thus, as Evelyn and James Whitehead conclude: "God's grace can be discovered at work within the structure of psychosocial development."[34]

Let us now summarize what we have said about adolescents and their spirituality. Today's youth are presented with many challenges. They must grow in self-identity, deepen relationships, move away from parental control, and strive to find their own place in an adult world. Most adolescents are resilient and capable of handling these developmental tasks. Moreover, it appears that youth today have not rejected American society but have opted, instead, for a middle-of-the-road approach concerning their own attitudes and values. As youth experience their adolescent years, they seek meaning in life, deepening relationships, and the necessary skills to realize their career aspirations as well as emotional and economic security—and economic security has become an increasingly important consideration in today's uncertain economy. But, although material success is certainly prized by adolescents, so also is the need to relate to and help others.

We are now ready to explore the meaning of adolescent spirituality in the hope of developing a pastoral theology for today's youth. In chapter 2, we look at the adult who relates and ministers to the adolescent. Chapter 3 explores the developmental psychology of adolescence, particularly as it pertains to youth's spiritual growth. In chapter 4, we examine the spiritual life of the adolescent and place special emphasis on prayer experiences in the adolescent years. Chapter 5 views the possibilities for spiritual direction during the adolescent years. The meaning of adolescent morality and its relation to the call of Jesus is discussed in chapter 6. Chapter 7 relates spirituality to the adolescent experience of sexuality. Chapter 8 integrates a developmental perspective to youth's growing social consciousness perspective. Finally, in chapter 9, we describe the goal of adolescent spirituality: the future adult Christian.

Notes to Chapter One

1. Armand M. Nicholi Jr., "The Adolescent." In *The Harvard Guide to Modern Psychiatry*, author (ed.), p. 520. Cambridge, MA: The Belknap Press, 1978. For an interesting perspective on the study of adolescence, see Thomas J. Cottle, "On Studying the Young," *Journal of Youth and Adolescence* 1, March 1972, pp. 3–11; and Eric H. Ellis, "Some Problems in the Study of Adolescent Development," *Adolescence* 14, Spring 1979, pp. 101–109.

2. Joseph Adelson, "Adolescence and the Generalization Gap," *Psychology Today* 12, February 1979, p. 34.

3. American Psychiatric Association, *A Psychiatric Glossary*. Washington, DC, American Psychiatric Association, 1975, as quoted in Nicholi, "The Adolescent," p. 519.

4. See Nicholi, "The Adolescent," pp. 522–527.

5. Ibid., p. 523.

6. Daniel J. Levinson et al., *The Seasons of a Man's Life*. New York: Alfred A. Knopf, 1978, p. 56.

7. John J. Conger, *Adolescence and Youth: Psychological Development in a Changing World*. New York: Harper & Row, 1977, pp. 30–31. *See also* David G. Oldham, "Adolescent Turmoil: A Myth Revisited." In *Adolescent Psychiatry, Developmental and Clinical Studies*, edited by Sherman C. Feinstein and Peter L. Giovacchini, vol. 6, pp. 267–279. Chicago: University of Chicago Press, 1978.

8. Joseph Adelson, "Adolescence and Generalization Gap," p. 37.

9. Dean R. Hoge, "Social Factors Influencing Youth Ministry in the 1980s." In *Hope for the Decade: A Look at the Issues Facing Catholic Youth Ministry*. Washington, DC: National CYO Federation, USCC, 1980, p. 12.

10. John J. Conger, *Current Issues in Adolescent Development*, JSAS Document, MS 1334. Washington, DC: American Psychological Association, p. 15. *See also*, Richard G. Braungart, "Youth and Social Movements." In *Adolescence in the Life Cycle*, edited by Sigmund E. Dragastin and Glen H. Elder Jr., pp. 255–289. New York: John Wiley & Sons, 1975.

11. Ibid., p. 18.

12. Daniel Yankelovich, *The New Morality: A Profile of American Youth in the 1970s*. New York: McGraw-Hill, 1974.

13. Jerald G. Bachman and Lloyd D. Johnston, "The Freshman, 1979," *Psychology Today* 13, September 1979, pp. 79–87.

14. "Fewer Liberals, More Moderates among This Year's Freshmen," *The Chronicle of Higher Education* 9, February 1981, pp. 5, 7–8.

15. Hoge, "Social Factors," p. 27.

16. Conger, *Adolescence and Youth*, p. 536.

17. Hilmar Wagner, "The Adolescent and His Religion," *Adolescence* 13, Summer 1978, p. 349.

18. Raymond H. Potvin et al., *Religion and American Youth with Emphasis on Catholic Adolescents and Young Adults*. The Boys Town Center for the Study of Youth Development, The Catholic University of America, commissioned by the U.S. Catholic Conference, Washington, DC: 1976. This document is an excellent survey of the religious behavior of Catholic adolescents and young adults.

19. John Devolder et al., "Religious Values and Practice of the College Freshman," *Counseling and Values* 23, April 1979, p. 163; Bruce Hunsberger, "The Religiosity of College Students: Stability and Change Over Years at University," *Journal for the Scientific Study of Religion* 17, June 1978, pp. 159–164; Potvin et al., *Religion and American Youth*, pp. 22–38.

20. Bruno Manno, "Distancing One's Self Religiously," *New Catholic World* 222, Sept/Oct 1979, pp. 207–211.

21. George Gallup Jr. "The Family and Evangelization," *Catholic Mind* 77, October, 1979, p. 30.

22. Ibid., p. 29.

23. Ibid., p. 33.

24. William C. McCready, "Spiritual Life in Contemporary American Society," *Chicago Studies* 15, Spring 1976, p. 23.

25. Andrew D. Thompson, "Alienation and Koinonia among Adolescents," *The Living Light* 16, Fall 1979, pp. 300–312.

26. *Spiritual Renewal of the American Priesthood*. Washington, DC: United States Catholic Conference, 1972. Pages 1–10 are an excellent observation on American culture and contemporary spirituality.

27. James J. DiGiacomo, S.J., "Socialization for Secularization," *New Catholic World* 223, March/April 1980, p. 61.

28. The posing of a term such as "adolescent spirituality" implies that emphasis can also be given to spiritualities that speak to other segments of the population. Examples of these spiritualities include a spirituality of marriage, a spirituality for the elderly, and a middle-age spirituality. Of particular importance for adolescent spirituality is the formation and nurturance of a family spirituality. For thoughts on this, see Francis W. Nichols, "Family Spirituality," *Spirituality Today* 31, September 1979, pp. 221–229.

29. John Paul II, "Two Addresses to Youth: Homily in Boston," *Catholic Mind* 78, January 1980, p. 29.

30. John Paul II, "Homily in New York City," p. 30. [The same publication and volume number as the preceding note.]

31. Megan McKenna and Bernarda Sharkey, "The Adolescent and the Sacrament of Reconciliation." In *The Rite of Penance Commentaries Implement-*

ing the Rite, edited by Elizabeth McMahon Jeep, vol. 2, p. 61. The Liturgical Conference, Washington, DC: 1976.

32. John Paul II, "Boston," p. 27.

33. *Spiritual Renewal of American Priesthood,* p. 3.

34. Evelyn Eaton Whitehead and James D. Whitehead, *Christian Life Patterns.* Garden City, NY: Doubleday & Co., 1979, p. 17. A primary emphasis in the theology of Karl Rahner, S.J. is the centrality of this grace-nature relationship. This includes, of course, an emphasis on the "development" of this nature. Rahner views grace as the "self-communication" of God wherein the person, as existing, is invited as a "partner" to carry out God's salvific plan. See Karl Rahner, S.J., "Concerning the Relationship between Nature and Grace," *Theological Investigations,* vol. 1. New York: The Seabury Press, A Crossroad Book, 1974, pp. 297–318; "Reflections on the Experience of Grace," *Theological Investigations,* vol. 3. New York: The Seabury Press, A Crossroad Book, 1974, pp. 86–90.

CHAPTER TWO

Adults Who Minister to Youth Some Reflections

Research on the developmental psychology of the child has usually concerned itself mainly with the child's physical, intellectual, and emotional growth. Recently, however, contemporary psychology has realized the inadequacy of this approach.[1] An exclusively child-centered orientation is both limiting and restrictive. Consequently, developmental studies are expanding to include other factors, such as the quality of the child's interactions with parents, the quality of the interaction between parents, and the influences of siblings and other socializing factors that might affect the child's life.

Similarly, psychological research has tended to concentrate on the effect that parents have on the individual child and has given less attention to the reciprocal aspects of this relationship. In other words, besides the parental effect on the child, developmental studies need to explore the effects of the child's behavior on the parents.

The above developments in academic psychology are instructive in a discussion of the adult-adolescent relationship. So often, when we minister to young people, we find ourselves concerned solely with the adolescent just as the developmental psychologist has, for so long, been concerned almost exclusively with the child. We ask questions such as: How is the young person developing? What are the adolescent's problems? How can we be of assistance to the adolescent? In what way can we be a sign of God's presence in this young person's life? Although these questions are certainly not inappropriate, they do not exhaust the possibilities, and although this "outer directedness" with respect to youth is important, ministering

15

to adolescents also involves *us* as individuals. Certainly attention must be given to the adolescent; but attention must also be given to *my* own mental-emotional outlook, *my* own role, and, equally important, the effect the young person is having on *my* own life. Adults often mistakenly assume that, given the age difference in the relationship, it is less necessary for those adults involved in youth ministry to engage in personal reflection; the attention must, for the most part, be directed to the developing young person. Such an attitude is limiting, however, and the effects of this restricted perspective often lead to a narrowness in the adult-adolescent relationship that deprives the adult of possibilities for personal and spiritual growth.

Before we proceed, though, we need to ask a preliminary question. Do adolescents turn to adults with their questions of meaning and faith? Although the empirical evidence is sparse, research suggests that youth do perceive the role of adults as important in helping them shape questions of personal value and meaning. A recent survey involving a large sampling of freshmen at a religious-affiliated liberal arts college found that students had a strong positive perception of the religious roles that are exhibited by adults. In comparison with adults who functioned in more secular roles, adults who interacted with adolescents in roles that were perceived to be religious in nature were more attractive to young persons when they had questions concerning values and life's meaning.[2] Clearly, adolescents prize adults whose roles are witnesses to the deeper meanings and values of life. From an experential standpoint, an adult who relates to high school or college youth knows the influence and impact of his or her own presence in the adolescent's life, provided the adult is viewed with positive regard and respect. By both being present and showing concern, adults exercise an integral role in helping the adolescent to clarify his or her own response to Jesus' call during these developing years.

Characteristics for Adults Ministering to Youth

As we review the developmental period of adolescence, it is helpful to examine the role of the adult, who in some capacity, by virtue of his or her role (e.g., campus minister, teacher, counselor, or even parent), dialogs with the adolescent.

16

Availability

An encounter with an adolescent requires an openness, a presence, and real availability. Dialogue with young people invites the adolescent's realization that there is someone to whom he or she can turn. To this end, there must first be a certain amount of adult visibility. A proper adult response includes a stance of receptivity toward the adolescent and an awareness and understanding of the adolescent's needs. An essential component of this receptivity is the adult's availability. Ideally, this means adolescents "know they are welcome to come and talk on their own terms."[3] As this encounter develops, the adolescent experiences this availability as the presence of someone who understands. This encounter must not be rushed or hurried, however. After all, there is probably enough frenzy in the adolescent's life as it is. In the same vein, this ongoing dialogue needs a sense of peacefulness in which the honest searching and reflection that are so needed by the adolescent can actually take place. This time might be one of the adolescent's few moments when he or she can just be, when he or she can "consciously" come to realize God's active working in his or her life. The adult's presence needs to nurture an atmosphere in which this reflection is possible.

For the adult, however, the scheduling of these encounters must always provide time for his or her own reflection and prayer. The adult, too, needs a place to experience personal solitude. "Rising early the next morning, he went off to a lonely place in the desert; there he was absorbed in prayer" (Mk 1:35).

The adult ministering to youth cannot ignore this fundamental need of the Christian life. It is for this reason that ministry to adolescents evinces a real tension. Alongside the need to witness and be present there exists the need to withdraw and explore one's own spiritual roots. This tension is frequently heightened by the fact that the adolescent's impulsiveness often triggers unreflected behaviors that demand the adult's immediate attention.

Acceptance

A second characteristic that should be discussed in relation to a ministry to adolescents is acceptance. Peter van Breemen speaks of our overpowering need for acceptance when he says that "every human being craves to be accepted, accepted for what he is. Noth-

17

ing in human life has such a lasting and fatal effect as the experience of not being completely accepted. When I am not accepted, then something in me is broken."[4] When we relate to youth, we need to understand *them*—their questions, their struggles, their concerns. Our acceptance helps us to appreciate the adolescent for who he or she really is—a person loved by God. "Love, then, consists in this: not that we have loved God, but that he has loved us" (1 Jn 4:10). This acceptance does not deny the importance of growth, penance, or true sorrow for failings. The adult realizes the adolescent's shortcomings, but this realization rests within the context of the future growth to which the adolescent is called and is communicated to the adolescent through open acceptance and trust.

Allied to acceptance is the need for tolerance and patience. The very nature of adolescence predisposes the young person to experiment, to, at times, unthinkingly take risky or foolish steps. Psychologically, the adolescent attempts to define the borders within which he or she can securely interact. Initially, the primary way to determine these limits is through experimentation, exploration, and observation of the reactions of others. In time, adolescents acquire more mature patterns of behavior that mirror the quest for a cohesive and integrated value system. The adult reveals an understanding of the adolescent's behavior by accepting the young person, but, at the same time, not necessarily approving his or her actions.

Adolescent behavior can challenge, test, and, in some instances, threaten the adult. In shifting through these youthful behaviors, the adult needs to sort out those adolescent behaviors that reflect real values quests, those that signify adolescent gropings on various life issues, and those that might indicate lingering developmental issues and emotional problems. The questioning of God's existence, for example, or belligerence toward the institutional church, or overly negative thinking, or alienation from the faith community can be reflected for any of the above reasons.

Authenticity

A third characteristic is the adult's expression of authenticity. One of the deepest desires of youth today is the quest for an honesty that brings some dimension of objectivity to their lives. This honesty is especially needed in relational experiences. The adult engenders this authenticity by responding with honesty and attentiveness to youth's questions and interests. No longer can a ministry to youth exist in a role-model perspective in which the adult functions simply in a "role" for the adolescent. Ministry to youth must involve adults who are willing to venture beyond such confines. Adolescents seek adults who can periodically speak of their own personal quest for Jesus—the struggles, hopes, and doubts that adults experience in their own lives.

There is, of course, a time and a place for this personal self-disclosure, and the timing must always take into consideration the developmental level of the adolescent. Nonetheless, there needs to be time for the authentic sharing of the adult's own faith experience. By this interaction with adolescents, the adult quietly demonstrates an inner acceptance of his or her own journey for personal meaning. Furthermore, an authentic ministerial style evinces a real sense of contentment in ministry with youth. This is not to say that the adult's life is immune from struggles, or that the adult has no developmental issues in his or her own life. It does say, however, that in the adult's life the peace that the Lord provides is being lived out *here and now.* Youth value this authentic witness, and this honesty speaks to the searching in which they honestly engage.

Vulnerability

Finally, there is the awareness of personal weakness. Probably one of the crucial changes in ministry to youth today is the movement away from "model" roles to a real humanness. Adults need awareness, understanding, and acceptance of their own mistakes and failures.

Adults who are capable of being vulnerable provide a tremendous support to the adolescent. In early adolescence the young person is increasingly self-conscious and aware of personal shortcomings and inadequacies. During this period he or she becomes aware of what others think, how he or she is perceived, and what behaviors are appropriate. Adults, especially those who are respected by the adolescent, exercise an integral role in allaying these feelings of inadequacy and personal shortcomings. The adult who is both aware of his or her own personal limitations and comfortable with them will often be an attractive figure to the adolescent, thus encouraging the adolescent's efforts at competency and the mastering of coping behaviors that are necessary for the adult world.[5]

In addition, a critical factor for adolescent growth is the adult's ability to admit limits. Whe the adolescent perceives an adult who is comfortable with personal limitations and capable of admitting failures, the way is opened for the adolescent's own personal self-acceptance. The adolescent then feels that mistakes can be made, yet growth can continue. A ministry to high school and college youth means bringing out not only one's strengths and gifts in the encounter, but also personal shortcomings and weaknesses, for "when I am powerless, then I am strong" (2 Cor 12:10).

Adult-Adolescent Friendships

When adults minister to adolescents, the question is often raised: "Can I really be a friend to the young person I am ministering to?" The question is provocative because it engages two different philosophical approaches to education. The first theory views the adult-adolescent relationship from a role perspective. This school of thought values power or some type of authority model wherein insight and knowledge are transferred from the adult to the adolescent. A second theory, which does not deny the learning that takes place or the necessity of roles in the educational process, emphasizes the quality of the relationships with the student as the primary focus for learning. The mutual interaction in the adult-adolescent relationship, and the consequent feelings and insights that emerge, are central to this second approach.

For early adolescence, of course, the possibility of friendship ties with adults is irrelevant. As the adolescent proceeds through middle adolescence, however, and, especially in late adolescence—the period that encompasses the later high school years and the college years—the possibilities become more frequent and the question becomes more real. There are difficulties in such a relationship that are not lightly dismissed. One is that friendship implies a real equality; yet, if the adult relates to the adolescent from necessary role (e.g., teacher or counselor), this equality becomes difficult. Another aspect of friendship is real sharing; but the young person's developmental stage, because of either inexperience or lack of reflection and self-awareness, might limit the possibilities for *mutual* sharing of selves. Finally, as the adult must realize, such a relationship involves a time commitment that is difficult in an already busy sched-

20

ule, and the particular environment (a school setting, for example) might make the building of such relationships difficult.

On the other hand, we must admit that friendship is a good thing. It exemplifies the New Testament notion of the love we share with one another as friends. Our Lord himself valued friendship. "You are my friends if you do what I command you" (Jn 15:14). Thus, there is an important value in adult-adolescent relationships, and, even though it is difficult to determine how often this might occur, it is a valuable experience "not only because such a friendship is instrumental to education, but also because friendship is in itself a rare and worthwhile thing, to be sought and cultivated for its own sake wherever it can be found."[6] Despite the difficulties that are involved, openness to this immensely satisfying and certainly important Christian form of human relating should be valued by adults. The beginnings of a friendship with an adult implants within the adolescent a profound sense of self-worth, which then helps to cement a foundation for later relationship-building. Such a relationship gives the adolescent great support during these developing years.

Cautions in the Adult-Adolescent Dialog

In addition to the characteristics that have already been discussed, there are several cautions that need attention if ministry to youth is to be effective. First, there is the adult's conscious realization of the time dimension. One physiological and psychological reality for all of us is the "growing-old syndrome." This is especially applicable in the school setting where, every year, adults experience the constancy of the same age group, yet continue to grow older. We slow down; we are not as capable of activity as we once were; our interests sometimes wander or our enthusiasm wanes. A typical (survival?) response often is boredom or a distancing of oneself from real involvement with young people. Moreover, for all the periodic novelties and fads, adolescents display many of the same basic developmental problems that were prevalent five or ten years ago. In other words, everyone is the same *except* me! This perception can often be subtle and unconscious.

Another common problem that adults face when ministering to adolescents is what social scientists have labeled burnout.[7] It is simply a fact of life that keeping up with youth is a full time job! The spontaneity and the enthusiasm of youth are often overwhelming. For the conscientious adult, there might not be enough time to work with, minister to, or simply be with the adolescent. In addition, in our work-oriented culture, an adult can feel guilt for not doing everything that should be done for the adolescent. This guilt is reinforced by many adolescents, especially younger adolescents, who find it difficult to understand the adult's need to seek privacy, to be away from ministerial work, and to have time for his or her family or religious community.

Another potentially troublesome aspect of youth ministry is a lack of feedback. Human relationships need a healthy give-and-take and reciprocity in feelings, thoughts, and goals. This is crucial for one's effective life in family, religious community, and friendship. The limited experiences of the adolescent and the developmental needs that are characteristic of the adolescent's age often preclude a relationship that truly is mutually fulfilling. Unless an adult is aware of his or her needs for intimacy and sharing, real frustration might result. Sometimes what an adult seeks in a relationship with youth actually reflects unresolved conflicts and problems from the adult's own past. The threatening feelings that result from adolescent behaviors often mirror areas in the adult's life in which unrecognized difficulties might still linger.[8] In this situation, real honesty is needed. When we approach ministerial work from need orientation (which is often unconscious) rather than from the freeing desire of availability and service for the Lord, then we are predisposed to frustration and dissatisfaction. Consequently, ministerial work with adolescents can become a frustrating experience rather than a time of openness and giving to the Lord. Instead of encountering spiritual consolation from witnessing and sharing an experience of Christ with the adolescent, we can become burdened and frustrated by unrequited needs. The inevitable question becomes: "Why can't I be satisfied?" Anger and frustration can emerge. What can ultimately result is a growing attitude of resentment toward young people.

Likewise, the pressures of overwork in ministry to adolescents are evinced both externally and internally. If ministering to adolescents—it does not matter what the activity is: counseling, teaching, or the like—precludes spending time with the religious community, the family, or significant others, then the adult's ministry needs examination. This issue must be faced by the adult at the personal level and, sometimes, by the religious community at the corporate level. The internal symptoms of overwork touch our spiritual lives. One of the first manifestations is a shying away from or downplaying of prayer. We begin to think "I'm too busy to pray," or "I'm too tired to pray." A related problem, especially at the secondary-school level, is the often insular nature of the school or the religious community. Sometimes the adult becomes so absorbed with students that they become the focus of concern and conversation for religious communities. Far too often, adults find that there is little time to minister to or just be with one another. Furthermore, ministerial work with youth can also be so absorbing that the ministers lose the wider perspective that is needed for other concerns in the school, not to mention the province, the diocese, or the church.

Another area of concern is the temptation to minister to the adolescent solely from one specific paradigm or model. In other words, it is possible to stress one particular way of ministering to adolescents, which supposedly fits *all* adolescents, simply because they are adolescents. Quoting Karl Rahner, youth specialist Michael Warren notes:

> A pastoral approach which recognizes only one recipe for everything, which aims at opening every door with one single key, which thinks itself to be in possession of an Archimedean fulcrum from which it can proceed to move the whole world, is refuted by the simple ontological reflection that man is a plural being; that this plurality, despite the fact that man is also a unity, is something that a man himself cannot get beyond; and that (if the existential significance of this plurality is not to be, in practice, denied) there can be no one single point for him from which everything can be surveyed, everything worked out and everything directed. . . . The humility and patience which goes with plurality . . . belongs to the creaturely humility to be found in truly Christian pastoral work.[9]

Certainly, in ministering to adolescents, this principle of pluralism is necessary. The behaviors, life challenges, and developmental issues that adolescents experience necessitate a personally-oriented pastoral approach that recognizes the unique developmental level (and needs) of each adolescent.

Finally, a phenomenon that can emerge in the adult-adolescent relationship is the insidious need for power. The adult's age, experience, knowledge, authority, and role can exert a profound influence over the adolescent. Guilt normally arises when one attempts to unduly influence or control another; such power needs are often unconscious, however, and are clothed in the banner of "the helpful ministerial work I am doing." Psychiatrist Adolf Guggenbuhl-Craig speaks of the "power shadow" and the deeper motivations that can underlie ministerial work.[10] Ministry to youth can provide great consolation; yet this work can give rise to the satisfying of inner needs for power. There is always the possibility that, beneath the advice and counsel, there lies the insidious personal need for control, which fashions and influences the response to the adolescent. Adults need to ask, "Can I honestly say that my ministery to youth does not encompass some deeper need for recognition or control?" No question like this is easily answered, but the very asking of the question is a stimulus for real reflection and prayer. It is extremely helpful if adults who minister to youth can find time to honestly explore such issues with one another—privately, in groups, in communal faith sharing, and in ministerial teams.

A Checklist

Adults can obviously profit from an honest examination of their own ministerial work with youth. The following is a checklist of questions that adult ministers might take time to reflect upon.

1 Does my ministry to adolescents allow time for prayer, family life, and/or my religious community?

2 When my ministering to young people becomes frustrating, could I be seeking more intimacy and support from them than they can possibly give to me?

3 Do I attempt to vicariously live out my own unnegotiated adolescence with the young that I minster to?

4 If I have been working with young people for several years, do I find myself growing in what St. Paul calls: "love, joy, peace, patient endurance, kindness, and generosity" (Gal 5:22)? If so, in what ways am I growing in these characteristics? If I am experiencing difficulty in this growth, in what ways is this being manifested in me? In my ministry?

5 Have I been able to find time for adult companionship that enables me to deal with my own affective needs?

6 For a religious: Has my apostolic work so absorbed me that I

24

have lost the wider apostolic vision that is needed for my province, my diocese, the church?

7 Do I have a spiritual director or trusted friends (other adults) who both challenge and nourish me to reflect on my life, thereby enabling me to explore the emotional and spiritual movements within me?

8 How do the young people that I minster to perceive me? What role do I play in their lives? Am I perceived as a parent, teacher, counselor, model, or friend? What role do I *want* to exercise in their lives?

9 Where do I see myself in five or ten years? If it is still working with young people, are there ways in which I can grow in this ministry? How might this growth affect me? If I do not plan to remain in this ministry, what preparations have I undertaken to prepare myself for a different ministry?

10 Finally, Sidney Callahan has remarked that adults, especially parents, learn from adolescents.[11] Adolescents are excellent teachers who keep us thinking, make us honest, and demand from us a real commitment to our Christian values. For adult ministers, then, an often unasked question is: In what ways have the young people that I've ministered to touched my life? Contributed to my growth? Helped me to realize what it means to follow Jesus?

The Adult As Counselor

Before proceeding to various issues in adolescent spirituality, it is helpful to briefly overview some basic counseling questions for adult-adolescent interactions. Adults need not be professional counselors in order to counsel adolescents. Yet an awareness of counseling perspectives or techniques fosters a helpful basis for youth ministry. This added dimension can provide the adult with an effective aid in ministering to adolescents.

Questioning Techniques

Questioning techniques are one of the most effective ways to dialog with adolescents. Questions provide the context for adolescent self-reflection, a critically important need during this developmental period. With the constant changes that adolescents undergo, a question format provides the adolescent with the opportunity for more in-depth reflection of personal life experiences and the consequences that these experiences have for future adult growth.

Insight questions   Insight questions allow the adolescent to make sense of life experiences, to place these experiences in a context, and to better understand the self. They provide the opportunity for deepening reflectivity and self-understanding of life experience. Examples of insight questions might include the following: "Does that behavior tell you anything about yourself?" "Mark, why do you think you do that?" "Do you think that says anything about you, Nancy?" "What do you think you have learned from all this?" "After that (name the experience) do you think your relationship with God is different?"

Exploratory questions   Exploratory questions center on a single theme or area of the adolescent's life experience. They are used to acquire a perspective or gain information about the adolescent's life situation. If the adolescent is experiencing a difficulty in a relationship, for example, exploratory questions would tend to identify the person(s) involved in the relationship, the background and history of the relationship, the issues that are important in the relationship, and the feelings involved in the interaction between the adolescent and the other person. Exploratory questions usually begin by posing open-ended questions: "Could you tell me more about that?" Then explore areas of this relationship or experience: "Are there other times that you have felt this way with . . . ?" "Are there other situations or people who make you feel this way?"

Comparison questions   Sometimes adolescents experience difficulty either in relating various life experiences to other experiences in their lives or in understanding their experience in light of their own development. Comparison questions are ideally suited for this situation because they provide the adolescent with an opportunity for comparing personal experience and reflecting on the personal growth that takes place. The following questions are examples: "How does this relationship compare to . . . ?" "Can you reflect on how this relationship is different now that you have started college?" "How do you feel about Jim compared to the last time we talked?" "Are your feelings and ideas about God any different from when you were a freshman?" "In what ways?" "Have you noticed any difference in what prayer means to you (or how you pray) over these past few months?"

Motivating questions   Motivating questions tend to focus on the future. They aid the adolescent in reflecting on the present but maintain an awareness of future possibilities and commitments. They encourage the adolescent to take responsibility for present experiences and future possibilities. Examples of these questions include the following: "How do you think we can deal with that question in the future?" "What do you think you'll do if that happens again?" "Do you have any ideas on where this might be leading?" "What ways do you think you might grow from . . . ?" "Can you get a sense of where your relationship with God is going?"

Having developed an overview of the adolescent experience in chapter 1 and having now discussed the role of the adult who ministers to the adolescent, we can proceed to chapter 3, in which we outline the developmental factors that pertain to the adolescent's spiritual growth.

Notes to Chapter Two

1. See William Kessen, "The American Child and Other Cultural Inventions," *American Psychologist* 34, October 1979, pp. 815–820; and Richard Q. Bell, "Parent, Child, and Reciprocal Influences," ibid., pp. 821–826.

2. James R. Golden et al., "Assessment of Student Perception of the Campus Religious," *Counseling and Values* 24, October 1979, p. 52.

3. Benjamin Winterborn, S.J., "Counseling the University Student," *Supplement to the Way*, no. 6, May 1968, p. 82.

4. Peter G. van Breemen, S.J., *As Bread That Is Broken.* Denville, NJ: Dimension Books, 1974, p. 9.

5. Eric Ostrov and Daniel Offer, "Loneliness and the Adolescent." In *Adolescent Psychiatry, Developmental and Clinical Studies,* edited by Sherman C. Feinstein and Peter L. Giovacchini, vol. 6, p. 41. Chicago: University of Chicago Press, 1978.

6. R. S. Downie et al., *Education and Personal Relationships: A Philosophical Study.* London: Methuen & Co., Ltd, 1974, p. 171.

7. For the effects of burnout on individuals in the helping professions, see Christina Maslach, "Burned-Out," *Human Behavior* 5, September 1976, pp. 16–22. An excellent discussion on the effects of burnout in pastoral ministry is contained in James J. Gill, S.J., M.D., "Burnout, A Growing Threat in Ministry," *Human Development* 1, Summer 1980, pp. 21–27.

8. Committee on Adolescence, Group for the Advancement of Psychiatry, *Normal Adolescence: Its Dynamic and Impact.* New York: Charles Scribner's Sons, 1968, pp. 95–99.

9. Karl Rahner, S.J., *The Christian Commitment.* New York: Sheed and Ward, 1963, p. 93. Quoted in "Evangelization of Young Adults," by Michael Warren, *New Catholic World* 222, Sept/Oct 1979, p. 216.

10. Adolf Guggenbuhl-Craig, *Power in the Helping Professions.* New York: Spring Publications, 1971, p. 11.

11. Sidney Callahan, "The Challenge of Living with Adolescents," *New Catholic World* 222, Nov/Dec, 1979, pp. 264–266.

12. For further reading on adolescents and counseling, the reader is encouraged to see: Peter H. Buntman and Eleanor M. Saris, *How to Live With Your Teenager.* Pasadena, CA: The Birch Tree Press, 1979; Eugene Kennedy, *On Becoming a Counselor: A Basic Guide for Non-Professional Counselors.* New York: Continuum Publishing Corp., 1980; Wayne W . Dyer and John Vriend, *Counseling Techniques That Work.* Washington, DC: American Personnel and Guidance Association Press, 1975; Helen G. Rabichow and Morris A. Sklansky, *Effective Counseling of Adolescents.* Chicago: Association Press, 1980.

CHAPTER THREE

Adolescence, Developmental Theory, and Spirituality

It is important that we continue on our course,
no matter what stage we have reached.

Philippians 3:16

New Testament teaching says the response to Jesus' call is never a decisive "yes," but rather a gradual process of continual conversion.[1] This perspective of spiritual development, which sees it as an ongoing process, necessitates a pastoral appreciation of the developmental level of all human experience. It is at our own particular level of human growth that each of us comes to understand and accept God's grace to respond to Jesus' invitation to follow him.

As a consequence, then, a spirituality for adolescents must pay particular attention to the developmental needs and issues that so preoccupy much of the adolescent's life. An understanding of adolescent development enriches the adult's ministry to youth, provides a foundation for this ministry, and ultimately enables the adult to challenge the adolescent gently toward future spiritual growth.

One of the striking changes that takes place during adolescence is the development of the cognitive self. Because cognitive growth is such a pivotal experience for the adolescent, we turn, first, to an examination of the cognitive developmental theory advanced by Jean Piaget.

Cognitive Development

Jean Piaget's theory of cognitive development has profoundly influenced both educational and developmental theory.[2] From his research with small groups of children, Piaget formulated a theory of cognitive growth that involves stages. Piaget said these stages were sequential (stages occur for individuals in a structured sequence) and invariant (all people go through the stages in the pre-scribed order).

Cognitive development results from both one's biological en-dowment and the normal processes of human growth. This devel-opment is similar to the way in which the body digests food. From a biological standpoint, the human organism digests food, which is then reconstituted to serve bodily needs. This same pattern emerges for cognitive development, that is, the human organism continu-ously takes in new information, which then constitutes the founda-tion for deepening cognitive growth.

Piaget states that two biological functions must be present for cognitive growth to occur: the first is organization and the second is adaptation. Organization refers to the arranging and structuring of various mental processes, such as memory and perception. Organ-ization could be labeled the "maintenance" component for normal human functioning in that it maintains the human organism as it experiences new information and encounters changing or even new environments. Organization, thus, provides continuity and stability to the self as it interacts and forms deeper levels of meaning.

Whereas organization represents the internal maintenance mechanism for normal human functioning, the ability to function and cope adequately with the environment in everyday life activity is called adaptation. As I interact in the world, I acquire new infor-mation about reality and, at the same time, reformulate my present ideas about reality as I process incoming information. This ongoing adaptation to reality is made possible by two intellectual functions—assimilation and accommodation. The new information that I en-counter is assimilated into my present cognitive view, while, at the same time, I accommodate my own understandings to the new in-formation I receive and, thereby, restructure my present thinking. Thus, "assimilation and accommodation are complementary proc-esses and through their continuous interaction they bring about con-ceptual adaptation and growth."[3]

It is this constant interplay of accommodation and assimilation that leads the self to experience deepening levels of understanding. Piaget also notes that the biological functions of adaptation and or-ganization are "inseparable," that they exist in a complementary fashion, with organization representing the "internal aspect" of cog-nitive development and adaptation representing the "external aspect." Piaget's model of cognitive development points out that humans are "active constructors of their own understandings."[4] From a Piagetan perspective, human cognition is a dynamic, developing system that continuously evolves to more complex levels. It is through this fluid, ongoing interaction that the adolescent gradually develops a deepening understanding of both the self and the world.

An example of this process is the adolescent's graduation from high school and departure for college. This separation from parents can have a beneficial effect on the late adolescent's relationship with his or her parents.[5] Attending college away from home may provide a healthy distancing and a time to reassess parental influence and realize its importance.

When the adolescent enters the new college environment, he or she must discover a way to mediate the self with the information from this new environment. Through organization, the adolescent brings his or her past life history to this new experience and enters an environment where he or she continues to perceive, to reflect, to act, and to relate to new realities. Organization maintains the integrity of the self as it encounters this challenging, new environment. The adolescent must simultaneously adapt to this new reality, however, for the adolescent self is confronted by new people, new living arrangements, new ideas, and new attitudes. Adolescent adaptation (through assimilation and accommodation) involves successfully negotiating with the environment to achieve deeper understandings of both the self and the environment. The fruits of this effort are evaluating one's beliefs, forming deeper relationships, increasing reflective thinking, and widening visions of reality. This dynamic interaction of the adolescent self also fosters deeper searchings, questioning, and the reformulating of previously held ideas and beliefs. Thus, the adolescent's questions about faith or the experience of a "faith crisis," which are common experiences in the high school and quite frequently the college years, are partly the result of this cognitve development. For adolescents, the ever-evolving experiences of entering and leaving high school, beginning college, entering into deepening relationships, and forming career and marriage plans become critical catalysts for the dynamic interplay of accommodating and assimilating the self to an increasingly complex world.

On the basis of his empirical findings, Piaget identified four stages of cognitive development. From birth to roughly two years of age, the child resides in the "sensorimotor stage." From age two until age seven, the child is in the "preoperational stage." The years from seven to twelve make up the concrete "operational stage" of thinking. As early adolescence begins, this stage of concrete thinking gives way to what Piaget characterizes as "formal operational thought." Because the time of concrete operations is the period prior to adolescence and the acquisition of formal operational thinking, it is helpful to sketch this period of cognitive development. Our description will facilitate the more detailed discussion of adolescent formal thinking that follows.

Before proceeding, however, it is helpful to explore Piaget's use of the term "operation." For Piaget, operation refers to the child's imaginative capacity to envision an object in thought. In one of Piaget's classic experiments, for example, he noted that when children are observing equal amounts of water being simultaneously poured into a tall glass and a shorter but wider glass, they invariably concluded the taller glass contained more water. Piaget maintains that the reason the children picked the taller glass was because height was the only characteristic of the glass that they perceived.

With continued growth, the child moves beyond preoperational thinking to concrete operational thinking and is now capable of imaginatively constructing images and can thus pay close attention to factors other than height. Yet this operational thinking is limited to imaginatively envisioning objects the child has personally experienced. In effect, concrete thought weds the child to the personal experience of concrete realities. One striking aspect of this stage is seen in terms of the child's relational capacities. For example, a child can begin to understand how an object can be "related" to color. A shirt need not necessarily be "blue" or "not blue," but can be shades of blue. In concrete operational thinking, the child also utilizes various mental operations such as "conservation." He or she comes to understand that the shape of an object can be altered while the quantity of the object remains the same (the example on water poured into two glasses of different heights but the same volume demonstrates the child's use of this mental operation of conservation). Thus, the child can imaginatively envision that although the shape of the object might change, the quantity of water would remain the same (conserved). Numerous other operations, such as commutability and reversibility, also appear at this stage.[6]

However, when we compare concrete operations of this age period to the formal operational thought patterns in adolescence, we find the younger child's ability to be limited. The concrete operational mode of thinking is tied to the concrete reality that the child experiences. And according to Piaget and his colleague Barbel Inhelder, "concrete thought remains essentially attached to empirical reality. The system of concrete operations . . . attains no more than a concept of 'what is possible,' which is a simple (and not very great) extension of the empirical situation."[7] Thus, the child is not capable of going beyond this experience to situations outside the realm of his or her immediate experience.

These limitations, however, are altered as the child enters adolescence and begins to attain formal operational thinking. Characteristics of this new found cognitive growth include the capacity to construct hypotheses, form generalization, and demonstrate abstract thinking. Thus, "in formal thought there is a reversal of the direction of thinking between *reality* and *possibility* in the subject's method of approach. *Possibility* no longer appears merely as an extension of an empirical situation or of actions actually performed. Instead, it is *reality* that is now secondary to *possibility*. The most distinctive property of formal thought is this reversal of direction between *reality* and *possibility*."[8]

Unlike the child, the adolescent can move from the concrete, personal experiences of life to the "possible" and "potential" aspects of situations and personal experiences. The adolescent constructs hypothetical situations of what might be and examines various alternatives and solutions to everyday problems.

This transition to formal thought allows the adolescent to consider answers to the burgeoning questions of life—which, of course, include questions of belief, the meaning of God and personal values. Initially, (age 11 or 12) such formal reasoning is quite rudimentary and requires much effort. At this stage, the adolescent, while attempting to deal with basic questions of faith and belief, can fall victim to "pseudostupidity."[9] In other words, formal thinking moves the adolescent, prompting him or her to ask complex questions and seek answers beyond his or her own ability to comprehend. The adolescent attempts to interpret reality by using his or her more complex reasoning, even when such reasoning is unnecessary or beyond his or her own understanding of it. Thus, no area of the child's life is sacred once he or she begins to ask "why?" or "what for?" about family behaviors or practices that previously have merely been taken for granted.

In the area of faith and religious practice, this aspect is readily apparent. The adolescent seeks motives and more complex answers to questions such as "Why is there God?" "Why do we go to mass?" "Why am I a Catholic?" No matter how obvious the situation is, simple answers are no longer sufficient. The adult's perception of adolescent inability to understand the obvious, or to accept family habits and practices, leads to a false impression of "stupidity." In reality, however, the adolescent is actually experimenting with his or her new-found cognitive powers. Although this does not mean that cognitive development explains the adolescent's faith questioning or incipient challenge to religious practice, this gradual development of formal thought does set the stage for later questioning and doubt.

As adolescent maturation continues through the middle and late adolescent years, the young person develops a growing, comfortable sense of his or her intellectual powers, along with deeper levels of hypothetical reasoning and intellectual abstraction, which he or she now employs to confront deeper questions of faith and meaning (and to find authentic and meaningful answers!).

Formal thinking becomes an integral component of the adolescent's quest for adulthood. Formal thought assists the adolescent in his or her yearning to plot strategies and consider a life plan for the adult world. Ideas surface that allow the adolescent to begin implementing various responsible behaviors in his or her preparation-for-future-adulthood (e.g., jobs, future studies, ways to behave). The adolescent now is characterized more as one who "thinks beyond the present." The adolescent is also increasingly viewed as one who reflects on his or her own thought processes. In essence, the adolescent thinks about thinking. This introspective quality gives rise to theories and ideas of how the world should be, what the adolescent's own place will be in this world, and how his or her future relates to the adult world that he or she will soon enter. Such reflection encourages the adolescent to begin constructing a personally meaningful value system that incorporates opinions and attitudes on political and social realities. The adolescent will more and more press these personal views and opinions on adults, often with a certain urgency. The adolescent tries out these newly acquired beliefs, values, and attitudes on both peers and adults (they have not yet been tested). Others' reactions (both peers and adults), coupled with his or her own continued reflection and desire to find meaning, lead to a modification and reformulation of these initial ideas. With time, this experimenting, reevaluating-formulating set the basis for constructing one's own philosophy of life, a sociopolitical value system, and ethical religious beliefs. It is this process of conceptual formulation that eases the adolescent's entrance into the adult world.

The adolescent's growth in abstract thinking parallels his or her growing realization of the need to take on future but-yet-to-be experienced adult roles and their accompanying uncertainties. As a consequence, the adolescent focuses on personal reflections and constructs a variety of beliefs and values that prepare him or her to deal with (and reform) the adult world. These self-absorbing ideas often form the basis for a true adolescent egocentrism, because the adolescent now views his or her own personal ideas as "the way" to save society. As Piaget notes: "We see, then, how the adolescent goes injecting himself into adult society. He does so by means of projects, life plans, theoretical systems, and ideas of political or social reform."[10] The adolescent becomes the reformer for adults and the personal conscience for the adult world! Unfortunately, although he or she is readily able to point out adult failures and shortcomings, the adolescent is often unable to understand his or her own inadequacies. When this factor is tied to religious belief and behavior, a certain critical and intolerant stance often surfaces in the adolescent's own judgment of the actual adult practice of faith.

Psychologist David Elkind notes that two characteristics, which commonly surface in the adolescent's development of formal thinking, can influence his or her personal behavior.[11] Elkind calls the first one the adolescent's construction of an "imaginary audience." We have noted that the adolescent often becomes preoccupied with the self. The adolescent's capacity for formal thinking also permits him or her to think about another's thought. As a consequence, the adolescent attributes his or her own personal preoccupation with self to other people. In effect, this tendency leads to a high degree of personal self-consciousness. Adolescents create an imaginary world in which they assume that everyone else is as personally interested in them as they are. This self-consciousness is often linked to a greater need for attention-seeking behaviors. But, because adolescents have wrongly assumed this intense interest by adults they engage in behaviors that seek to attract adult attention. Young adolescents are often preoccupied with what others are thinking because they are often thinking that there is an audience that is fascinated by their own personal appearance and behavior. In short, "young adolescents, then, take it for granted that the audience shares their assumptive realities about themselves."[12]

Another characteristic of formal thinking, which arises during this period, is the "personal fable." Just as adolescents view an audience, so too they perceive themselves as special and, therefore, create a personal mystique in which they can do nothing wrong (or are immune to personal injury or hurt). We need only witness the sexual acting out and drug experiences of many adolescents to see the effects of this mistaken notion of invincibility.

These characteristics help to explain many of the behaviors that appear during the adolescent years. Assuming an ever-present audience, adolescents can foist upon adults their own personal thinking and demands, which then compel adult attention and response. Likewise, adolescents might not realize the implications and consequences of their personal statements that question various adult values, such as religious practice and belief. Using their new-found intellectual power, adolescents may make foolish statements reflecting their own sense of power and uniqueness (personal fable). In both instances, the growing capacity for formal thinking sheds light on these behaviors.

Piaget called the adolescent fascination with his or her own thinking "egocentrism." This does not mean what adults typically refer to as selfishness. Rather, what Piaget interprets as egocentrism is the adolescent's fixation on his or her own reflective capacity. In time, however, the adolescent begins to shed this self-absorption. Two reasons make this shedding of egocentrism possible. First, the adolescent increasingly interacts on deepening levels with peers, forcing, on the adolescent's part, comparison and re-examination of existing personal theories and ideologies. This self-comparison with other adolescents' views and beliefs leads to modification and alteration of personal beliefs and values. Second, the adolescent takes on adult roles through work, career, vocational training, or advanced schooling, thus accentuating a need for other perspectives that encourage a widening social vision. Gradually, the adolescent casts off egocentrism, which has colored his or her thinking patterns, and acquires an adult perspective toward both reality and his or her interpersonal relationships. The diminution of egocentrism clears the path for the adolescent's entrance into adulthood.

As the adolescent proceeds into the undergraduate college years, this deepening understanding of the complexity of the social world and human relationships is reinforced. Through the school environment, curriculum, and so on, the late adolescent becomes attuned to broader, in-depth discussions of complex and social issues. Reflections on such abstract topics as "freedom," "the good," "what is moral?," become more important and more focused. It is only during the college years that the adolescent engages in such topics with an expanded understanding of his or her own self and the role he or she will soon be acquiring in the world of adulthood.

Piaget also noted that affective responses are linked to the growing formal thinking patterns that are set in adolescence. As the adolescent develops the capacity for abstract thinking, affective responses toward ideas (justice, liberty, freedom) and the various dimensions of social reality (poverty, capitalism, social issues) also unfold. In the concrete operational stage, the child has no real feelings about the various ideas and ideals that preoccupy the adolescent. The child is limited to feelings concerning concrete experiences and persons such as parents and family. Beginning at around 13 to 15 years, however, the adolescent develops affective responses toward more abstract ideas, for "the notions of humanity, social justice . . . freedom of conscience, civic or intellectual courage, and so forth, like the idea of nationality, are ideals which profoundly influence the adolescent's affective life."[13] The adolescent can become impassioned about selected causes and values, and much time and energy are involved in whatever the adolescent deems important.

We see, then, that formal operational thinking sets the stage for a cognitive leap in the adolescent's thinking patterns. The high school student's newly found reflective capacity leads him or her to ask more profound questions regarding religion, values, and personal morality and, inchoately, to construct a system of belief that is both personally meaningful for the present and functional for later adult roles. The fact that adolescents in the secondary school years so often ask serious questions—such as "Why go to church?" "Why be a Catholic?" or "Who is Jesus?"—reflects in part this growing cognitive capacity. And this increased cognitive capacity meshes with other developmental issues, such as identity (to be treated later in this chapter), to bring about the adolescent faith crises that will be discussed in chapter 4.

As maturation continues and the adolescent enters young adulthood, this cognitive development translates into deeper reflection concerning morality, ethics, and deepening ideological values. Ideally, throughout his or her life, the adolescent uses his or her cognitive powers to derive meaning from the diverse experiences of human relationships, social interactions in adulthood, and experiences of socio-political realities. Along the way, the adolescent constructs a role that is functional for adult living, but is suffciently flexible to allow for continued adaptation to arise from these divergent experiences.

Piaget's perspective allows us to view the adolescent's cognitive development as a rich, dynamic process of growth. Yet it is important to note that the world to which and in which the adolescent is adapting is also in flux. This point is crucially important to us, as we view the adolescent's growing understanding of both the church and his or her own maturing faith response. Based on a more substance-oriented or classical view of the world (see chapter 4), the pre-Vatican II church tended to foster a message that life's problems, difficulties, and complexities could be accepted and managed through conformity to church pronouncements and teachings. Catechetical instruction and the manual teaching in moral theology underscored this assumption. Since Vatican II, with the emphasis on church-as-a-pilgrim-people and on the Kingdom of God as "already" and "not-yet" realized, the church has dialoged with other groups on the pressing issues of our world (take, for example, the profound issues that surround medical ethics and the challenging perspectives of liberation theology). As a result, the church is also in the process of both engaging in dialog and attempting to seek better ways to relate to the world and understand the pressing issues of the day.

This new-found emphasis on dialog, interaction, and continued searching forms a fruitful foundation for today's youth ministry. Since the acquisition of formal thinking leads the adolescent to interact with new experiences in a dynamic way and with ever-expanding cognitive richness, we are faced with the challenge to tie such a developmental process to this world of change that the adolescent is now experiencing. Three points can be made:

1. It is important in ministering to youth that attention is directed to the actual "experience" of the adolescent—how he or she really experiences reality and what this experiencing means for this adolescent.

2 Adults can be helpful by sharing with the adolescent their own journey of faith and how they have experienced personal growth in faith over these many years.

3. The church should be portrayed as a community of faith whose own experience leads to a continual searching for and discerning of the "signs of the times" in its attempt to understand more deeply the message of Jesus' call in our world.

In our discussion of Piaget's theory, it is important to note that not all adolescents acquire formal operational thinking. There are wide differences in the acquisition of formal thinking during the adolescent years. Likewise, the level of formal thought in the adolescent's thinking pattern varies from one adolescent to another, but most adolescents do demonstrate some evidence of formal thinking.[14] In our ministry to adolescents, especially in group settings, this phenomenon is striking. What is correctly perceived through one adolescent's correct perception and analysis might well be out of reach of another adolescent who is the same age.

From the perspective of spirituality, formal thinking exercises an integral role in the adolescent's quest for spiritual maturity. Formal thinking sets the stage for more profound reflection on fundamental questions of life and personal meaning. Once the adolescent has acquired some formal thought, he or she begins to ask about meaning and value, and how these notions and beliefs are relevant for his or her own life. With his formal thinking, the adolescent can also begin to comprehend, at a much deeper level, Jesus' call (Mk 10:21) and what this call entails "for me." Formal thinking, in effect, makes it possible to now ask what the invitation to "come, follow me" really means.

In light of the importance of cognitive thinking to youth's spiritual growth, adults might profitably employ some of the following questions and techniques in their ministry to adolescents.

1. Does the adolescent show evidence of a developing capacity to reflect on his or her own life, his or her relationship with God and its significance in his or her life, as well as the ability to ponder what role he or she might have in the adult world? How deeply can he or she engage each of these issues? Does his or her reflection involve itself with personal values and beliefs? Does his or her reflection show evidence of an overly critical view toward God, the church, society? If so, what reasoning does the adolescent offer for this criticism? What is the quality of this reasoning?

a) Formulate questions that involve a time dimension. Reflect with the adolescent on how his or her views and ideas have changed about God or the church over the past few years. This developmental perspective enables the adolescent to realize some form of continuity with his or her own reflection over time. This reflection can be especially helpful when the adolescent experiences a crises of personal commitment to religion, relationships, work, politics, and so forth.

b) Ask the adolescent to articulate specific criticisms he or she has about God, the church, authority, or society. Explore with the adolescent the basis of these criticisms. What are the "reasons" the adolescent offers for negative views in these areas? Are they really "reasonable?"

2. Through the adolescent's later years of high school and during the undergraduate years of college, the adult might note the "pattern" of the adolescent's reflection. Is the adolescent's reflection uneven? That is to say, does reflection take place in some areas but not others—for example, in areas concerning the adolescent's personal life, but not political or social issues? Is the adolescent growing in the ability to thread personal and religious meaning into his or her reflection on interpersonal relationships and social and political ideas?

a) One possibilitly is to reflect with the adolescent on areas of life where little reflection seems to be experienced (sexuality, politics, personal relationships).

b) Another possibility is to note how, when the adolescent reflects, he or she can see the positive and healthy aspects of a situation as well as the critical and negative aspects. In other words, is there a sense of balance in the adolescent's reflection? Is it uneven? Can the adolescent realize this?

3 Does the adolescent find time for reflecting on the self? It is helpful here to note the level of the reflection—its depth, its insight. The adult might also try to see whether the adolescent can experience a conscious presence of God as part of his or her reflection? A very approachable theme here is simply to talk with the adolescent on where he or she finds God in his or her present life? Also, try to determine whether there are ways that this presence has changed over the years as the adolescent has continued to grow and mature.

4 Does this adolescent's view of God, of values, and of personal meanings mesh with his or her everyday experience of life? Does he or she speak about experiences and various subjects of interest with a certain urgency? Does he or she gradually integrate personal experiences into an overall life approach that mirrors an essential acceptance and openness towards both the self and others? We might question the adolescent about what subjects he or she finds most important in life at this moment. Is there a gradual deepening of the level of understanding accorded these topics? Are values consciously expressed regarding these various topics?

5 How open is the adolescent to new ideas and experiences that impinge on the beliefs and values he or she presently holds? How does the adolescent deal with new experiences and ideas? Are they denied? accepted? seriously examined in depth? Is there an overall sense of acceptance toward new experiences and ideas? Is this openness dependent on the specific type of experience? Do some areas remain unattended to in the adolescent's reflection? It might be helpful here to present new ideas to the adolescent on particular subjects. "What if . . ." questions are particularly helpful, since they engage the adolescent's newly discovered capacity for hypothetical reasoning. How does the adolescent react to these hypothetical situations? Is there a degree of defensiveness?

6 How realistic is the adolescent's interpretations of relationships? personal experiences? social and political events? Is there an idealistic view toward life or a pessimistic view present in the adolescent's thinking? A growing understanding of realism is especially crucial to the adolescent's growth in career and vocational goals. Does the adolescent evince a realistic understanding of his or her talents, strengths, weaknesses, etc? Does this understanding seem to be deepening with time?

7 As the adolescent reflects more deeply, is there a gradual

learning from this reflection? That is to say, does this reflection tend to alter existing patterns of thought (ideas, stereotypes, interests) and/or lead to more open reflection? deeper reflection? Comparison and motivating questions are helpful here (see Chapter 2). Another exercise is to take a topic of conversation that one has been discussing with an adolescent. If the adolescent has brought up a new experience that relates to this theme, ask him or her how this topic has affected his or her life. In other words, help the adolescent to profit from his or her experience. The model used here is an action-reflection-action model. It is helpful to aid the adolescent in experiencing the connection between these two behaviors. Specific Christian themes can then be introduced. If, over a period of time, for example, the adolescent has been discussing the importance of relationships and has mentioned personal experiences with a friend, we can ask the adolescent how (if at all) this experience has altered the relationship in any way (reflecting on experience). Then, from this dialog, we can use motivating questions to reflect on the future possibilities and growth that might occur. The adult can then reflect with the adolescent on what values or meanings are found in this experience: "What does this tell you about yourself?" "What is the most important thing you found in that experience?" The adult can introduce considerations of how Jesus might have responded and reflect with the adolescent on how Jesus might make a difference in the adolescent's life.

Moral Development

Piaget's developmental theory is not limited to cognitive development. In his early research, the Swiss psychologist explored the importance of cognitive development in the forming of the child's judgment.[15] Piaget's work in cognitive and moral development has influenced Harvard psychologist Lawrence Kohlberg, who has written extensively on the development of moral reasoning.[16] We will examine Kohlberg's theory. Then, we will explore the importance of his theory for the adolescent years. In order to take our understanding of adolescent moral development one step further, we will then turn to Harvard educator William Perry, who has written specifically on the development of ethical reasoning in the late adolescent years (college undergraduate). And finally, we will look at the role of moral reasoning in an adolescent spirituality and examine techniques to encourage spiritual growth by developing the adolescent's moral reasoning in the context of a Christian commitment.

1. Kohlberg

Kohlberg developed his theory of the stages of moral development in a longitudinal study of teen-age boys, ages 10 to 16 (and in later confirmatory studies). He presented young people with hypothetical situations called "moral dilemmas." For each of these situations, the subject was instructed to provide "reasons" for the behaviors of the character in the dilemma.

A well-known example is the famous Heinz case. In this dilemma, the subject discovers that Heinz's wife was near death from cancer. A local druggist had discovered a drug that could cure Heinz's wife, but was charging the customers ten times the actual cost of the drug. Unable to either borrow enough money or cajole the druggist into lowering the price, Heinz thought about stealing the drug. After reading the Heinz story, the subject then responds to a series of questions exploring the reasons for advocating a certain course of action for the character.

From these responses, Kohlberg developed his theory of the stages of moral development. His theory consists of three distinct levels, with two stages at each level. It has been highly popularized in educational circles, and discussions have ensued that foster the hopes of increasing the moral developmental level of primary, secondary, and college students.

A brief summary of Kohlberg's three levels and two stages for each level follows.

Preconventional Level

The dominant influences at the preconventional level of moral reasoning are the external demands of authority and the child's own hedonistic orientation toward pleasure and away from pain.

The punishment-and-obedience orientation (Stage 1). Moral reasoning at stage one uses the criterion of avoiding punishment to determine the right or wrong. At this stage, the child is dependent upon others. The preoccupation of moral reasoning, therefore, is to deter punishment and avoid the adverse consequences of one's actions.

The instrumental-relativist orientation (Stage 2). At stage two, the child is more concerned with personal needs and desires. Whether something is right or wrong is determined by reasoning whether the actions are instrumental in satisfying the wants and desires of the child, and only infrequently the needs of others. At this stage, the child might do something for another, but some reciprocity is expected. In other words, reciprocity becomes a matter of "you scratch my back and I'll scratch yours."

Conventional level

At the conventional level, the young person is increasingly aware of the external demands of various social groupings—family, school, government, society—that begin to make demands on him or her. This awareness of others who are beyond the self is concretized in loyalty and "conformity" to groups, one's nation, and the current social order. The young person respects and uses others as reference points in his or her reasoning about the rightness and wrongness of personal acts. This level emerges in later childhood and early adolescence. Most adolescents and adults are found to reason at this level.

The good boy-nice girl orientation (Stage 3). At stage three, the person is motivated by the desire to gain the acceptance and approval of others. Conformity is prized, and personal actions are planned to meet with the acceptance and social approval of the person's own group. The individual places value on conforming types of behavior. The behavior of others tends to be evaluated by intention ("He or she means well"). Being "nice" becomes the norm for earning the approval of others.

The law-and-order orientation (Stage 4). At stage four, the person places a high emphasis on "law and order." A person's duty within the social environment becomes increasingly important. Rules are prized, and authority is given greater respect. The individual believes that right or wrong correspond to "doing one's duty," that is, fulfilling the demands made on the individual by observing the law and performing expected group behaviors.

Postconventional Level

An individual who obtains the postconventional level of moral reasoning begins to prize values that exist independently of groups and the culture. He or she recognizes universalizing moral principles that are followed for their own sake. At this level, the person's moral principles are focused on higher values such as equality and justice for all. Right and wrong are determined according to these universal principles.

The social contract-legalistic orientation (Stage 5).   At stage five, the person realizes that law is for the common good of all, that laws protect the rights and welfare of all members of society. He or she sees that although conflicts between individuals and the law can exist, the law must prevail because the generalized acceptance of this law promotes the welfare of all. At the same time, the individual who is at this stage of development, unlike the person who is at stage 4, perceives law as a benefit to the common good; laws are, therefore, not rigid, but rather are subject to alteration to meet changing human needs.

The universal-ethical-principle orientation (Stage 6).   At stage six, the individual uses universal principles to determine the morality of personal acts. Of particular importance are the ethical principles, which are derived from the individual's personal conscience, that have universal application (e.g., equality, justice). The law is still thought to be important, but there are higher values that deserve human allegiance.

The individual's advancement in Kohlberg's schema shows a movement away from self-absorption (preconventional) toward an awareness of the thinking and the feeling of others (conventional). Finally, attention is given to universal moral principles that respect the rights of all human beings. Cathy Stonehouse has summarized the characteristics that correspond to Kohlberg's three levels of moral development.

This summary tends to show that at Level I the primary concern is with the self. At Level II, the individual's growth outward leads to greater respect for law and for society's demands. Finally, at Level III, universal moral principles that prize justice and equality toward all men and women are fostered through principled moral reasoning.

Characteristics of Levels of Moral Development

	Level I	Level II	Level III
Source of Authority	Self-Interest	External Standards— models and rules	Internal principles
Definitions	Right is what adults command or what brings reward. Wrong is what I am punished for—what brings pain.	Right is what good people do or what the law says one should do. Wrong is what good people do not do or what the law says one should not do.	Right is living out moral principles and being just. Wrong is violating a moral principle and being unjust.
Intentions	Oblivious to intentions.	Makes allowances for intentions. Lenience tempered by sense of duty.	Consider intentions but also concerned about justice.
Justice	What adults command. Later, equal treatment.	Defined by society.	Equal consideration for all.
Value of Persons	Valued in material terms. "Persons are valuable for what they do for me."	Valued because of relationships of affection and for their contribution to society.	Valued because they are persons. Human life is sacred.
Stimulus to Right Actions	Fear of punishment and desire for reward.	Desire to please important persons and perform one's duty to society.	To be true to oneself one must act upon the moral principles to which one is committed.
Ability to Take Another's Perspective	Understands the perspective of persons in situations which he has experienced.	Understands the perspective of friends, family, and eventually society.	Understands the perspective of a wide range of persons including minority groups.

Reprinted from Cathy Stonehouse, "Moral Development: The Process and the Pattern," *Counseling and Values* 24, October 1979, p. 6. By permission of the American Personnel and Guidance Association.

Kohlberg's theory has a distinct developmental perspective, for it discloses how individuals progress through a sequence of stages in their moral development. Each stage (which Kohlberg also labels a structure) helps the individual to realize the importance of personal life values, as well as the reasoning behind why he or she cherishes a particular value. Kohlberg views life as basically a living out of various value choices that a person makes in a variety of concrete, everyday situations. The values from which a person chooses continuously pose dilemmas from our everyday actions; they include "punishment, property, roles and concerns of affection, roles and concerns of authority, law, life, liberty, distributive justice, truth, and sex."[17] Kohlberg suggest that "a moral choice involves choosing between two (or more) of these values as they conflict in concrete situations of choice."[18] An individual who has reached a particular level of moral reasoning will therefore reflect through his or her reasoning what he or she believes to be important about a particular value. A person at a preconventional level of moral reasoning, for example, will reason that truth (the value) is primarily for the self-interest and furtherance of personal desires. On the other hand, a person who reasons at a postconventional level will view truth as valuable because of the honest openness and respect that he or she shows everyone because all human beings are deserving of respect.

Kohlberg also maintains that justice is central to moral reasoning. He states that "there is a natural sense of justice intuitively known by the child."[19] Like the above values, the person's understanding of justice depends upon the stage of moral development at which he or she reasons. The moral reasoning of both the child and the adult is based on justice; each one, however, actually understands justice in quite distinct ways. Thus a young adult might understand justice solely in terms of the necessity of law for society (stage 4) or see the need to alter laws that are unjust (stage 5). The adolescent's growing sense of maturity, coupled with social interactions and cognitive development, leads to a deepening understanding of the universal demands of justice. At the principled level of stage 6, justice is concerned with maximizing every human's freedom and treating everyone with equal respect. Ideally, then, the way to resolve the conflicting claims of society is through mutual respect and treating every person in an equitable manner. For Kohlberg, justice becomes the universal moral principle that allows us to treat others with the respect they deserve as human beings. He says that justice is treating "every man's claim impartially regardless of the man. As a reason for action, justice is called respect for persons."[20]

Kohlberg, like Piaget, asserts that his theory is invariant and that individuals progress in moral development through the stages that he has outlined. Cross-cultural studies have also confirmed that Kohlberg's developmental theory is not a particular reflection on American society but is a "cultural universal," that is, it has universal general applicability. Kohlberg has found a consistency in moral reasoning; a person will think in one stage over half of the time, and then the rest of his or her thinking will be either one stage above or one below the dominant level. Finally, he notes that people comprehend all the stages below their own level, but they reason only one level above their own. He remarks: "Adolescents prefer (or rank as best) the highest stage that they can comprehend."[21]

Before proceeding to a discussion of how we advance in moral reasoning, we need to mention two critical points that are often overlooked in discussing Kohlberg's theory.

First, Kohlberg's emphasis is *not* on the actual behavior of the person. For Kohlberg, moral reasoning is concerned instead with the actual *reasoning* one uses to determine which actions are right or wrong. In other words, it is the reasoning that the adolescent utilizes to choose a particular value over another that is the object of Kohlberg's inquiry, not the actual behavior itself. Taking the Heinz dilemma that was mentioned earlier, Kohlberg's emphasis was not on Heinz's behavior (whether he stole or did not steal), but rather on the reasoning that was used to justify or not justify Heinz's behavior.

Second, Kohlberg is concerned not with the "content" of the moral reasoning, but only in the moral reasoning itself. In other words, the values (the content) that a person prizes are not Kohlberg's concern; his interest lies in the reasoning that the person utilizes in choosing a particular value or explaining the meaning that is given to a value. Again, taking the Heinz dilemma as an example, let us say that Heinz steals the drug. Whether we decide that Heinz should or should not have stolen the drug is called the "content" of the dilemma. This is not Kohlberg's concern. Kohlberg is concerned, instead, with the reasoning behind Heinz's choice. What reasons did the subject give for either advocating stealing or objecting to stealing? It is this reasoning (structure) that determines the stage of one's moral development.

Thus, although the actual values (content) and behaviors are important, the determinent of levels of moral reasoning relies on the actual reasoning that is employed in response to the dilemmas. In discussing the adolescent's spiritual growth, then, these two points are highly significant. Although Kohlberg has contributed extensively to our knowledge about the complexity of moral reasoning, his theory in itself is inadequate when we are speaking about a spirituality for adolescents. An adolescent spirituality must consider both the values that the adolescent actually possesses (are they Christian?) and the actual behaviors that the adolescent manifests in everyday life (are his or her actions oriented toward love of God and neighbor?).

Having summarized Kohlberg's theory, there are several avenues through which moral reasoning advances to higher stages. The first avenue arises from Kohlberg's view that cognitive disequilibrium can be a significant factor in advancing a person's moral reasoning. This disequilibrium process represents the person's attempt to reason at one stage above his or her present level of moral reasoning. When the person is presented with a dilemma that requires level of reasoning one stage above his or her present level of reasoning, the resulting contradictions and confusions (disequilibrium) lead the person to make sense of this inner imbalance by advancing one stage in moral reasoning. Adults can aid the moral reasoning advancement of their students, therefore, by presenting dilemmas and reasoning that stimulate the young persons to reflect on these dilemmas from a different perspective and thereby foster advancement in moral reasoning.

A second method of advancement arises out of the social interactions within which the adolescent operates. Emphasis here should be placed on encouraging the person to assume another's role. This "role-taking" can be a positive force in contributing to the advancement of moral reasoning (see Selman later this chapter). Additionally, Kohlberg has maintained that the environment in which the person interacts must be evaluated with regard to the actual values that are presented and promoted. Specifically, the level of justice must be assessed. How are rewards distributed? Punishment handed out? Responsibilities shared? Environment exercises a critical influence on the person's own perceptions of another's actions as well as his or her understanding of justice. This environmental emphasis stresses the critical importance of social interactions, both in the family and at school, in helping to foster the young person's sense of justice.

In his earlier writings, Kohlberg argued that although the majority of adolescents (and adults) function at the conventional level, they possess the potential for more principled moral reasoning. With his colleague, Carol Gilligan, Kohlberg described the adolescent's development of moral reasoning. Kohlberg and Gilligan have noted the clear relationship between cognitive development and moral reasoning, for "the existence of moral stages implies that moral development has a basic cognitive-structural component."[22] Although few individuals over age 16 demonstrate postconventional thinking, Kohlberg has noted that individuals who do have principled moral thinking also possess formal operational thought. This fact led Kohlberg to assert that formal operational thinking is a condition for principled moral reasoning. Because we have already learned from Piaget that the attainment of formal thinking can be somewhat limited in adolescence, there arises the question of how much principled reasoning is really possible during the adolescent years.[23]

Yet we do need to see the relationship between principled reasoning and adolescent growth in both the high school and—most especially—the undergraduate college years. Even though there might be limits to the adolescent's capacity for formal thought and even if the extent of principled reasoning is questionable, the fact remains that adolescence is the time when questions about deeper meaning are initially asked and values are critically examined. As we have already seen with Piaget, adolescence is a pivotal time in the development of a deepening reflective capacity for relating to and finding meaning in the world. The questions, quandaries, and dilemmas that adolescents encounter can stimulate the beginning of reasoning that will eventually reflect postconventional thinking.

In his earlier writings, Kohlberg envisioned the secondary school years as marking the adolescent's use of conventional moral reasoning as well as setting the stage for later moral development. He and Gilligan state that "it is in adolescence, then, that the child has the cognitive capability for moving from a conventional to a postconventional, reflective, or philosophic view of values and society."[24]

The adolescent's acquisition of formal thought, combined with the new experiences of the secondary school years, i.e., diverse attitudes, greater possibilities, and wider perspectives, provide the opportunity for advancing moral reasoning. Yet in this advancement other experiences also enter the adolescent's life. The adolescent's increasing interactions and experiences of other people, events, and situations bring about a growing sense of relativity. The adolescent discovers that right and wrong vary according to the cultural expectations and norms of society. This growing awareness of relativism is enhanced by the adolescent's own personal life experiences that reflect diversity and ambiguity. Most important, however, the adolescent, in the midst of this relativity, lacks commitment to deeper values and principled reasoning. Thus, in the midst of numerous transitions and yet-to-be-realized-commitments, the adolescent will often display behaviors that fail to take into account the wider demands and commitments that all others deserve. Instead, adolescents often seem to be locked in a sort of rugged individualism that seeks solace and security from peer behavior. In delineating this phenomenon, Kohlberg remarks that one of the most striking characteristics of adolescents is their oft-repeated remark "do your own thing, and let others do theirs."[25] Such reasoning lacks a universal concern for others and focuses instead on personal desires and needs.

Kohlberg also discovered that, as the adolescent proceeds to college, an interesting phenomenon occurs. The late adolescents who previously evidenced conventional moral reasoning regressed to stage 2 thinking upon entering college.[26] The explanation for this regression was two-fold: (1) the middle-class student realized that adult behavior was inconsistent, and (2) the student encountered the diverse points of view that are so much a part of the college experience. The adolescent's encounter with diversity jolts his or her conventional thinking, and he or she regresses to the hedonistic orientation of stage 2. This phenomenon has been labeled "transitional" by Kohlberg, since the college students returned to the post-conventional level by age 25.[27]

Psychologist Elliot Turiel has offered another explanation for this regressive tendency. Turiel believes that, instead of really regressing, the adolescent is actually experiencing the breakdown of his or her current level of moral reasoning, a step that is essential to the emergence of a more mature or advanced level of moral reasoning. The late adolescent experience in the college years brings both conflicts and contradictions. This is especially influential in the transition from stage 4, and conventional morality, to stage 5, and the beginnings of principled morality. Among the areas that the late adolescent questions are the diversity of value systems, questions of external standards, authority, and God. As a result, the late adolescent shows increasing concern for individual rights, freedom, equality, and the construction of personal values. (Society, says the late adolescent, can no longer impose morality on the individual; hence one has a right to do one's own thing.) From this standpoint, the adolescent might well reject more traditional notions of morality. What is really happening for the adolescent, says Turiel, is a transformation of the adolescent's present moral reasoning level, and the foundation is laid for movement to a higher stage of moral reasoning. As a consequence, during this in-between stage, there is much confusion and questioning.[28]

Psychologist Martin Hoffman offers still a third perspective on this phenomenon, which surfaces in the college years. What might simply be happening, says Hoffman, is that if adolescents "are confronted both by evidence for relativism as well as the fact that their prior moral values do not fit the real world, their prior values will be undermined, thus creating a void of meaning. To fill this void they may search for new values, which, for some individuals, entails selecting from an array of available ideologies."[29]

Theologian James Fowler, in his book *Stages of Faith,* has reported that Kohlberg now concludes that his early assertion that adolescents might obtain a level of principled moral reasoning was inadequate. Using "new scoring criteria," Fowler reports that "no true stage 5s" emerged before the age of 24.[30] Several reasons are offered for this revision. First, the adolescent needs to resolve his or her identity crises to allow him or her to make full, free commitments to others. Second, the adolescent needs to undergo two types of "experiences" in order to make his or her way toward principled reasoning. These are: (1) the adolescent must leave home (hence, we

51

are talking about the post-high school years) and encounter the diversity and ambiguity of new experiences, where he or she can shift and sort out values to find his or her own commitments to specific ethical principles; and (2) the adolescent must take upon himself or herself a commitment to be responsible for others and live with the experience of having made "moral choices" that are "irreversible." Both of these experiences are usually beyond the capabilities of even college undergraduates. It thus appears that principled reasoning is more the task of young adulthood, although, as we have seen, the experiences of middle and late adolescence prepares the way for this moral advancement.[31]

Finally, recent work on this regressive phenomenon that occurs during the college years might well be a consequence of the scoring procedures used in analyzing the answers to dilemmas. Perhaps a central component in the developing adolescent's capacity for moral reasoning is the notion of "context" in moral reasoning. In other words, the adolescent increasingly subjects moral reasoning to the actual concrete situation in which his or her value choices are made. Personal values, life experiences, and questions of meaning and faith must now be submitted to the particular situation in which they are found. No longer can there be an appeal to the simplistic absolute that is found in earlier childhood years. Such simplistic appeals seem woefully inadequate to the late adolescent, in light of the complexity and diversity that he or she now confronts. The use of an alternative scoring procedure, based on the work of Harvard educator William Perry, takes into account this contextual basis for moral reasoning. When this alternate scoring procedure is used to measure moral dilemmas it is discovered that late adolescents actually progress rather than regress in their level of moral reasoning. In other words, the regression in moral reasoning that was found in adolescents might well be attributable to the type of scoring that was used in examining adolescent response to moral dilemmas.[32]

2   Perry

Because the encounter with relativism is a crucial factor for the late adolescent in determining his or her moral reasoning, we shall examine the work of William Perry, who incorporates this dimension within his developmental schema for late adolescents. Perry's work enriches the understanding of adolescent moral reasoning because of his attention to two critical phenomena: the experience of relativism and the need to form an initial commitment.

William Perry's work shows how the late adolescent develops ethical reasoning in the undergraduate college years.[33] His subjects were undergraduate students from Harvard and Radcliffe. For Perry, the key to the college undergraduate's development is the experience of commitment, which germinates in the college years. The college undergraduate, according to Perry, progresses through nine positions in his or her quest for mature ethical reasoning. These nine positions are divided into three developmental stages: Dualism (positions 1, 2, 3); Relativism (positions 4, 5, 6); and Commitment (positions 7, 8, 9).

A brief outline of Perry's nine positions follows:

Dualism

In this first sequence of positions, the adolescent moves from an absolute and simplistic conceptualization of situations and life experiences (good-bad, right-wrong) to a more diversified view, which Perry labels "multiplicity."

Position 1: Basic duality. The adolescent views the world in a simplistic way. All difficulties and complex situations are resolved by appeal to an absolute—some type of authority. In this position, obedience and authority are prized. In a liberal arts setting, Perry believes that no student who passes through his or her freshman year maintains this position because the climate of the liberal arts college is opposed to such a value position. Thus, the college experience and this duality are "incompatible."

Position 2: Multiplicity prelegitimate. Now the adolescent becomes aware of positions that are disparate from his or her own. It is at this stage that the encounter with pluralism begins. This experience, however, of pluralism (multiplicity) is seen as "alien" or "unreal" to the undergraduate. There is still a simplistic right or wrong threaded through the student's perception and thinking. He or she views diversity as confusion on the part of authorities (which they will eventually correct). Or this diversity is perceived in a more benign way as the authorities' attempt to present new experiences to the student so that he or she can profit from them.

Position 3: Multiplicity subordinate. The student now recognizes diversity and pluralism, but this phenomenon is temporary. There is still the "absolute," which remains to be discovered. The student believes that, in time, the authorities will find the true answer. The crucial point of this position is that the adolescent now admits the diversity that he or she is experiencing and accepts it as real. The adolescent is puzzled because answers that were present in previous years are simply no longer there, or at least they are not readily available.

The portrait that emerges from position 3 is especially significant for the Catholic adolescent. If the adolescent is raised in a home environment in which explicit Christian values are articulated without any reference to other points of view, then the adolescent might well leave this home environment with a set of values and beliefs that have not been submitted to much personal reflection. The college environment might well lead the adolescent to experience situations in which views that had never before been challenged prove to be distressing and threatening. If the adolescent's faith tends to be unreflective and taken for granted, these new experiences may well lead to cynicism, disillusionment, and a rejection of long-held beliefs and religious practices.

Perry's theory poses interesting questions concerning attempts by the Christian family and school to accomplish religious socialization. The experience of late childhood and adolescence requires opportunities for the young person to reflect on and discuss his or her personal religious values and the significance of these values in his or her own life. Opportunities for the adolescent's gradual experience of diversity and complexity of life experiences also need to be fostered. The adolescent's developmental need to witness a clear faith articulated by the family, the school, and other adults is accompanied by another need to experience diversity and ambiguity and to reflect on them, so that the adolescent can eventually integrate personal meaning and moral commitment within these developing years.

Relativism

In the stage of relativism, the adolescent realizes multiplicity and accepts it. The student not only encounters diversity but also mediates this pluralism of values, ideas, and the like into his or her own worldview.

Position 4: Multiplicity correlate or relativism subordinate   Within

54

this position, we can put adolescents into one of two groups. Some adolescents will emerge from position 3 and accept relativism, the multiplicity of competing values and ideas. In this instance, the student internalizes a relativistic stance, which then becomes the framework within which to negate authority. The position leads to such statements as "everyone has a right to his or her own opinion." Thus, in this position, authority is now opposed to relativism, the newly discovered ally of the late adolescent.

A majority of students at this stage choose a second alternative, however. In the "relativism subordinate" position, the adolescent views authorities as permitting yet overseeing the presence of relativism. At times, however, the adolescent recognizes his or her need to admit the inevitability of relativism and also notices that authorities, too, must admit this inevitability.

Position 5: Relativism correlate competing or diffuse   Once the adolescent enters this stage, he or she sees the necessity of relativism. The duality of right-wrong is now subordinate to the situation (context) in which life experiences occur. We note, therefore, a fundamental shift in the adolescent's thinking. Up to and including position 4, the adolescent attempts to fit divergence of views and ideas into a dualistic stance. Now, however, relativism itself is accepted on its own terms as a legitimate mode of perceiving and thinking, inasmuch as "relativism is perceived as the common characteristic of *all* thought, *all* knowing, *all* of man's relations to his world."[34] The dualistic position that was previously so common is now an exception in a relativistic world. This fundamental altering of the late adolescent's thinking is a gradual process of unfolding that goes almost undetected; yet it emerges as a commonplace, pivotal form of thinking in the late adolescent years. In this relativistic stance, however, the student still needs to realize the consequences of his or her personal actions.

We should take special note here of the place of religion in this relativistic position. First, Perry notes that position 5 represents the point of departure between belief and faith. Belief itself is an acceptance that "requires no investment by the person."[35] In order to arrive at faith, there must first be some form of doubt. It is only when one's faith is problematic that the adolescent moves to an acceptance of faith that involves the Transcendent.

When the adolescent accepts faith in the relativistic framework, he or she makes a commitment in the midst of relativism; however, the student's acceptance of relativism leads him or her to support this differing faith stance while, at the same time, he or she affirms personal faith. What arises for the adolescent is a personalized commitment to the absolute in a relativistic world.

Position 6: Commitment foreseen   The adolescent now views the consequences of a relativistic world: the need for some type of commitment. Perry defines commitment as "an act, or ongoing activity relating a person as agent and chooser to aspects of his life in which he invests his energies, his care, and his identity."[36] Commitment, then, becomes the affirmation of self within a pluralistic world. The importance of this commitment cannot be overstressed when we are discussing the spiritual growth of the adolescent. Now, upon entering this position, the adolescent finds himself or herself facing real questions of faith: What are the values that I hold? Are they Christian? Do I treat others in loving and caring ways? What does real friendship require of me? What are my personal political and philosophical beliefs? What does life, God, and the church really mean to me? It is at this time, of course, that Jesus' call to "come, follow me" takes on increasing meaning for the adolescent.

Commitment arises after the adolescent perceives this relativistic world and accepts it. Commitment means personal decision-making in a world of many choices and possibilities. The adolescent makes his or her commitment in a variety of life areas: career, marriage, religion, politics, friendship, and personal values. The adolescent personally decides the extent to which previous values and behaviors will now form a part of his or her personal commitment.

In addition to commitments made in the various areas that have already been mentioned, the adolescent's commitments also reflect various styles in which these commitments are acted out. Perry notes that adolescents must balance various styles when they invest themselves in commitments. He says there are two types of balances: external and subjective. External balances are acted out in styles that include narrowness vs. breadth, number vs. intensity, and self-centered vs. other-centered. The styles of subjective balances include action vs. contemplation, immediacy vs. detachment, stability vs. flexibility, continuity vs. diversity, control vs. openness, and maintenance vs. growth. Styles provide the adolescent a fuller, richer expression of self as he or she increasingly accepts commitments. An adolescent, for example, who says "I enjoy a variety of people and friends" displays commitment to relationships that involve stylistic approaches that are other-centered, encompass a breadth or spectrum and are both diverse and open. The adolescent constructs his or her personal identity through a variety of both commitments and stylistic approaches.

At this point, the adolescent has yet to experience the actual commitment in various areas of his or her life. Yet the adolescent does foresee commitment as the answer to a relativistic world, which he or she is personally experiencing. With time, this realization of commitment's necessity leads to further acceptance of authentic choices such as vocational aspirations, moral values, and relationship choices.

Commitment

When the adolescent enters the commitment stage he or she consciously affirms various ideas and values within a relativistic world. Positions 7, 8, and 9 describe the late adolescent's deeper understanding of what commitment entails.

Position 7: Initial commitment   The adolescent might, for example, give real consideration to a particular field of study, such as business, social work, or law, but does not yet realize the implications or consequences of such a commitment.

Position 8: Orientation in implications of commitment   The adolescent gradually comes to realize the consequences of his or her commitment. At the same time, there is a growing awareness that he or she must take responsibility for personal actions. The adolescent must decide issues such as how much to trust himself or herself—and others—in forming commitments, how much to listen to other's opinions, or to what extent should he or she identify with other's commitments. At various junctures, the adolescent sorts out these numerous questions as he or she slowly comes to make commitments in various areas of his or her own life.

Position 9: Developing commitment(s)   This position is really an extension of positions 7 and 8. The person is now capable of true commitment to many facets of life. One encounters life with a real sense of personal identity. The adolescent affirms his or her identity while realizing that commitment is an ongoing, unfolding process that encompasses his or her entire future.

Additional Patterns

In describing his schema, Perry notes that late adolescents often deviate from his growth patterns. Perry identifies three additional patterns that portray the nongrowth tendencies that are commonly experienced in the late adolescent years. Perry expressed the growth of the adolescent as "wavelike," inasmuch as this growth tends to come in "surges." Between these spurts of growth, the adolescent at times waits, reasons, or retreats, until the arrival of the next period of growth. Thus, during these college years, the adolescent's development does not follow a linear pattern but, rather, is subject to numerous fluctuations characterized by turbulence, rethinking, and reassessment.

The first type of adolescent regression during the college years is labeled *temporizing*. In this position, which can last a year, the adolescent pauses before making any future attempts toward continued growth. The adolescent reassesses and solidifies personal experiences to gain an increased sense of self in the process. Sometimes adolescents appear to be pausing, waiting for the next surge in growth. Other adolescents, however, might simply wait for a personal experience that will resolve all the difficulties and dilemmas he or she is now experiencing.

The second haven from growth is known as *retreat*. Although retreat can occur at any stage, it usually occurs as a return to stage 2 or 3. In the retreat stage, the adolescent often finds solace in the authority that emanates from position 2. We might recall that this position exhibits a dualistic stance toward the world. Through this regressive state, the adolescent finds comfort in the support that is provided in a dualism that shields the undergraduate from an ambiguous, complex, and relativistic world.

The final form of the adolescent's pause in growth is labeled *escape*. This escape can take several forms. The first is known as *dissociation*. In this form, the adolescent disengages from involvement and refuses responsibility, self-confrontation, and commitment. A second form is *encapsulation* and is normally found in positions 4, 5, 6. Here the adolescent uses relativism and multiplicity as defenses. The adolescent resorts to relativism and multiplicity to shield himself or herself from opposing values and ideas. As a result, he or she does not have to make a commitment and, thus, actually escapes any real commitment in the process. The adolescent reasons that if relativism is everywhere, then no real commitment need be made.

A final form of escape is the *over commitment* of some adolescents. In this form of escape, the adolescent concentrates all his or her energy on one activity or goal. The adolescent, in effect, eschews the challenge of relativism and the demands made by commitment. This false type of commitment can be seen in the adolescent's total absorption in one academic subject, school activity, school politics, or relationships.

Perry's schema provides an overview for the adolescent's acquisition of a personal, meaningful value system. For the most part, the student who completes freshman year of college cannot really remain in Basic Duality (position 1). High school adolescents are found in these stages, but most college freshmen advance to positions 3, 4, or 5. On the other hand, seniors are more likely to evince positions 6, 7, or 8. Position 9 is a level of maturity that is usually most ascribed to the college graduate. Some student responses, however, appear to show evidence of this position.

3   Kohlberg and Perry Compared

It is helpful, now, to compare the developmental schemas of Kohlberg and Perry. Both theorists are concerned with the moral development of the adolescent. Perry's study, however, concerns older adolescents in a certain environment (liberal arts college). Perry's theory also tends to view moral development as encompassing some form of ethical commitment that the adolescent must make despite his or her growing encounter with relativism. Perry's theory enriches the notion of adolescent development, concentrating as it does on what the adolescent ethically commits the self to as he or she enters the world of young adulthood.[37]

In summary, then, Perry finds that the adolescent progresses through a variety of growth positions. Dualistic responses typify the early years of life inasmuch as the adolescent perceives the world in a simplistic way. By the high school years, however, the adolescent usually sees the complexity of life and the inadequacy of a dualistic stance. In the college years, the late adolescent experiences the world's inherent relativity. At the same time, though, the need arises to place this relativity in some type of order that will lead to an initial commitment. Adolescents can find themselves in various positions regarding various dimensions of their lives, such as relationships, personal values, vocation or career choices. Furthermore, adolescents pass through various positions at varying rates depending on their own personal life situations. Some adolescents may be well along the way in a commitment to a career choice yet still lack a philosophy of life or a sense of personally thought-out values. On the other hand, the adolescent might find a great personal meaning in relationships, but lack any real sense of direction regarding career choice. Finally, along the way to commitment, many adolescents will experience periods of doubt and confusion from time to time as they pursue the quest for commitment in a relativistic world.

A crucial aspect of Perry's schema is the adolescent's growing awareness of complexity and divergence in life, coupled with the attempt to understand the resulting ambiguity and make sense of it. These experiences are, first, seen in multiplicity; varying opinions and values are perceived but labeled illegitimate and unwarranted. Later, the perception of relativism emerges. This acceptance of relativism realizes the second aspect of Perry's schema whereby some positions are seen as better than others, thus laying the foundation for future commitment.

We see, therefore, the critical role that commitment exercises in the spiritual growth of the adolescent. The question posed by a spirituality for adolescents is: How can the adolescent more fully integrate a sense of commitment to Jesus' call to "come, follow me" with his or her growing acceptance of a personally held value system that he or she finds meaningful? The adolescent can ask: What, in effect, am I really committed to? In what ways do my behaviors manifest the values that I hold? How important is the call of Jesus in my life and how am I committed to this call? Likewise, in what ways am I still growing in commitment to this call? The hedonistic or dualistic utterances of the child are far removed from the statements of a college graduate, who can reflect a profound sense of commitment to Gospel values.

As we discuss moral reasoning and commitment, however, we should be mindful of the limits of moral developmental theory. Theologian Donald Gelpi has noted that Kohlberg's analysis illuminates a humanistic ethic but is inadequate for an ethic of faith.[38] In other words, morality must be grounded on Gospel values and the life of Jesus. A human, naturalistic ethic must not be substituted for faith, the values of the Gospel, and Jesus' invitation to "come, follow me." What the moral developmental theory has done, however, is complement the adolescent's spiritual growth by offering a perspective that allows him or her to integrate Christian values more and more within normal developmental growth patterns. We agree, therefore, with Ronald Duska and Mariellen Whelan when they assert that the Christian commitment offers "content for the formal structure that Kohlberg identified."[39]

Along the same lines, Rick Ellrod has argued that Kohlberg's schema is inadequate in the way it addresses the "complexity of the human life situation."[40] Making moral decisions needs more than a principle of justice. It requires an explicit statement of values and a prioritizing of these values in the "concrete" situations of human experience. A maturing moral stance for the adolescent years, then, must provide a conscious realization of what these values are and how the adolescent's behaviors mirror these values in everyday life situations.

4   Moral Development and Spiritual Growth

Having examined moral developmental theory, we can now integrate Jesus' Gospel invitation to "come, follow me"—the cornerstone of adolescent spirituality—into the developmental perspective offered by Kohlberg and Perry. With this in mind we now turn to ways to foster spiritual growth in adolescents in the context of moral developmental theory.

1 Adolescents differ greatly in their own understandng and reasoning about personal values. The adolescent's developmental level influences how he or she perceives personal problems and life situations. It is helpful for the adult to be able to understand how an adolescent reasons about life dilemmas and moral problems. Some points and questions the adult will want to keep in mind include the following:

• What is the adolescent's stance toward authority? Does authority seem threatening to the adolescent? Does he or she feel estranged from authority? If so, from what particular types of authority is he or she estranged—parents? the institutional church? school authorities? Is there an affective level of fear or mistrust?

• Can the adolescent perceive that many different values are often involved in life situations, personal relationships, and moral problems? Can he or she articulate what values are important in his or her own life? Can he or she prioritize values, that is, can the adolescent determine what values have priority for him or her in this particular situation?

• How capable is this adolescent of going outside himself or herself and understanding the perspective of others? Can he or she understand on an interpersonal level the feelings and ideas of others?

• How much continuity is there between the values articulated by the adolescent and his or her actual behavior? Can the adolescent perceive any disparity between what he or she proclaims and what he or she actually does? Can the adolescent discuss these disparities and gain insights from these differences?

2. The adolescent often goes through a gradual process in which he or she questions previously held values and comes into a period of confusion and questioning in his or her life. We might note how comfortable this adolescent is with the ambiguity of his or her own personal values. Can the adolescent discuss this confusion in various areas of his or her life?

Likewise, the adolescent also gradually learns that personal values are not equal. Life situations and experiences sometimes force him or her to choose some values over others. Often, when the adolescent is making value choices, he or she is hesitant and unclear about what his or her values actually are. "Scaling" is an excellent technique to help the adolescent examine his or her personal values and prioritize them. This technique has two variations. In one, the adult offers the adolescent a list of values such as love, honor, self-worth, money, and success and asks the adolescent to rank which values are most important.[41] The adult and adolescent then reflect together on various situations the adolescent has experienced to see if those values that ranked highest also appear in this personal experience.

In the other variation of this technique, the adult focuses on a personal experience of the adolescent—it would be especially wise to pick one to which the adolescent has devoted some thought and consideration—or one that is important for the adolescent, and reflect with him or her on what values are in the experience. Insightful questions are helpful here for eliciting values. The adult might ask, for example: "Does that tell you anything about yourself?" Or, "Do you think you were saying anything about yourself when you did that?" Once the adolescent mentions various values, then time can be spent ranking these values or discussing which values are most important to the adolescent. There can then be a discussion of the behaviors that portray these values.

Whatever technique that is used to elicit values, the adolescent and adult can also spend time considering "why" the young person selected these values. A variation on this is to carefully evaluate the top three to five values and the lowest three to five that the adolescent has ranked. Then time can be spent exploring any differences between these two sets of values. The adolescent might consider if there are any differences in the content of the top and lowest values? Does this say anything to the adolescent?

3 A counseling technique that invites moral development in a spiritual context is the experiencing of a "sense of dissatisfaction."[42] In this state, the adolescent experiences inconsistency in the self because of the discrepancy between the values one desires to display and the actual behaviors one portrays in life. The feeling of this discrepancy leads the person to experience dissatisfaction with his or her life. When the adult engages the adolescent in reflection on this area, he or she should emphasize concrete situations that mirror this dissatisfaction in the adolescent's own life. A helpful scripture passage that points out this sense of dissatisfaction is Romans 7:15 in which Paul talks about his own inner struggle. The adult should provide positive support for the adolescent as they reflect, together, on these various experiences. Then, the adult can explore with the adolescent various ways to integrate Christian values and personal behavior.

4 Since adolescence reflects the gradual learning of how ambiguous life situations can actually be, a good point for discussion is how the adolescent's value structure is represented across the various developmental tasks he or she faces. Psychiatrist Frederick Coons, for example, speaks of four tasks that the late adolescent must accomplish: (1) to resolve the parent-child relationship, (2) to solidify one's sexual identity, (3) to develop the capacity for true intimacy, and (4) to choose one's life work.[43] An adult can concen-

trate on any one of these areas with the adolescent and reflect on how values are present in each developmental task that the adolescent must accomplish.

5 Theologian Donald Gelpi has applied his notion of religious experience to the Kohlberg schema. For an adolescent who is in stage 3, Gelpi suggests reflection not only on the critical importance of loving others as one loves the self, but also on the Biblical command to love God "with all your mind, all your heart, and all your strength." In other words, the adolescent's gravitation toward approval from others needs to be tempered by the command to love God. The adult might profitably spend time with the adolescent reflecting on ways the young person might show love and care for others in his or her own concrete life situation. The adult and the adolescent can also reflect on the extent and depth of the adolescent's love for others. Another profitable approach is to spend time reflecting on how the adolescent's experience of love has deepened with time, has grown over these past years.

We can recall that the stage 4 adolescent or adult focuses on a law-and-order reasoning. Gelpi suggests that law must be seen as a *means* rather than as an ultimate end for the adolescent at this stage. That is, Jesus has come to fulfill the law, not to abolish it. The adult might explore with the adolescent the extent that behaviors conform to the adolescent's own peer group or other authority figures in his or her life. A productive question to put to the adolescent is, "Do your peers unduly influence your life?" Reflection should emphasize the role of Jesus in the young person's personal actions and His influence on them. Adolescents need to seriously consider the tyranny of peer influence and what role this influence has on their lives. Pressure to conform to peers becomes, in effect, its own law. The adolescent must subject his or her relationship with peers to the command of Jesus to love God and one another.[44]

Principled reasoning incorporates a more universal type of value—a sense of universal respect and justice toward all men and women—whereas the Christian ethic reflects a universal commitment to love. The adult might then reflect with the adolescent not only on how he or she shows love, but also on the universality of this love toward others. With younger adolescents, the adult can place the emphasis on how the young person shows love in the family, at school, with friends. With older adolescents, a good format is simply to ask the adolescent for his or her own definition of love. It is important to note here the extent to which the adolescent can speak of love from affective, intellectual, and religious dimensions. Thus, the adult can reflect with the adolescent on personal relationships, intellectual understandings of social and political issues, and the place of personal values in his or her own life. The adult can then ask about the ways that love is shown in these experiences or reflections.

One way to aid the adolescent to realize the place of love is to portray the "ideal" situation of love in its fullest realization in a personal relationship, a social issue, or an issue or experience that has great personal meaning in the adolescent's life. Two comparisons can be made: (a) consider the adolescent's situation with him or her and compare it to the "ideal" situation that he or she has talked about, the way that Jesus would respond, or the way the Gospel would ask us to respond; (b) with the ideal situation in mind, explore with the adolescent his or her various personal habits, tendencies, and external influences that threaten this ideal sense of love or keep it from being realized. Then, reflect with the adolescent on the ways this love is presently realized and/or compromised, and whether there are possible ways to alter this situation in order to more fully realize the ideal of love (John 15:17).

6 From William Perry's perspective, the late adolescent confronts relativism and needs to emerge from the college experience with a sense of commitment. The adult reflects with the adolescent not only on how relativity is handled, but also on what types of commitment the adolescent can and wants to make in personal life choices, in areas such as relationships, career, philosophy of life, and, of course, his or her own faith stance. What is the place of Christian commitment in this adolescent's life? Can the adolescent translate a commitment to love or to the Gospel into different areas of his or her life? The adult can reflect with the adolescent on what he or she is willing to commit the self to and what place the Gospel has in this commitment.

There also has been research to indicate that when adolescents engage in moral reasoning they reason at levels below the levels that have been reported when they are confronted with hypothetical situations. In other words, everyday life dilemmas might result in levels of moral reasoning that vary from findings that have been reported in the literature.[45] It is critically important that adolescents have the opportunity to reflect on the everyday life situations of their own lives—personal relationships, career choices, and so on. It is in everyday living, not in hypothetical dilemmas, that the adolescent has the actual opportunity to enact the experience of the Gospel in his or her life. The adult can offer opportunities for the adolescent to reflect with him or her on the everyday, typical experiences of these developmental years. Time spent with the adolescent can be used to clarify and articulate personal values that surface during these everyday experiences. The adult might then invite the adolescent to share his or her reflections on how these everyday life experiences point to commitment to personal values. And lastly the adult might ask the adolescent to delineate ways in which Gospel values and Jesus' call to "come, follow me" are part of this commitment.

Faith Development

According to Kohlberg, as the child develops a sense of being a moral philosopher, he or she creates a parallel understanding of himself or herself as a theologian. Just as the child demonstrates an increasingly complex structure of moral reasoning, he or she also shows a deepening understanding of his or her faith. Kohlberg hypothesizes that a moral stage precedes the development of a faith stage because a longer period of time is needed to conceptualize and construct a faith system than is needed to construct a moral stance. He also concludes that universal moral principles cannot be founded on faith because not all people subscribe to the same beliefs.[46]

Theologian James Fowler, on the other hand, maintains that faith is neither derived from morality nor grounded in it.[47] Rather, one's moral view is supported by the beliefs and loyalties that one cherishes.

Fowler provides an extensive theory of faith development that is influenced by the developmental perspective of Jean Piaget and Lawrence Kohlberg. Just as Kohlberg has argued for a clear distinction between the structure and content of moral reasoning, so too Fowler has maintained a similar distinction between the structure and content of faith. In this regard, Jesuit educator Edwin McDermott points out that Fowler's distinction is "not new" to Catholic teaching, but rather incorporates recent theological insights concerning faith.[48]

Fowler studies *how* adolescents come to conceptualize their faith view (the structure) and develop it. This is clearly separate from the actual content of faith, that is, what one believes and values, such as specific dogmas, and the value one places in a particular religious tradition. At the same time, however, Fowler cautions against dismissing the content of faith. Why? Because faith cannot be understood as a structural process, unless it arises out of actual, lived experiences that incorporate personally held values and beliefs—in other words, the content of faith itself.

Fowler accepts many of the stage theorists' premises concerning developmental growth. Each stage, for example, builds on the prior stage; the stages are sequential and invariant, and they grow increasingly complex. Fowler has yet to claim universality for his stages, however, because his studies are still in process. But in one critical area he distinguishes himself from the work of Piaget and Kohlberg. According to Fowler, Piaget maintains a distinct separation between cognition and affect. From a theoretical standpoint, Kohlberg accepts this distinction, but, in reality, cognition and affect remain inseparable. Fowler, however, maintains that, in faith, "cognition and affection are inextricably bound up together."[49] According to Fowler, any discussion of faith must blend this affective dimension with a cognitive understanding.

For Fowler, faith is best understood as a *verb* instead of a noun. Too often we associate faith with *what* we believe, that is, with the actual dogmas, rules, or tenets of religion. This is the content of faith. Faith, for Fowler, however, is *relating* to someone or something in a way that invests our heart, our care, and our hope. He says that "faith is a person's way of seeing him- or herself in relation to others against a background of shared meaning and purpose."[50] From this perspective, we realize that faith is a verb; it is an active, dynamic process playing "a central role in shaping the responses a person will make in and against the force field of his or her life."[51] Likewise, faith is posed in relationship to something else, because "faith is an irreducibly *relational* phenomenon."[52]

It is a commitment to "someone or something." Faith is the commitment we make to others, to groups, and to communities.

There is a deep sense of trust in this commitment. There also exists the commitment to share community values. These values are ideals that deeply touch our hopes, perspectives, and sense of purpose. Faith, then, is in relation to both a transcendent (something beyond the self that enters our lives) and the human community of which we are a part. In summary, Fowler says: "Faith, then, is a person's or a community's way-of-being-in-relation to our neighbors and to the causes and companions of our lives."[53]

Fowler states that the transitions through the stages of faith do not occur without difficulties. It is often a long, arduous process that can sometimes be painful. A person is frequently in the process of terminating one stage of faith and attempting to construct the next one. Adolescents, for example, are often seen as attempting to leave stage 3 and enter stage 4—a process that is customarily fraught with doubt and pain. Fowler is also careful to point out that individuals must not be judged by the stage of faith in which they reside. An individual's passage from one stage to another underscores his or her personal attempt to construct ways to know, value, and relate to others.

Fowler bases his theory of faith development on interviews that he has conducted with both children and adults. These interviews elicited responses on a variety of issues, such as death and afterlife, evil and suffering, the meaning of life, and ideal manhood or womanhood. From these interviews, Fowler and his associates could evaluate a person's perspective of himself, as well as the person's thinking on these various issues. Fowler's concentration on these issues allowed him to bypass any specific religious tradition and to stress critical questions that face all men and women.

A summary of Fowler's stages of faith development follows. In our discussion of these stages, we will give particular attention to those that involve adolescence. We will then address how Fowler's theory can be used to help foster the spiritual growth of the adolescent.

Stage 1: Intuitive-Projective

Children ranging in age from four to eight are typically found in the Intuitive-Projective stage. This stage places great emphasis on important others in the child's life, especially parents and family members. Likewise, the child relies on the parents as a source of authority regarding religious matters. At this stage the child has difficulty in determining cause and effect, divorcing fact from fantasy, and understanding the sequential nature of various events. Symbols and images at this stage mirror for the child the reality that they represent. A drawing of a flower, for example, actually *is* the flower. The challenge for this stage is to develop a more conscious focus on the future.

Stage 2: Mythic-Literal

The years for stage 2 come approximately between 6 or 7 and 11 or 12—the threshold of adolescence. Fowler notes, however, that some adults possess structural patterns that reflect this stage. Usually this stage begins in middle-to-late childhood. The transition to this stage can often take one or two years, but usually by age 12, the transition to stage 3 is already in process.

At this stage, the child gradually comes to bring his or her attention to rest on the world and to distinguish the real from the unreal. The stage 2 child also reflects a private world of thought and fantasy. Cognitively, the child now functions at the concrete operations level. The child can reason causally and develop categories for classifying various experiences. The child acquires some mastery of the surrounding environment, but this is usually on the concrete level. Therefore, he or she still has no capacity for abstraction and reflection. The child who has reached this stage manipulates stories and myths in order to find personal meaning. There also emerges a role-taking capacity, for the child now realizes that others may see and understand things differently.

During this stage, authorities for the child include not only the family, but also teachers and religious leaders, customs and traditions. The child makes nascent personal judgments, but still yields to trusted adults for conclusions and guidance, since a deep reflective capacity is still beyond his or her ability.

Moreover, the child at this stage envisions a sense of order and dependability. He or she acquires a sense of how things are and what they might become. There is a deeper comprehension of the real world, cause and effect, the actions of others, and the need for reciprocity in relationships. At this stage, God is viewed as being both faithful and lawful. Yet the world is still uncertain, and in many ways the child remains powerless. Thus, by embracing and involving himself or herself in religious belief and ritual, the child finds security while he or she expresses his or her faith in anticipation of the future and all it holds.

Stage 3: Synthetic-Conventional

Stage 3 encompasses both adolescents and adults. The average age of entry into this stage varies from 12 years to adulthood; departure from the Synthetic-Conventional stage can begin as early as 17 or 18, but a person can remain in this stage through middle or even late adulthood.

The salient characteristic of this stage, which coincides with the emergence of adolescence, is the concern with the interpersonal. Simply stated, the world for the adolescent is viewed in interpersonal terms and when the adolescent refers to other groups or entities, the language becomes decidedly personal. When speaking of government, for example, the adolescent will often refer to the *leaders* by name (and his or her personal dislike for them) rather than the structures of government itself.

The adolescent also acts in a conforming manner, that is to say, the ideas, expectations, and views of others are internalized in order to foster a growing identity. The adolescent begins to question and rely on the views of significant others to help construct his or her own value system. At the same time, the world for an adolescent in stage 3 grows increasingly complex. There are roles to be played in family, work, sports, friendship, and so on. Mutual expectations of self and others emerge along with deepening relationships with significant others.

At this stage, the complexity and lack of consensus among significant others can lead the young person to "compartmentalize." In this defensive strategy, the adolescent (or adult) acts one way with friends, for example, and another way at home, thus compartmentalizing his or her behaviors among various groups.

There is another defensive strategy that can be employed called "hierarchy." In this strategy, the adolescent places one group or authority in a dominant category of influence and relegates all others to a secondary role. Thus, the adolescent might prioritize the peer group, and, as a result, downplay commitments to family, school, and other important figures.

At stage 3, cognitive functioning has now reached the formal

operational level. The adolescent engages in abstraction, hypothetical thinking, and deeper reflection. As noted in our discussion of
Piaget, the adolescent is now focusing on his or her own thought.
The adolescent is also now capable of initially developing a value
system that incorportes rudimentary philosophical and ideological
underpinnings.

Authorities who deal with adolescents at this stage need to be
"sincere," "genuine," and "truthful." We can note, of course, how
responsive high schol youth and college undergraduates are to
adults who are committed, warm, and open to their students. This
point is critically important for adults who minister to young people
who are in their adolescent years. As we have noted, adolescents at
this stage are in the process of beginning to form their own personal
value systems, yet, even with their deepening critical reflection,
they often need to fall back on and rely on trusted others for direction and needed advice. The inviting presence of an adult serves as
a pivotal event for the adolescent's deepening quest for values.

Furthermore, the boundaries of the adolescent's social environment are also expanding. Groups, races, and social classes are appreciated and loyalty to them is emphasized. Consequently, the
adolescent achieves a greater awareness of others outside his or her
own age group. This awareness of others is somewhat limited, however, because the impression of outsiders is often tinged with a
stereotypic image. Thus, the adolescent might well become aware of
the social injustice with which a racial or ethnic group has been
treated, yet still speak of them in stereotypic ways.

Of particular importance to an adolescent spirituality is the role
that symbols take on for the adolescent. Symbols are understood as
more than their mere physical presence or commonly used name,
such as "God"; symbols possess a distinctive personal quality.
Thus, Jesus Christ can be both a friend and companion whom the
adolescent can relate to. Relating with God, in effect, becomes much
more personal for the adolescent.

Faith at this stage sustains and supports the adolescent as he
or she encounters and experiences an increasingly ambiguous,
complex world. The reinforcement that this stage provides, however, does little to allow the adolescent the time to experience the
views and perspectives of others in deep, meaningful ways. As a
result, denial and oversimplification are defenses that the adoles-

cent utilizes to assuage the fear that emanates from future and unknown experiences.

The "dangers" of this stage are a reliance on significant others to such an extent that personally held beliefs and values are never consciously adopted or reflected upon. In other words, what arises is a truncated value system in which the adolescent simply "buys into" the values of those others in his or her life who are admired. Another danger that emerges during this stage is the failure of interpersonal relationships, which, of course, are so pivotal during this age period. Such failure in interpersonal relating might lead the adolescent to despair of any ultimate being (and meaning), or lead him or her to seek an intense and unrealizable (and false) intimacy with God as a way to compensate for the failure in interpersonal relationships.

Fowler identifies numerous experiences that aid the breakdown of stage 3 faith and brings the adolescent to the transition between stages 3 and 4. Among these instances that lead to the breakdown of stage 3 faith are: (1) contradictions and disagreements among the significant others who are valued; (2) the discovery that personally held beliefs, which are thought to be inviolable, are alterable (Fowler uses the poignant example of the Catholic who felt betrayed by the change from Latin to English in the mass); (3) instances which force the adolescent to reflect critically on his or her own beliefs and values and how he or she has formed them. Fowler notes that the adolescent experience of "leaving home" can set the stage for the examination that leads to the breakdown of stage 3 faith.[54]

Stage 4: Individuative-Reflective

The transition from stage 3 to stage 4 can be a protracted process. The onset of this transition roughly parallels college entrance (age 17 or 18) and lasts through the undergraduate college years (the early 20s). Fowler notes that numerous adults are in this stage 3–4 transition and that this process can often take place in the 30s and 40s.

Upon entering college, the adolescent can entertain the possibility of a faith that is both individuating and reflective. The transition to stage 4 faith allows the late adolescents to begin viewing a faith that is more and more "their own." Furthermore, this faith is not only more personal but ushers in the need for a faith expression that is both consistent and coherent. The late adolescent begins to be held responsible for a recognizable, logical expression of his or her faith. The college undergraduate not only senses the need for deepening reflectivity, but also the need to be open to both present and future experiences.

Late adolescents who have reached this stage are challenged to critically reflect on their own life and its meaning. Fowler notes that it is in this transition from stage 3 to stage 4 faith "that the late adolescent or adult must begin to take seriously the burden of responsibility for his or her own commitments, lifestyle, beliefs, and attitudes."[55] Stage 4 faith provides the adolescent with needed guidance "for religious or ideological orientation" and for "ethical and political responsibility in a world where the reality of relativism is threateningly real."[56] Although a full expression of this faith does not take form until young adulthood, it is in the college years that the demands of stage 4 faith surface for the college undergraduate. It is in the successful resolution of these transitional struggles that the adolescent emerges with a faith expression that is personally held and valued.

Two more stages, which emerge in later adulthood, follow stage 4. We shall mention them briefly.

Stage 5: Conjunctive Faith

The emergence of stage 5 is rarely seen before the age of 30. This stage evolves from the person's deepening life experience, which includes suffering, loss, and injustice. Stage 5 assumes a deepening knowledge of the self in which one explores the depths of his or her own being. In stage 4, the self has emerged as individual and responsible. Now the person must undo the somewhat hasty construction of stage-4 thinking and reconstruct a far more meaningful system that takes into account the deepening, newly discovered aspects of one's self.

At this stage, what an individual accepts as worthwhile is verified by not only external others, such as authorities, experts, Scripture, and the like, but also his or her own inner method of relating to the transcendent. The individual realizes the deepening dimension of his or her own relationships and loyalties and becomes aware of the need for a more universal community within which he or she can find meaning. The person realizes that relating to transcendence demands commitment; yet, the person also realizes the inadequacy of his or her commitment and the consequent need for openness to an uncertain future. A deeper commitment to political and ethical values emerges. Fowler notes that "the structural characteristics of stage 5 are not a *content* that can be taught but rather are the products of one's reflective interaction with other people and with the conditions of one's life."[57]

Stage 6: Universalizing Faith

The final stage is best described by listing a few of the individuals who have exemplified this stage: Martin Luther King, Mother Teresa, and Dag Hammarskjöld. Individuals who have reached this stage show an overwhelming passion and commitment to the demands of love and justice. Whereas a stage 5 person is caught up in the perduring tension between his or her own needs and the welfare and demands of others, the stage 6 person is caught up in an unending desire to serve and help his or her fellow human beings. Fowler notes that individuals who reach this stage frequently care little for themselves and are often martyrs.

Fowler easily admits that there exists a transcendent element of faith and that human "models" of faith go only so far in explaining one's relationship to transcendence. There is present, says Fowler, an "extraordinary grace" which is "the unpredictable and unexpected manifestations of God's care and of God's claims upon our loves and our passions."[58] The purpose of "faith developmental theory" is to help explain our own human "nature" upon which this grace interacts.

At this point in our discussion it is useful to stress the following: First, it is important to note the difference between Christian faith and faith development. Christian faith is concerned with a particular content: the message of salvation proclaimed through the words and actions of Jesus Christ. Faith development, on the other hand, is concerned with how the individual understands and reinterprets this content as he or she matures in relationships and interactions within the environment.[59]

Second, as we have already mentioned, an individual must not be judged or evaluated by his or her particular stage of faith. Each individual responds to the experience of grace at a particular moment when relationships and events interweave to help construct his or her life story. Grace's offering is a highly personal event, which is communicated to this unique human project. Fowler has captured the grace moments of the individual as they occur in human experience.[60] Hence, we are attempting to help the adolescent reach a greater understanding of Jesus' message as it applies in his or her own life. As a consequence, we hope to open to the adolescent the experience of a deepening call of Jesus and help him or her respond to this call.

Strategies for Ministering to Faith Concerns

The adolescent's faith perspective is concentrated in stage 3 (Synthetic-Conventional) and the questioning and turmoils characteristic of the transition to stage 4, which is associated with the late adolescent or college undergraduate. With this in mind, the adult who is ministering to adolescents might use some of the following strategies.

1. The adolescent who is in stage 3 often relies on the views of others to help support his or her own faith stance. As Fowler notes, significant others in the adolescent's life become critical influences for defining himself or herself and for bolstering his or her personal sense of faith. In encounters with the adolescent, therefore, it is often helpful for the adults to share their own life experiences that relay themes of personal relating and personal commitment. Such sharing often helps the adolescent better understand his or her own life situation. A sense of structure sometimes facilitates this sharing experience. For example, one very helpful question is: "Who have I known that has had a profound effect on me as a Christian?" or "Can you share with me an experience that helped you understand what it really means to be a Christian?" Such dialog awakens the adolescent to the deepening influences of others who exercise a significant role in helping shape the adolescent's own sense of faith.

2. Because compartmentalizing and constructing hierarchies are common defensive strategies employed by adolescents during the high school and college years, it is helpful for the adolescent to realize the various roles he or she is experiencing (often for the first time), such as student, worker, son or daughter, athlete, friend, and the like. There are several strategies here: For example, we can have the adolescent list the many roles he or she finds in life. The adoles-

cent might then be asked to rate these roles according to various characteristics, such as "feeling good," "when I am most myself." Or the adolescent might be asked to reflect on the role that he or she finds most comfortable in order to determine why this might be so. The adult might then help the adolescent compare the feelings that he or she has in the role to feelings that are experienced in other roles. In this comparison, both similarities and contrasts can be noted. Reflection can then take place on why these differences might exist. A specific theme might then be introduced; for example, the adolescent might be asked to reflect on which role he or she finds most loving, caring, understanding. Reflection can then concentrate on how each of these roles measures up to each of these Christian themes. The focus on the dialog should be to both help the adolescent realize the compartmentalizing behaviors and hierarchical defenses that he or she employs and, at the same time, encourage the adolescent to show more uniform behaviors across the many roles he or she experiences.

3 At stage 3, the adolescent has beliefs, values, and ideas that are grounded in both significant others and peer-group consensus. Inquiry questions can be helpful. "Why" questions tend to elicit the young person's beliefs and values. The same questions can be posed in reference to the group from which the adolescent draws support. "Why do you think the group does it that way?" "Why do your friends do that?" "Why do others in your dormitory or on your floor act like that?" "How much do you buy into that?" The goal in such discussions is to aid the adolescent in responding to Jesus from a growing inner sense of self rather than relying on external influences. At the same time, however, respect must be given to the adolescent at this current developmental level, wherever that might be. No attempt should be made to force the adolescent to relate at a different developmental level or to articulate more sophisticated understandings of values and beliefs than he or she is ready for. The question for adults should always be, How can we aid *this* adolescent's faith experience to be a more personal response to Jesus' call to "come, follow me?"

4 Another critical factor in helping the adolescent at this stage is the presentation of perspectives that differ from his or her own limited view. Recall that Fowler noted one of the dominant characteristics of adolescents during this stage is the tendency to categorize

others through stereotypic images. It is important to engage the adolescent in discussions that broaden his or her own social environment and point to faith commitments and relationships that differ from his or her own. Studies and discussions of other cultures, religions, and the sharing of personal views that vary from the adolescent's own ideas can provide this important perspective.[61]

5 As we have seen, this stage of faith allows one to view God in a more personal way. Hence, the adolescent might be asked to reflect on the experience of God as friend or companion. We can explore with the adolescent what this means for him or her on an intellectual, affective, and moral level (see chapter 4 for further discussion of Jesus Christ as friend).

6 For late adolescents who are beginning to experience faith as a more autonomous undertaking, there can be exploration of what it means to be a Christian, a person of faith, and an individual who holds distinct, personal views. The relating that takes place at this stage is indicative of the growing individuating of faith. Hence, concrete questions concerning commitment (What types of commitment?), values (What is important in my life?), and beliefs (What do I believe?) are essential. It is profitable to relate this transition in faith to the adolescent's deepest sense of self. When the adolescent experiences a deep, personal relationship, for example, the adult might evoke a more autonomous and personal response by inquiring "What does this say about *you*?" "How is this relationship influencing and changing *your* life?" Increasing attention might then be paid to helping the adolescent take personal responsibility for his or her actions and behaviors in the relationship.

7 Because adolescents (especially late adolescents) are beginning to look for a personal and comprehensive philosophical-ideological value system, it is helpful to foster in the adolescent a reflective critique of his or her own personal and social values. How do the adolescent's values, for example, lead him or her to critique American culture, the government, and the values of society such as consumerism? Can the adolescent also critique his or her own personal value system and admit weaknesses in his or her own beliefs and thinking? The goal in this activity is to foster a continued openness in the adolescent's thinking as he or she encounters the future. From another perspective, the adolescent might be asked "Where is God in all of your ideas?" or "How is

being a Christian part of your thinking?" or "What does being a Christian have to do with your thinking about all these issues?" "Does it make a difference in your thinking?"

Identity in Adolescence

No word is more used when discussing adolescence than the term "identity." Identity refers to the person's acquisition of a meaningful sense of self, of who he or she is, of what he or she is about, and of where he or she is going. Adolescence represents the critical juncture at which truth of identity must now be faced. In adolescence, the young person grapples with questions of meaning, lifestyle, and relationships. It is during this period that the adolescent begins to find and take personal responsibility for the direction of his or her life.

Why does identity occupy center stage during the adolescent years? There are several reasons. First, as we have seen from Piaget, adolescence represents a crucial time in the adolescent's cognitive development. The attainment of formal operational thought fosters greater abstraction and reflective capacities. As a result, the adolescent views the self from outside, asking "Who am I?" "What am I really like?" Questions begin surfacing that press for answers. The adolescent can no longer cuddle in the security of childhood, but rather must answer this deepening cognitive inquiry.

Second, this cognitive reflection leads the adolescent to face more directly his or her own life history. What emerges is not only a past that can be reflected upon, but also a growing sense of a future that *I* must face and take responsibility for. Present experiences are contrasted with earlier experiences in his or her life, thereby helping the adolescent to question his or her current life experience and gain insight into it. Finally, there is the growing encounter with new ideas and the realization of issues and questions, as well as their attending complexities. The adolescent must begin to address issues and questions and fashion his or her own thinking into a more coherent system that gives personal meaning.

Third, the adolescent now experiences the increasing complexity of everyday life. In high school, the student is presented with a growing list of information and facts. The adolescent gradually realizes that life's questions and problems are not so simple. The ready-made answers of the childhood years now seem incredibly insufficient. Paralleling this growing realization of the world's complexity is the adolescent's needs to find personal values and an ethical sense of how he or she is to act, as an *individual,* in the midst of this growing complexity.

All of the above reasons lead the adolescent to face his or her own identity. As the high school years pass by, identity questions become more pressing; indeed, research indicates that "grade 10 may be the crucial age for identity formation."[62] This initial sense of identity, however, is rendered inadequate in the face of the late adolescent's entrance into college. As he or she experiences the college environment, the late adolescent is confronted with questions of religious belief, politics, personal relationships, and future life choices. All in all, the adolescent, who is no longer supported by the simple life perspective of earlier years, finds that he or she must successfully deal with the numerous questions and issues that so dominate the college experience.

Erikson's Theory of Psychological Development

The developmental thinker most associated with the adolescent quest for identity is Erik Erikson.[63] From his own study and interviews, Erikson has formulated a theory of psychological development that has had a profound impact in psychological and educational circles.

Erikson based his theory of personality development on the "epigenetic principle." This principle maintains that various organs of the body develop within a specific, designated time frame. As these organs develop, they also come to form a unity—namely, the human person. Erikson's theory of ego development proceeds along a similar vein. The personality has a basic plan, says Erikson, and the ego, which progresses through a variety of interrelated stages, emerges from this fundamental beginning. At each particular stage there is a developmental task that needs to be mastered and a potential danger that appears if the developmental task is not successfully negotiated.

Erikson's stages are well known and will be mentioned only briefly. In infancy, the critical task for the infant is to develop personal trust for the self and others. If this trust is not realized, then a sense of mistrust is fostered. Early childhood confronts the task of autonomy, that is, the striving to be one's own personal self. And if this autonomy fails to develop, the child begins to doubt. With autonomy, the child begins to take initiative, but guilt is realized if initiative is not achieved. The child's growing sense of self then leads to industry—to being actively engaged in the environment. Without industry, the child develops feelings of inferiority.

With the dawn of the adolescent years, the task of identity appears. Experiencing the immense changes that are so much a part of this developmental period leads the adolescent to ask, "Who am I really?" Failure to solidify a personal identity leads the adolescent to a diffuse state of endless wandering and escape.

As adolescence enters the late stage and grows into young adulthood, the person feels the need to relate this personal identity in a deepening sharing of self with others. Failure to realize this need for intimacy can produce in the adolescent a growing sense of isolation. Identity and intimacy are not distinct entities but are, rather, interrelated components of healthy, positive personality growth. Psychologist James Marcia describes the interplay of identity and intimacy when he writes: "It is the paradox of intimacy that it is a strength that can be acquired only through vulnerability; and vulnerability is possible only with the internal assurance of a firm identity."[64]

Two additional tasks arise in later adulthood. In middle adulthood, the central task becomes generativity, seeing oneself in others, and developing the deepening capacity to care for others. If this generative capacity fails to emerge, then the adult is left with a narrowing self-absorption. Finally, in late adulthood, the task becomes integrity—the acceptance of the self as who one really is. Failure to meet this task renders life a despairing experience for the adult.

Erikson concluded that the successful meeting or coming to terms with one developmental stage allows the person to proceed to the next. Each task is sequential; one task builds on the previous developmental task and opens the way for the next. At the same time, the stages are related to one another, and each is nascently present before its own developmental period.

The crises of identity and the developmental needs of intimacy preoccupy the high-school adolescent and later the college undergraduate. The physiological changes lead the adolescent to sense a growing difference in who the adolescent was, is, and hopes to become. Furthermore, a more intense, highly personal sense of questioning develops, a sense of wondering what the self and life really mean. Concomitantly, the adolescent grows to experience changing relationships within the family. "Distancing" appears as the adolescent intensifies his or her separation through efforts to establish his or her own personal identity. Psychologist Ruthellen Josselson states that the advent of early adolescence fosters a false sense of power, because the adolescent begins to experience more autonomy and freedom. This false sense of strength can lead the adolescent to act with a sense of impunity, while, at the same time, he or she attributes shortcomings and defects to others. As a consequence, the early adolescent often engages in disruptive, vexing behaviors that force the adult to take notice and, in turn, lead to an acknowledgement that the adolescent is indeed separate and distinct from other family members.[65]

To fill the void arising from this separation, the adolescent seeks the solace of the peer group. Although the peer group fosters a needed sense of security, the peer group itself can become oppressive as it exerts its conforming behaviors on the adolescent; deviation from the peer's way often leads to personal insecurity and stress.

Coupled with these developing ties, the adolescent comes to learn the importance of sex roles, namely, what it means to be a man or woman in today's society. In early adolescence, a markedly rigid behavior in sex role perspectives can develop. Acting very masculine or very feminine facilitates a sense of one's sexual identity. The conforming, stereotypic styles of thinking and behaving can assuage the adolescent's wondering and doubts about sexuality. With time, however, a more balanced, less oppressive sense of sexuality emerges, one that reflects a healthy, balanced mixture of masculine and feminine traits.[66]

The early adolescent begins to see that there are new demands and expectations. The secondary school offers new challenges. A first job, homework, driving a car, and an increased load of school activities all present the adolescent with new questions and demands. Deepening relationships with both sexes foster intense feelings and a developing, more enhancing sense of "who-I-am." At the same time, the adolescent grows to realize that adults—parents, teachers, coaches—expect more responsible, more mature behavior. These challenges and expectations are not always easy to resolve, and the adolescent is often left with lingering questions and doubts.

It should be pointed out that although a person initially faces the question of identity during the adolescent years, the questions about and preoccupations with identity do not terminate with adolescence. As Josselson notes: "Identity formation may be the 'star' of adolescence, but it has been rehearsing and will continue to act throughout the life cycle."[67] It is not difficult to see that the high school experience offers adolescents the opportunity for real growth along with the possibility of real frustration. From a spirituality perspective, the adult who encounters the adolescent in spiritual dialog—whether individually, in group experiences, or through retreat experiences—needs to speak to these developmental needs.

First, a sense of *security*, which can allay the demands and potential threats of the early adolescent years, should be created. As we have seen, the early demands of identity can often leave the adolescent bewildered, questioning, and unsure. Thus, it is a prime consideration for the adult to foster an atmosphere of trust and security in which the young person can face many of these experiences and articulate them within a spiritual dialog. Second, a climate of trust and security more easily sets the stage for a gentle *challenge* to the adolescent to continue his or her personal and spiritual growth. In other words, the adolescent is increasingly beset by changes that are pointing somewhere. The needs of this age are directional and lead to deeper and even future questions of growth. The adult might use these spiritual dialogs as a way to help the adolescent clarify issues and future life tasks, which are yet-to-be-experienced.

Strategies for Relating Personal Identity to Spiritual Growth

There are several approaches that adults might use in helping the adolescent relate his or her deepening sense of personal identity to his or her own spiritual growth.

1 We can label the first technique "positive enhancement." As already stated, this germinal period of adolescence is the initial stage for articulating deeper questions regarding life's meaning. What the adolescent often needs is a reinforcing perspective that will allow him or her to consciously experience the important "enhancing" moments of his or her own religious experience. This conscious celebration of such experiences can promote a security that is grounded in the Lord's love and, in turn, reinforce the young person's later spiritual growth.

There are many ways to use this technique. A group of adolescents, for example, can be given a sheet of paper and asked to write down two or three specific instances when they felt very close to God. The adolescent should be encouraged to be honest and to use everyday experiences. The adult can then comment and expand on these instances and invite reactions from the group. Emphasis should be placed on seeing the action of God in each adolescent's life. This realization of God in the adolescent's life is important, because in later years, particularly in the college experience, the adolescent's relationship with God will be open to more intense questioning and criticism. These God experiences, in effect, serve as touchstones in the adolescent's own journey of faith. This pilgrimage of faith will often lead to questioning and doubting in years ahead.

When an adolescent does speak about God experiences, it is important for the adult to capture a sense of the adolescent's affective response to God. Theologian Donald Gelpi notes that the affective response is an essential component of any conversion experience.[68] From another vantage point, priest-sociologist Andrew Greeley has stated that an affective response elicited through imagination can have a positive effect on behavior during the adolescent years.[69] The adult can look for particular manifestations of warmth, insecurity, intellectualizing, hope, joy, and so on as the adolescent describes his or her personal experience of God. These feelings can help the adult develop a sense of how the adolescent views God and what role personal needs and emotions exercise in the adolescent's God experiences. If, for example, an adolescent speaks about a certain experience of God that creates a sense of "goodness" or "aliveness," the adult might respond: "It sounds as though feeling good and being loved are important to you and that God provides this for you in some way." It is also important for the adult to continue with follow-up questions. Summarizing statements and inquiry questions enable the adolescent to reflect his or her own experience through another; clarify what is really important in his or her life; and explicitly articulate the basic affective and intellectual dimensions of his or her God experience.

There are various other possibilities for "enhancing moments." For example, because young people frequently have their first serious encounter with scripture during the high school years, a survey

83

of significant events and persons in the Old and New Testaments can be used. A good example here would be the story of Israel (or, more specifically a character such as Moses). The adult can help the adolescent discuss particular "God moments" in either Israel's journey or Moses' life. This example of God's faithfulness can then be related to the adolescent's own life. Emphasis should be placed on the continuity of God's love, God's call to the adolescent at a personal level, and God's faithfulness—all of which should be followed by the adolescent's consideration of his or her own readiness to respond. We can highlight this action-response model as follows: God invites and we respond. The prophets or New Testament characters like Paul can be profitably used in this approach.

Still another variation is to develop a list of themes in a discussion of "God-filled moments." In this technique, the adolescent centers on a specific aspect of his or her life, such as people, family, friends, or personal experiences that have involved an awareness of God. An important benefit of this approach is that it helps the adult view particular experiences of God over a broad list of adolescent behaviors and specific situations. It also tends to highlight areas where the adolescent may be experiencing difficulty. If the adolescent speaks quite openly about friends, for example, but is reticent to talk about school experiences, then perhaps the adult might encourage a discussion of this latter area.

All in all, the use of "enhancing moments" helps the adolescent to ground a sense of continuity in the faithfulness of God's love. As the adolescent experiences future identity issues, which increasingly grow intense in the years ahead, the open expression of God's love can become a welcoming experience.

2 We have already noted the critical importance that peer groups exercise during the high school years. Thus, the emphasis on relationships and group exercises can be profitably utilized. Peer relationships provide a tremendous reaffirming experience during these years of adolescent change.

There are numerous exercises that can be carried out in a group. The group, for example, might be asked to fill in the following blanks:

For me, God is _____.
I feel closest to Jesus when _____ :
Jesus _____ :

It is often helpful for the adult to also share his or her own responses in this.exercise. The adult can facilitate the discussion by noting some common themes that emerge from the group. In this group context, the adolescents should be encouraged not only to respond to one another's questions, but also to offer affirmation to the sharing that each one does.

3 Adolescence brings about the emergence of diverse roles. The adolescent must balance the roles of son, daughter, athlete, worker, student friend, and the like. Sometimes the role conflicts that emerge evoke a certain perplexity and frustration in the adolescent. As we have already noted, James Fowler comments on this role compartmentalization as a defensive strategy commonly employed by the adolescent during these developing years (although we certainly observe this behavior in adults, too!) During the high school years, we should stress a positive presentation of these roles because they wield an important influence in the adolescent's identity formation. Because these roles are often confusing, one technique that might help clarify them is to have the adolescent write down all the roles he or she presently experiences. This exercise in itself can be insightful. Many adolescents have no prior experience of consciously reflecting on the numerous adult roles in their lives. Here the adult might want to select the roles with which the adolescent feels most comfortable. Some open-ended questions in this regard include the following:

Positive question—What do you like best about ___(role)___?
Inquiry question—Why is being ___(role)___ important to you?
Relation question—How is Jesus present in ___(role)___?

From questions such as these, it is often not too difficult to assess what roles the adolescent is most comfortable in.

Another profitable exercise is to help the adolescent understand role conflict, a factor that is probably important for the young person's maturing sense of self. For this purpose, the adult can propose a situation that demonstrates potential role conflict, such as: "A friend wants you to go to a movie and your mom wants you to clean the garage." The adult can then discuss this dilemma with the adolescent. Even more profitable is to encourage the adolescent to bring up an actual experience of role conflict that the adolescent is experiencing and then discuss this situation with the adolescent. When using this strategy, the adult's main interest is to help the adolescent clarify exactly what criteria the young person utilizes to determine how to resolve these very human situations. The adult might also discern what affective responses the adolescent gives in facing various conflicts. The adult should encourage the adolescent to reflect on other experiences of role conflict or potential role conflicts that the adolescent might confront in the future.

In addition to the insights that can be gathered from these reflections with the adolescent, the adult can also suggest comparisons between the adolescent's behaviors and various Gospel norms. In comparison with John's Gospel (John 15), for example, we can mention the way Our Lord beckons us to love one another. The point is to help the adolescent realize how love can be expressed in the various roles that make up his or her life at this moment. This conscious pinpointing of love in numerous life roles helps the adolescent to interweave the Gospel with the various experiences of his or her own self. It is important to consider the Gospel value of love, because in later years the adolescent will experience a variety of situations and relationships in which he or she will be challenged to show love, even in the midst of numerous role conflicts.

4. In our discussion of identity in early adolescence we have noted that younger adolescents might resort to behaviors that are irritating to parents and other adults in order to prove their growing sense of an independent identity. High school teachers and parents of adolescents can readily attest to this statement. At this point in the adolescent's development, the adult's main contribution is to channel the adolescent's actions into positive, constructive behaviors that enhance his or her growing personal identity. The adult should encourage those behaviors that demonstrate independence, those that meet an adolescent's needs in his or her identity struggle, and those that simultaneously give witness to Gospel values. Chores at home, volunteer activities, and extracurricular activities at school can all be encouraged as responsible ways to confirm individuality and express true Christian maturity and service.

At the same time, the adult can challenge the adolescent peer group. The peer group's conforming behavior must be confronted and discussed in relation to the Gospel. Questions of "why" and "how" should be encouraged, that is, we can explore *why* we behave this way and *how* our actions conform to the Gospel's command to love. Sometimes it may be helpful to mention a particular value, such as justice or love, and discuss the value in terms of concrete examples from the adolescent's life, or in the behaviors of the peer group. The adult should not hesitate to challenge an adolescent group to both explore their behaviors and reflect on the way these behaviors mirror the Gospel. Then, the group should be encouraged to reflect on future actions and how these actions might fulfill the Gospel.

As the adolescent approaches the end of high school and moves on to the college experience, he or she encounters a greater realization of the urges, stresses, and demands of identity consolidation. As this process continues, the adolescent notices a growing need for intimacy in personal relationships, a clearer understanding of "who I am" based on these deepening personal relationships, a clearer outlook and worldview based on his or her undergraduate education, and, finally, a clearer notion of "what my own place in the world might be." College majors, occupational choices, and the world of work become more pressing as the late adolescent attempts to carve his or her place in society. Ideally, the resolution of the identity crisis finds the adolescent capable of entering into intimate relationships, developing a socio-ideological stance toward the world, building a personally meaningful and coherent value (ethical-religious) system, and taking personal responsibility for both his or her own present life and the future actions he or she will eventually be committed to.

Identity Achievement

Once the adolescent has successfully achieved a sense of identity in one area of his or her life—in relationships, value systems, occupational choice, or a socio-political orientation—then he or she has experienced *identity achievement*. In identity achievement the adolescent accepts responsibility for an emerging self that is capable of personal, responsible decisions in a particular area of his or her life. The adolescent (now the young adult) takes responsibility for personal life decisions and for making commitments to both society and others.

It should be noted that achieving a solid, stable identity is beyond the capability of the secondary-school adolescent.[70] To achieve the adolescent's growth in identity encompasses the resolution of various issues in his or her life; as a result, he or she has a deepening sense of a personal commitment to self, others, and the adult world. Ministry to adolescents in the secondary-school years should focus on affirming the adolescent's growing sense of a personal selfhood while, at the same time, reinforcing the need for a continued "openness" on the adolescent's part to the future experiences (college studies, deeper relationships, and so on) that no doubt will critically influence the adolescent's later identity struggles.

The resolution of the adolescent identity crisis rarely occurs without some sense of personal struggle. Psychologist James Marcia has studied the achievement of identity based on the criteria of crises and commitment.[71] During the adolescent experience of crises, adolescents reevaluate their present views and behaviors, explore various life options, and make numerous choices concerning basic life issues in the areas of religion, occupational choice, personal relationships, and political ideology. Commitment is defined as the adolescent's personal investment of the self toward one of these life issues (for example, taking on a personal ideology, a commitment to an occupation or area of study). In studying identity growth at the college level, Marcia classified adolescents into one of the following four categories:

1 *Identity achievement*   Adolescents who have achieved identity have experienced a crisis and now appear to have found some sense of commitment in their lives.

2 *Moratorium*   Adolescents in the moratorium category are presently in a state of crisis and are attempting to resolve the crisis through examining various life options.

3 *Identity foreclosure*   Adolescents in the identity foreclosure category are committed to a certain set of beliefs, often as a result of parental influences, and are not open to examining or questioning their present beliefs.

4 *Identity diffusion*   Adolescents in the identity diffusion category are found to lack personal commitment and, at the same time, appear not to be making any effort to find commitment for their lives (or at least not in some areas of their lives).

Defense Mechanisms

Psychologist Richard Logan points out several defense mechanisms that adolescents might adopt in order to assuage the anxiety of an identity-diffuse state.[72] For one, says Logan, the adolescent can engage in "temporary escape." There are many examples that involve an obsession with any kind of activity such as intellectual or physical pursuits, partying, drug taking, or even TV watching. This escapism counterbalances the sense of drift that permeates the adolescent's life.

Second, some adolescents find "substitutes" for their diffuse identity state. The adolescent can find gratification from a specific role, such as being an athlete, a leader, or a scholar. This limited role acquisition provides a respite from his or her identity confusion. A variation of this substitution finds the adolescent overidentifying with a particular cause that provides an identity substitute. In my own pastoral work I have found an example of this substitution can be the college student who uncritically embraces a fundamentalist religious outlook toward life. This time-consuming devotion to dogma and Scripture offers the adolescent a socially acceptable substitute for a secure identity.[73] Another way for the adolescent to substitute for his or her lack of identity is to be obsessed with material goods. Thus, purchasing clothes, an automobile, or taking a trip might promote a substitute identity that the adolescent presently lacks.

A third approach to solve the confused and meaningless drift of role diffusion is to engage in expressions that reinforce the present state of confusion. Fast driving, taking drugs, and sexual acting out, for example, can all be immediate palliatives that enhance the mistaken sense of well-being. A variation of this third approach occurs when the adolescent attempts to compete with peers scholastically or athletically, or in other ways. The experience of competition gives the adolescent the sense of being someone, thus mitigating his or her confused, drifting state. Still a further variation of this approach is for the adolescent to enhance a secure sense of self by exhibiting prejudicial attitudes toward others. His or her personal attacks on others seem to augment his or her own sense of personal well-being. Thus, degrading others becomes the vehicle for enhancing one's own self.

A fourth way for the adolescent to counter diffusion is to engage in a variety of meaningless activities such as fads, games, and ridiculous behaviors. When the adolescent invests psychic energy in these meaningless activities, he or she unconsciously asserts that the present state of meaninglessness is in fact legitimate. Thus, his or her own meaninglessness is legitimatized by meaningless behavior.

The final way for the adolescent to refute his or her diffuse state of identity is to adopt a value structure that is opposed to authorities and adults—to, in effect, deviate from the behaviors that adults expect. In this case, the adolescent takes on a "negative identity" whereby he or she responds to society's expectations by differing from them, if not openly opposing them. In a negative-identity state, the adolescent engages in behaviors that question adult expectations and undermine them. This negative identity can become important in the adolescent's rejection or questioning of adult values and religious practices. In chapter 4 we shall explore how this negative identity is at times caught up in the adolescent crisis of faith.

In summary, then the late adolescent years provide the time when adolescents must confront their own identity quest. It should be noted that through continued schooling, particularly the college years, the adolescent tends to grow in his or her achievement of identity.

Identity and Intimacy

It is not difficult to see the importance that identity plays in leading to the adolescent's experience of intimacy. Erikson notes that "it is only when identity formation is well on its way that true intimacy—which is really a counterpointing as well as a fusing of identities—is possible."[75] Erikson views intimacy as having a central role in developmental growth. Without intimacy, the adolescent is resigned to isolation. Intimacy is the capacity to make commitments beyond the self; it is the ability to share deeply, to risk mutually, and to be honest with another. As adolescents complete high school and enter college, the need for intimacy becomes an increasingly important task. The development of deep, trusting personal friendships—with members of the same sex and members of the opposite sex—are signs of this growing capacity for intimacy.

The development of close personal relationships provides the adolescent with a wonderful opportunity. Through deep friendships, the adolescent realizes that he or she is really accepted and loved. At the same time, personal friendships offer the adolescent real insight into others as well as into the personal self. A deep friendship makes the adolescent capable of seeing himself or herself as both normal and worthwhile. Through shared thoughts and activities, the adolescent discovers what is most deeply yearned for,

90

namely, the overpowering need for acceptance and love—to be "who I am" and to really be accepted by others.

As this developmental period progresses, the adolescent attempts, cautiously at first, the sharing of self. These initial experiences of sharing are often wedded to groups, but in the later high school years, and most certainly in the college years, the adolescent seeks out close friends more and more, trying to find those special others with whom self-revelation is desirable. The adolescent soon longs for such authentic self-disclosure. Psychologist John Mitchell has identified "the attribute most essential to intimacy is *honesty*. Intimacy demands honesty because authentic self-disclosure requires that the individual show himself as he is, without pretense or facade."[76]

Yet, even as the need for intimacy comes increasingly to the forefront, the adolescent must continue his or her identity quest. This will involve academic and career choices as well as the need to discover one's own personal value system, which will allow the adolescent to dialog and make sense of a world that is growing increasingly complex. The adolescent's values, which surface in both interpersonal relationships and occupational commitments, become an important dimension of his or her identity.

Identity, Intimacy, and Spiritual Growth

From the foregoing discussion we can conclude that personal growth arising through identity and intimacy are signficant underpinnings for an adolescent spirituality. No other developmental need so profoundly captures the adolescent's relationship with Jesus as does the adolescent's quest for identity and intimacy.

We will have an opportunity in chapter 4, which focuses on adolescent prayer, to consider the significance of identity and intimacy in the adolescent's spiritual life. Still, there are several brief observations to be made here.

1 The acquisition of identity allows for a personal, deeply relational experience with Jesus Christ. This is enhanced by the adolescent's developmental need for intimacy. See chapter 4, on adolescent prayer, for a deeper exploration of this dimension of the adolescent's spiritual growth.

2 The critical sense of self that develops in adolescence leads the young person to reach outward toward future Christian adult-

hood. In this process, the need for relationships, an occupational role, and a socio-ideological value system are integral for identity solidification. The call of the Gospel resonates with the emerging identity to foster spiritual growth that accepts the adolescent as he or she is, and yet beckons him or her to future growth.

3 The doubts of this developmental period create for many late adolescents deeper questions concerning roles, institutions, and values. The quest for identity becomes fused with this new-found openness and doubting stance. As a consequence, the question often becomes: "What does it mean for *me* to be a Christian?" or even "Why believe?"

4 Some of the deepest experiences in any human being arise from the development of intimate relationships. These relational experiences express what being Christian means, namely, the sharing of myself based on the life, death, and resurrection of Jesus. Thus, attention to this relational sphere of adolescent growth is critically important, because relationships mirror both a personal experience of God's love and a conscious presence of this love in the young person's life.

Techniques for Addressing Identity Issues

There are a variety of techniques and approaches that we can use when addressing identity issues in the context of adolescent spirituality.

1 One very simple question (which, unfortunately, often goes unasked) might well be presented to the adolescent in the later years of high school or college—"What does it mean for *you* to be a Christian?" "What does it mean for you to be a *Catholic*?" Since the adolescent is more and more developing a sense of identity, it is important to consciously pose the function and place of Christian commitment in the young person's life. As the adolescent converses on this topic, the adult might find it profitable to assess what significance Christianity or Catholicism exercise in the young person's life, in his or her various roles, and in his or her relationships. Because the adolescent, at this stage, has acquired the cognitive capacity to reflect on previous experiences, he or she might be invited to reflect on how the meaning of being Christian has changed over the years, and what demands and understandings are now present that were absent even a few years ago.

2. We have already mentioned the place of relationships in the young person's life. We can ask the adolescent, then, how he or she views this present relationship with Christ. It is often useful to have the adolescent talk about what friendship is for him or her, and then ask that he or she consider how friendship is tied to his or her feelings about Jesus. One can structure this dialog by follow-up questions that concern "affective," "intellectual," or "value" responses. From another perspective, since the adolescent has now developed a sense of history, the attention might shift to how this adolescent's relationship with God has changed or is different from that of the early high school or childhood years. These insights are often quite helpful to the adolescent. Follow-up questions exploring this change and the adolescent's sense of his or her deepening or changing relationship with the Lord are often quite enlightening. Jesus can become, then, a touchstone in the midst of the shifting and change that is occurring in the adolescent's life. This time perspective can allow the adolescent to perceive a relationship with Jesus as an ongoing, deepening process. The adult might also reflectively examine with the adolescent how open he or she is in this relationship or what challenge it evokes within him or her.

3. Because the adolescent is more and more looking to a future, it is sometimes helpful to have the adolescent reflect on how various life experiences capture the call of Jesus to "come, follow me." The adolescent comes in contact, for example, with numerous instances of change and loss such as leaving grade school, making and losing friends, leaving high school, entering college, and finding new friends.[77] Each of these experiences can be a positive avenue for furthering identity growth and enhancing the call of Jesus. The adult might reflect with the adolescent how each of these experiences, when they occur, touch the young person's life. The adult might then focus on how these experiences of "loss" might challenge the adolescent to future growth. The adult can use comparison questions and have the adolescent reflect on his or her life "before" and "after" these experiences. The adult might ask, "Do you see any difference in yourself?" The adult might also ask: "How is Jesus part of your life as this change is going on?" or "Does knowing Christ help you deal with leaving school?" or "Does Jesus' presence say anything to you as you feel all the hurt from this broken friendship?"

4. An excellent scripture passage to aid the adolescent in the

internalizing of a deepening identity and intimacy with Jesus is Luke 24:13-35—the road to Emmaus. The adolescent can identify with one of the disciples and reflectively examine how he or she has grown in a relationship with Christ. We can point out to the adolescent how we need to reflect and wrestle with the message of Jesus and gradually gain insight, just as the disciples did. An important realization in this passage (and a good theme for adolescents) is the disciples' growing realization of who Jesus is. This theme ties in well with the adolescent's own developmental stage. The adolescent, who is experiencing the deepening commitments of identity and intimacy, sheds old patterns and attitudes and incorporates new understandings of his or her continuing development. Another useful passage is 1 Samuel 3. In this passage, Samuel replies to the Lord about *who he really is*. Like Samuel, the adolescent, too, can respond with all his or her personal talents, and shortcomings, with his or her own questions, doubts, and concerns that might be problematic at this particular age. The adolescent can identify with Samuel and explore his or her own personal sense of God's call in his or her own life in order to realize the deepening response that faith demands.[78]

5 In discussing identity, we have noted how adolescents often oscillate between various phases of crisis and commitment. The adult might wish to explore any of these many areas with the adolescent. Religion, for example, is often a topic of real conversation for the late adolescent. The adult might simply question the adolescent about his or her understanding of religion for his or her own life or how a relationship with God is part of religious practice. Furthermore, the adult might ask what part institutional structures play in determining this adolescent's feelings toward religion.

6 In her writings on Erikson's stages of development, professor Ruth Whitney suggests that characteristics for development might include identity, fidelity, intimacy, interdependence, and community.[79] The adolescent might be asked to share instances of these characteristics in his or her life—fidelity, trust, commitment, openness, dependence, and community. To focus on concrete, positive examples of these experiences can enhance the adolescent's own identity and self-worth. The adolescent can also be asked to describe how love and Gospel values are part of these various experiences.

7 Because identity acquisition is fraught with change, question-

ing, and sometimes doubt, it is important that the adolescent enjoy some great measure of self-esteem. Individuals benefit from a positive self-image, and adolescents who are immersed in questions about emotions, values, ideas, meaning, and relationships can especially profit from the enhanced view of the self. Priest-psychiatrist James Gill has suggested that one way to assess the level of self-esteem is to ask the adolescent to complete the following sentence, "I like myself because. . . ." He notes that responses to this question generally reveal one of four attitudes about the self: (1) what they are, (2) what they do, (3) what they make, (4) what they have.[80] These statements reflect the reliance on external sources of support. Thus, the person is enhanced not because of *who* they are, but because of *what* they have become. This commonplace answer is particularly troublesome for adolescents because (a) many adolescents have not yet accomplished anything in which they can invest a sense of self-worth, and (b) adolescents are periodically (if not more often) preoccupied with negative images of self ("I can't do that") or at least with nonenhancing features of themselves ("Why am I different?" "What am I going to do?").

The first way to help the adolescent deal with this self-esteem issue is to bring up important life situations, such as experiences in the family, experiences with friends, or personal experiences that provide enhancement for the adolescent. The adult should help the adolescent consciously articulate these enhancing moments in his or her life. The adult can also share his or her own positive acceptance of the adolescent as a means of self-enhancement.

Second, the adult can encourage the adolescent to probe his or her own experience of God's love for him or her. As Peter van Breemen has noted, one of the best examples of this love is found in 1 John 4:10: "Love, then, consists in this: not that we have loved God but that he has loved us." In other words, as van Breemen points out, our love for God is secondary. What is important, indeed, uppermost, is God's love for us. We are accepted for who we are; God loves us first for that which we are, not for anything that we accomplish.[81] The adult might share some personal experiences of God's love in his or her own life with the adolescent. The adult can then encourage the adolescent to reflect on personal experiences of God's love in his or her own life.

Third, the adolescent can be helped to see personal relationships—we have seen that they are critically important in the adolescent years—as personal signs of God's love for the adolescent. Friends are signs to us of God's love and care. In the same light, the adult can reflect with the adolescent to see that he or she is also an instrument of God's love. God uses us to be these signs to each other. The adolescent, therefore, not only is loved by God, but also is a visible sign of God's love to the world. The adolescent can then shift to consider how he or she meets and finds this love in his or her life and shares it with others (in attitudes, in relationships, in actions).

8 Priest-spiritual writer Henri Nouwen has written: "Jesus Christ reveals to us that our real identity is not to be found on the edge of our existence where we can brag about our own specialties, but in the center where we can recognize our basic human sameness and discover each other as brothers and sisters, children of the same God."[82] Far too often, says Nouwen, we seek to discover our identity in the differences that exist, that is, we think about the ways in which we are different from one another. In this context, adolescents come up against a two-fold struggle. On the one hand, there is an attempt to establish a separate identity that reveals a distinct sense of self; concomitantly, there is the need to feel like others and be like them. For the Christian, the resolution of this dilemma lies in enjoying the uniqueness of our self in the service of others. The adolescent should be encouraged to think of his or her talents and gifts with the recognition that they are for the service of others. Since notions of community and personal relationships are important in the adolescent years, the adult can suggest how these gifts and talents can be used for others. From another perspective, this sharing of gifts allows us to see our own weaknesses and our need for support from others. Scripture passages that emphasize love and service are helpful.

9 Religious educator Gabriel Moran says that the issue of identity, which has been so much a part of the adolescent experience, is an issue that threads itself through the years of young adulthood (the 20s and 30s).[83] In seeking their own identity, adolescents who enter their 20s are especially concerned about security in both personal relationships and economic matters. The demands of emotional commitment and financial security interplay with the struggles for identity, intimacy, and a meaningful values system. Adults need to give

careful attention to these concerns, because they constitute a large part of the adolescent's focus in the early adult years.

In concluding our discussion of identity formation, we might note that in all likelihood there exists in the adolescent a relationship between growing development of formal operational thinking, advanced moral reasoning, and identity achievement. Evidence seems to indicate that there is a relationship between these various developmental dimensions of human growth.[84] The critical task for an adolescent spirituality is to endow these intellectual, affective, and moral dimensions of the adolescent's life with *Gospel values*, in order to deepen Jesus' call to "come, follow me."

Interpersonal Development

Throughout our developmental perspective of adolescence, we have noted the adolescent's growing capacity to be aware and understand others. This deepening awareness of both our selves and others is termed social reasoning. Robert Selman is the psychologist most associated with the study of this growing developmental capacity of human growth.[85]

Selman notes that, as a child interacts in the social world, a deeper capacity to appreciate another's perspective develops. The child becomes more and more capable of understanding the content and manner of another's perceptions, thoughts, and feelings. Selman labels this deepening capacity of the person as "role taking." He notes that role taking "refers to the process by which a person is able to take the perspective of another and relate it to his or her own perspective."[86] The development of this capacity proceeds through a sequential process (stages) that grows increasingly complex. Using an interview method that is similar to the methods employed by Piaget and Kohlberg, Selman delineates a sequential level of social reasoning that reflects both this growing role-taking capacity and the child's increasing capacity to understand "the relation between the perspectives of self and others."[87] The levels are briefly discussed in the following pages.

Level 0: Undifferentiated and Egocentric Perspective Taking

The child, from age 3 to 6, is incapable of taking the perspective of another. Although the child can differentiate between the self and others, the child is without the capacity to distinguish his or her own motives from another's. Thus, what the child believes to be his or her motive for an action becomes the motive for another, too. Likewise, for this child, the actions of the individual are paramount, rather then the reasons and motivations behind one's actions.

Level 1: Differentiated and Subjective Perspective Taking

Between the ages of 5 and 9, the child grows to comprehend that people can think and feel differently in various situations. Others are viewed as having intentions and motives that are different from one's own; yet these inner feelings are construed in simplistic ways, which lack mixed or multiple motives for actions.

Level 2: Self-reflective/Second-person and Reciprocal Perspective Taking

This level occurs between the ages of 7 and 12, and it is at this level that the child can not only reflect on his or her thoughts and actions, but also realize that others, too, enjoy this capacity for self-reflection. The child can now place himself or herself in another's shoes and realize, at the same time, that others can also do this. He or she appreciates that the outer appearances of a person can be deceptive and belie that person's true, inner feelings. Although the child can now conceive of both his or her own subjective state and that of another, the child is still incapable of focusing on the dynamics of the relationship itself.

Level 3: Third-person and Mutual Perspective Taking

This level has its onset around age 10 and can last until age 15, although it can remain even into adulthood. At this level, the young adolescent can take a third-party perspective. The person can step outside himself or herself and consider both parties in the relationship—the feelings, actions, and the needs of those within the relationship. Thus, relationships at this level can take on more mutuality. Trust, friendship, and loyalty become significant factors in relationships.

Level 4: In-depth and Societal-Symbolic Perspective Taking

When the young person moves from level 3 to level 4—this transition normally takes place in adolescence, although it can occur in adulthood—the adolescent finds a much broader perspective that encompasses the self and the peer group as well as others. The attitudes and views of the larger group are increasingly understood and taken into consideration. The adolescent now realizes that other individuals are acting out of a complex web of beliefs, attitudes, and values that may differ from his or her own belief system. The adolescent can view others as acting from predictable patterns; at the same time, however, he or she comes to understand the deeper complexities of the self, and the inner self or unconscious can exercise an important role in personal behavior. The adolescent can now realize the complexity of his or her own life story and begin to appreciate his or her own developmental history as it has influenced his or her life.

In his research, Selman acknowledges a close relationship between cognitive, moral, and social reasoning. Role taking emerges as a natural ally of social reasoning. Thus, as the child grows in his or her ability to understand another through interpersonal action, there develops an increasing capacity to take on the role of another. Research indicates that this role-taking capacity increases as moral reasoning increases.[88] Still, as with formal thinking, there appears to be limits to the adolescent's ability to advance in social reasoning.[89]

The development of social reasoning fosters two realities for the adolescent. First, by moving from levels 3 to 4, the adolescent is capable of comprehending more deeply the motives, feelings, and thought patterns of other individuals and groups of peoples, such as nations and classes. At the same time, however, there is a mutual interaction whereby these other influences now affect the adolescent and exert a profound impact.

This capacity to demonstrate social reasoning is rich in implications for adolescent spirituality. The widening understanding of others permits the young person to appreciate others and to care more deeply for them. At the same time, it enables him or her to develop a social consciousness perspective that is attentive to the needs of those who are hurting and oppressed. Among the possibilities that rise, then, from a discussion of social reasoning are the following: a deepening interpersonal relationship with Jesus Christ; a greater sensitivity and understanding of communal concerns at various levels; the capacity to grasp the diverse motives, complexities, and values that are present in human encounters; and the capacity to appreciate the corresponding ethical demands of these human encounters.

Adolescent Spirituality and Interpersonal Development

From the perspective of adolescent spirituality, there are several suggestions for our consideration in discussing the social reasoning of the adolescent.

1 Obviously, the first suggestion at this stage of developmental growth is the increasing attention to the adolescent's relationship with Jesus. A discussion with the adolescent can concentrate on who Jesus really is—on his values, his intentions, his motives, and his attitudes as well as what he really proclaimed and how this relates to the adolescent's own life. The adolescent might be invited to consider his or her personal perception and understanding of Jesus, to see whether it is primarily affective or cognitive, or whether there is a notion that the adolescent is growing in his or her sense of really "knowing" Jesus and "experiencing" a relationship with him.

2 Since the adolescent who has reached level 4 can increasingly comprehend the motives and feelings of wider social groupings, such as races, classes, and countries, the adult might reflect with the adolescent on his or her awareness of others. Scriptural passages, such as Matthew 25, for example, can be used. The adolescent can be invited to consider "others" and notice the caring and compassion that Jesus evinces in the Gospel. This can then be related to broader social groupings. We might ask these questions: How does the adolescent respond in this reflection? Is the adolescent's awareness and response primarily cognitive, affective, or judgmental? The adult might also note the adolescent's capacity to be open to others.

3 Because the adolescent can now experience a "third-person perspective," this technique becomes an excellent way to look at the adolescent's relationships. If the adolescent discusses a difficulty that he or she is experiencing with a peer or friend, for example, the adult can ask the adolescent to take the role of a third party who then observes and reflects on the behaviors and attitudes that arise in the relationship. The adult can suggest Christian themes, such as compassion, care, and forgiveness, and encourage the adolescent to comment on the way these themes are reflected in the relationship.

4 Role playing can be another way that the adolescent can use his or her capacity for social reasoning to enhance personal spiritual growth as well as self-understanding. The adolescent and the adult

can role play life or personal problems, difficulties with parents, friends, teachers, dorm floor residents, etc. The adult can then pose reflections for the adolescent that help him or her to consider (a) his or her understanding and reactions to the feelings that arise from this role playing; (b) possible strategies for personally coping with these difficulties and effectively dealing with them; and (c) the possibility that this relationship can embody Christian values such as care, understanding, and openness.

Vocational Development

There is a final aspect of developmental theory that is often overlooked, namely, the adolescent's development of a vocational commitment. The adolescent gradually comes to realize the numerous expectations that society has of him or her while, at the same time, wonders more and more about his or her own role in society as an adult. As we have already noted, Erikson views work on occupational commitment as a critical component in the growth of identity. Moreover, a developing sense of an occupational identity is an important, integral need during the adolescent years. Commenting on this developmental need in adolescence, psychologist Milton Shore has remarked: "It is during the adolescent phase that the young person is clearly exposed to the values which are inherent in the society with regard to occupations and vocations."[90]

For adolescent spirituality, the development of a vocational identity is critical. First, Vatican Council II has noted the call of all men and women to a life of Christian holiness. And, at this critical juncture of the adolescent's life, vocational goals need to be seen in the context of this universal call to holiness. Second, the confluence of spirituality and social justice (see chapter 8) has pointed to the significant role assigned to the social dimension of Christian living. Care, concern, and compassion for others must be realized and appreciated in the Christian's lifestyle and everyday life activity. No longer can the Christian stand detached from the problems and sufferings in society.

We know that the adolescent's concerns and interests in the secondary and undergraduate college years go beyond mere cognitive and emotional development. The adolescent increasingly faces the pressure of future adulthood and the precise role and place he or

101

she will have in society. Among the questions forming in the adolescent's mind are the following: "What kind of job can I have?" "How happy will I be in my future work?" "Should I really take these courses and consider this type of career?" or even more basic "What do I *really* want to do?" An adolescent spirituality must concern itself with these questions. Contemplating questions of career, occupation, and job prospects creates a climate in which the adolescent can dialog on this even more vital and immanent facet of his or her life. Because adolescence offers a time for the adolescent to discover how he or she really "fits" in the world, it is helpful to explore the adolescent's pursuit of a vocation and to consider how this vocational commitment can be integrated into the young person's spiritual life.

Vocational Theory

Psychologist Donald Super has formulated perhaps one of the most extensive, sophisticated theories of vocational development.[91] The importance of developmental theory is central to Super's theory. Through interaction with the environment, the adolescent gradually comes to formulate a commitment in the working world. For Super, the importance of the self-concept underlies this orientation to future work. By self-concept, Super means the impression we have of ourselves. He defines self-concept as "the individual's picture of himself, the perceived self with accrued meanings."[92]

Self-concepts have various levels of complexity. With the use of our growing abstraction and generalization powers, we come to form more complex self-concepts from simpler ones. Every individual has self-concepts of himself or herself as parent, daughter, worker, friend, and so on. Taken together, these self-concepts make up a person's self-concept system. Super has emphasized the development of a vocational self-concept. By this he means a self-concept that relates to the vocational choices and commitments that we make.

Critical to Super's theory is the developmental process one undergoes in order to achieve a viable vocational identity. In his earlier work, Super viewed the person's vocational development as proceeding through a growth stage of early childhood years to an exploration stage that emerges in adolescence. During the adolescent years, there is a tentative substage regarding occupation (15 to 17), which then moves to a transition substage, in which reality bears much greater weight, and then finally to a trial substage, in which the first job is often acquired. Of course, the adolescent might prolong substages through more professional training in young adulthood.

In his later writings, Super has concentrated on delineating two primary tasks for the adolescent years. The secondary-school student is concerned with "crystallizing" a vocational choice, whereas the college undergraduate's concept is "specifying" various vocational possibilities. As a person's developmental growth proceeds, the tasks of implementing one's vocational preference, becoming stabilized in a vocation, and consolidating and advancing in a vocation follow. But because we are specifically concerned with the adolescent years, we will detail the importance of crystallizing and specifying the adolescent experience of these years.

Crystallizing vocational choices. The crystallization of various vocational possibilities occurs in the middle adolescent years (ages 14 to 18). Super says: "During this period the teen-ager is expected by society to begin to formulate ideas as to fields and levels of work which are appropriate for himself and occupational concepts which will enable him, if necessary, to make tentative choices, that is, to commit himself to a type of education or training which will lead him toward some partially specified occupation."[93]

The preference that the adolescent has at this time might be vague, but this exploration does take place, nevertheless. Although this crystallizing of a vocation is commonly found in early and middle adolescence, college graduates can also be crystallizing a vocational choice. An engineering student, for example, who is attempting to decide what type of graduate school to attend, can still be in the process of crystallization. Super identifies the crystallizing process as basically cognitive in orientation. In this process there are the following specific behaviors and attitudes that the adult might keep in mind.

1. *Awareness of the need to crystallize.* If the adolescent can realize the importance of crystallization, then the crystallizing process is facilitated. This awareness evolves from the adolescent's interaction with teachers, parents, counselors, and friends. These individuals inquire about the adolescent's future life; their questioning, in turn, leads the adolescent to discuss and explore future vocational possibilities.

103

2 *Use of resources*   The use of resources involves the actual behavior of the adolescent. The young person might have a part-time job, talk to a counselor, or read an article about a possible career.

3 *Awareness of factors to consider*   The adolescent cognitively assesses his or her own self and situation. The adolescent's own self-knowledge, such as understanding of intellectual capabilities and various interests, fosters a vocational preference that is increasingly crystallized.

4 *Awareness of contingencies that may affect goals*   When the adolescent becomes aware of contingencies in vocational preference, then some vocational preferences may be reinforced and others discarded. For example, the presence of financial or parental support, or the time involved in preparation for a particular vocation are factors that are taken into consideration in developing a vocational preference.

5 *Differentiation of interests and values*   When the adolescent gradually becomes aware of interests that gravitate toward particular occupations and away from others, then the basis is set for some type of decision and action on the adolescent's part.

6 *Awareness of present-future relationships*   The awareness of present-future relationships occurs when the adolescent is aware that a present behavior will influence future vocational choices. For example, certain science and math courses at the secondary school level (and, of course, their successful completion!) allow the adolescent to pursue a science or preprofessional program in college undergraduate study.

7 *Formulation of a generalized preference*   The adolescent verbally refers to a possible general vocational goal that is realized at some future date.

8 *Consistency of preference*   Consistency of preference for a particular occupation is shown, for example, when the adolescent takes a selected series of courses or verbally expresses interest in a certain area over a specific time period.

9 *Possession of information concerning the preferred occupation* For understanding to take place, the adolescent must have some knowledge concerning requirements of the occupation, training involved, and so on. In the specification stage, this knowledge is more advanced and specific with regard to particular occupations.

10 *Planning for the preferred occupation*   Planning for the preferred occupation is very similar to the behavior described in number nine, but stresses the decision the adolescent must make regarding vocational preference.

11 *Wisdom of the vocational preference*   Wisdom about the vocational preference is demonstrated by the adolescent's conscious reflection and verbalizing about the particular vocational preference.

Specifying vocational choices   When we reach the specification stage, which is relevant to the college undergraduate years, we find that these eleven general vocational preferences regarding the secondary-school student now emerge in more specific detail. In this stage, we find the adolescent demonstrating a firmer sense of commitment to his or her occupational choice. There is an increased sense of realism as the adolescent shows more interest in planning vocational goals. The behaviors and attitudes summarized above are also exhibited by the late adolescent in the college years. Now, whenever the adolescent seeks some type of preference in occupational choice, however, there is a specification of a particular preference rather than an attempt to crystallize choices. The one behavior that is added during this specification period is "*Confidence in a specific preference.*" During the college years, the adolescent usually develops a growing confidence in a particular vocational choice. The adolescent's confidence in his or her vocational commitment can be evaluated in terms of his or her verbalization, personal rating of self, and various acts concerned with making vocational preferences realizable.

Implementing vocational choices   After crystallization and specification of a vocational preference, the third task of the adolescent is the implementation of a vocational preference. The implementation begins in the secondary-school years when the adolescent makes various curricular choices. Super notes that this process is already going on by age 21 and is completed before the mid-twenties. During this stage, there are four behaviors and attitudes that need discussion.

1 *Awareness of the need to implement preference*   The awareness of the need to implement a preference is manifested in the young person's actions. For example, the adolescent actually applies to a particular college or graduate/professional school. Evidence of this need arises when the adolescent verbalizes the need to apply to

school, passes a qualifying examination, or actually ventures forth to get a job.

2 *Planning to implement preference*   Planning to implement a vocational preference occurs when the adolescent actually determines a means for implementing a vocational preference. It is seen in the adolescent's conversations with friends, counselors, parents, and others. It is also seen in the actual behavior of the adolescent in his or her planning, goal setting, or formulation of ideas on various vocational options.

3 *Executing plans to qualify for entry*   Executing plans to qualify for entry is manifested in the adolescent's behavior, such as participating in training programs, taking qualifying exams, and making necessary contacts for one's life's work.

4 *Obtaining an entry job*   This final stage, obtaining an entry-level job, is implemented in the actual entry into the job market — that is, the securing of employment.

In discussing Super's vocational theory we must keep in mind that cultural and economic factors might well influence the occupational commitment of the adolescent or young adult. No doubt many young people go several years before deciding on a specific occupational commitment. Nevertheless, Super's developmental theory of vocational preference poses several challenges to a spirituality for adolescents. On one level, there is the adolescent's actual involvement in the social world, how the adolescent will actually function in an adult role. Second, there is the adolescent's own attempt at personally integrating his or her vocational self-concept (what he or she will be) with his or her personal self-concept (who he or she is). Third, and most important for a spirituality for adolescents, we must ask what deeper meanings arise when we speak of a vocational commitment. More specifically, we need to ask how the adolescent's commitment to the working world reflects deeper values that resonate with Christian commitment in the world.

Vatican II reminds us that every Christian is called to the common vocation of Christian holiness and Christian service (ministry) in the world. This call to Christian holiness presents adolescent spirituality with two tasks for any vocational theory. First, spirituality must speak to the development of the person's own sense of self as a productive, working member of the world. For the adolescent, this call must be transposed into spiritual insights and experiences that the adolescent can bring to decisions about future career choices. Second, this career focus and its integration with spirituality must help articulate for *this* adolescent an explicit realization for future Christian ministry in-the-world. The adolescent needs to view how conscious career choices help him or her to realize the Gospel invitation to "come, follow me."

A Theology of Vocation

Theologian Laurence O'Connell has attempted an initial formulation of a theology of vocation and urges continued theological study in this uncharted area. O'Connell recalls that the word vocation comes from the Latin word *vocare*, which means "to call." The call of God has been present from the beginning of creation. God not only has created humankind, but also has given all men and women a vocation, which is "to cooperate with Him in the ongoing process of creation."[94] In Old Testament history, this "calling" is reflected in the various covenants that God has made with Israel. Furthermore, this call is realized in New Testament history through Jesus Christ, because "Jesus has come to invite or call humankind back to their original vocation or calling, namely, sharing deeply in the very life of the Creator."[95]

O'Connell says that, therefore, just as the disciples are *called* (Mt 4:21), so, too, we are also *called* to continue to labor and bring about the saving work of creation through our own lives that are given over to Christian service. Each human being responds to God's call through the concrete, personal experiences of life. And the call is, moreover, ratified by the actions and commitments of one' lifestyle, career, and relationships. Here we can see the active, personal emphasis by which each person can respond in experiencing God's call. Every Christian is beckoned by Jesus through his or her baptismal commitment to the Kingdom. The adolescent's response to Jesus' invitation to "come, follow me" can reflect this call in his or her own life.

St. Ignatius also talks of the importance of God's call and the retreatant's response to this call in his classic *Spiritual Exercises*. Talking about the decision that a person makes regarding life choices, Ignatius says: "In making a choice or in coming to a decision, only one thing is really important, to seek and to find what God calls me to at this time of my life. I know that his call remains faithful; he has created me for himself and my salvation is found in that love." Thus, the aim of the Christian "should be to seek and to serve God in whatever way his call might come to me." For Ignatius, this call must be rooted in a personally meaningful experience of the life of Jesus Christ. Just as Jesus, through the experiences of his own life, grew to a greater knowledge of the destiny to which he was called, so, too, the Christian, through the experiences of his or her life, must respond to the personal call of God through Jesus Christ.

During the stage of adolescence, then, an important task can be to help the adolescent through his or her own vocational development to realize Jesus' invitation to "come, follow me" in a vocation that is devoted to Gospel values. Through vocational development, we hope to encourage the adolescent to understand the richness of his or her gifts and the possibility of using his or her personal talents in the context of responding to Jesus' call to build the Kingdom.

We can conclude that the process of crystallizing, specifying, and implementing a vocational commitment is tied to an experience of the Lord through working for the Kingdom and is realized in the occupational identity one undertakes.

Adolescent Spirituality and Vocational Theory

Combining vocational theory with adolescent spirituality, we offer the following points as possibilities for the adolescent's growth in his or her spiritual life.

1 It is of critical importance that the adolescent's knowledge of his or her own strengths be enhanced. We often discover how easy it is in life to talk of faults and weaknesses. This is especially true regarding adolescents; young persons can develop a stance of largely unwarranted self-criticism. Thus, providing a young person with time to reflect on personal gifts and talents can be quite affirming during the adolescent years. This can be done by suggesting that the adolescent reflect on his or her personal talents and gifts; afterwards, the adult can encourage the adolescent to be thankful for who he or she is and what he or she has been given. The Thanksgiving Examen at the end of the next chapter provides a format for reflecting on these feelings.

2 Because the discussion of developmental theory has centered on the adolescent's growing capacity to develop personal and intimate relationships, we can give some attention to the adolescent's

personal relationship with Jesus. Incidents in the Gospel, such as the call of the Lord (Mt 4:21), can be used to give some direction and structure to the adolescent's deeper awareness of his or her own call from the Lord. Common open-ended questions that can be used are, "What do you think this call means in your life now?" "What do you think Jesus might be saying to you?" It is important that the adult aid the adolescent in making Jesus' call *concrete*. This might include a discussion of various life options, careers, courses, majors, college choices, and so on. It is also helpful, especially with middle and late adolescents, to reflect with them on the values that might underly these specific behavioral choices. The adolescent might also be encouraged to reflect on the self-in-the-future, and how Jesus' call might be experienced then. Although the future might be uncertain, the adolescent needs to begin seeing that current actions and behavioral choices will influence what options will be available in the future.

3 Paul speaks of the gifts of the Spirit in the Corinthian community (1 Cor 12:4–11). Paul's exhortation reminds every Christian of the personal gifts that he or she has been given to build up the community. As we have noted earlier, this emphasis on gifts is very important in the adolescent years. Adolescents (like many adults) will often define themselves by what they possess. It is important, then, to consider these gifts. We can ask: "What do you experience as gifts in your life?" A question of equal importance for the adolescent's Christian commitment is: "How will these gifts be used for building up the Kingdom?" From our discussion of developmental theory, we see opposing tendencies in the adolescent. On the one hand, there is the desire to reflect and personally define the self through reflection, relationships, and personal activity—a sense of self-preoccupation that influences the adolescent. On the other hand, however, there is a growing awareness of others and their growing demands as they intrude on the adolescent's life. Hence, we must aid the adolescent in articulating his or her personal gifts— how are these an important part of this adolescent's life and how do they help him or her follow Jesus' call. Likewise, we need to help the adolescent clarify his use of these gifts—how can they be used in meaningful Christian service to others.

4 A useful technique that can be utilized in aiding the adolescent's understanding his or her vocational commitment is called the

"ideal self." The adolescent imagines what he or she would like to be if there were no limitations on the self. For example, you might say to the adolescent, "If you could imagine yourself being anything that you wanted, what would you be?" There are several useful strategies that can be used here. The adolescent can be asked to outline what Gospel values are present in this ideal self. (Is there a place in the adolescent's ideal self for compassion or care? How is this shown?) The adolescent can also reflect on this ideal self as a "goal" for his or her life. Then, we can explore with the adolescent what particular experiences, characteristics, or aspects of self have led the adolescent to pose this as a goal for his or her life. Open-ended questions, which explore "why" this career or job was chosen, can be posed. As the adolescent talks, the adult might note the level of realism in the adolescent's reflections. (Do the adolescent's capabilities, personality fit the goal he or she is attempting to achieve?) From another perspective, the adult might explore any limitations the adolescent might have that could preclude the obtaining of this goal. (Is the adolescent aware of these limitations? Can he or she discuss them? Equally important, can he or she accept them?) Finally, the adult can explore with the adolescent the actual steps that might have been taken to initiate actions toward achieving this goal. (Has the adolescent talked with a counselor, for example, taken specific courses, or done further reading?) Specifically, the adolescent needs to reflect on the connection between thought and action, on how his or her behavior contributes to or inhibits the attainment of goals, and on how present behavior might enhance or limit future possibilities.

5. Because the secondary-school years (and even the college years) can be a time for crystallizing vocational preference, the adult might explore various vocational options with the adolescent. It is often helpful to examine with the adolescent the extent of the adolescent's knowledge and understanding of possible careers. Gospel values such as care, compassion, and openness can also be applied to these possible careers, thus inviting comparisons on the adolescent's part.

As the late adolescent attempts to specify what particular careers he or she might desire, the attention can shift to the specifics of careers and occupations. A good technique for accomplishing this is to have the adolescent imagine himself or herself in a particular career. Then we can pose questions such as, "What is the first thing you think about or feel in this type of work?" or "What types of personal satisfaction come to you when you imagine yourself in that type of work?" This exercise provides insight because it offers a glimpse into the affective and cognitive commitment that the adolescent might be investing in a particular type of occupational choice. It also affords the opportunity to explore what values the adolescent might possess and what he or she is bringing to his or her vocational identity. Also, the adult can ask the adolescent to "step outside" his or her own self (see Selman) and imagine viewing this person that he or she has now become. Ask the adolescent to verbalize what he or she sees in this person. This exercise can be very helpful because it allows the adolescent to reflect on personal attitudes and values and where these might be leading the young person in his or her future life.

6. A variation of the previous suggestion is to have the adolescent imagine himself or herself some thirty years hence. Once the adolescent has imagined what he or she will be doing thirty years from now, suggest that the adolescent reflect back on the thirty years that have gone by. We can pose information-producing questions to aid the adolescent in this experience: "What have you seen yourself accomplishing during these thirty years?" "What do people say about you or what do they think of you?" "What are the most important things you have done during these thirty years?" "What do you most regret about these thirty years?" This exercise can allow the adolescent to profitably reflect on Gospel values. Read with the adolescent the Gospel passages that deal with the sowing of seed (Mk 4:1–20); the adolescent can then be invited to look at what seeds he or she has sown during these imaginary years. Especially consider what seeds the adolescent has brought to fruition, during these thirty years, through Christian service to others.

Summary

We have examined the various aspects of developmental theory as they pertain to the adolescent. Now we include the following table in an attempt to capture the various areas of adolescent development as well as the specific points that adolescent spirituality brings to this developmental theory.

111

DEVELOPMENTAL THEORY AND ADOLESCENT SPIRITUALITY: A SYNTHESIS

APPROXIMATE AGE	Cognitive (Piaget)	Moral (Kohlberg)	Values (Perry)	Identity (Erikson)	Faith (Fowler)	Interpersonal (Selman)	Career (Super)
EARLY ADOLESCENCE (12–15)	•Leaving Concrete thinking •Early formal thinking	•Stage 3: Approval from others	•Dualism	•Industry/ Inferiority	•Synthetic-Conventional	•Third-Person Perspective	
MIDDLE ADOLESCENCE (15–18)	•Formal thinking	•Stage 4: Law and Order	•Relativism	•Identity/ Diffusion		•In-depth Perspective of self, others	•Crystallize career
LATE ADOLESCENCE (18–22/5)	•Increasing capacity for abstraction, reflection, and critical thought	*Youth often regress to earlier stage* •Movement toward Stage 5: Principled Reasoning	•Possibility of Commitment in the midst of Relativism	•Intimacy/ Isolation	•Transition to Individuative-Reflective		•Specify career
FOCUS FOR ADOLESCENT SPIRITUALITY	•Encourage deeper reflection on faith and life's meaning	•Encourage moral reasoning that reflects Christian values	•Aid in attempts to cope with relativism and how personal faith gives meaning in a complex, ambiguous world	•Help in formation of a deeper sense of self •Encourage intimacy for deeper relationship with Jesus and others	•Help foster the development of a perspective that centers on Jesus Christ, Gospel values, and the faith community	•Encourage growing sensitivity to others, especially those who are hurting and oppressed	•Aid development of a career choice that accepts Christian responsibility for others
PASTORAL TECHNIQUES, STRATEGIES FOR ADULTS MINISTERING TO ADOLESCENTS	•Pose questions, hypothetical situations •Challenge statements as to their implications	•Present Christian values •Help adolescent clarify personal values	•Reflect on the diversity of beliefs and values and youth's own personal commitments	•Pose questions that reflect on who the adolescent is •Reflect on meaning of love, feelings, self	•Discuss how the adolescent finds meaning •Discuss how are values related to this meaning	•Role-playing •Explore ways that adolescent understands others and their perspectives	•Pose various jobs, careers •Reflect on ways Christian values are present in these careers

We can conclude our discussion of developmental theory with several observations concerning developmental theory and adolescent spirituality.

1 Although developmental theory reveals the tendencies and characteristics that can be generalized to the entire adolescent population, as pastoral ministers to youth we must always respect the *uniqueness* of each adolescent we minister to. Equally important, this adolescent's experience of God is the unique beckoning of God through His offer of grace to this adolescent. The adult should always respect the uniqueness of this adolescent. Thus, in the context of a spiritual dialog with the adolescent, the adult should always keep in mind both the unique life story and the unique relationship with God that this adolescent brings to the encounter.

2 A second point that emerges from our developmental perspective is the *relational* character of adolescence. Relational tendencies in adolescence encompass relating to the world, various roles, and friendships and personal relationships. More and more, the adolescent comes to develop a self-in-relation-to-others. Central to all these relationships is the presence of Jesus in the adolescent's life. As the adolescent constructs these relationships and attempts to make meaning out of them, he or she must balance and place these many relational encounters in their proper perspective. We might view this developing adolescent self as a puzzle in which each relationship in the young person's life is a piece that helps to give meaning to the puzzle as it is slowly put together into a more meaningful whole. In this regard, a relationship with Jesus becomes the central piece in this puzzle of the self. The goal of adolescent spirituality is to offer Jesus as a central relationship in the adolescent's life from which all other relationships can draw meaning and support.

3 A third dimension of the developmental perspective is the process of *change*. Adolescence is a period in which change is ever present, even if it is not always recognized. In emotions, attitudes, values, knowledge, and even the physical self, the adolescent experiences a process of redefinement. Quite naturally, the adolescent's perception and understanding of God, the Transcendent, and Jesus is part of this change. Thus, adolescent spirituality considers each adolescent's attempt to make sense of and relate to a changing view of God, which flows, to a great extent, from the ongoing developmental changes that are so much a part of the adolescent's experience.

4 Adolescence is also a time of growing, reflective *criticism*. This critical stance is touched by the deeper demands of society and the deepening of the adolescent's own life experience. As a result, the adolescent develops a nascent, personally constructed philosophy of life that includes ideas, attitudes, and values that are internally examined as he or she prepares to enter the world of young adulthood. It is not unlikely, then, that a facet of this critical reflection is a re-evaluation by many adolescents of the role that Jesus exercises in their lives. As we shall see in the next chapter, this critical stance might include a questioning of God's existence and the place of Jesus in the young person's life.

5 The final aspect of adolescent developmental theory is its *integrative* nature. The adolescent is experiencing profound changes at the intellectual, emotional, and physical levels. A spirituality that is sensitive to adolescent development attempts to integrate all aspects of adolescent growth in a self that is capable of making a commitment to the Gospel and the forming of a personal relationship with Jesus in the context of a growing sense of adulthood. At the same time, from a spiritual perspective, the integration of the Transcendent gives meaning to the emotional and intellectual changes in the adolescent's life. Morever, an adolescent spirituality views as inadequate any attempt to deal with changes in the adolescent's life that do not focus on the integration of the Transcendent with the personal changes and life experiences of the adolescent.

This chapter has focused on the place that developmental theory has in adolescent spirituality. We have concluded that the spiritual growth of the young person is only realized when all facets of the adolescent's life are exposed to the call of Jesus. Thus, the cognitive, moral, faith, emotional, interpersonal, and vocational growth that the adolescent experiences must be sensitive to Jesus' call to "come, follow me." Through an awareness of the developmental experiences that adolescents undergo, the adult's stance in ministering to the adolescent is enhanced.

Having examined the developmental changes in adolescence, we now turn to various aspects of adolescent spirituality and view the place of this development in the spiritual life of the adolescent.

Notes to Chapter Three

1. Karl Rahner, S.J., "Reflections on the Problem of the Gradual Ascent to Christian Perfection." In *Theological Investigations*, vol. 3, pp. 3–5. New York: The Seabury Press, A Crossroad Book, 1974.

2. For an overall view of Jean Piaget's theory of cognitive development, I rely on the following: Jean Piaget, *Six Psychological Studies*, trans. David Elkind and Anita Teuzel, pp. 1–74. New York: Random House, Vintage Books, 1968; with Barbel Inhelder, *The Growth of Logical Thinking from Childhood to Adolescence*. New York: Basic Books, 1958; *The Origins of Intelligence in Children*. New York: W. W. Norton & Co., 1963; John L. Phillips, Jr., *The Origins of Intellect: Piaget's Theory*. San Francisco: W. H. Freeman, 1975; Ruth M. Beard, *An Outline of Piaget's Developmental Psychology for Students and Teachers*. New York: Mentor-Basic Books, 1972; Rolf E. Muuss, *Theories of Adolescence*, pp. 178–207. New York: Random House, 1975.

3. Muuss, *Theories of Adolescence*, p. 182.

4. Cathy Stonehouse, "Moral Development: The Process and the Pattern," *Counseling and Values* 24, October 1979, p. 3.

5. Kenneth Sullivan and Anna Sullivan, "Adolescent-Parent Separation," *Developmental Psychology* 16, March 1980, pp. 93–99.

6. For a more detailed description of concrete operational thinking, see Phillips, Beard, or Muuss, all cited in note 2 above.

7. Inhelder and Piaget, *Logical Thinking*, p. 250.

8. Ibid., p. 251.

9. See David Elkind, "Understanding the Young Adolescent," *Adolescence* 49, Spring 1978, pp. 128–129.

10. Piaget, *Six Psychological Studies*, p. 67.

11. See Elkind, "Understanding the Young Adolescent, pp. 129–132, and "Child Development and Counseling," *The Personnel and Guidance Journal* 58, January 1980, pp. 353–356.

12. Elkind, "Child Development and Counseling," p. 354.

13. Inhelder and Piaget, *Logical Thinking*, p. 349. For an extended overview of adolescent cognitive development, see Chapter 18, "Adolescent Thinking," pp. 334–350. For a detailed treatment of formal thinking in adolescence, see Muuss, *Theories of Adolescence*, pp. 178–207.

14. The work in this area is extensive. See Daniel Keating and Lawrence Clark, "Development of Physical and Social Reasoning in Adolescence," *Developmental Psychology* 16, January 1980, pp. 23–30; David Elkind, "Recent Research on Cognitive Development in Adolescence," in *Adolescence in the Life Cycle*, ed. Sigmund Dragastin and Glen Elder Jr., pp. 49–61. New York: John Wiley & Sons, 1975; and Everett Dulit, "Adolescent Thinking a la Piaget: The Formal Stage," *Journal of Youth and Adolescence* 1, December 1972, pp. 281–301.

Piaget, *The Moral Judgment of the Child*. New York: The Free Press, 1965. For an excellent summary of Piaget's theory of moral development, see Ronald Duska and Mariellen Whelan, *Moral Development: A Guide to Piaget and Kohlberg*. New York: Paulist Press, 1975, pp. 5–41.

16. For an overall view of Lawrence Kohlberg's work, I rely on the following: Lawrence Kohlberg, "Moral Development," in *International Encyclopedia of the Social Sciences*. New York: Macmillan Free Press, 1968; with Carol Gilligan, "The Adolescent as a Philosopher: The Discovery of Self in a Postconventional World," *Daedalus* 100, Fall 1971, pp. 1051–1086; "The Cognitive-Developmental Approach to Moral Education," *Phi Delta Kappan* 56, June 1975, 670–677; "Education, Moral Development, and Faith," *Journal of Moral Education* 4, October 1974, pp. 5–16; "Stage and Sequence: The Cognitive-Developmental Approach to Socialization," in *Handbook of Socialization Theory and Research*, ed. David A. Goslin. Chicago: Rand McNally and Co., permission of Houghton Mifflin Co., Boston, MA, 1969; Ronald Duska and Mariellen Whelan, *Moral Development*, pp. 42–79; Rolf E. Muuss, "Lawrence Kohlberg's Cognitive-Developmental Approach to Adolescent Morality," *Theories of Adolescence*, pp. 208–229; Martin L. Hoffman, "Moral Development in Adolscence," in *The Handbook of Adolescent Psychology*, ed. Joseph Adelson, pp. 295–343. New York: John Wiley and Sons, 1980. For a critique of Kohlberg's theory, see Howard Muson, "Moral Thinking: Can It Be Taught?" *Psychology Today* 12, February 1979, pp. 48–68, 92; Martin L. Hoffman, "Moral Development in Adolescence," pp. 299–304; Paul J. Philibert, O.P., "Some Cautions on Kohlberg," *The Living Light* 12, Winter 1975, pp. 527–534; Rick Ellrod, "Morality and Interests: A Critique of Kohlberg's Ethical Theory," *Communio* 7, Fall 1980, pp. 259–268; D. M. Wonderly and J. H. Kupfersmid, "Promoting Postconventional Morality: The Adequacy of Kohlberg's Aim," *Adolescence* 15, Fall 1980, pp. 609–631. Wonderly and Kupfersmid, in particular, give a devasting critique of Kohlberg's theory regarding both its "philosophic adequacy" and its "empirical evidence." Kohlberg now admits to some reservations about his own theory regarding principled moral reasoning. His research indicates that none of his subjects have obtained stage six moral reasoning. This lack of empirical evidence leads one to question what stage of moral reasoning is truly possible for the human person. Cf. Lawrence Kohlberg, "Educating for a Just Society: Updated and Revised Paradigm," in *Moral Development, Moral Education, and Kohlberg*, ed. Brenda Munsey, pp. 456–459. Birmingham, AL: Religious Education Press, 1980. Personally, I have much sympathy with many of the criticisms leveled against moral developmental theory; this is especially true regarding its incorporation into the Catholic school system without any meaningful critical review. Yet, in terms of the adolescent experience, Kohlberg's developmental theory provides a format for the emergence of Gospel values and Christian commitment. By integrating Kohlberg's work and Perry's work with spirituality, we can help nurture the development of the adolescent's Christian commitment in the face of increasing ambiguity and relativism.

17. Kohlberg, "Cognitive-Developmental Approach," p. 672.

18. Ibid. [The same page as the preceding note.]

19. Kohlberg, "Education, Moral Development, and Faith," *p. 5.*

20. Ibid., p. 11.

21. Lawrence Kohlberg and Elsa R. Wasserman, "The Cognitive-Developmental Approach and the Practicing Counselor: An Opportunity for Counselors to Rethink Their Roles," *The Personnel and Guidance Journal* 58, May 1980, p. 561.

22. Kohlberg and Gilligan, "Adolescent as Philosopher," p. 1075.

23. For a critique of Kohlberg's theory of principled reasoning, see especially Wonderly and Kupfersmid "Promoting Postconventional Morality," pp. 609–631.

24. Kohlberg and Gilligan, "Adolescent as Philosopher," p. 1072.

25. Ibid., p. 1074.

26. Lawrence Kohlberg and R. Kramer, "Continuities and Discontinuities in Childhood and Adult Moral Development," *Human Development* 12, no. 2, 1969, 93–120.

27. Kohlberg and Gilligan, "Adolescent as Philosopher," p. 1075.

28. Elliot Turiel, "Conflict and Transition in Adolescent Moral Development," *Child Development* 45, March 1974, 140–179.

29. Martin L. Hoffman, "Moral Development in Adolescence," p. 304. I am indebted to Hoffman for the above reference to Turiel.

30. James W. Fowler, *Stages of Faith.* San Francisco: Harper & Row, 1981, pp. 81–84.

31. Fowler gives an excellent summary of the developmental theories of Piaget, Erikson, and Kohlberg through the various stages of human development (Ibid., pp. 41–88), which is highly recommended.

32. John M. Murphy and Carol Gilligan, "Moral Development in Late Adolescence and Adulthood: A Critique and Reconstruction of Kohlberg's Theory," *Human Development* 23, no. 2, 1980, pp. 77–104.

33. William G. Perry, Jr. *Forms of Intellectual and Ethical Development in the College Years.* New York: Holt, Rinehart, and Winston, Inc., 1968.

34. Ibid., p. 111.

35. Ibid., p. 131.

36. Ibid., p. 135.

37. For an interesting comparison of Kohlberg and Perry, see Glenn R. Pellino, "Student Development and Values Education," *Counseling and Values* 22, October 1977, pp. 41–51.

38. Donald L. Gelpi, S.J., *Experiencing God.* New York: Paulist Press, 1978, pp. 299–306.

116

39. Duska and Whelan, *Moral Development*, p. 83.

40. Ellrod, "Morality and Interests," pp. 267–268.

41. For an excellent example of the use of values in the counseling situation, see Milton Rokeach and John F. Regan, "The Role of Values in the Counseling Situation," *The Personnel and Guidance Journal* 58, May 1980, pp. 576–581.

42. Ibid., p. 580. See Also, Alan L. Lockwood, "Notes on Research Associated with Values Clarification and Value Therapy," *The Personnel and Guidance Journal* 58, May 1980, pp. 606–608.

43. Frederick Coons, "The Developmental Tasks of the College Student," in *Adolescent Psychiatry Developmental and Clinical Studies*, vol. 1, ed. Sherman C. Feinstein and Peter L. Giovacchini, New York: Basic Books, Inc., 1971, pp. 256–274.

44. Gelpi, *Experiencing God*, p. 304.

45. James S. Leming, "Intrapersonal Variation in Stages of Moral Reasoning among Adolescents as a Function of Situational Context," *Journal of Youth and Adolescence* 7, December 1978, pp. 405–416. The March 1978 issue of the *St. Anthony Messenger* is devoted to the facing of everyday life situations. Seven moral theologians tackle real-life dilemmas such as alcoholism, paying one's income tax, and school busing; for adolescents there are several issues of interest—smoking marijuana, the draft, and premarital sexuality. Adolescents are in need of facing decisions in everyday life situations. Discussion of specific, concrete issues that relate to the adolescent's everyday life concerns are quite helpful.

46. Kohlberg, "Education, Moral Development, and Faith," p. 14.

47. For an overall view of James Fowler's theory, I rely on James W. Fowler and Sam Keen, *Life Maps: Conversations on the Journey of Faith.* Waco, Texas: Word Books, 1978; "Faith Liberation and Human Development," *The Foundation* 79 (Gammon Theological Seminary, Atlanta), Spring 1974, pp. 1–29; "Stages in Faith: The Structural-Developmental Approach," in *Values and Moral Development*, ed. Thomas Hennessey, S.J., pp. 173–213. New York: Paulist Press, 1976; "Faith Development: Theory and the Aims of Religious Socialization," in *Emerging Issues in Religious Education*, ed. Gloria Durka and Joanmarie Smith, pp. 187–208. New York: Paulist Press, 1976; "Moral Stages and the Development of Faith," in *Moral Development, Moral Education, and Kohlberg*, ed. Brenda Munsey, pp. 130–160. Birmingham, AL: Religious Education Press, 1980; *Stages of Faith: The Psychology of Human Development and the Quest for Meaning.* San Francisco: Harper & Row, 1981.

48. Edwin J. McDermott, S.J., review of *Stages of Faith* by James W. Fowler, *Human Development* 2, Winter 1981, p. 46.

49. Fowler, "Faith Development," p. 193.

50. Fowler, *Stages of Faith*, p. 4.

117

51. Fowler and Keen, *Life Maps*, p. 25.

52. Ibid., p. 18.

53. Ibid., p. 21.

54. Fowler, *Stages of Faith*, pp. 81–83.

55. Ibid., p. 182.

56. Fowler, "Stages in Faith," p. 199.

57. Fowler, *Life Maps*, p. 80.

58. Fowler, *Stages of Faith*, p. 303.

59. Gary L. Chamberlain, "Faith Development and Campus Ministry," *Religious Education* 74, May–June, 1979, p. 323. This article is an excellent introduction to the application of Fowler's theory at the secondary-school level.

60. James E. Hennessy, "Reactions to Fowler: Stages in Faith or Stages in Commitment," in *Values and Moral Development*, p. 219.

61. Chamberlain also argues for this. See "Faith Development and Campus Ministry," p. 318.

62. Sue Street, "Social Self-Concept in High School Students," *The School Counselor* 28, May 1981, p.. 320.

63. For an overall view of Erik Erikson's theory, I rely on Erik Erikson, *Childhood and Society*. New York: W. W. Norton, 1963; *Identity, Youth, and Crisis*. New York: W. W. Norton, 1968; "Reflections on Dr. Borg's Life Cycle," *Daedalus* 105, Spring 1976,, pp. 1–28. Also, the following works: Kathleen M. White, "Problems and Characteristics of College Students," *Adolescence* 15, Spring 1980, pp. 23–41; Philip R. Newman and Barbara M. Newman, "Identity Formation and the College Experience," *Adolescence* 13, Summer 1978, pp. 311–326; Ruth Whitney, "Beyond Erikson's Eight Stages," *Counseling and Values* 23, April 1979, pp. 174–183; John J. Conger, *Adolescence and Youth: Psychological Development in a Changing World*. New York: Harper & Row, 1977, pp. 91–99, 249–251; James E. Marcia, "Identity in Adolescence,' in *Handbook of Adolescent Psychology*, ed. Joseph Adelson, pp. 159–210; and Muuss, *Theories of Adolescence*, pp. 54–84.

64. James E. Marcia, "Identity in Adolescence," p. 160. For a discussion on the relationship between identity and intimacy see Mary Ann Jacerquis and Gerald R. Adams, "Erikson Stage Resolution: The Relationship between Identity and Intimacy," *Journal of Youth and Adolescence* 9, April 1980, pp. 117–26.

65. Ruthellen Josselson, "Ego Development in Adolescence," in *Handbook of Adolescent Psychology*, ed. Joseph Adelson, p. 194.

66. For a discussion of this issue, see White, "Problems and Characteristics of College Students," pp. 26–27.

67. Josselson, "Ego Development in Adolescence," p. 191.

68. Gelpi, *Experiencing God,* pp. 307–310.

69. Andrew M. Greeley, "A Post-Vatican II New Breed? A Report on Contemporary Catholic Teen-Agers," *America* 142, 28 June 1980, pp. 534–537.

70. Dennis Raphael and Helga G. Xelowski, "Identity Status in High School Students: Critique and a Revised Paradigm," *Journal of Youth and Adolescence* 9, October 1980, pp. 383–389.

71. See James E. Marcia, "Development and Validation of Ego Identity Status," *Journal of Personality and Social Psychology* 3, May 1966, pp. 551–558; "Identity in Adolescence," *op. cit.,* pp. 161–166.

72. Richard Logan, "Identity Diffusion and Psycho-Social Defense Mechanisms," *Adolescence* 13, Fall 1978, pp. 503–507.

73. Another, more extreme variation is the adolescent commitment to religious youth cults in order to cope with identity needs. For a discussion of this issue, see E. Mansell Pattison, "Religious Youth Cults: Alternative Healing Social Networks," *Journal of Religion and Health* 19, Winter 1980, pp. 275–286; George H. Klumper, "Youth and Religious Cults: A Societal and Clinical Dilemma," in *Adolescent Psychiatry* 6, ed. Sherman C. Feinstein and Peter L. Giovacchini, pp. 75–89. Chicago: The University of Chicago Press, 1978.

74. Philip W. Mielman, "Cross-Sectional Age Changes in Ego Identity Status During Adolescence," *Developmental Psychology* 15, March 1979, pp. 230–231.

75. Erikson, *Identity, Youth, and Crisis,* p. 135.

76. John J. Mitchell, "Adolescent Intimacy," *Adolescence* 11, Summer 1976, pp. 275–280.

77. See, for example, Richard L. Hayes, "High School Graduation: The Case for Identity Loss," *The Personnel and Guidance Journal* 59, February 1981, pp. 369–371.

78. I am indebted to J. Peter Schineller, S.J. and his article "The Newer Approaches to Christology and Their Use in the Spiritual Exercises," *Studies in the Spirituality of Jesuits* 12, September–November, 1980, pp. 37–39, for the mention of these scripture passages.

79. Ruth Whitney, "Beyond Erikson's Eight Stages," p. 176.

80. James J. Gill, S.J., "Indispensable Self-Esteem," *Human Development* 1, Fall 1980, p. 34.

81. Peter J. van Breemen, S.J., *As Bread That Is Broken.* Denville, NJ: Dimension Books, 1974, pp. 12–15.

82. Henri Nouwen, "The Faces of Community," *The Catholic Worker,* March–April, 1978, p. 3.

83. Gabriel Moran, "A Precarious Age," *New Catholic World* 222, September/October, 1979, pp. 199–200.

84. In support of this, James Fowler notes a doctoral dissertation by Eugene J. Mischey, "Faith Development and Its Relationship to Moral Reasoning and Identity Status in Young Adults," University of Toronto; see Munsey (ed.), *Moral Development, Moral Education, and Kohlberg*, pp. 154–156.

85. For an understanding of Robert L. Selman's work, I rely on: Robert L. Selman, "The Development of Socio-Cognitive Understanding: A Guide to Educational and Clinical Practice," in *Moral Development and Behavior: Theory, Research, and Social Issue*, ed. Thomas Lickona, pp. 229–316. New York: Holt, Rinehart, and Winston, 1976; with Ellen Ward Cooney, "Children's Use of Social Conceptions: Towards a Dynamic Model of Social Cognition," *The Personnel and Guidance Journal* 58, January, 1980, pp. 344–352; *The Growth of Interpersonal Understanding*. New York: Academic Press, 1980, pp. 11–47.

86. Selman and Cooney, "Children's Use of Social Conceptions," p. 345.

87. Selman, "Development of Socio-Cognitive Understanding," p. 301.

88. Ervin Staub, *Positive Social Behavior and Morality Socialization and Development*, vol. 2. new York: Academic Press, 1979, pp. 83–86.

89. Keating and Clark, "Development of Physical and Social Reasoning in Adolescence," pp. 23–30.

90. Milton F. Shore, "Youth and Jobs: Educational, Occupational, and Mental Health Aspects," *Journal of Youth and Adolescence* 1, December 1972, p. 316.

91. For a discussion of Super's work, see Donald E. Super et al., *Vocational Development: A Framework for Research*. New York: Bureau of Publications Teachers College, Columbia University, 1957; and Super et al., *Career Development: Self-concept theory*. New York: College Entrance Examination Board, 1963. In the second text, see specifically "Self-concept in vocational development," pp. 1–11; "Toward making self-concept theory operational," pp. 17–32; and "Vocational development in adolescence and early adulthood," pp. 79–93.

92. Super, *Career Development*, p. 18.

93. Super, *Career Development*, p. 82.

94. Laurence J. O'Connell, "God's Call to Humankind: Towards a Theology of Vocation," *Chicago Studies* 18, Summer 1979, p. 151. The entire article (pp. 147–160) presents an interesting perspective on vocation.

95. Ibid., p. 152.

CHAPTER FOUR

Spiritual Life
of the
Adolescent

From our examination of developmental theory in chapter 3, we can readily see the place of human development—its issues and concerns—in the growth of the adolescent's spiritual life. When we discuss topics such as prayer, the church, and the sacraments, we must understand the lived experience of the adolescent who is attempting to find meaning and value in the midst of the numerous changes that are taking place in his or her own life. Having examined the adolescent in a developmental context, then, we now turn to various aspects of the adolescent's spiritual life to see how we might integrate our developmental perspective with youth's attempt to answer the Lord's call.

Prayer and the Adolescent

One fundamental principle of Christian living is the need for prayer. In addition to Jesus' own example of a prayerful life, we know that He spoke of how we have a need for prayer in our own lives (Mt 7:7). "He gave us a formula of prayer in what is known as the Lord's Prayer. He taught us that prayer is necessary, that it should be humble, vigilant, persevering, confident in the Father's goodness, single-minded and in conformity with God's nature."[1] Yet, adults who are ministering to youth must ask how the experience of prayer can be made meaningful in the midst of the adolescent's own developmental growth. As pointed out in the preceding chapter, adolescents are at a stage when questions of faith, the meaning of Jesus Christ, and one's relationship with the larger Christian community

121

become more pressing and genuine. Thus, as the adolescent's need for relating and sharing becomes more intense, it behooves adults to discuss prayer in the context of these developmental needs.

All too often, however, we overlook the point that prayer does not just happen. Prayer deserves some type of preparation on the part of the individual. St. Ignatius notes that the first step for prayer is maintaining a "spirit of deeper reverence before God." Reverence is the capacity to be open—a state of mind, an attitude that allows one to be present and truly respectful of another. In marriage, in friendship, indeed, in any relationship, we must experience the other's presence. It is through reverence that this special appreciation for the other allows that person to enter our lives, to touch us in a profound and special way. In short, reverence makes this relational dynamic both feasible and permissible.

Solitude becomes one prerequisite for reverence. In the *Spiritual Exercises,* St. Ignatius suggests a number of advantages to seclusion from others: (1) Seclusion is difficult and shows one's true disposition and will, one's true intent before the Lord; (2) seclusion is the absence of distractions that allows the person to concentrate on the encounter with God; (3) the more solitary we are, the more disposed we are to seek "grace and gifts" from God. Ignatius' observations can be applied to our personal life of prayer. One's own solitude disposes the self to really face the Creator and Lord, to actually experience the message He intends.

It is instructive that other writers have also spoken of the need to find solitude for prayer. Thomas Merton, in quoting the Syrian monk Issac of Niniveh, says "if you love truth, be a lover of silence. Silence, like the sunlight, will illuminate you in God and deliver you from the phantoms of ignorance. Silence will unite you to God."[2] And the popular priest-writer Henri Nouwen speaks of the benefits of the Christian call to solitude, for "a life without a lonely place, that is, a life without a quiet center, easily becomes destructive." He goes on to say that "in solitude we can slowly unmask the illusion of our possessiveness and discover in the center of our own self that we are not what we can conquer, but what is given to us. In solitude we can listen to the voice of him who spoke to us before we could speak a word, who healed us before we could make any gesture to help, who set us free long before we could free others, and who loved us long before we could give love to anyone."[3]

For the adolescent, however, especially in the early years of adolescence, this solitude is often difficult. The hustle of everyday life, the experiences of newly found freedom, and the attempts and trials of new opportunities often militate against setting aside time for being alone by oneself, not to mention time in solitude with God. What is more, adolescent solitude can be difficult for a significant reason: spending time alone opens up the possibility that loneliness can emerge. For youth, "the process of separating and maturing is tinged with loneliness."[4] Solitude opens the young person up to the vulnerability of internal questioning, anxieties, and the possible inordinate focusing that comes with family difficulties that are potentially threatening. Psychiatrists Eric Ostrov and Daniel Offer have noted that this feeling of loneliness is more common among early adolescents than among late adolescents. As we have noted in chapter 3, the young person begins to face psychological and physiological changes without a firm foothold in identity. He or she is only beginning the voyage to self-discovery. On the other hand, as adolescents grow older, they "typically become less focused on their own internal changes and on departing from parents and childhood roles and beliefs. Instead, they concentrate on realizing interpersonal and vocational goals which promise relatedness to significant others and the larger society on a new, more mature basis."[5] Thus, one question we must pose when discussing prayer for adolescents is: How can we convert solitude from a threatening possibility to an inviting occurrence in the early adolescent's life?

For younger adolescents, it is often helpful to work within a group setting. (Although this group experience provides a usually appreciated shield against loneliness, more mature young adolescents might enjoy periods of solitude and actually find such experiences nonthreatening.) Group experiences can take place during a retreat, in a classroom, or in a group discussion. We might ask the adolescent to close his or her eyes, be silent, and think of something very positive, something that he or she really enjoys—a certain activity, for example, or being with a close friend. We let the student just sit with these feelings and enjoy the experiece for several minutes. The adult can then announce, "I am going to read you something from Scripture" (John 15:9–17 is appropriate). The group as a whole is then asked: "How is Christ speaking to you personally? What is he saying to you?" After a few minutes we ask everyone to

123

open their eyes and lead a discussion that focuses on the topic of love or on the meaning of a personal relationship with Jesus. Some questions to stimulate the discussion might be: (1) What was this experience like? Can you describe your feelings of this experience? (2) How did you react when Jesus' words were spoken? (3) Did you feel Jesus speaking to you personally?

Other possibilities include having the adolescent compose an autobiography or keep a journal or write about his or her personal strengths. These strengths can then be discussed in the group, and everyone can be asked to comment. In any group experience with adolescents, a trusting atmosphere is essential. Group experiences provide a format for the adolescent to learn social skills and to develop positive, constructive ways for relating with others. It is also important to remember that numbers can often be critical in determining the outcome of a group experience. Five to seven young people in a group is often ideal for this type of exercise. Finally, in group experiences it is often helpful to have older adolescents work with younger ones. This format provides an essential learning experience and a chance to develop real Christian leadership among the older adolescents. It can also provide a tremendous amount of peer support for the younger adolescents.

For middle and late adolescents, more private, directed encounters with solitude are usually possible. A few possible exercises will be developed later in this chapter.

In addition to the need for solitude, it is important to understand the nature of prayer. In his book *Letters from the Desert*, Carlo Carretto shares with us his thoughts on the need to be alone with God, to experience God in the desert of our lives. Carretto says "understanding prayer well means understanding that one is speaking with God."[6] In his splendid little book *Beginning to Pray*, Archbishop Anthony Bloom reminds us that "if we cannot meet God within, in the very depth of ourselves our chances of meeting Him outside ourselves are very remote."[7] We glean from these authors that prayer is a personal experience of speaking-to and listening-in-relationship. It is a relationship that is dialogic, in which we experience our selves with God and, at the same time, experience God within us. Robert Ochs captures this theme nicely when he notes that we need real honesty in our relationship with God. We must level with God from where we truly are and present to Him what we are really about. This honesty with God means "letting the 'true' nature of our relation with him come to the fore, convinced that however distorted or unchristian it is, it is where God and we actually are, and thus provides contact."[8] Our relationship with God, then, is above all a relationship that is *honest*.

The Element of Friendship

Yet we might ask how this honesty in prayer, indeed, how prayer itself is made meaningful for the adolescent. If we return for a moment to a concept that we have explored in chapter 1, we recall that friendship is highly valued by adolescents; in chapter 3 we noted that friendship is, in fact, a critical factor in the adolescent's experience of the developmental tasks of identity and intimacy. It is on this point that we now come to rest. Simply stated, therefore, it is Jesus Christ who is the adolescent's friend. The model we propose for adolescent prayer is Jesus Christ *as friend*. French catechist Pierre Babin captures the essence of this model when he writes that "adolescence constitutes a sensitive period for knowing Jesus Christ as Friend and the ultimate meaning of the universe. It is a passage through the depths, which will liberate the young person from his selfishness and help him to live as a friend of men in Christ, opening him more and more to the full dimensions of life in his earthly task."[9] This realization of Jesus as a friend parallels James Fowler's observation of the deeper symbolization that takes place in adolescents concerning God. It is during adolescence that God can now be symbolized as a personal friend who can offer the young person a deepening relationship that is based on both openness and trust.

The nature of human friendship is one of the important topics for Christian living. Priest-psychologist Ignace Lepp has remarked that friendship is the most noble form of all human communication. In friendship, says Lepp, we discover the authentic part of ourselves and realize in the deepest way what it means to be truly human.[10] Friendship with Jesus seeks to affirm this truth. A friendship model in the adolescent's relationship with the Lord seeks to touch the deepest yearnings of the adolescent's desires and dreams, to speak of the adolescent's need for closeness, understanding, intensity, security, and growth.

Jesus as friend   The model of Jesus as friend attempts to ask ultimate questions of the adolescent, thereby enabling him or her to find in Jesus as friend the source, as well as the terminus, of ultimate meaning. Through friendship with Jesus, the adolescent more deeply experiences who he or she really is. When the adolescent truly relates to Jesus as *friend*, he or she comes to see more than a simple relationship. Friendship with Jesus is, in the deepest possible way, what Andrew Greeley is describing when he talks of friendship as an "invitation."[11] Friendship is the inviting of another into one's life. The adolescent relationship with Jesus is an invitation to the deepest of relationships, a relationship in which the young person grows to understand more deeply both who he or she is and what his or her life is made for. In this friendship with Jesus, the adolescent comes to experience Jesus' invitation to more intimately know Jesus' own life—His struggles, His joy, and His passion, death, and resurrection—in short, His call to "come, follow me" through discipleship.

For the adolescent, for whom the building of relationships is a primary developmental need, recognizing Christ as a friend and relating to him in this way can elicit bountiful rewards. For the adolescent, friends help to define the self-concept, offer security, and foster intimacy—all of which are integral for development. Truly relating to Jesus as a friend presents the adolescent with the opportunity (and, because Jesus is experienced as a friend, with the psychological possibility) to grow in real openness and freedom in both the spiritual and emotional dimensions of his or her life. As the years go by, this friendship with Jesus can develop and become richer because it exemplifies a relationship in which the young person is accepted, in the deepest possible way, for who he or she really is.

Recent theological reflection in Christology (the theological study of Jesus Christ and the implications of Jesus' life for humankind) help to give us an insight into friendship with Jesus. In contemporary theological circles, there has been a movement away from a "high Christology," or a Christology "from above," to one that is concerned with the reality of Jesus Christ that is based on the experience of His humanity, that is, a "low Christology," or a Christology "from below."[12] In theological thinking, both of these perspectives are important because each approach stresses a vital aspect of God's salvific love. Each way helps the Christian penetrate "more deeply into the reality and mystery of the Christ event."[13]

A "high Christology," which is more representative of older theological thinking, tends to be concerned with Jesus Christ in terms of His divinity; it emphasizes Jesus as God. The humanity of Jesus, although certainly accepted, recedes into the background and often receives little attention or consideration. This approach can at times enshrine Jesus to such an extent that in many ways He appears to be remote from the daily life of the ordinary Christian. Although emphasis on Jesus as divine is absolutely necessary from the standpoint of salvation history, it sometimes distorts or blurs the humanity of Jesus in the minds of many young people. For adolescents, who are increasingly caught up in what it means to be human (and very often feeling this condition in an acute way), a "high Christology" approach can set up unnecessary barriers. Young people are inclined toward a Jesus who can relate to the self, a Jesus who shares the young person's feelings, fears, and joys—all that it means to be human. Extremely inviting for the adolescent, then, is a Jesus who experiences the life that the young person is presently experiencing.

This need to feel and experience Jesus in His humanity receives support from the new "low Christology." "Low Christology" focuses on the humanity of Jesus—the life, work, and message of the Jesus of scriptures. Central to the thinking of this "low Christology" is the place of the Kingdom of God, that is, Jesus' saving message. As religious educator Thomas Groome remarks, in lower Christological thinking "the central theme in the preaching and life of Jesus was the Kingdom of God."[14] This thinking emphasizes the human nature of Jesus. This approach to Jesus often leads the Christian to use scripture to grow more deeply into an understanding of who this man really is and to what His life, death, and resurrection call the person in daily life. Moreover, this approach does not dismiss the divinity of Jesus. On the contrary, when properly presented, "low Christology" elucidates more clearly the profound mystery of God's love that is revealed to humanity through the event of the Incarnation.

There are four reasons why this approach is particularly appealing to high school and college students and can be a useful resource in working with them.

1. The humanity of Jesus offers the adolescent a model of *personal relatedness* in which he or she can experience his or her own

identity and the need for intimacy. This need for identity and intimacy, as we have already noted in chapter 3, is an integral factor for adolescent development.

2. Emphasizing the humanity of Jesus allows for the development of a personally meaningful *value* system. Through a personal relationship with Jesus, the adolescent does not simply ask questions about values, but also experiences who has realized these values to their fullest. The adolescent is thus challenged to relate Jesus' life to his or her own life and ask, "What does Jesus' life mean for *me*?" The adolescent also has a personal model for answering these crucial questions.

3. The "low Christology" approach provides a new level of *commitment*, which is part of the adolescent's search. The adolescent is faced with the questions: "What do I live my life for?" "How do I (and how will I) respond to Jesus' call?" As the adolescent matures, a deeper sense of this call and what it entails emerges.

4. Emphasizing the humanity of Jesus in the "low Christology" approach is oriented toward continued *growth*, which parallels the adolescent's own personal experience. A study of the life of Jesus allows us to realize that He, too, "grew in wisdom" as He learned what was demanded of Him. So, too, in the adolescent's life there emerges the need to grow, to develop, and to understand more deeply the meaning of Jesus' words, "come, follow me."

The notion of God might appear abstract to adolescents, but, as Hilmar Wagner observes, young people can experience "a greater understanding of Jesus and His mission and His ministry."[15] A focus for adolescent spirituality is to provide a deepening experience of what it really means to be a follower of Jesus, what it calls the young person to in his or her life, and how the call, "come, follow me," is made a part of the adolescent's lived experience.

This developing relationship with Jesus is no doubt influenced by the religious training that has taken place in early development. Early religious training is marked by an acceptance of adult beliefs and ideas so that what parents and other authority figures relate to the child is socialized in the child's behavior in the world. As we have seen, James Fowler notes that this synthetic-conventional stage can last long into adolescence, or even into adulthood, and is marked by the dependence on adult authority to give meaning to the person's value system. With the advent of adolescence, however, more focused developmental needs appear. The need for identity and intimacy, which translates into the adolescent's search for deeper relationships, presses firmly into the forefront during this period. This developmental process of identity-intimacy acquisition leads the adolescent to seek out others and to share with them the deeper yearnings of the self.

In chapter 3, we noted that friendship—this actually is the finding of significant others in the adolescent's life—allows for this deeper sharing of self. As the adolescent matures, he or she enters into more relationships and comes to experience the faithfulness and joy of some, while simultaneously suffering through the insecurity, brevity, and disappointment of others. From these experiences, all of which are essential to growth, the adolescent comes to realize the real joy and richness of Jesus' love, because, unlike the adolescent's other relationships, his or her relationship with Jesus is grounded in Jesus' faithfulness, acceptance, and love. This, of course, does not mean that the adolescent will not have an existential doubt of his or her faith, or that the relationship with Jesus will not, at some future time, be tinged with doubt or questioning; on the contrary, these doubts are possible and even quite likely in the adolescent years. What this does say, however, is that Jesus' love, manifested in a relationship with the adolescent, is there. It is ever present and offers support and understanding during these developing years. Jesus is a responsive friend; He is ready to accept the young person, despite the adolescent's doubts, hesitations, and questions. This developing friendship with Jesus can be crucial for later spiritual development because it cements a foundation to which the adolescent can return in the midst of his or her later experiences and growth. Thus, Jesus' friendship can be a source of support, encouragement, and value in the adolescent's later adult years.

The Element of Time

How does this experience in solitude with Jesus as friend come about for the adolescent? The answer rests with a well-known principle in social psychology. In order for someone to like us and for us to be personally attracted to him or her, the person must be familiar to us. We must have *time* to interact, to be *with* each other. We must have both the environment and the opportunity to experience this other. When time is spent with another, the barriers and defenses erode and attitudes and perceptions are reformed or altered. We come to know the other as who he or she really is.

The adolescent experience of Jesus can be modeled on this principle. We must encourage the adolescent to have time for Jesus, to be with Him, and to experience His friendship. We can provide the adolescent with a real *challenge* in this regard. It is only when friends invest time with one another that they can really speak and share their hearts. We should not hesitate to be direct about the importance of spending time with Jesus. We might ask the adolescent to mention friends with whom he or she spends time and inquire how much time is actually spent in these relationships. We can then ask the adolescent how much time is actually spent with Jesus. Adolescents, when they are confronted by someone in a trusting encounter, are often able to admit their own shortcomings when they are challenged. Such direct and loving challenge offers something the adolescent can really take to heart. This reflection, coupled with the adolescent's own developmental needs for deeper understanding, can lead him or her to realize how little time has been given to friendship with Jesus in comparison to the time given to significant people in his or her life.

The Ignatian Method for Experiencing Jesus as Friend

Let us now come back to the point made earlier in our discussion: It is solitude that allows the adolescent to experience Jesus as friend. Thus, we need to discover what method allows this friendship with Jesus to be experienced.

St. Ignatius' method of prayer may prove useful. The ancient monastic tradition spoke of prayer in several stages: *lectio*—reading the mystery of scripture; *meditatio*—applying this reading to myself; *oratio*—petitioning, asking God for help and enlightenment; and *contemplatio*—contemplation, the unique personal experience of God in prayer.[16] St. Ignatius was influenced by this tradition, and it is revealed in his own spiritual writings. For St. Ignatius, contemplation is an "organic" experience that involves the total self— thoughts, memory, feelings, imagination, and will. We experience the self with God through the mystery of scripture. We can propose that the adolescent try to encounter God in this way. It is this friendship model, one which is crucial for adolescent development, that provides the opportunity for the adolescent to experience Jesus in this most intimate way. Let us now examine three ways in which we can adapt the Ignatian method of prayer to fit the adolescent's life.

1. Scripture and the friendship model.   One way to adapt the Ignatian method to the adolescent's life is to work with scripture and the friendship model. By encountering Jesus in scripture, the young person experiences a deepening knowledge of Jesus as a friend. By contemplating the actual words of Jesus (and incorporating the perspective of a "low Christology"), the adolescent can become better acquainted with Jesus as friend. The adolescent can then share Jesus' own feelings, thoughts, and experiences. In other words, Jesus becomes a real friend with whom the young person can share his or her own life.

Just as the adolescent allows the Lord into his or her life, so too does Jesus (as a real friend would) invite the adolescent to share His life with Him. This, of course, does not mean that every event in the Gospel is a literal, historical occurrence in Jesus' life. Our knowledge of scripture tells us that the Gospel writers wrote to understand more deeply the message of salvation that Jesus had proclaimed. At the same time, though, we can view the scriptural words and accounts of Jesus as not only relating much of what the real Jesus was actually experiencing, but also giving us glimpses into who this man Jesus was. We invite the adolescent to penetrate scripture with his or her imagination so that he or she can experience more deeply the personal call and actual life of Jesus in friendship.

In attempting to capture the experience of Jesus as friend, we can turn to the Gospels and view passages that reveal to us who Jesus is. The following list suggests some passages that might help us to capture the humanity of Jesus:

Prayer. Mk 1:35 (withdrawing to pray); Mt 6:9–15 (the Our Father); Lk 5:16 (Jesus retiring to pray); Lk 9:29 (prayer before the Transfiguration).

Being tempted. Lk 4:1–13 (Jesus enduring temptation).

Compassion. Mt 15:32–38 (Jesus feeds the hungry); Lk 7:11–17 (Jesus has compassion for the widow).

Hunger. Mk 11:12 (leaving Bethany); Mt 4:2 (fasting in the desert).

Anxiety. Mt 26:36–46 (agony in the garden).

Surprise. Mt 15:21–28 (encounter with the Canaanite woman).

Friendship Jn 11:1−44.

Tears Lk 19:41 (viewing Jerusalem).

Frustration Lk 22:38 (response to the disciples).

Forgiveness Lk 23:34 (on the Cross).

Relaxation Lk 10:38 (visiting Mary and Martha); Lk 11:37 (dining with Pharisees); Jn 2:1−11 (wedding feast at Cana).

Discipleship Lk 9:23−27; Mt 10:16−27; Lk 9:57−62; Mt 16:24−28; Mk 10:17−22.

Anger Mt 21:18−19 (the fig tree); Mt 23:25−26 (warning to the Pharisees); Jn 2:13−16 (driving money changers from the temple).

Love Mk 12:28−34 (the great commandment); Lk 10:25−37 (the Good Samaritan); Mk 10:43−44 (serving others); Jn 15:9−17 (the command to love).

Openness to others Mk 3:31−35.

Reading these passages helps us to see that Jesus really assumed a human nature (a fact we intellectually concur with, but often cannot really believe). These passages speak of a real humanity—from someone who, through His feelings, actions, and words, lived life in a full and profound way. For many young people, similar experiences are acutely felt in the adolescent years. These passages certainly do not exhaust everything in scripture that portrays the life of Jesus—the reader is encouraged to develop additional lists of Jesus' experiences and feelings—but these incidents in Jesus' life give us a chance to encounter the person of Jesus Christ, to be with Him, and to experience His life, just as any friend would.

St. Ignatius is particularly useful in capturing prayer experiences for adolescents. In a colloquy (paragraph 53) of the *Spiritual Exercises*, Ignatius invites us to enter into such an experience with Jesus and to pose the questions: In the past, what responses have I made to Jesus? How do I respond to Jesus now? What responses should I make to Jesus in the future? This colloquy is one of several integral sections of the *Spiritual Exercises*. Ignatius asks us, first, to place ourselves in preparation to pray (some moments of solitude, an act of reverence, the right frame of mind). Second, we are asked to beg God for the grace we desire (sorrow, knowledge of sin, thanksgiving). Third, we are to place before ourselves an incident of Jesus' life (such as one of the incidents described earlier) and to imagine our own experience with Jesus. What are we doing? What are we saying and feeling? Such a framework is ideally adapted to an adolescent and the friendship model. Robert Schmitt notes that one image of Jesus that can be gathered in the *Exercises* is that of friendship. He says that "the word 'friend' is chosen but it must be emphasized that it is meant to point to the deepest of loves possible between persons."[17] Jesus' love for us, in other words, is understood in the deepest form of human friendship.

Borrowing from the Ignatian method, an adaptation of the format for adolescents might include the following forms of prayer:

Preparation Suggest that the adolescent imagine the importance of friendship: What does a friend really mean to the young person? How important are friends to him or her? Spend a few moments on this.

Grace Have the adolescent ask Jesus to share His life with him. The adolescent can ask Jesus some questions about Himself, His life, His experiences.

Setting Read about a scripture passage, such as John 11:3–6, for example, which describes the friendship of Jesus, Martha, Mary, and Lazarus. Then, ask the adolescent some questions dealing with the theme of the passage. In this instance, the young person could imagine himself or herself with Jesus when He learns of Lazarus' death. Or the adolescent could go with Jesus as He talks with Martha and Mary, or accompany Jesus to the tomb.

Colloquy Reflect with the adolescent (or have the adolescent reflect alone) on what his or her reactions are. Ask the following questions: What are you feeling? What are your reactions to Jesus now? What kind of friend do you find yourself being to Jesus?

Many other scripture passages can be included and this format can easily fit into a classroom setting, a weekend retreat, or an individual spiritual counseling session. In addition, the use of scripture and the friendship model offers several advantages for the adolescent. First, these exercises allow the adolescent to be aware of his or her affective life and to incorporate this aspect of the personality in his or her relationship with Jesus. Other benefits are also derived from this approach; for example, insights about how the adolescent relates to others can often emerge. Second, the adolescent experiences Jesus in a relationship that is both personal and special. Third, this model takes into account the current developmental level of the adolescent and provides support for it. As the adolescent proceeds through high school, goes through college, and continues into later life, he or she develops an increasing capacity for intimacy. The adolescent's relationship with Jesus can mirror this developmental process into one of real openness in which Jesus becomes more and more an integral part of the adolescent's life.

2 *Ignatian application of the senses*   A second method of prayer for adolescents involves using the Ignatian "Application of the Senses." St. Ignatius viewed the application of the senses as a way to enter more deeply "into the mystery of Christ's life." This prayer involves using one's senses—sight, touch, hearing, smell, and taste—in order to be more deeply with the Lord. A profitable way to do this is to select a character from scripture and meditate on this character's experience in the Gospel.

Some of the characters from scripture that might be used include: Zacchaeus (Lk 19:1–10); Mary and Martha (Lk 10:38–42); the prodigal son (Lk 15:11–32); the rich man (Mt 19:16–30); the centurion (Mt 8:5–13); and the woman and the ointment (Lk 7:36–50). Let us take the Zacchaeus story and see how this scene can be placed in a prayer atmosphere for adolescents.

Read the story aloud, or read it together with the adolescent, and then reflect on the story. The adolescent can make an application of the senses. We can provide him or her with some guidance by instructing him to: *Watch* Zacchaeus as he talks to Jesus; *hear* what Zacchaeus is saying. Then, ask the adolescent the following: What can you *smell* in this story as you are thinking about it? Can you *touch* Zacchaeus' cloak?

After the adolescent has contemplated the scene of Zacchaeus, ask him or her to turn his or her attention to Jesus: What is *Jesus* saying? What is Jesus doing? After this part of the exercise, ask the adolescent to put himself or herself into the conversation, to become a "third party" in the story. Note carefully what role the adolescent takes. What is his or her involvement in the story? When you talk to the adolescent after one of these meditations, bring up the following distinct points:

• Does this experience make Jesus more real for the adolescent?

• Consider the way the adolescent relates to this exercise, that is, the extent of personal involvement in the exercise, how freely he or she experiences the exercise, and so on.

• Reflect with the adolescent on where this experience now

leads him or her. Or on how this exercise can lead to actions that are more Christian. This reflection is very important for the adolescent. The adult needs to aid the adolescent in seeing the relationship between the contemplative life and the active life (a favorite Ignatian theme). How does prayer lead the adolescent to *act* to further the Kingdom in the world. The ideal Ignatian vision is found in the term "contemplative action." For our day, this phrase describes prayerful men and women who minister and labor in the world to bring about God's Kingdom of peace and justice.

3. Meditation   A third method that can also be used with adolescents is meditation. Meditation exercises work well with many young people and are quite popular with today's youth. Ideally, meditation exercises should be presented in a more structured way at first and then oriented to the individual needs of the adolescent.[18] These exercises can be a source of deepening insight as well as spiritual growth. When we are using meditation exercises with adolescents, knowledge of self is an important starting place for prayer's inception. There must be leisure just to be, to relax, to become aware of one's own inner self. This process can be time consuming, but it should be emphasized to the adolescent that if Jesus is to speak to us, we have to be *receptive* to His message. We should discuss with the adolescent the importance of communicating with a friend, listening to a friend, and sharing with a friend. When the notion of Jesus as friend is offered to the adolescent, we might inquire from the adolescent about the need to just be with Jesus. If the adolescent can make the transition from simple affectional bonds to an authentic relationship with Jesus, then an opportunity for real spiritual growth has entered the adolescent's life.

The following meditation exercises are specifically oriented to the adolescent's experience.

Exercise 1

1 Use a standard relaxation technique such as a breathing exercise or focusing on a particular object.

2 Help the adolescent to slowly enter a relaxed state of peace and quiet.

3 Then, ask the adolescent to imagine a very close friend—

someone who is very close and special to him or her. Suggest the following to the adolescent: "Now tell this friend something very personal, very confidential about yourself." Continue, periodically making other suggestions, such as, "Watch how your friend responds. Is it in a loving way?" "Is this friend bothered by what you say?" Reflect with the adolescent on the reactions that he or she discovers during the course of the meditation.

4 After a designated amount of time, request that the adolescent allow Jesus to join him or her and the special friend. Continuing the meditation, ask the adolescent what Jesus says to him or her and the friend. Ask the adolescent if Jesus' presence alters in any way the relationship between the adolescent and his or her friend. This exercise can furnish a wealth of insights into how the adolescent relates with others. After the adolescent has reflected with you on this experience, he or she might continue the reflection along several themes:

• What feelings are there in the relationship?
• What is the level of communication in this relationship?
• How does the adolescent *listen* in a relationship—with the friend, with Jesus?
• What role does the adolescent see Jesus exercising in the relationship? Does Jesus' presence make a difference in this relationship?

A variation of this exercise involves having Jesus appear as the adolescent's friend. Ask the same questions. Reflect with the adolescent on the experience of Jesus as friend.

Exercise 2

1 Use some type of relaxation technique (as before).
2 Encourage the adolescent to be in a relaxed, peaceful state.
3 Ask the adolescent to fantasize a parent. Then ask: "What is the happiest time you have had with this parent?" Ask the adolescent to fantasize this experience. Then inquire: "What are the feelings you have toward this parent?" "What does your parent say to you?" "How do you respond to your parent?"

Feelings toward the parents can be explored through this exercise. In addition, this exercise can be altered to include siblings and other relatives. You can also bring Jesus into this exercise. For example, ask the adolescent how Jesus is present in his or her family. This exercise is an excellent method of exploration with the young person, who often experiences mixed and ambivalent feelings during the adolescent years.

Life as Prayer

The growing presence of Jesus Christ in the adolescent's life and the experience of Jesus in a life of prayer orient the young person to an essential aspect of Christian living. On the other hand, perhaps we might be able to expand the meaning of prayer to include a more universal and encompassing view of God's presence in life. The adolescent is embarking on a search to determine both "who I am" and "what my life is about." If prayer is above all the presence of God in life, perhaps we might attempt a confluence of this God-presence and the adolescent's quest. From this standpoint, the adolescent can then view life itself as a response of prayer.

Theologian Matthew Fox has pointed out that Jesus' prayer was filled with a response to life itself. In this sense, we might see prayer as a "radical response to life."[19] Theologian Nicholas Lohkamp maintains that Jesus' command to "pray always" means, in its fullest sense, the call to "speak of prayer as a way of being, as an attitude of mind and heart, as a dimension of our whole life and *all* our activity."[20] Thus, for the Christian, prayer can be viewed as an openness to experiencing life in its fullest. It is the experience of living—in all its joys, its struggles, its frustrations—under the banner of Christian hope.

The Experience Model of Prayer

We propose, then, an approach to prayer that allows the deepening of this God-presence in life. The model offered here is that of "experience." This model is a focal point for the adolescent search, because adolescents are attempting, in their own lives, to appropriate a richer understanding of their own experiences. The cognitive gropings of the adolescent seek new answers and deeper meanings to life's questions. Affectional strivings are more acutely felt as the adolescent attempts more and more to encapsulate the deeper sense of "who I am." Experience becomes, for adolescents, a mode for forming and shaping the self. It emerges as the tool for the adolescent discovery of "who I am."

Attention to experience highlights the profound changes that have occurred in how we view the human person. Historically, Catholic teaching has utilized a classical model as the dominant force to share the notion of experience. In this perspective, the human person has primarily been seen as a conforming agent. Human experience was enhanced and made whole through conformity to rules and regulations, which arose out of a basic, static, essentialist view of the human person. The nature of the person was an abstraction from which stipulated forms of behaviors could be judged in terms of their conformity or nonconformity to this abstraction of the human person. Thus, "according to the classicist mentality, the meaning of reality is to be found in the eternal, the abstract, the essential, and the unchanging. God made the world; all that is in it has its own given essence; that essence can be known in itself apart from the concrete existence; the concrete existence has no substantial impact on the essence which is therefore unchanging."[21] This essentialist perspective has had a profound impact on Catholic thinking and likewise has shaped the consciousness of most adult Catholics.

This view has been challenged in modern times by a newer interest in experience. Attention has shifted from the notion of essence to the *experience* of the human person. Thus, a person feels, reflects, and acts—in other words, one experiences life—in the reality of his or her concrete existence in the world. In this model, the self becomes the vehicle for interior self-reflection. As theologian John Shea has noted in his remarkable book *Stories of God*, "human experiencing is the reciprocal flow between the self and its environment."[22]

Contemporary thinkers such as Michael Place view this new notion of experience as leading to the presence of Mystery. When reflecting on the self, the person comes to an understanding of something that is more than that which is present; there is something "new," something "sacred." It is in this reflection that we find Mystery. As we experience life, we discover the desire "to make sense" and find personal meaning in the world. It is this fusion of meaning and Mystery that reflects "the drive for ultimate meaning."[23] This new notion of experience has broad appeal in the adolescent years. Adolescents today gravitate toward this experience model as the way to discover meaning in relating to the world.

From the practical standpoint, we can ask how the adolescent can discover this sense of Mystery through personal experiencing. Religious educator Robert Knopp has proposed a four-tiered ladder of experience that coincides with the concept of prayer-as-life-experience.[24] Through the encounter of these life experiences, says Knopp, the adolescent is coming into contact with the transcendent mystery of God through Jesus Christ. This "hierarchy" of life experience consists of: (1) discovery of nature's marvels, (2) crisis experiences, (3) strong insights, and (4) interpersonal relationships.

The person encounters in the *marvels of nature* a deep appreciation of the works of the Creator. The person's natural surroundings—trees, waterfalls, mountains, and the natural habitat—reflect the wonders of creation and the loving hand of God's guidance.

In *crisis experiences*, the adolescent is drawn to a deeper confrontation of who the self really is. In adolescence, the facing of such traumatic experiences as death, a family divorce, or broken relationships confronts the core of the adolescent identity in attempting to discover "who I am."

In reflecting on nature's marvels and the crisis moments of human living, the mature adolescent is led to appreciate in a deeper way what life is, what goodness means, and of what beauty consists. But even more important, the adolescent discovers who God is and how He calls the adolescent to experience life. The rich *insights* that can come from this reflection can be enhanced by attention to artistic endeavors such as plays and movies.

Interpersonal relationships are the highest form of experience that can prove most beneficial in the adolescent years. These relationships are the experiences that "more than all others can become the approaches to the supreme religious experience of relationship with God."[25] Through forming relationships, the adolescent's emerging self comes to understand more deeply what it means to be human. And the deepening experience of relationships, most readily realized in friendship, provides the foundation for a relationship with God through Jesus Christ.

The hierarchy of experiences provides a wonderful vantage point for the adolescent. The adolescent's emotional state, combined with greater sensitivity and awareness, provides a heightened consciousness in which nature's marvels can be appreciated. High school or college retreat directors often remark, for example, that in small group retreats adolescents can experience with greater intensity the beauty of nature. In late adolescence, this capacity is enhanced by the adolescent's growing capacity for ever deepening reflection, so that even the everyday experience of life can be a source of a heightened sense of being.

With adolescent maturation there also develops a more realistic sense of crisis occurrences. As the adolescent becomes more mature, he or she relinquishes the more mythical and idealized perceptions that had characterized the childhood years. The ability to confront ambiguity, admit relativity, face disappointment, and accept the everyday uncertainty of life grows with more maturity. Life, then, no longer seems unmanageable. The healthy adolescent develops the capacity to share experiences, to tackle difficult problems, and to live without clear-cut answers, even if these tasks engender frustration and ambiguity. Likewise, in the adolescent years, conflicts take on increasing significance. Crisis situations provide the maturing adolescent the possibility for experiencing personal growth in meaning, values, and commitment. Furthermore, the adolescent's cognitive growth permits a greater level of abstraction and a more thorough understanding of life experiences. The adolescent can now see possibilities and answers that, in previous years, seemed remote. This cognitive adventure of problem solving and thinking through difficult life dilemmas enables the adolescent to both profit from his or her life experiences and take increasing control for his or her future life direction.

Finally, concern with interpersonal relationships occupies a considerable amount of attention in the adolescent years and becomes an integral factor in consolidating identity and developing the capacity for a deepening commitment. Through the personal encounter of relationships, the adolescent faces the deepening dimension of love, caring, compassion, and, through these experiences, the Christian challenge for true self-emptying (Phil 2:6–11). When the adolescent experiences friendship, he or she feels love, greater loyalty to another, and a turning away from preoccupation with self because he or she is now committed to another. At the same time, the adolescent slowly comes to let go, to open up. His or her secrets, concerns, doubts, fears, and disappointments can be shared along with his or her joys and hopes. Defenses slowly break down while greater trust emerges. The developing of such relationships is a profound event in the adolescent years. It is through these relationships that the adolescent is drawn toward Mystery, to a greater saying of "yes," and a greater realization of God's unique and special concern.

The Personal Story Model of Prayer

In recent theological writing, this sense of the self-as-experiencing takes on added significance in the description of a personal life story. Theologian John Shea, in *Stories of God*, captures the personal experience of the person's encounter with the Transcendent. Shea notes that we are all storytellers; each person has a unique life history that influences that person's perception of God who enters his or her life. Stories, myths, and fables evoke messages that reflect the Transcendent in our own experience. According to Shea, the formation of a person's life story involves four basic underpinnings that give structure and meaning to who we are.

First, there is the mystery of the personal self, a mystery that allows for self-reflection. Second, we all possess an environment that includes family and friends, those who have nurtured and supported us through the years. It is from these people that we seek solace and support, and to whom we relate the deepest part of self. Third, there is the environment that is made up of the influence of society and its institutions. We all find ourselves tied to diverse groups and social bodies such as schools, cities, governments, churches, and organizations that influence and help define persons and, at the same time, contribute to our own self-identity. Finally, all of us have a relationship to a far more encompassing reality, the universe.[26]

Shea notes that human experiencing takes place in the self's interrelationship with the environment. Through this encounter, we come to confront the Ultimate. This encounter has numerous forms. "The experiences of contingency, dialog, communion, moral ambiguity, and disenchantment are a few of the paths which people travel to become aware of their relatedness to Mystery."[27] As we experience these different facets of life, the presence of mystery becomes more evident. It is in these very dialogs, ambiguities, and disenchantments that adolescents experience the mystery of their own selves and, finally, that Mystery which is Ultimate. In this Mystery, the adolescent confronts what is above and beyond the self. This Mystery is ambiguous and at times fleeting, but it is the foundation for all human activity.[28]

Referring to Shea's *Stories of God*, priest-sociologist Andrew Greeley remarks that adolescents have developed their own unique stories of who this God is and how this God is meaningful in personal life experience.[29] Greeley notes that the "religious consciousness" of adolescents had helped to create a phenomenon that he labels a "new breed." He says that Catholic adolescents in the secondary school years are much more apt than young adult Catholics (those in their twenties) to view God as a "lover" and a "mother." This group of young adolescents tends to see God as tender and loving in their own personal story of God. Sandwiched between Catholic adolescents at the secondary school level and Catholic young adults who are in their twenties are Catholic adolescents in the undergraduate college years; these adolescents generally reflect characteristics of the younger adolescents.

In order to explain the age differences, Greeley remarks that possibly the "religious formation" of current Catholic adolescents is different from their older counterparts. Says Greeley: "the New Breed of the 1980's is more likely to think of God as a mother and a lover, and of heaven as a life of action and pleasure . . . a change apparently caused by Vatican Council II and transmitted by devout mothers, sympathetic parish priests, and passionately loving spouses."[30] Greeley's research has also discovered that warm religious imagery exercises an important role in the marriages of young Catholic families. Young people who possess a capacity for warm religious imagery are much more likely to have more satisfactory marriages, including the ability to share love and sexual fulfillment.[31]

It seems from this evidence that the stories of God that adolescents formulate are critical components in their own sense of relatedness to the Transcendent. Adults ministering to adolescents might well find it useful to reflect on ways to encourage religious imagery in the childhood and adolescent years, and to dialog with the adolescent on the meaning of these images for the adolescent's own life. The religious image may well be a critically important influence in helping the adolescent respond to Jesus' call to "come, follow me."

142

Faith and the Adolescent

When the quest for ultimate meaning, which arises from human experience, leads to the creation of a "stance" toward life and of all human reality, then personal faith emerges.[32] And, as can be expected, the development of personal faith coincides with human development itself. Psychologist Gordon Allport has noted that children adopt religious gestures and rituals, even when they have no understanding of what these behaviors signify. He goes on to say that, with the emergence of adolescence, however, these behaviors begin to take on meaning and significance.[33]

This search for meaning leads to further questioning as the adolescent uses his or her life experience to construct personal values that forge for him or her a sense of life's purpose. When this drive for meaning and purpose spills over into a religious context and raises questions of religious and ethical significance, then the stage is set for the emergence of the adolescent crisis of faith.

The Adolescent Faith Crisis

The adolescent faith crisis, which can arise in either the high school years or undergraduate college years, can take many forms. For some adolescents, the crisis results in a complete break with traditional value systems and a retreat within the self to discover new meaning. Other adolescents dramatize their reactions to the faith crisis by assuming values and behaviors that explicitly reject the religious traditions from their childhood. For other adolescents, the crisis might lead to the questioning of a limited scale of behaviors or certain religious practices such as mass attendance. Still other adolescents might adapt their own religious upbringing without recourse to any sense of rebellion or rejection.

Although we can never really predict what behaviors and questions will emerge during these developing years, it is helpful to consider the following "reasons" that offer some explanation of why adolescents experience faith crises during these years.

1 *Peer pressure*   As we have already noted, it is difficult to overestimate the importance of peers in the adolescent years. Identity acquisition often finds support in a peer group or in close interpersonal relationships with one or more friends. Consequently, this group support often provides reinforcement for the personal reli-

gious questioning that the adolescent experiences. This peer influence likewise combines with environmental factors to reinforce personal doubts and questions. An adolescent, for example, who is moving into a college dorm as a freshman often notices that his or her peers do not participate in any religious practices. This peer behavior becomes, then, not only a subtle pressure to conform, but also a factor that legitimates the adolescent's own withdrawal from religious practice.

2. *Institutional alienation.* In chapter 1, we noted that individuals often show a disinclination toward accepting the larger, more impersonal, so-called institutional forms of worship. Although a relationship with Jesus Christ may be of major importance to the adolescent, the larger, more impersonal settings that characterize traditional religious practice often distract the adolescent and actually militate against his or her developmental need for more personal, relational forms of worship. The adolescent suffers a lack of meaning from these impersonal forms of worship that, in turn, reinforces a growing sense of alienation from the church.

3. *Separation from parents.* Parents often ally themseves with institutional attitudes and values. For this reason, distancing oneself from traditional attitudes and practices (whether this means disbelief in God or attending mass) reflects the adolescent's attempt to separate himself or herself from parental authority and discover what God means for *me*. There is truly a need for the adolescent to come to a *personal* understanding of faith that is just that—personal and clearly distinct from parental beliefs.

4. *Rebellion.* The identity acquisition can easily follow along the lines of what Erikson has termed "negative identity"—adolescent rebellion. In acting out negative behaviors (refusing to attend mass, questioning beliefs, doubting God's existence), the adolescent may well find ways to attack parental authority. Such negative behaviors often elicit negative reactions from parents and other authority figures, thereby facilitating the adolescent's own sense of separate identity. In other words, the behavior-reaction cycle reinforces the adolescent's conviction that "my ways really are my ways, and I don't need yours."

5. *Search for meaning.* During the adolescent's develoment, he or she often searches for the real meaning of life by constructing his or her own personal value system. The later years of high school

(and most certainly the undergraduate college years) are a time during which the adolescent realizes a new intellectual power that seeks to understand and ask important questions of life—"Why is there evil?" and "What is the purpose of life?" In this context, the answers of the past, which had been accepted for so long, simply do not suffice. The adolescent finds that he or she has traveled down a road from which there is no turning back: the childhood years of uncritical acceptance are gone; yet commitment to a future course is unsure and uninviting. Perplexed, the adolescent must, in a sense, pause and reassess by asking: "Where am I going?" "What is important for me?" "Where is life taking me?" "What do I really believe?" This pause can be short or it can extend over several years. The adolescent must nonetheless find in his or her own life experience some type of meaning that attempts to answer these questions. For many adolescents, it is possible that no real commitment or honesty with the self appears until he or she stops to reflect and work through the answers to these and other life questions. From my own pastoral work with high school and college youth, I have found that this search for meaning is a very significant factor in the adolescent's crisis of faith.

6 *Disillusionment*   The adolescent's confrontation with relativism in the later high school years (and certainly in the years of undergraduate study) can trigger a crisis of disillusionment that calls for reassessment before any commitment can be made. For many adolescents, the entrance into the adult world—with all its complexity, ambiguity, and relativity—can be a time for what William Perry calls "reevaluation." Contributing to this reevaluation is the realization that many adults themselves do not live up to the ideals and practices that reflect true Christian values. In this light, we can see that the questions, doubts, frustrations, anger, and alienation that appear may be the adolescent's response to the disappointing adult world.

7 *Personal difficulty*   The adolescent's personal life history, which obviously influences the questioning of the adolescent years, can be a significant factor in the faith crisis. Thus, emotional conflicts (especially in the home environment), personal insecurities, and adjustment problems can militate against a call to a deepening faith commitment. When these difficulties are combined with the uncertainties of adolescence, there can often be a distancing from

145

any deepening faith response. Adolescents who are experiencing such difficulties often require a ministry that directly addresses these hurts and crises rather than a ministry that attempts to engage them in formal spiritual dialogue. For these adolescents, the journey of faith must first invite the acceptance of personal life hurts and working through them.

8 *Environment*   Finally, we cannot dismiss the cultural and environmental factors that influence the adolescent. The 1980s are certainly not a decade in which adolescents are receiving great cultural support for their faith expressions. Cultural influences such as the arts and media, or American society's drift toward a consumer mentality can certainly obfuscate the adolescent's quest for a Christian commitment. Of course, this does not mean that adolescents should be shielded from or should run away from such cultural pressures. Instead, the Christian faith response should concern itself, first of all, with forming during adolescence a *critical* Christian perspective that can challenge such environmental influences.

As we have noted, there are a variety of reasons for the adolescent crisis of faith. It is important, therefore, that the adult who is ministering to youth to spend time considering what particular factors are influencing each adolescent's crisis. This is not as easy as it sounds because, as adults who have ministered to youth can attest, this crisis truly seems to permeate the adolescent years.[34] The questions of doubt and the decline in religious practice, however, need not necessarily be viewed as negative phenomena. As we noted in chapter 3, William Perry views the presence of doubt as a prelude to the formation of religious commitment, which he defines as faith. When the adolescent experiences doubt, there can arise a movement from belief, which, according to Perry, requires no real commitment, to a commitment to the Absolute. This commitment (faith in the Absolute), however, is internalized in the midst of an ambiguous and relativistic world. Thus, adolescents are capable of authentic commitment, even in the midst of ambiguous and uncertain surroundings and futures.[35]

The role of doubt in the faith crisis   I believe that an authentic adolescent spirituality can view doubt as part of youth's search for meaning and truth. Philosopher Robert Baird notes that doubt can be a catalyst in the search for authentic faith.[36] First, advises Baird, doubt offers a conscious awareness of human and personal limitations. Doubting can also provide a check on the person's own unreflected, taken-for-granted assumptions. Furthermore, if faith is viewed as a commitment to what "one believes to be of ultimate value,"[37] doubt can guard against one's faith stance becoming narrow or shortsighted. And, of course, even if this "ultimate" underlies an acceptance of God, doubt could possibly open the person's understanding of God to deeper truths in the years ahead.

Second, one's beliefs and notions of faith always need the challenge of further stimulation and refinement. Doubt challenges a person to ask himself or herself to confront how little he or she has actually reflected on who God is. Ironically, I have discovered that in family situations, adult family members quite often have given little attention to their own definition of God until adolescent questions such as "Why do I have to believe in God?" or "Who is God?" or "Why does God allow evil?" emerge. In many ways, adolescents become catalysts for an adult's growth in faith.

Third, Baird reasons that symbols and religious language can become inadequate expressions of the meaning of God in life. By creative doubt, however, we are continually challenged to rethink and reappraise the existing religious language of God in order to make our personal reflection on God more adequate and meaningful.

Fourth, an unreflected acceptance of "the faith" can often serve as a temptation to remove the burden and responsibility for authentic personal decision making. If the search for faith leads to a simple acceptance of the authority of others, which, of course, frees one from responsible decision making, then the quest for faith's certainty is, in reality, the opposite of an authentic growth in faith. Doubt, then, can serve as a tempering influence for avoiding personal responsibility.

Doubt, thus, can exercise a positive role in the adolescent's experience that can actually encourage growth rather than retard it. We must add the caution, however, that we are not prescribing that adults who minister to adolescents should foster needless doubt and negativity. The adult's role should be that of a creative agent who aids the adolescent, when doubts occur, to achieve from the experience an understanding that points to a future commitment toward Jesus and Gospel values.

Life Experiences and Adolescent Faith

The questions and behaviors of adolescents cannot be divorced from the deeper question of what constitutes faith. Heavily influenced by a scholastic tradition and an insular, communal life (what some have referred to as a "ghetto" theology), Catholics have traditionally defined faith as an acceptance of beliefs. In the past, faith has often been understood as the acceptance of church rules, which fashioned a behavior that was distinctly Catholic. Logically, then, many Catholics tied authentic faith to receiving the sacraments, practicing prescribed behaviors, and accepting church rules.

Recent theological scholarship has moved beyond the traditional, if simplistic, understanding of faith and has considered faith in a much broader context. Theologian Joseph Powers, for example, has argued against a faith that is based on a simple assent of the intellect. For Powers, a person's faith "takes place in the actual investment of a person's intellectual, emotional, and physical energies in the people, the things, and the relationships of his or her life."[38] From this perspective, then, Christian faith is an all-encompassing, continual reaffirmation of a "response" that lives out a personal life story. As this life story unfolds, the person continues to develop a greater sense of his or her own life history. The experiences of relationships, crises, and ordinary life events (as well as the more unexpected happenings) invite one to deeper self-understanding. Through this continual self-discovery, the person grows to discover what is beyond the self. The person grows more open to Mystery, that is, more open to how God is actually revealing His message in the person's life through the concrete adventures in human experience.

This growing sense of faith does not take place in a submissive manner. Powers says it is a "creative assent," which engages life, seeking to find new, more satisfactory meanings and eventually the One who provides all meaning. "Faith can be seen, then, not so much as a set of 'answers' to the 'problems of life' but rather as a growing confidence and courage to live with the mysteries of life."[39] This response, which is courageous, creative, and confident, is, however, marked by limits; the person must confront his or her own finiteness, which ultimately is realized in death. In the process of life, the person learns to accept this limiting nature and experience life in a creative way that will enable the person to more fully realize his or her very self. Powers notes that "it is in this complex of freedom, ambiguity, struggle, accomplishment, and failure that one comes to recognize the reality and meaning of God."[40]

Theologian John Wright also grounds the meaning of faith in life experience. Wright says that faith exists as the central investment of a person's life, an investment that leads him or her to believe in "an existential certainty which is neither self-evident nor demonstrable, and yet is somehow grounded in experience."[41] Through this voyage of self-discovery, the person begins to seek some type of meaning, order, and sense for his or her world, as well as a personal life commitment that is grounded in this life but ultimately rests in that which is Mystery.

Faith as personal activity   Religious educator Thomas Groome has delineated faith in the context of a three-fold activity. According to Groome, faith is best viewed as believing, trusting, and doing.[42] Christian faith is, first of all, *believing* because it is a commitment to belief. Initially, this commitment takes place through the illuminating power of God's grace within the person. Unfortunately, a limited intellectualist approach in the Christian tradition has tended to overshadow this illuminating presence; as a result, faith has veered toward a cognitive acceptance of intellectual truths that divorces faith from daily life. In this perspective, then, faith becomes an intellectual summons initiated by God's gift of grace. Yet, we must go beyond this summons to incorporate a dimension of trust and activity if faith is to be lived in daily life.

Groome points out, secondly, that a relationship with God is a *trusting* encounter. Above all, "the call to God's Kingdom is an invitation to a relationship of unbounded trust in the faithfulness of God and in the power of God's saving grace."[43] This trust finds fruition in a life of prayer. Likewise, this trusting relationship with God is proclaimed by the Christian through personal activity, which Groome labels *doing*.

"Doing" means living one's faith in the world. Although faith is a believing and trusting encounter that leads to action, action also nurtures and sustains belief and trust. True faith, then, is immersed in, rather than isolated from, the everyday activity of life experiences.

Faith as communal activity   Faith is not only personal but also communal. The believing community occupies a central focus in the faith story of each individual. It is this communal nature of faith, as least the way it is often expressed, that often leads the adolescent to question his or her faith. Heretofore, the more privatized, insular nature of Catholic faith provided a safe avenue for expression of Catholic belief. It must be admitted, of course, that even in pre-Vatican II days, Catholic adolescents asked questions about faith. But these questions were received with less urgency, for there existed a strong sense of Catholic identity. Today, however, adolescents are asking important questions such as "What is the lived community of church?" and "*How* do I belong to this faith community that is Catholic?"

Adults who minister to Catholic youth need to ask how they can provide a context in which adolescents can experience a community of faith that is called Catholic. Theologian John Wright addresses this issue when he notes that "the central feature of Catholic faith is to regard the Church as the ongoing effect of the saving power of Christ through the gift of the Holy Spirit."[44] Crucial to explaining a faith that is Catholic, then, is the presence and activity of the Spirit in the believing faith community. The Spirit animates the community as a source of life, truth, knowledge, and love.

Authentic Catholic faith   To better understand the significance of faith's meaning, Wright proposes three perspectives from which to acknowledge the structured underpinnings of faith: openness, acceptance, and commitment.[45] *Openness*, says Wright, is the capacity of the believing Catholic to affirm that Jesus is Lord in spite of the many evils, weaknesses, and obstructions to faith in the world. The Catholic Christian readily and willingly confronts the world and its reality, in all its hope and all its failings. The believer must be able to squarely face questions, inconsistencies, and doubts, and willingly accept them because to decry any of these human experiences is tantamount to admitting that faith is unreliable.

The second characteristic of an authentic Catholic faith, *acceptance*, is the result of one's conversion, which "is experienced as a divine attraction, as a personal invitation to enter into communion with God."[46] Human experience becomes the vehicle for God's communication in the activities of everyday life. Acceptance then leads to the sharing of values in a community where Jesus Christ is realized to be the self-communication of God. This acceptance is manifested in both the community and the believer's personal life as

150

he or she experiences community under the guidance of the Spirit. The Catholic's acceptance leads him or her to encounter the Trinity through Father, Son, and Spirit as the fullest expression of God.

Finally, the underpinnings of faith are realized in *commitment*—a faithfulness to God's purpose. It is a commitment to Jesus and His word. Faith, thus, is acting in the world to carry out Jesus' saving message. It means living on both the personal and the communal level, that is, living a life that seeks human dignity, care for others, and humankind's freedom from the bondages of social injustice.

Wright's description of Catholic faith as openness, acceptance, and commitment resonates with the adolescent's own experience. Adolescents are confronted with the need to be open to experiences in their personal lives. They need openness to developing relationships, unexpected happenings, and disappointments, as well as a more profound, greater awareness of their own intellectual, affective, and sexual selves. The adolescent's faith experience is a gradual openness to Jesus' presence, in light of a present self and future course that are not always clear.

Likewise, the adolescent's experience is characterized by a growing sense of the self that includes an acceptance of who he or she is in all dimensions of life. The adolescent's faith is lived in a growing acceptance not only of Jesus' presence, but also of Jesus' demands on the adolescent's life. The adolescent's daily activities gradually demonstrate, both in personal living and in the shared experience of community, Jesus' centrality for his or her life. The adolescent's acceptance of self actually makes possible a growing personal experience of Jesus, who sustains and nourishes the adolescent's own experience of self-acceptance (1 Jn 4:10).

Finally, the adolescent's experience of faith is realized in the personal experience of a growing commitment to the Gospel. The adolescent's own journey of faith shows a growing sense of his or her "personal role" in proclaiming the Kingdom of God.

The Meaning of Faith

The following paragraphs summarize the meaning and import of faith as it was developed in the preceding discussion.

1 Faith is a gift. It is God's self-communicating presence, which is encountered in the context of human experience within the activities and events of daily life.

2 Faith includes not only the present existential situation of a person's life, but also the past life story that brings him or her to the present moment, as well as a future to which the person must remain open and which is yet to be experienced.

3 Faith is more than an intellectual assent, although an intellectual notion remains an important component of faith. Faith is viewed as an all-encompassing response of "yes" in one's present life situation. This affirming response emanates from the person's unique life experience. From this life story, the person forms impressions and images of God, who beckons him or her, through the person of Jesus Christ, to a life of faith that is dedicated to proclaiming the Kingdom.

4 Faith involves a profound relational commitment. First, a personal life stance emerges that reflects a trusting and loyal relationship with the Transcendent. Second, there is a relationship to the self that invites yearnings of the person to be open to search for Mystery. And third, there is the relationship to the lived community that has nurtured and sustained faith from its inception and that now offers support and encouragement in the day-to-day living of the Gospel's message.

The Church, the Sacraments, and the Adolescent

As we have noted, faith finds meaning, support, and challenge in the experience of community. This community, called the church, offers the believer both support and challenge through witness, teaching, and sacramental invitation.

Theologian Richard McBrien maintains that we have no phrase or word that can adequately reflect the meaning of church.[47] Rather, McBrien uses a three-fold description of the church; it is, in his words, "the community of those who are called to acknowledge the Lordship of Jesus, who ratify that faith sacramentally, and who commit themselves thereby to membership and mission for the sake of the Kingdom of God in history."[48]

A key question that adolescents frequently ask is, "If I believe in Jesus, why do I need the church?" This question often results from the adolescent's experience of dull liturgies or the human limitations of church leaders, or the failure of Catholics to personally live the Gospel. When they view these limitations, adolescents frequently become very critical, sometimes rigidly so. When we dicuss these themes with adolescents we need to point out that Jesus was more than an historical figure. He left a message to be carried on by his church (how else would we know of him?). This suggestion does not imply that we should not take seriously the adolescent's frustration with present or past limitations and failures of the church. Certainly any Catholic should be sensitive to these inadequacies. Yet the fact remains that the church exists to proclaim the saving message of Jesus. Without the church's proclamations and guidance through history, how would such a message be proclaimed?[49] When discussing these or related issues with an adolescent, a sound pastoral approach shows sensitivity to the adolescent's experience. At the same time, however, the adult needs to challenge the adolescent: how can this particular young person be *part* of proclaiming this message. Even in the midst of human limitations and inadequacies, what will this adolescent be willing to contribute to help bring about God's Kingdom? The focus here should be on challenging the adolescent to commit himself or herself as a member of the believing community.

A key element in this model of church is the role of the sacraments and their activity in the church's life. John Lynch argues that the key to present-day evangelization rests with the sacraments. Lynch says that there is a great movement in the church to bring back fallen-away Catholics, to make the church community meaningful—in essence, to once again evangelize the Catholic who has already been initiated (baptized). Evangelization challenges the docile attitudes previously practiced by the church community. Lynch maintains that many Catholics have lived under the aegis of what Dietrich Bonhoeffer called "cheap grace." Too many Catholics live in the context of a salvation that is taken for granted and, therefore, demands little of them. In this situation, grace is "cheap," that is, it demands little or no sacrifice on the Catholic's part. Within this mindset, frequent reception of the sacraments resulted in a "reverse evangelization." That is to say, people became accustomed to receiving the sacraments without regard for what the message of Jesus really calls us to.[50]

The focus on sacraments presents a notable challenge for both adults and for the adolescents to whom they minister. Religious educator James DiGiacomo suggests that evangelization of the adolescent implies a devotion by the adult to his own life of faith. He calls for an existential encounter of personal faith on the part of adults who minister to adolescents. DiGiacomo says that the adult must "be open to the transcendent, hungry for the fullness of life."[51]

In our ministry to high school and college youth, we must share with them the importance of love as the foundation of human relationships. Furthermore, we must also convey to adolescents that growth in Christian adulthood is much more than living a life that is dedicated to a group of shared values. It is a commitment to the message of Jesus Christ that is lived out in a life sustained and nurtured by the believing community through the sacraments. The sacraments are ways in which the adolescent is strengthened for a life that is committed to Jesus and His message.[52] The role of the sacraments in Christian living, therefore, cannot be overestimated.

Far too often we work with adolescents for whom the Eucharist has no attraction. In many cases, this indifference is no doubt the result of developmental issues (and often a good dose of laziness!). We need to convey to young people not only the richness of the sacramental life, but also the opportunity for strength and nourishment that the sacraments can bring, as well as the fundamental need that we have to worship. For adolescents, however, the experience of Jesus is central. The Eucharist will hardly be of interest or meaningful if a relationship with Jesus is not an important focus for the adolescent.

Suggestions for Fostering Adolescent Spiritual Growth

Having examined the adolescent's spiritual life, let us now look at a variety of approaches to aid the adolescent's deepening experience of Jesus' call.

Suggestion 1

One of the primary influences in the development of the adolescent's faith is the presence of adult relationships. Indeed, as we have frequently noted, relationships are pivotal events in the adolescent years. Survey research supports the notion of the salutary effect that adult relationships have on the adolescent's religious practice.[53] Patrick O'Neill, a priest-specialist in youth ministry, has noted that young people are "not so much interested in dogmatic truths as they are in personal stories. Why do *you* believe? Why do *you* still bother with organized religion? What does Mass mean to *you*? What makes church and religion real for *you*?"[54] Likewise, theologian John Dunne remarks that coming to understand the life of another (which he terms "passing over") enriches and empowers our own life of faith.[55] In "passing over," the adolescent experiences the reality of the adult's faith commitment. This adult sharing contributes to the adolescent's deepening quest to find religious meaning for his or her own life. An adult who can prudently convey his or her own struggles, questions, joys, beliefs, and commitments becomes a tremendous ratifying force in the young person's life.

There are several ways to approach this theme. One involves the adult posing the question to himself or herself: How has God made a difference in my life? The adult can then share his or her own response with the adolescent(s). Other areas that can be explored are how God has led me in my life, what are the significant events in my life (relationships, crises, unexpected happenings) in which God has spoken to me? The adult should also consider how the community of believers, the church, sustains and supports him or her. The adult might ask himself or herself: How do I find nourishment and support in this faith community? The adult can invite the adolescent to share his or her own experiences in these areas, along with the doubts, hesitancies, and insecurities, too.

Since imaging appears to have a positive effect on the adolescent's faith life, the adult might share his or her own image of God. The adult might reflect on the following questions: How do I view God? What feelings, symbols, images does my notion of God evoke? The adult might also reflect on how these images touch and nurture his or her life of faith. The adult might then ask the adolescent a few open-ended questions on this same subject: What do you think when you think of God? How do you feel when you imagine God? The adult might also wish to consider with the adolescent how this imaging influences the adolescent's own behavior. If God is viewed as Father or Mother, as loving or authoritarian, then is this image translated in the adolescent's relationships? To what extent does the adolescent's treating of others mirror his or her image of God?

A third variation on this approach is to transfer to human experience the notion of God and God's working through Jesus Christ. Can the adolescent view significant others or special friends as signs of God's love and acceptance? Can significant others be seen as "gifts" from God that draw the adolescent more deeply to a richer sense of God's personal love for the adolescent? It is hoped that, when the adolescent examines his or her relationships, he or she will, as John Dunne puts it, enter "more deeply into self and others and inevitably find in Jesus that which no other can provide. In Jesus we come to understand the mystery of ourselves and others that no one else can give."[56]

This approach can also be applied to other significant events in the adolescent's life. The adolescent can explore crises, ambiguities, great moments of peace and contentment, and other experiences to find within them the deeper messages and truths that lead to a deeper sense of Mystery.

Suggestion 2

Experiences with adolescents, especially late adolescents, are oftentimes far removed from formal modes of religious practice such as liturgies. Thus, when we dialog with the adolescent we often find ourselves focusing on areas that are rather removed from "religious" topics. Consequently, when we dialog with adolescents, regardless of the theme, a primary focus for adults should be "value focusing." Through reflection with the adult about his or her feelings, attitudes, and behaviors, the adolescent should be led to understand what are his or her personal values that thread themselves through his or her many behaviors.

Suggestion 3

For many people, the use of symbols can enlarge the meaning and perspective that the person gives to his or her life. Through symbols, myths, and personal images, a person can come to experience a deeper sense of meaning. Symbols provide insights that yield deeper truths from human experience. Thomas Lay notes that symbols foster a deeper sense of a person's own "self-identity."[57] As we know, the adolescent quest is touched deeply by this identity search. Symbolization can thus provide a chance for deeper self-knowledge and foster deeper integration and wholeness in the adolescent's journey of faith. The adolescent can be queried about the symbols that reflect his or her own self. What would symbolize personal value and meaning for him or her? What symbol would summarize this adolescent's life? What metaphor would seem appropriate for this adolescent to use? Insights can be gleaned from these answers. When the adolescent offers a symbol for his or her life, we might inquire from the adolescent what this says to him or her about himself or herself? How does this symbol or metaphor of self contribute to the adolescent's own sense of personal meaning? Are there parts of the adolescent self that this symbol does not reflect? Are there parts of the self, such as certain emotions, sexuality, or personal limitations, that are distorted, rejected, or unacknowledged? We might explore with the adolescent not only what a personal symbol says, but also what it does not say.

Symbols provide the adolescent with a chance for self-expression that moves beyond the intellectual sphere. Just as faith expression has all too often been identified in an intellectual framework, so too the definition of the self has too often been restricted to an intellectual dimension. For many adolescents, focusing on symbols can serve as a format within which ongoing questioning can take place.

Some helpful exercises to further symbolization involve asking the adolescent to depict his or her life in a picture or to portray his or her life in an image. What is this image? What does it say to the adolescent about himself or herself? Or we might ask the adolescent to name something that reflects who he or she is or what he or she presently feels about himself or herself? Why was this image chosen? Another related exercise is to have the adolescent reflect over previous years on the meaning of this symbol? Has this symbol's meaning changed? How is it different? Does this change say anything to the adolescent?

Suggestion 4

Thomas Groome points out that the faith experience of Christian people is best viewed as a "pilgrimage."[58] With this in mind, the adult might reflect with the adolescent on the latter's own journey. This might take on specific Christian themes when we enter into discussions with the adolescent. The discussion might involve, for example, reflecting on how God has worked through the adolescent's life and brought him or her to where he or she is today.

As we have noted in several of the previous exercises, in a less specifically Christian context, this reflection might be devoted to particular values and meanings the adolescent finds important in his or her life. The adult might reflect with the adolescent on where his or her journey might be going? Where are his or her values leading? What values might take on increasing importance in later years? How do future goals of the adolescent reflect the values he or she now holds?

Suggestion 5

We have already noted that adolescent religious practice declines as the adolescent proceeds through the adolescent years. Moral theologian Charles Curran notes that legalism has exercised a far too influential role in the lives of Catholics.[59] This is demonstrated by the misconception that Catholics are merely to "pray, pay, and obey." In order to counteract the legalism that clouds the liturgy, for example, we need to address the issue of *why* the Eucharist gives meaning and support to the life of a person who is a member of the faith community, rather than rely solely on a law that compels religious observance. Religious educator James DiGiacomo says that when we dialog with an adolescent on the need for the Eucharist in life, we can emphasize the difficulty of living the Christian life in the world.[60] The Christian life *is* difficult. This fact leads us in turn to the Eucharist, which provides support and strength. If we want to give to others, we ourselves need sustenance, and the Eucharist provides this nourishment. The most important point, of course, is for the adult to share with the adolescent the meaning and strength that the Eucharist provides for the adult's life. Not that every liturgy is exciting or emits a message of profound personal meaning. Sometimes I may not be in the mood, I may be tired or distracted, but I know that I am weak and that I need strength and nourishment and that the Eucharist provides this, because Jesus has shared himself— his very self—with me, and it is in the Eucharist that I find the strength to live out the commitment I have made to Him.

In many families a difficult problem occurs when the adolescent proclaims: I get nothing out of Mass. It doesn't mean anything to me. Why do I have to go? Or the adolescent may arrive home from college, show resistance to going to church, and appear indifferent to the Mass. Parents are no doubt often challenged by this behavior.

This challenge often compels the adult to think about his or her own reasons for attending Mass and evaluate them. It is somewhat ironic that it is often the questions and challenges posed by adolescents that stimulate family discussions on questions of faith and meaning. Such discussions can be an opportunity for the entire family to think about their own faith commitment in a reflective way.[61] In dealing with the attitudes and questions of adolescents, it is unwise to appeal to "law"; moreover, from a developmental perspective, such appeals do not encourage growth. Adolescents deserve deeper explanations of the reasons and motives that lead adults to commit themselves to personal faith.

In pastoral terms, I believe that the wisest approach to ministering to adolescent questions about religious practice is to engage them in discussion, keeping in mind several important themes: The adult conveys to the adolescent his or her own faith commitment and speaks of the importance that the Eucharist holds for his or her own life. The adult then helps the adolescent consider the values in his or her life. Where does the adolescent find strength and support for his or her values? The adolescent should also be asked to reflect on how he or she receives support and strength for his or her own religious commitment. Also, the adolescent should consider how his or her own values reflect a personal religious commitment. These gentle challenges need not be presented in a forceful manner, yet the adolescent needs to see that a faith commitment requires nurturance. Moreover, the adolescent needs to reflect on how he or she will provide for this nurturance in his or her daily life if the Eucharist is not a priority.

Suggestion 6

We have already discussed the importance of friendship in the adolescent's life. Patterns of friendship in adolescence vary with the developmental age of the adolescent. As the young person proceeds through adolescence, friendships become more individualized and less a focus for anxiety.[62] Thus, in early and middle adolescence, more emphasis may be placed on how the adolescent finds security in the friendship, whereas in late adolescence the attention shifts to the needs of intimacy. Hence, presenting Jesus as a friend in a friendship model can meet different needs at the various stages of adolescence. With young adolescents, for example, the friendship model can focus on the support and security that Jesus can provide. With older adolescents, more emphasis can be given to the reciprocal nature of friendship, that is, its demands, its responsibilities, and the level of its communication. At every level, however, the adolescent should be encouraged to reflect on how much time is devoted to and spent with Jesus-as-friend. The adolescent might be asked: Do you invite Jesus into your life? Does He make a difference in your life? How? Is there time to communicate with Him? To be alone with Him? How has this friendship deepened over the years? How has this friendship changed you?

Equally important is the adolescent's capacity to be honest and open with Jesus. True friendship demands a real openness and honesty. The adult might explore with the adolescent the extent to which he or she openly shares feelings and hurts. The noted spiritual writer William Connolly captures the importance of sharing one's affections with God when he says: "It is only by expressing feelings (at first relatively superficial ones) that people can come to allow their deeper affective attitudes to enter prayer and continue to operate there. If they let themselves tell God what they feel at the moment, they will at some point begin to express those deeper attitudes and allow themselves to be vulnerable to God's action."[63] The adult should encourage the adolescent to share personal feelings in his or her relationship with Jesus. This increasing capacity to share feelings not only opens the adolescent to being touched in a deeper way by the Lord's saving grace, but also encourages a sense of deepening trust that can then be of benefit in the adolescent's relationship with others.

Suggestion 7

Theologian John Dunne states that Jesus was touched by several significant events in His life. As a result of His baptism by John the Baptist and hearing of John's imprisonment and then his impending death, Jesus grew to understand a deepening sense of what His own mission was.[64] Jesus' gradual discovery of His mission in life parallels the process of faith discovery that the adolescent experiences. When reflecting with the adolescent on his or her life of faith, the adult might wish to discuss with the adolescent what he or she believes are the significant events in Jesus' life that led to His growing sense of mission and understanding of the Father's will. Likewise, the adult can explain how significant experiences in his or her own life have helped to develop a personal faith stance. In addition to this dual reflection from Scripture and from the adult's own life story, the adult might invite the adolescent to share significant events that have led to a growing faith discovery. Through this reflection, the adolescent can come to realize that his or her own growth in faith often results from significant events and significant happenings (often unexpected) that he or she experiences.

Suggestion 8

Late adolescence presents a particularly challenging time in which to discuss questions of faith. Theologian Matthew Kohmescher notes that college undergraduates might be characterized as being "pregnant with faith." Borrowing John's allusion from the Last Supper Discourse (Jn 16:21), Kohmescher notes that pregnancy is a unique experience in life that is an apt description of the late adolescent's journey toward an adult faith stance. The journey of faith is unique for each adolescent. Some undergraduates will emerge unscathed, whereas others will find the experience challenging, confronting, and even convulsive.[65] Furthermore, as campus minister Kenneth McGuire notes, issues and questions change for the late adolescent as he or she proceeds from the early years of college to graduation and possibly to graduate school. As students mature, "their attention shifts. They are more concerned with finding values and appropriate means for understanding and articulating the fullness of their experience."[66] Youth specialist Michael Warren suggests that in many instances the late adolescent might be in need of counseling and healing before he or she can deal with questions of religious significance.[67] Pastorally speaking, I believe this observation is quite sound and it deserves the attention of adults who work with late adolescents at the undergraduate college level.

We have noted in the discussion of faith crises that adolescents often experience a period of doubting or even rejecting traditional belief and practice. We have also seen that such cases can be a source for the adolescent's strengthening and deepening his or her faith commitment for future adulthood and for coming to understand it more fully. With this in mind, several points can be made when working with the late adolescent:

• Encourage the adolescent to be *honest* with himself or herself about what he or she is experiencing at this time.

• Aid the adolescent in *clarifying* the significant issues in his or her life. Likewise, encourage serious thinking about what values and meanings are important for the adolescent.

• When it is appropriate to do so, the adult might *share* with the adolescent significant events in his or her own faith journey.

• *Focus* on adolescent behaviors that reflect the young person's own values and discuss these with the adolescent.

• *Challenge* the adolescent to reflect on and question his or her own experience in order to continue personal growth through self-discovery.

• Offer *flexibility* in the dialog, that is, be prepared to discuss the significant issues and questions that the adolescent has, even if these issues are not explicitly related to questions of religious faith. Dealing with such issues as career, relationships, disappointments, and personal hurts is often a prelude for a direct encounter with the adolescent's deeper faith questions.

Suggestion 9

The place of Jesus Christ is central to Christian faith. Adolescents may at times ask in a very pressing way, "Who is Jesus? Was he really human? Is he really God? In essence, when adolescents ask questions about Jesus Christ, they are often asking questions that have deep significance for themselves. Reflecting on the relevancy of Jesus Christ as both God and man, Scripture scholar Raymond Brown notes that only if Jesus is God can we truly grasp the depths of God's love, the total giving of Himself to humankind, because "God's love was so real that He gave Himself for us."[68] Our experience of God is one of self-giving; this is where love resides. Likewise, God took on our humanity. Only when we comprehend His humanity do we understand that God's love was so immense that He freely gave Himself to our humanness by suffering our weaknesses, our doubts, our fears, and our joys. He truly was one of us. A Christology from below, which we have already examined, especially allows us to capture this humanness.

At the same time, however, we need to interject one caution when we discuss with adolescents a Christology from below and stress a model of Jesus as friend. Residing in the Synthetic-Conventional stage of faith, adolescents easily, if not effortlessly, gravitate toward the interpersonal. Yet, if this interpersonal tendency becomes all-absorbing, there is the danger that a conscious awareness of Jesus' divinity will be eclipsed. As a consequence, the adolescent might perceive Jesus as simply human and lose an awareness of His divinity. This tendency can be offset by reflecting with the adolescent on Jesus as "other." Religious educator James DiGiacomo addresses the issue when he discusses how today's youth portray a "religious experience" that is much more "horizontal" than "vertical."[69] Young people today are more predisposed to see how God is like them rather than to reflect on the "otherness" of God—His majesty, His lordship, His holiness—and adults must be prepared for this reaction from adolescents. A helpful technique in this regard is for the adult to share with the adolescent how the adult's own experience of Jesus is "other" for him or her—how Jesus is Mystery "for me." Also, the adult might share his or her need to worship. Why worship is important for him or her.

Pastorally speaking, the central importance in reflecting with the adolescent should be assigned to the place of Jesus Christ in the adolescent's life. A fruitful way to do this is to start with the adolescent's own *experience*. It is often helpful, for example, to consider with the adolescent how he or she is loved. What have been the experiences of love in this adolescent's life? How is this love described? Is it self-giving, life-enhancing, other-enriching, selfless? Where does the adolescent find the source for his or her love (1 John 4:7–8)? The life of Jesus can then be reflected on in light of these experiences. How, for example, does Jesus' love convey to the adolescent that it is self-giving, life-enhancing, challenging? The adult might consider and share with the adolescent his or her thoughts on how Jesus' love mirrors the adolescent's love relationships in family, friends, and various other relationships in the young person's life. Through this reflection, the adolescent can come to view love as based on and sustained through Jesus Christ.

Suggestion 10

The question of God's existence invariably surfaces in the adolescent's reflection, most often in the late high school years or in the undergraduate college years. The problem of evil also arises in many discussions. Questions that the adolescent brings up that relate to these themes include the following: Is there a God? Why is there evil? How can a loving God allow evil? Of course, one can see how important persistent questions of the adolescent can be as a source to stimulate the adult. How do we adults, for example, attempt to understand the meaning of evil? Adolescents often force such discussions by their probing (and often threatening) questions.

The question of God's existence has special importance in adolescence. Psychologist Martin Hoffman suggests that the questioning of God's existence might possibly influence the adolescent's moral behavior, for without the presence of a God who demands certain behaviors, the adolescent might unreflectively engage in heretofore proscribed behaviors.[70] During the later stages of adolescence, the young person encounters the complexity and ambiguity of the adult world and may well come to associate God with his or her own disillusionment with adult forms of behavior. Hence, to dismiss God becomes an important attempt to construct one's own growing sense of independence and adulthood. As adolescents confront this confusion, which includes the area of moral values and behaviors, the rejection of God affords them an opportunity to somehow begin constructing a personal value system.

When we assess the adolescent's questioning of God, then, we might point to three key factors that have an impact on this line of questioning.

(1) The adolescent's growing cognitive maturity invites a more critical stance and results in questions such as: Why is there evil? Is there a God? What is life all about?

(2) The adolescent's confrontation with increasing relativism and ambiguity, along with his or her growing disillusionment with adult behaviors that fail to live up to measured ideals, can lead the adolescent to serious questioning, to wondering about ultimate meaning and about God's existence.

(3) The pressing demands of identity compel the adolescent into questions about his or her personal value system. The struggle with an identity crisis might well include a period in which the existence of God is questioned or even rejected.

Questions about God's existence have usually been answered by appealing to intellectual arguments such as causality. Likewise, the question of evil has been approached by arguments that describe evil as a lack of good or the result of Original Sin, and by appeals to some sort of "rule of efficacy," such as out of evil good can arise. These arguments, however, are not helpful in pastoral work with adolescents because so often they do not fit the adolescent's experience. They attempt to give "reasonable" answers to experiences that are often anything but clear. Pastorally speaking, it is not wise to attempt to "solve" these types of questions for the adolescent. Although this inclination is well intentioned, it is nevertheless short-sighted because it deprives the adolescent an opportunity for real growth in facing the complexities inherent in his or her own development. A more fruitful and meaningful approach is to dialog with the adolescent at his or her own developmental level. This means taking into consideration the many cognitive, affective, moral, and faith issues that appear in the adolescent years and that often influence the adolescent's questioning.

A helpful way to address adolescent questions about God is to talk not about whether God exists but, rather, about *who* God is?[71] And in reflecting on who this God is, the Gospel of John is particularly helpful, especially the Last Supper Discourses on love. The approach can move from an abstract discussion of love to the personal level of the adolescent's own experience: How do you love? How is love kept alive in your life? We can reflect with the adolescent on how this God has shown love most of all through the self-giving of his Son, His faithfulness to His people, His faithfulness to the individual adolescent, and the way He has gifted this adolescent (talents, friends, relationships, etc.). In the reflection on the place of God in the adolescent's life, the adults might wish to reflect on how God "is love" in their own lives. In other words, what does this God call me as an adult to? What values arise out of my saying, "I believe in God." Adults should be willing to share with adolescents how a relationship with God helps them find value, meaning, and purpose in life. If the adolescent has decidedly rejected God, however, then adults can spend time reflecting on what values the adolescent prizes. Adults might reflect with the adolescent on how he or she supports and sustains these personal values? Adults might also observe if the adolescent reflects a certain openness to life that allows him or her to continue questioning and reflecting on his or her own values?

When adults attempt to deal with the problem of evil, it can be helpful to reflect on the necessary connection between love and freedom. Ask the adolescent how love is defined? Is it not a free experience of the self in relation to another? Expand on this approach by reflecting with the adolescent on the importance of freedom and how it is used in the adolescent's own relationships. How is the adolescent growing in freedom? How does the adolescent freely commit himself or herself in relationships? How is this freedom shown in the adolescent's present relationships? At the same time, also reflect on how freedom is often misused, how there is often misunderstanding in the adolescent's relationships, or how possessiveness, jealousy, or using another are often present in relationships.

Adults can further dialog with the adolescent on how all of us can reject God's love, refuse to accept a relationship with God, or choose to ignore His grace in our personal relationships. Ask whether the price of the freedom to love might not be the evil that we can choose as we make the decisions that influence our lives. Adults can also reflect with the adolescent on his or her relationships, decisions, and the consequences of his or her personal actions. How does the adolescent use his or her own "freedom" in the various instances of his or her life? What place does love occupy in the adolescent's actions? This response is not meant to "solve" the question of evil for the adolescent. Rather, it invites the adolescent to think through his or her own experience and draw from it a sense of these issues by attempting to address these questions through a growing reflectivity.

Conclusion

From these reflections, several points need to be kept in mind when adults are dialoging with the adolescent.

• The adolescent's views on these various issues must be *respected*. This respect is fundamental if any growth is to occur and for any fruitful dialog to take place.

• The adult should be prepared to *speak* about and *reflect* on how he or she has personally dealt with these issues in his or her own life.

• The actual *experience* of the adolescent should be stressed in his or her personal reflection.

• The adolescent should be engaged at both the affective level and the cognitive level. The *total* adolescent self should be engaged in the dialog.

• The adolescent should be encouraged to remain *open* and *reflective* on these issues, to search for truths and levels of commitment as his or her life continues.

• The adolescent should be lovingly *challenged* to take responsibility for his or her questions, ideas, and responses. The adolescent should be asked to reflect on the statements he or she makes. What behaviors or consequences might these statements lead to? What are the consequences for the adolescent and for others?

Notes to Chapter Four

1. "General Instruction of the Liturgy of the Hours," in *The Liturgy of the Hours*, vol. 1. New York: The Catholic Book Publishing Co., 1975, p. 24.

2. Thomas Merton, *Contemplative Prayer*. New York: Herder & Herder, 1969, p. 33.

3. Henri Nouwen, *Out of Solitude*. Notre Dame, IN: Ave Maria Press, 1975, pp. 21–22.

4. Eric Ostrov and Daniel Offer, "Loneliness and the Adolescent," in *Adolescent Psychiatry*, vol. 6, ed. Sherman C. Feinstein and Peter L. Giovacchini, p. 36. Chicago: University of Chicago Press, 1978.

5. Ibid. [The same page as the preceding note.]

6. Carlo Carreto, *Letters from the Desert*. Maryknoll, NY: Orbis Books, 1972, p. 36.

7. Anthony Bloom, *Beginning to Pray*. New York: Paulist Press, 1970, p. 19.

8. Robert Ochs, S.J., *God Is More Present Than You Think*. New York: Paulist Press, 1970, p. 45.

9. Pierre Babin, *Crisis of Faith: The Religious Psychology of Adolescence*. New York: Herder & Herder, 1963.

10. Ignace Lepp, *The Ways of Friendship*. New York: The Macmillan Co., 1971.

11. Andrew M. Greeley, *The Friendship Game*. Garden City, NY: Image Books, 1971, pp. 27–29.

12. For a recent theological work that reflect this thinking (low Christology), see: John Sobrino, *Christology at the Crossroads*. New York: Orbis Books, 1978.

13. J. Peter Schineller, S.J., "The New Approaches to Christology and Their Use in the Spiritual Exercises," *Studies in the Spirituality of Jesuits* 12, September–November 1980, p. 5.

14. Thomas H. Groome, *Christian Religious Education: Sharing Our Story and Vision*, New York: Harper & Row, 1980, p. 39.

15. Hilmar Wagner, "The Adolescent and His Religion," *Adolescence* 13, Summer 1978, p. 350.

16. Merton, *Contemplative Prayer*, pp. 32–38.

17. Robert L. Schmitt, S.J., "The Christ-Experience and Relationship Fostered in the Spiritual Exercises of St. Ignatius of Loyola," *Studies in the Spirituality of Jesuits* 6, October 1974, p. 241.

18. Anthony de Mello, S.J., *Sadhana: A Way to God*. St. Louis: The Institute of Jesuit Sources, 1978. This book is an excellent source for meditation exercises.

19. Matthew Fox, *On Becoming a Musical Mystical Bear*. New York: Paulist Press, 1976, p. 49.

20. Nicholas Lohkamp, O.F.M., "Communing with the Spirit," *Religion Teacher's Journal* 14, April 1980, p. 31.

21. Michael D. Place, "Philosophical Foundations for Value Transmission: Part I," *Chicago Studies* 19, Fall 1980, p. 310. *See also* pp. 307–313.

22. John Shea, *Stories of God*. Chicago: Thomas More Press, 1978, p. 15. Also quoted in Michael D. Place, "Philosophical Foundations," p. 315. Place discusses the historical change from an essentialist to an experiential model, pp. 310–316.

23. Place, "Philosophical Foundations," p. 316.

24. Robert Knopp, "Not Just Experiences—Relationship Experiences," *The Living Light* 17, Spring 1980, pp. 34–43.

25. Ibid., p. 37.

26. Shea, *Stories of God*, pp. 11–15.

27. Ibid., p. 36. *See also* pp. 25–36.

28. Ibid., p. 38.

29. Andrew M. Greeley, "A Post-Vatican II New Breed? A Report on Contemporary Catholic Teen-Agers," *America* 142, June 28, 1980, pp. 534–537.

30. Ibid., p. 537.

31. *See* Andrew M. Greeley, *The Young Catholic Family*. Chicago: Thomas More Press, 1980.

32. Place, "Philosophical Foundations," p. 316.

33. Gordon W. Allport, *The Individual and His Religion*. New York: Macmillan Publishing Co., 1960, pp. 31–49.

34. *See* chapter 1, footnote 19.

35. William G. Perry, Jr., *Forms of Intellectual and Ethical Development in the College Years*. New York: Holt, Rinehart, and Winston, Inc., 1968, p. 131.

36. Robert M. Baird, "The Creative Role of Doubt in Religion," *Journal of Religion and Health* 19, Fall 1980, pp. 172–179.

37. Ibid., p. 37.

38. Joseph Powers, S.J., "Faith, Mortality, Creativity: Toward the Art of Believing," *Theological Studies* 39, December 1978, p. 665.

39. Ibid., p. 667.

40. Ibid., p. 678.

41. John Wright, S.J., "Catholic Faith," *Theological Studies* 39, December 1978, p. 703.

42. Groome, *Christian Religious Education*, pp. 57–66.

43. Ibid., p. 60.

44. Wright, "Catholic Faith," p. 708.

45. For a discussion of these three characteristics see Wright, "Catholic Faith," pp. 711–717.

46. Ibid., p. 714.

47. Richard McBrien, "Church," *Chicago Studies* 12, Fall 1975, p. 242.

48. Ibid. [The same page as the preceding note.]

49. For an interesting discussion of the church and Jesus, see Patrick McCloskey, O.F.M., "Is the Church Necessary—If I have Jesus?" *Catholic Update*, St. Anthony's Messenger Press, November 1975.

50. John Lynch, "Sacraments: Key to Evangelization," *America* 141, October 13, 1979, pp. 190–191.

51. James J. DiGiacomo, S.J., "Evangelizing the Young," *America* 141, October 13, 1979, p. 187.

52. Ibid., p. 189.

53. Dean R. Hoge and Gregory H. Petrillo, "Determinants of Church Participation and Attitudes among High School Youth," *Journal for the Scientific Study of Religion* 17, December 1978, pp. 359–379.

54. Patrick O'Neill, "Ministry with Single Young Adults," *New Catholic World* 222, September–October 1979, p. 203.

55. John S. Dunne, C.S.C., *A Search for God in Time and Memory*, Notre Dame, IN: University of Notre Dame Press, 1977, pp. 1–7.

56. Ibid., p. 7–8.

57. Thomas N. Lay, S.J., "Symbols to Grow On," *Journal of Religion and Health* 19, Fall 1980, pp. 180–185.

58. Groome, *Christian Religious Education* pp. 14–15.

59. Charles E. Curran, *Themes in Fundamental Moral Theology*. Notre Dame, IN: University of Notre Dame Press, 1977, pp. 88–89.

60. James J. DiGiacomo, S.J. (with Edward Wakin), "How to Talk Religion with Teenagers," *U.S. Catholic* 38, July 1973, pp. 9–10.

61. *See* Sheila F. Stanley, "Family Disputes: A Means of Stimulating Adolescent Development," *Counseling and Values* 25, February 1981, pp. 110–118; and, Martin L. Hoffman, "Moral Development in Adolescence," in *Handbook of Adolescent Psychology*, ed. Joseph Adelson. New York: John Wiley & Sons, 1980, p. 337.

62. John C. Coleman, "Friendship and the Peer Group in Adolescence," in *Handbook of Adolescent Psychology*, pp. 409–413.

63. William J. Connolly, S.J., "Exploring Relational Prayer," *Human Development* 2, Winter 1981, p. 44.

64. Dunne, *Search for God*, pp. 10–11.

65. Matthew F. Kohmescher, S.M., "Profile of College Students Studying Religion in the Eighties," *New Catholic World* 224, January–February, 1981, pp. 22–24.

66. Kenneth McGuire, C.S.P., "A Spirituality for Searching People," *New Catholic World* 222, World 224, January–February, 1981, pp. 22–24.

66. Kenneth McGuire, C.S.P., "A Spirituality for Searching People," *New Catholic World* 222, September–October, 1979, p. 229.

67. Michael Warren, "Evangelization of Young Adults," *New Catholic World* 222, September–October, 1979, p. 217.

68. Raymond E. Brown, *Jesus: God and Man*. New York: Macmillan Publishing Co., 1967, pp. 103–105.

69. James J. DiGiacomo, S.J., "Teaching the Next New Breed," *America* 144, June 27, 1981, p. 520.

70. Hoffman, "Moral Development in Adolescence," p. 334.

71. John Dunne, C.S.C., *Time and Myth*. Notre Dame, IN: University of Notre Dame Press, 1975, p. 37.

CHAPTER FIVE

Spiritual Counseling
of the
Adolescent

A valuable experience for any adolescent during the high school or college years is the opportunity to reflect and dialog with an adult on personal understandings of life's meaning—particularly as it pertains to God, prayer, and spiritual growth. An adult can be a channel for positive reflection from which the adolescent can draw personal meaning. This spiritual counseling (or spiritual direction) that the adult provides can be a stimulus to growth, providing an important focus for the adolescent's questions and life search.

The Nature of Spiritual Direction

The goal or central focus of spiritual direction is to help a person "focus his life with an awareness and honesty in response to God's loving, creative, and saving action."[1] As adults, we should give our attention to how our relationship with an adolescent can foster a conscious and growing focusing on God in the young person's life. In general, then, spiritual direction provides a format, in the context of a relationship, that allows one person to aid another in clarifying the presence of God's love during the course of his or her own life experience. David Fleming terms this type of spiritual direction "incarnational," for the focal point is the conscious, growthful presence of God's call in everyday life experience.[2] The incarnational relationship emphasizes how God's call is integrated into my life and how my personal actions reflect an honest and open response to God's call.

In the adolescent-adult context, then, spiritual direction is a dialog that invites the adolescent to be aware of, understand, and respond to Jesus' call, in the context of his or her own developmental growth and personal experience. St. Ignatius has said that "we can become discerning persons by examining carefully our own experience." Noted spiritual director William Connolly sustains this view when he observes that "in spiritual direction, the point of our beginning with the person's experience is that when God does communicate, it's liable to be through the person's experience."[3] The adolescent's personal experience is heavily influenced by developmental issues and personal needs. The adult aids the adolescent in understanding these experiences, and from them flow a deeper internalization and integration of Jesus' call, which points more and more to a maturing, future-oriented Christian response. Adolescent spiritual direction, then, has as its goal the development of a conscious presence of the Lord in the young person's everyday life activity—in work, in play, in study, in relationships, or in whatever the experience might be.

Spiritual direction, of necessity, must be differentiated from the more personally oriented counseling of the adolescent. The similarities between the two are great because both counseling and spiritual direction deal with the person's experiences and growing self-awareness. Nonetheless, it is important to distinguish between these two modes of interaction.[4] Spiritual direction focuses on the relationship that one has developed with Jesus Christ, how one is growing in that relationship, and how one responds to His call. In spiritual direction, there is an intentional focusing on God that is lacking in personal counseling. A young person who is now capable of realizing the demands of personal faith needs the opportunity to reflect on these experiences of God. Spiritual direction can provide the needed format for focusing on these very experiences in his or her life.

Adolescence is a time when the critical questions about faith can be asked and shared; it is a special time when the young person can reflect on and question his or her own life in the light of this deeper questioning; it can also be a time for more personally-oriented counseling, if this is necessary. Such counseling may, of course, be used in the spiritual dialog between the adolescent and the adult. The time for spiritual direction presents an occasion in the adolescent's life for focusing on God. This opportunity for an awareness of God through dialog constitutes a significant occurrence during these years of development.

One might well ask whether spiritual direction is appropriate for adolescents and, if so, when. Certainly spiritual direction is needed for young people because, during their adolescent years, they must integrate a growing and maturing faith commitment in preparation for adulthood. It is also important to be aware, however, that spiritual direction with those in the adolescent years is distinct in some ways from spiritual direction with those who are older, regardless of the form that the later direction might take. Speaking of young people, Jean LaPlace has observed: "At this age, spiritual direction is simple and almost rudimentary in its manifestations, but is such as to permit the emergence of grace from within the searches and developments of adolescence."[5] In the early adolescent years, any type of spiritual direction is usually very elementary and often group-oriented (during classroom time, for example, or group retreats). In the last years of high school and most certainly in the college years, however, increasing time can be given to individual encounters with an adolescent.

The Beginning of Adolescent Spiritual Direction

In contemplating the onset of spiritual direction with adolescents, it will be helpful for us to consider the nature of the initial session(s). Although there are certainly exceptions, it can quite often be assumed that adolescent direction takes place over a shorter period of time than the typical direction or spiritual counseling of adults. For youth in middle and late adolescence, this direction often parallels the emergence of a specific problem, event, or crisis that the adolescent might be experiencing and needs to work through. Time must be given to the exploration of the particular experience, problem, or whatever the situation might be: a school grade, a difficult home condition, the choice of a college major, or a troubled relationship. Just listening to the adolescent often furnishes him or her a tremendous amount of relief. In such situations, a primary task for the adult is to place the adolescent's personal experience in the context of his or her developmental self (see chapter 3). In other words, the young person needs to learn the extent to which this difficulty is part of "normal" adolescent development. After exploring and dealing with the difficulty at hand, he or she can be invited to meet periodically for discussions in which a greater amount of time can be spent reflecting and focusing on the young person's personal life situation. Adolescent spiritual direction provides the time to both focus on those distinct developmental questions and difficulties that the young person might be experiencing and to reflect on them in the context of his or her level of faith experience. Such direction provides the opportunity for the adolescent to share reflections on how Jesus is really present and being experienced in his or her own life.

In contrast to the counseling and direction of adults, adolescent direction is usually less formal and is certainly an aspect of student retreats, long discussions, and occasional get-togethers. Many times, adolescents have a specific area on which they wish to focus, and it is these particular conversations that can be a source of real strength and inspiration. Regardless of the format, however, during these initial contacts, it is helpful to concentrate on the folllowing areas:

Significant events   Explore significant events or persons in the adolescent's life and the ways in which these events or persons have emerged and influenced his or her present spiritual life. Determine what influence is exerted in this adolescent's life by significant others, that is, parents, siblings, friends. What experiences have he or she had that convey the message of God's love? What is his or her felt experience of God's love? Can he or she articulate this experience? In experiencing God's love it is sometimes helpful to use other analogies or images in the dialog. Examples include: "Talking to Jesus is like talking to my best friend" or "For me, being with God and feeling His love is like feeling really free and alive."

Relationship with God   Develop an overall view of the adolescent's relationship with God and how prayer fits into this relationship. Find out whether the adolescent prays. If the adolescent does pray, *how* does he or she pray? What form does his or her prayer take? How peaceful can this adolescent be with himself or herself? Is time alone important for this adolescent?

Life situations   Appraise the adolescent's ability to assess his or her personal life situation (realistic orientation). This appraisal should include discussing assets, strengths, weaknesses, goals, and so forth. Does the adolescent's experience signify a realistic orientation and perception of the self? How is this adolescent aware of God's presence? How does he or she experience God relating to his or her life in concrete situations, personal relationships, home life, school, and so on?

As spiritual direction proceeds, increasing emphasis can be placed on the various characteristics of adolescent spiritual direction. The adult and young person can explore various facets of the young person's life and the ways these areas mesh with the adolescent's growing in true Christian maturity.

Four Characteristics of Adolescent Spiritual Direction

1 Focus on God

As we have noted, the major emphasis must *focus on God* as He is present in the young person's life—particularly on how God is leading and guiding the adolescent. Because adolescence is a state of life in which reflection is often limited, or is just beginning to occur at a deeper level, adults must first of all aid the adolescent in developing an awareness of God's active presence. Some of the questions the adult might keep in mind as he or she dialogues with the adolescent include the following:

• What is this adolescent's experience of God at this moment in his or her life?

• What is the adolescent's emotional experience of God? Is there an affective component in his or her relationship with God?

• Cognitively, what does this adolescent understand by "God?" By "Jesus Christ?"

• What is his or her perception of God? That is to say, is God a father figure? A mother figure? Warm and trusting? Distant and far removed?

• How is Jesus perceived? Is there a relational experience of Jesus? Is He a friend? Is He perceived as more human than divine? More divine than human? Can the adolescent share with Jesus and talk with Him?

• When does the need for God arise in this adolescent's life? In time of personal need? In what type of situations or experiences? Is there a central focus on God in this activity?

2   *Relational in Scope*

A second characteristic of adolescent spiritual direction, which has particular importance for the young person, is the *relational scope* of direction in the spiritual dialog. This means that the relationship with God gets the primary accent; but there is also attention given to how this relationship with God affects the relationships with family, peers, friends, and those at work and school, and so forth. Conversely, there must also be an exploration of how these relationships mirror the loving presence of God in the young person's life. Because adolescence is especially concerned with the forming and nurturing of relational needs, it is proper, at this developmental stage, to focus on how personal relationships are formed, how relationships support and continue the young person's growth, and how Jesus is present in these relationships. Some questions the adults might keep in mind when ministering to adolescents are the following:

• How does this adolescent form relationships? Is the level of these relationships commensurate with his or her level of developmental growth? What, for example, is the level (capacity) of the adolescent's vulnerability, intimacy, defensiveness, and so on in his or her relationships? Does the experience of God enter into any of these relationships? Can the adolescent reflect on and discuss what meanings and values are present in these relationships?
• Is there any similarity between how he or she relates to God and how he or she relates to others, that is to say, are the relationships characterized by fear, control, level of openness?
• Does he or she make a conscious effort to relate to others in charitable ways that mirror Gospel values?
• Does he or she engage in self-defeating or nongrowthful behaviors in personal relationships?
• What is this adolescent's capacity for insight into his or her relationships? Can he or she learn from experiences in his or her relationships?
• Do relationships draw him or her into a deepening awareness of God's love?
• Can this adolescent admit difficulties in relationships? How does he or she cope with frustration and conflicts in relationships? How does he or she react when confronted with these difficulties? Can he

or she use these events for growth? Does he or she experience relationships primarily out of need, or is there a real sense of growth and mutual dependency in his or her relationships?

3 Functional in Approach

A third characteristic of adolescent spiritual direction arises because adolescence is an inchoate stage for more in-depth strategies that will allow the young person to relate and participate in the adult world. This stage of development provides a necessary time for devising the ways to deal with the adult world in which the adolescent is rapidly acquiring membership. Hence, adolescent spiritual direction is *functional in approach,* in that it relates the Gospel to the strategies and adaptive capacities that the adolescent is now exploring. As we related in chapter 3, the adolescent's growing cognitive capacity allows for deeper critical reflection regarding social, political, and personal views on many diverse topics that, in earlier years, were only of passing interest. The adolescent begins his or her quest for meaning in life and starts formulating a social and political philosophy to understand and interpret the world. He or she begins acquiring goals or strategies for dealing with new interests and experiences. Various jobs are taken on and careers are explored. Some roles become more important than others, and conflict occasionally arises between two roles (e.g., friend vs. daughter or son conflicts, athletics vs. job conflicts, career vs. relationship conflicts, etc.). The adult who is ministering to an adolescent needs to aid the young person in reflecting on how these experiences, goals, roles, and strategies reflect the Gospel's presence in his or her life. Some questions the adult can keep in mind are the following:

• How does this adolescent use his or her developing freedom? Does he or she fear it? Accept it? Apply this freedom to time, activities, and relationships? Does this freedom allow opportunities for the presence of God to touch him or her?

• How does this adolescent experience various life encounters? As a planner? As an attacker? Methodically? Reflectively? Cautiously? With a free spirit?

• Does this adolescent welcome new experiences? Does he or she demonstrate a capacity to grow and deepen from these experiences? Can he or she reflect on how these relationships influence his or her life?

• Does he or she handle various roles with a certain equanimity? What happens when conflict arises between various roles? Is his or her faith commitment pervasive in all roles or only in certain ones (son, daughter, student, athlete, worker, etc.)?
• Is there a developing sense of service toward other people in the adolescent's life? That is to say, is there a growing sense of "my life as lived for others" (Mt 16:24–26)?

4   Future Oriented

A fourth characteristic of adolescent spiritual direction is that it is *future oriented*. The adolescent is a person who looks to the future. Thus, a critical component of the spiritual direction of the adolescent involves offering him or her an understanding of where he or she is being led by the Lord as well as a growing realization that his or her life is leading to an ever increasing sense of Christian adulthood (see chapter 9). The adult encourages the adolescent to reflect on his or her various vocational goals, possibilities, future career choices and, in addition, to think about the place and role of his or her future relationships (friendship commitments, marriage plans, and so on) and the ways these future states in his or her life might reflect a call to the Gospel. Some of the questions that might help the adult to explore this future with the adolescent include the following:
• Can the adolescent conceptualize a future adult role? Does this role become consonant with his or her temperament, abilities, goals, and the like as he or she acquires greater understanding and experience?
• Does he or she show a growing sensitivity about how this role will influence, touch, and affect others. In other words, is the adolescent developing a broadening interest in others beyond the work or career that he or she envisions? Can he or she deal with questions about how this role will allow him or her to help others and demonstrate true concern for them? Does he or she display interest in such issues?
• Can principles of social justice be related to future roles? Is social consciousness part of his or her thinking?
• Do relationships, deepening friendships, or possible marriage plans give evidence of a deepening capacity to love others? What place does Jesus occupy in these relationships?

The Spiritual Director of Adolescents

In chapter 2 we discussed several points concerning the adult who ministers to adolescents. There are, in addition, some specific aspects of ministering to adolescents that relate to the spiritual counseling or spiritual direction that takes place during the adolescent years.

First, the adult must have some understanding of the adolescent experience—especially the developmental aspects of adolescence, including its social, emotional, intellectual, moral, and faith dimensions (see chapter 3). When working with young people, especially young adults, there is a temptation to prematurely assume an adult orientation that really does not exist, or, at most, is still in a formative state. In such cases, the adult fails to realize that the adolescent lacks experiential knowledge of many life situations and their attendant complexities. With experience and time, the adolescent increasingly develops the capacity for reflection and adult behaviors that mirror this reflective capacity. The adult must be careful not to expect a given level of reflective capacity until the adolescent passes through the necessary experiences to allow this reflective capacity to develop. The spiritual director can, however, concentrate on (1) questions and observations that enable the adolescent to increasingly develop this capacity, and (2) newly discovered insights that are associated with a maturing reflective sense of both himself or herself and his or her faith. In a sense, then, we should note that adolescent spiritual direction has the potential for being somewhat frustrating, if the adult expects adolescent responses to contain insights or reflective responses that are beyond his or her developmental level.

Second, the adult needs to possess some understanding of the dynamics of the adult-adolescent relationship. One of the most vexing pitfalls in this relationship arises because adolescence is a developmental period during which change occurs rapidly. An adult who is ministering to an adolescent can all too often respond to an adolescent's particular experiences or statements without viewing the wider context in which this encounter takes place. In other words, the adult needs some understanding of both the current status or dynamics of the relationship and the future direction in which this relationship is pointing. It is insufficient (and inadequate) simply to "solve" or "work through" a difficulty with an adolescent. What is also needed is a total perspective that situates the adolescent's current life situation and future growth possibilities. We can examine this aspect in the form of a question: How is my particular response to this particular adolescent leading him or her to future spiritual growth? The following diagram seeks to place the adult-adolescent interaction that occurs during spiritual direction into a larger context. The diagram puts the adult-adolescent dialog into this larger context, takes into account the various aspects of the adult-adolescent dialog, and provides a general goal orientation for this interaction. In chapter 9, we shall identify specific characteristics to which the adult can refer in assessing the adolescent's growth in the spiritual life.

Third, the adult who ministers to adolescents as a spiritual director must have a sense of quiet openness. The adult must be able to really listen to what the adolescent is saying and have the capacity for deep reflection on it. The adult should be a source of profound reflection that can move the adolescent to realize deeper meaning. "The greatest service the [spiritual] director can render to the one who seeks his help is that of truly hearing what he is trying to say, so that the Spirit working within him can release His saving power."[6] A caution, however, is warranted here: There is a tendency in adolescent spiritual direction to "anticipate" what the adolescent might say. Because we ourselves have gone through this developmental period and might have already ministered to many young people, we are tempted to assume that an adolescent will fit into a definite stage or a particular stereotype; we therefore *expect* certain things to happen. Yet, as we know from chapter 3—it has been a central thesis of this book—adolescence is a developmental stage. Although there certainly are sequential aspects and common characteristics in adolescent behaviors, thoughts, and feelings, the Lord's working within each of us is unique. The spiritual director who works with adolescents must be wary of temptations to stereotype and remain open to the uniqueness that each adolescent brings to an encounter. A productive way to temper this tendency is to periodically reflect on the mysterious ways in which God has graced your own life. Such experiences of grace are both personal and unique. For the adolescent, too, such experiences are unique and deserving of personal attention.

SPIRITUAL DIRECTION (COUNSELING) OF ADOLESCENTS

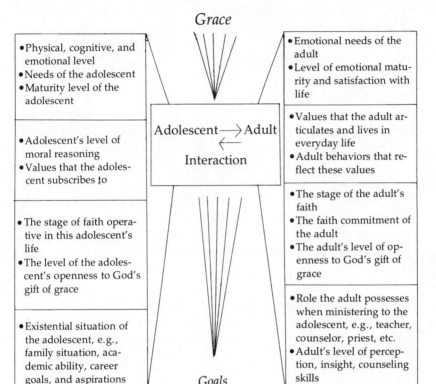

Grace

• Physical, cognitive, and emotional level • Needs of the adolescent • Maturity level of the adolescent	• Emotional needs of the adult • Level of emotional maturity and satisfaction with life
• Adolescent's level of moral reasoning • Values that the adolescent subscribes to	Adolescent ⟶ Adult ⟵ Interaction	• Values that the adult articulates and lives in everyday life • Adult behaviors that reflect these values
• The stage of faith operative in this adolescent's life • The level of the adolescent's openness to God's gift of grace	• The stage of the adult's faith • The faith commitment of the adult • The adult's level of openness to God's gift of grace
• Existential situation of the adolescent, e.g., family situation, academic ability, career goals, and aspirations	*Goals*	• Role the adult possesses when ministering to the adolescent, e.g., teacher, counselor, priest, etc. • Adult's level of perception, insight, counseling skills

1. The growing awareness and sense of God's presence in the adolescent's life; the nurturing and presence of a deepening prayer life that reflects a deepening faith commitment.

2. The developing sense of the adolescent's relational life reflecting deepening commitments and love for others—family, peers, friends.

3. The development of everyday values, perceptions, attitudes, and goals consonant with the Gospel; focusing on behaviors in the present life of the adolescent.

4. The development of a future orientation that integrates the Gospel with future relationships, career goals, and vocational aspirations.

A corollary to this openness is an acceptance of the distinct role that silence might exercise in the adult-adolescent dialog. The adult who can communicate that he or she is at ease with silence may prove to be of tremendous benefit to the young person. Adolescents are so often simply unaware of the human need to be alone with oneself. Moments of silence in the dialog can, of course, be unsettling; yet, in time, the adolescent develops the capacity to use this period for self-reflection, for deepening his or her understanding of the Lord's call, and for realizing the profound insights that arise from this silent reflection. During intervals of silence in the dialog, the adult might just be with the adolescent in this silence, and, after a while, pose open-ended questions, such as the following: What are you feeling (thinking)? Do you think God might be saying something to you now? Can you think where we might go from here? Increasingly, the adolescent might be encouraged to reflect on personal experience in order to discover further insights and understandings about where God's call might be leading. Here, of course, the adult acts as a ' self-clarifier'' whose presence enables the adolescent to reflect on where these experiences might be heading. Many adolescents may have difficulty articulating exactly what they are experiencing. The adult's presence might well serve, therefore, as a source of feedback to help the adolescent clarify what is really taking place.

This leads to the fourth characteristic of the adult spiritual director who ministers to adolescents—the ability to reflect on his or her various diverse experiences. Although any spiritual director or counselor needs this characteristic, it takes on special significance in the adult-adolescent dialog. The adolescent often lacks an understanding of the deeper meanings and consequences of relationships, life dreams, and experiences because of his or her stage of development. As the adolescent experiences life, he or she often finds it difficult to understand the meanings of life's experiences. For example, what does a particular experience say about my relationship with God and/or with others?

The wise spiritual director of adolescents must not only listen to and reflect on what the adolescent says, but also comment in a way that invites the young person to reflect on and inquire more deeply into what those life experiences really say and how God is present in them. An excellent technique to accomplish this reflection and inquiry is to summarize what the adolescent has said about an experience and then direct back to the adolescent some open-ended questions concerning this experience. An adolescent, for example, might tell about a difficult experience regarding relationships. The adult can summarize what the young person has said, and then pose questions that concentrate on the adolescent's developmental level and its attendant difficulties, such as, What feelings have you been having since that difficulty occurred? What do you think, Mary, this difficulty says to you about yourself? Once the situation and various feelings have been explored, the adult can then reflect with the adolescent on how meanings, values, and God are part of this experience. The adult might ask, for example, How have you grown from . . . ? Are there any ways you see yourself as different now that this has happened? After the adolescent responds, the adult might continue, asking such questions as, Why do you think you were affected in those ways? Do you find God present in any of this? How have you grown from this? Have you shared this experience with God? These open-ended questions—oriented toward a particular experience—offer the adolescent a chance to both reflect more deeply on these experiences and reorient thinking and perceptions. In addition, they gently challenge the adolescent to look beyond the immediate circumstances to the deeper truth that is contained in the experience. In this way, the adolescent can realize and understand more fully the Lord's call to "come, follow me."

Strategies and Techniques for the Spiritual Direction of Adolescents

We have said that adolescence is a developmental stage during which diverse thoughts, feelings, and behaviors are manifested. In the following pages, we have presented some typical adolescent behaviors and attitudes. These manifestations can often be dealt with in a counseling situation, using standard counseling techniques that will produce positive results, provided the adult understands adolescent development. The standard counseling approaches can be adapted to the adult-adolescent spiritual dialogue and incorporated into it. In the examples presented here, the behavior of the adolescent is mentioned first. Next, an approach that might prove

183

helpful in dealing with the adolescent is suggested. Lastly, there is discussion of a focus for spiritual direction that will allow the adult to work within the context of a spiritual-direction format.

Example 1: The Dilemma of Decision Making

Adolescent behavior   In making decisions about life and relationships, young people sometimes act out of what might be called the fallacy of perfect choice. Because adolescence is a stage of newfound freedom, the adolescent grows to realize that he or she is presented with many choices in life, and when one choice is made, other choices are effectively eliminated. Or, as is often the case in adolescence, when no choice is made—for example, putting off writing a term paper, or applying to a college, or dealing with a troubled relationship—a choice is, in effect, often made for the adolescent.

Choosing requires decision making that is clear and insightful. Inasmuch as adolescents often lack experience and frequently worry over the choices that must be made, however, making decisions can sometimes be difficult and frustrating for them. Thus, in order to simplify the ambiguity and anxiety that is present in these choices, many adolescents engage in the fallacy of perfect choice. Adolescents (and many adults, too) will sometimes picture one choice as totally good, offering "everything that I am looking for." In making a decision about college, for example, one school might be rated as *the* school to attend and no other will do. Or, in a relationship, an adolescent might be attempting to either find the *perfect friend* or construct an ideal of how a friend must act. Frustration often develops out of these unmet ideals. The adolescent needs to perceive the limitations inherent in any choice that he or she makes. Additionally, the adult might help the adolescent realize there are other choices which might combine the original choices that the adolescent thought were the only ones available.

Clarifier approach   When the adult confronts circumstances such as those described in this example, the role for the adult is that of "clarifier." The adult aids the adolescent in clarifying the issues and dynamics of everyday life decisions. The adult also helps the adolescent to see beyond the narrowing perceptions that are inherent in the fallacy of perfect choice. A sequence of stages can be used in helping the adolescent to clarify the important elements in various decisions. The adult might use guidelines such as the following:

Information stage.   Explore with the adolescent the intent behind and the purposes of selecting this choice. What were the antecedent factors that influenced the adolescent? Reflect on these with the adolescent. It is important for the adolescent to realize that other influences in his or her life might favor one choice over another or might cloud the decision-making process. Do certain past experiences bias the choices that are made? Can the adolescent recognize these influences?

Option stage.   What viable alternatives are available to this adolescent? Sometimes it is good to have the adolescent write down his or her various options, listing the advantages and disadvantages of each alternative. Does the adolescent perceive the real difference between the various choices that are available?

Consequence stage.   Does the adolescent understand the consequences of each stage? Can he or she admit the limitations of the choice he or she is making? In other words, the adolescent needs to realize that no choice is perfect and that there will no doubt be times when the choice that is made is less attractive and/or beneficial than another.

Spiritual direction focus.   We can explore with the adolescent various values that exist in making a choice. If the adolescent chooses college, for example, what are the values that are influencing him or her to attend this school. What do these values say about the adolescent? If the adolescent faces the choice of a job or career decision, what values underlie the choice of this type of work? Especially when adults are directing college undergraduates, time may be profitably spent exploring the values that are involved in deciding on a particular college major. What value does this particular major reflect? What does it say to the adolescent about himself or herself? If the adolescent is unsure about college, work, career, or the like, the adult can present hypothetical situations that invite the adolescent to imagine various choices and their attending values. The adult might wish to suggest that the adolescent examine how a particular Gospel value, such as compassion, peace, or care for the poor, meshes with the choices that are under consideration. If the choice that is being considered involves a relationship, the adult might explore with the adolescent a variety of responses in that relationship, and then examine the values and intentions behind the various behaviors that the adolescent is considering. The overall atmosphere should be one of helping the adolescent to see clearly the attendant factors, along with the underlying values, in all decision making, as well as the possible Gospel values that can be part of his or her future decisions. The adolescent needs encouragement in reflecting on these values and on the place they exercise (or do not exercise) in his or her life.

Example 2: The Dilemma of Behaviors

Adolescent behavior.   Young people often need clarity to help them see their own behaviors and perceptions in their interpersonal behaviors. Sometimes the adolescent is engulfed in a variety of different emotions, needs, and attitudes. The college undergraduate, for example, might not understand how an overbearing manner might be mistakenly perceived by those who live on the same dormitory floor. In an effort to gain a sense of belonging, a high school student involved in school activities might be overly assertive, not realizing the harmful approach that this behavior has on peer relations.

Scaling technique approach.   In this situation, a good technique is the scaling technique.[7] Ask the adolescent to imagine a linear scale from 1 to 10. The scale should focus on a distinctive criteria such as likability or maturity. Then, describe to the adolescent a behavior that mirrors the behavior you have noticed in this young person, or a behavior that the young person has experienced or discussed. Have the adolescent rate the behavior on a 10-point scale (10 is high and 1 is low) in terms of the distinctive criteria (e.g., likability). When the adolescent rates the behavior, explore with him or her why the particular rating was selected. Reflect with the adolescent what this rating says about him or her and about the behavior. This approach is helpful because it "objectifies" the adolescent's behavior rather than focusing too directly or too personally on the adolescent (which some young people find threatening). The scaling technique enables the adolescent to view a behavior from outside the self. It enlarges the perspective of personal behavior and provides a format for discussing ways to deal with the behavior at hand.

Spiritual direction focus   Follow the scaling technique, but instead of rating criteria such as likability or maturity, this time relate the behavior according to a Gospel value or a quality from Scripture, such as peace, patience, or kindness (Gal 5:22). Continuing with the procedure, discuss this value or quality with the adolescent. Focus on how it is reflected or not reflected (and possible ways it might be realized) in the adolescent's behavior.

Example 3: The Dilemma of a Worldview

Adolescent behavior   From our discussion of Piaget in chapter 3, we know that an increasing capacity for critical thinking emerges when a child reaches adolescence. Through the high school and college years, the young person's cognitive capacity engenders a growing complexity of evaluative notions toward the world and society. The young person develops ideals and complex attitudes that translate into social, political, and philosophical questions and criticisms. As a result, adolescents, who lack sufficient reflection or experience, tend to become overly critical of others and can develop a perspective or viewpoint that narrows their ability to evaluate life situations in ways that are positive and growthful.

Hypothetical questioning approach   In light of what we have said, we can see that an adolescent might develop a worldview that is either overly critical (that is, narrowing) or idealistic (that is, one that can subject the adolescent to much frustration). It is common for an adolescent to generalize these views with statements such as, "Everyone is out for themselves," or "People should be able to do whatever they want" (or some other all-inclusive statement). A productive way to deal with this adolescent tendency is to use hypothetical questioning.[8] Because the adolescent is now capable of more complex forms of reasoning, we can challenge him or her to logically look at what he or she is really saying. When an adolescent says, for example, "Everyone should be able to do whatever they want" (a common statement in the high school and college years), suggest that the adolescent imagine a world in which this is really true. Then ask the adolescent: What are the results? What are the personal consequences for the adolescent? After discussing this matter, invite the adolescent to take responsibility for his or her statements. Such discussions can help the young person to see the growing complexities and realities that come with adolescence.

Spiritual direction focus A way to attach some spiritual significance to this technique is to have the adolescent imagine a world that is perfect—a utopia. What type of world would this be? Have the adolescent talk about the values that are important in such a world or society and try to relate the values in this hypothetical world to the values that are consciously part of the young person's life. Are there similarities or differences? What are they? The adult might suggest various scriptural passages that either mirror the young person's values or are at variance with those values. Another approach is to spend time together reflecting on the various values in the adolescent's life and how these values are similar or dissimilar to Gospel values. This technique provides the adolescent with the opportunity to confront his or her own self and examine his or her personal values.

Example 4: The Dilemma of Evaluating Values

Adolescent behavior Adolescence is a time during which deeper reflection and thinking on values commences and life questions are asked and dealt with. Some young people find it quite helpful to keep a diary or journal in which they write down their reflections and thoughts.

Journal writing approach Talk with the adolescent about the possibility of keeping a journal. The young person can be left to work out the specific content, but a few suggestions might be helpful. It might be valuable, for example, to emphasize concrete experiences or situations, followed by the young persons's subsequent reflections. Some themes that might be suggested include trust, love, and friendship. The adolescent writes from a personal understanding of what these themes mean. The adolescent, for example, could be asked to write out what friendship really means. For college undergraduates, the emphasis might involve deeper and yet more practical applications. A class discussion after a lecture on "ethics" or "freedom" might be a useful theme for the adolescent to write about in his or her journal. Another possibility is to have the adolescent describe in his or her journal the perfect job or career choice—a detailed description of what he or she is really looking for in life. This task can be a helpful and thoughtful form of written reflection.

Spiritual direction focus   Ask the adolescent to select a particular Gospel passage or a specific Psalm. The adolescent can then write out his or her reactions to the scripture passage. It is helpful to give some structure to the adolescent's reflections. A good model is to suggest that the adolescent write down his or her reflection in a three-fold process, that is, (a) the meaning of the passage for him or her, (b) the importance of the passage for his or her present life, and (c) what the passage calls him or her to do with his or her life, what responses the adolescent can make to this passage here and now. St. Ignatius often made the point that love is shown through service to one's fellow men and women. It is helpful to point this out to adolescents, who sometimes become absorbed in their own thought and reflection. A component of adolescent reflection should be forward looking, focusing on the actual *doing* of some behavior that mirrors Christian service. The proper focus is always what the Lord is both telling us *and* leading us to.

Example 5: The Dilemma of Understanding Others

Adolescent behavior   As we noted in chapter 3, the adolescent's growing awareness of himself or herself allows for a greater sense of another's perspectives. The adolescent increasingly acquires a deeper cognitive and affective awareness of other people. In this context, then, role-playing is a useful technique for encouraging the adolescent to grow in his or her own understanding of both himself or herself and others.

Role-playing approach   If the adolescent is facing a difficult time in either a relationship or a home situation, spend some time role playing with the adolescent. Alternate with the adolescent the roles of friends, parents, peers, or teachers, and then experience the situation as it evolves.[9] Role playing provides the adolescent with the opportunity to experience another person at a much deeper level than is usually possible. In this way, the exceptions, attitudes, and behaviors of another can be better understood. At the same time, there are three things to keep in mind when using the role-playing approach. First, the adult must clearly explain the purpose or reason for this exercise—why it is being used—so that the adolescent can gain some insight into and knowledge of self, another, and of a particular situation. Second, be sure to stress the reality of the role-playing situation as it is actually being experienced. This emphasis will provide some measure of authenticity in the role-playing situation. Third, following the role-playing exercise, time should be spent exploring the insights that have been gathered from this experience, the adolescent's level of awareness, and the behavior this experience might elicit from the adolescent sometime in the future.

Spiritual direction focus   Role playing can be used to more deeply understand Scripture. The adolescent can examine and meditate privately on various passages and then assume the role of one of the characters (see chapter 4 for possible suggestions). The adult can explore with the adolescent the feelings and insights that have emerged from this role-playing experience. As a follow-up to this exercise, ask the adolescent to compare new understandings or insights into his or her relationship with Jesus with understandings and peceptions that he or she had before the role-playing exercise. This direct discussion helps the adolescent focus on growth in his or her own relationship with Jesus. The follow-up questions in role-playing exercises should concentrate on insights and understandings that deal with the adolescent's cognitive understanding, affective experiences during the role playing, and motivational and/or practical applications in the young person's own life.

Example 6: The Dilemma of Goal Striving

Adolescent behavior   Much of our behavior can be better understood by examining he goals we have developed for ourselves. Our goals often underlie much of our behavior, that is, when we desire something, we strive for it. This very human reaction can lead to problems if we do not fully understand these goals and the effects the goals and our goal-attaining behaviors have on both ourselves and others. It is important for us to keep this goal-striving in mind when we are working with adolescents. The demands of adolescence, including the needs for independence, separation from parents, self-understanding, and one's growing identity often lead the young person to pursue various goals that facilitate developmental tasks and give potentially stressful situations a sense of stability. In striving for goals, adolescents often engage in a variety of "typical faulty goals."[10] These faulty goals include superiority, popularity, conformity, defiance, sexual promiscuity, inadequacy, charm, beauty and/or strength, sexism, intellectualizing, and religiosity. In one way or another, these goals represent the adolescent's attempt to obtain self-esteem and a sense of relatedness to others.

Goal probing approach. Ask the adolescent what goal is underlying a particular behavior. Then, attempt to identify what goal the adolescent or young adult is seeking to fulfill. When doing this, ask inquiry questions concerning these various behaviors, such as, *Why are you doing this?* It is helpful to summarize past concrete situations and experiences in the adolescent's life that portray these behaviors, and then challenge the adolescent to consider more deeply what is *really* going on when these behaviors are manifested. If a high school adolescent relates various incidents that imply difficulty with parents, for example, present a summary of these experiences based on previous statements or discussions with the adolescent, and then, to explore the adolescent's behavior, raise inquiry questions such as the following: What do you think you were trying to accomplish when that happened? What are you really looking for when this happens? Gather insights from these questions so that you can have some understanding of what is behind the adolescent's behavior. But, always remember that when you are working with the adolescent's mistaken goals, it is important that you do not reinforce goals by praise and encouragement. If an adolescent is over-intellectualizing, for example, it is important that you offer alternative ways to behave without overly stressing the intellectual endeavors. Thus, it is important for the adult to reflect with the adolescent on possible alternative behaviors.

Spiritual direction focus. An adult who is ministering to adolescents might want to explore ways in which Christian values might mesh with adolescent goals. Discuss with the adolescent some concrete instances from Scripture, for example, in which Jesus' actions benefited others. Then, suggest that the adolescent reflect on these passages and discover for himself or herself what specific goals Jesus had. Also, pose questions such as, What values or qualities of being a Christian do you find most appealing? Then, ask the adolescent to reflect on his or her own behavior and what steps the adolescent has taken to obtain and demonstrate these qualities in his or her own life. A direct relationship of means to end is then established for the adolescent. In other words, the adolescent must determine to what extent his or her actions, behaviors, and attitudes have really led this adolescent to portray the Christian values he or she

191

admires? The adult can then reflect with the adolescent on acceptable and appropriate behaviors that truly mirror these values.

Another positive behavior technique that can be used is the "best-self-forward" technique. With this technique, the adolescent is asked to imagine his or her "best self." The Christian values that are present in this self are then explicitly explored and discussed with the adolescent. In this discussion, the adolescent is encouraged to both think of his or her own values and explore ways to express these values in his or her life. Incremental behaviors (ways to act, various types of reflection) to achieve Christian values (patience, understanding, charity) can be suggested. Be cautious, however, in suggesting incremental behaviors; do not instill unrealistic goals in the adolescent; encourage the adolescent to set *obtainable* goals.

Example 7: The Dilemma of Maturity

Adolescent behavior   When adolescents encounter particular situations, they often function at a level that is below their own developmental capability. Quite often, when adolescents come to an adult, it is because the level of their behavior in a particular situation is below the culturally acceptable level of maturity that is expected of them. Psychologist Clifford Swensen has noted that the level of functioning that we portray through our behaviors can be at a level that is below our overall level of ego functioning.[11] Priest-psychologist Eamonn O'Doherty notes that "if we are to be effective in dealing with youth, the temptation to attribute to them higher levels of maturity in one area simply because they have obtained a certain level in another must be resisted."[12]

Functional-level approach   An adolescent might, at times, be impulsive, overly preoccupied with self, or withdrawn. The adolescent needs to inwardly examine his or her own behaviors and develop an inner capacity to deal with such behaviors. There are several techniques for dealing with regressive tendencies when they occur. Sometimes a gentle challenge or even a confrontation can be helpful to elicit more effective, maturing responses.[13] Such initiatives, however, should only be taken when the adult has an overall understanding and adequate knowledge of both the adolescent and his or her behavior. Futile challenges can be self-defeating and can even isolate the young person. Another technique that can be used is the "comparison technique." If the adolescent's difficulty involves a relationship, suggest that he or she rank several relationships according to specific criteria, such as satisfaction, honesty, and understanding. Explore with him or her common characteristics—both positive and negative—that are threaded through these relationships. Look for common themes and discuss these with the adolescent.

Spiritual direction focus   Adults should always express acceptance and encouragement of the adolescent, regardless of his or her shortcomings. Together with the adolescent reflect on the fact that the road to the Lord is a never-ending path because there will always be human shortcomings (Phil 3:12–14). One of the important components of any healthy spirituality is the acceptance of one's own shortcomings alongside continued striving forward, no matter what difficulties and obstacles are experienced. This is especially crucial for adolescents who, in their idealism, intense desire, or introspection, can sometimes become excessively preoccupied with accomplishment or success. Yet spiritual growth as well as personal growth is often slow in coming because it requires an amount of experience and reflection that is often necessarily beyond the adolescent. In being with adolescents through their struggles for growth, encouragement and support should always be the norm.

Example 8: The Dilemma of Past-Life Experiences

Adolescent behavior   Evelyn and James Whitehead have suggested a technique for dealing with memories and life experiences that can be utilized in adolescent spiritual direction.[14]

Memories approach   In this approach, a person recalls an event or incident from his or her past. This memory represents some experience that has touched the person's life, often in a significant way. The person reflects on this experience and attempts to capture what the experience represented *then* as well as what it means *now* in his or her present life situation.

Spiritual direction focus   Adolescents have, as a developmental task, the need to reflect on their own growth and deepening awareness of how they are actually growing and maturing during the developing years of adolescence. An adolescent can do this by reflecting on a significant life experience from the past few months or years. Suggest that the adolescent reflect on a significant relationship, a family experience, a secret desire, or a developing career goal. Along with the adolescent, reflect on what this event meant when it occurred; then, reflect on what this experience means in the adolescent's life now, and discuss together the differences that have emerged. What do these say *to* him or her? What do these say *about* him or her? His or her growth? His or her value system? Is the adolescent aware of God's presence during any of this change?

Spiritual Discernment in Adolescence

As human beings, we react to many things. Some experiences in life excite us, some attract us, and some repel or disgust us. When we reflect on life, we realize that there are few experiences to which we react without some form of attraction or aversion. Understanding this dynamic is crucial for us becaue it conveys the true meanings and values within our inner selves. Whatever we find ourselves drawn toward, or fantasizing about, or reflecting on often discloses the objects of real value to us—those persons or things that have special importance in our lives.

Regarding these inclinations that we all have, St. Ignatius says that one's relationship with other people and things, as well as one's relationship with the self, should be seen as "gifts" that we receive from God; we should, therefore, "appreciate and use all these gifts of God insofar as they help us develop as a loving person." Ignatian theology stresses ordered affection in all that we experience. An ordered affection is the love of people, places, or things and their use in a love deeply rooted in God. In other words, all things have their place in God because all things are loved through God. Thus, ordered affection disposes me to love all things properly—in and throught God.

The difficulty in life arises when a particular person or thing, a particular friend, job, or interest becomes so central that our life becomes distorted. Therefore, "if any of these gifts become the center of our lives, they displace God and so hinder our growth towards our goal." This distortion in life is what Ignatian theology labels "disordered affectivity"—it is an inclination that disengages us from that for which we are truly made. The goal of life is the freeing of the self from these disordered affections and the finding of God in all the activities of one's life.

In order to have a life that is ordered toward God, we must discern what the Spirit wants and where the Spirit is leading us in our life. From an existential standpoint, discernment is seeking God's will in the concrete situations of one's existence—in work, play, relationships, in short, in all that we do. Ignatius found this movement of the Spirit to have a central significance in his own spiritual life. Where was God leading him? Where was the greater good that was required of him in his life? In discovering the Spirit's movements, Ignatius was more and more able to give his life in service to both God and his church. It is through spiritual discernment that we recognize, and are sensitive to, the movements of God within our own selves.

St. Ignatius is often viewed as the father of discernment, because his *Spiritual Exercises* contain the "Rules for the Discernment of Spirits." Yet, discernment of spirits has had a long, rich life within the church and has evolved as a rich source for describing a person's interior experience of God's movement in his or her life.[15]

It might appear that spiritual discernment is a phenomenon that is well beyond the capability of all high school students and most college students. But, despite appearances, the development of a truly discerning spirit is possible in adolescence. The developmental capacity of the adolescent, especially his or her growing cognitive development and firmer sense of identity, can lead him or her to an increase in a discerning vision of life. Because the adolescent will one day be an adult Christian, it is important to aid the young person in learning to shift through various interior movements, so that, as the years progress, he or she can grow in sensitivity and respond freely and lovingly to Jesus' call to "come, follow me."

It is redundant to point out that Christian discernment requires serious reflection, and that an integral part of this reflection is an honest searching of one's life. St. Ignatius called this process of reflecting on one's life the "examen." More recently, George Aschenbrenner, S.J., has used the term "consciousness examen" when this examen is tied to a discerning reflection on everyday activities.[16] This examen does not require an exhaustive examination of a person's every action. Instead, it is crucial for the person to listen to where the Spirit is leading him or her at this point in his or her life. Concomitantly, the person must discern how his or her actions mirror this call of God, and how this call of God is beckoning the person forward into a life that is dedicated toward the service and love of others.

Arriving at spiritual discernment during adolescence can be difficult, especially because a young person's life is complicated by developmental issues. The struggle for identity and maturity frequently leave adolescents perplexed. It is often difficult for young persons to reflect on life because they are not at all sure what they really believe, where they are going, or even who they, as individuals, really are. Thus, it is sometimes, perhaps even frequently, difficult for adolescents to understand and internalize a Christian value system that is both meaningful and functional with an identity that is yet to be formed. Adolescents are attempting not only to formulate values, but also to construct a sense of self-identity that will reflect these Christian values. How can adults who minister to adolescents aid in the development of this discerning Christian sense of the self? It is helpful to use the Ignatian mode of examen to suggest a model of "consciousness examen" that can be adapted for the adolescent's use.

Three models of this examen are suggested as appropriate. First, a model of examen is suggested for the late adolescent who reflects a deep interior disposition and maturity, and truly seeks an explicit way to follow the call of Jesus in his or her life. Second, a model of examen is suggested either for the young adolescent or for the late adolescent who has not yet reached the level of maturity achieved by the adolescent who uses the first model. Third, a model of examen is suggested for the adolescent who, for intellectual and emotional reasons or because of a personal life situation, is disinclined to accept an explicit discussion of either Jesus Christ or a personal relationship with God. This adolescent might be, for example, the college student who professes no belief in God, or an adolescent who is alienated and estranged from the church.

Model 1

A crucial axiom for Christian living is the need to pray. Jesus asks us in the Gospel to pray to the Father for our needs (Mt 7:7–11). This initial offering before the Father is translated in the examen through a prayer for *enlightenment*. We ask Jesus to aid us in knowing our true selves, our weaknesses and strengths. Thus, the first criterion for real self-reflection is knowing our own self through the Spirit.

Encourage the adolescent to spend a few moments asking Jesus for strength and insight into where he or she really is in his or her life. This is important, because "it is not possible for me to make an examen without confronting my own identity in Christ before the Father."[17] The word "identity" draws us to the heart of adolescence. Because adolescents are in the process of forming their individual identities, they often ask themselves *who* they really are. This can be an excellent introduction to the examen. In fact, encourage the adolescents in their petitions for enlightenment to ask for deeper self-knowledge, a clearer sense of who they reallly are. In order to concretize this notion for an individual adolescent, direct the young person (in the sense of spiritual direction) to focus on various roles such as daughter, son, student, worker, friend. Then, suggest that the adolescent pray for a deeper understanding of what these roles are in his or her own life. In other words, help the adolescent concentrate on experiences in his or her life and how he or she responds to these roles. This technique helps the adolescent to develop a growing sense of self-acceptance that is based on his or her own concrete life experience.

Following this "enlightenment stage," invite the young person to spend some time reflecting on his or her personal *gifts* from God, such as intelligence, athletic skills, personality, helping skills, sensitivity in relationships, or other attributes, abilities, or accomplishments. Emphasizing the adolescent's positive qualities and skills will help to counter any punitive tendencies the young person might have. A positive foundation will also foster a sense of serenity and peacefulness that will prepare for later reflection on ways in which the young person might not have responded to the Lord's call. Also, ask the adolescent to focus on occurrences during a particular day that have given him or her a sense of self-worth, a feeling of acceptance, and a deepening love of self. Encourage the young person to be as concrete and specific as possible in this reflection. In this way, the adolescent is led to perceive tangible signs of God's love in his or her own life.

Instilling in the adolescent a conscious understanding of how he or she is really *gifted* in the Lord's presence is critical. Many adolescents who are burdened by inappropriate feelings of inadequacy lack a sense of self-worth and, therefore, have difficulty viewing

God as both personal and loving and often experience guilt in their relationships with God. In other words, an adolescent who has low self-worth might intellectually see God as forgiving; yet, in his or her own affective life, the adolescent might still need to prove himself or herself in order to feel personally accepted.[18] A brief period of reflection on the young person's positive points will militate against these deprecating tendencies.

After you have stressed positive acceptance, invite the adolescent to reflect on his or her personal life and any *limitations* that might be restricting his or her relationship with God at this time. Caution, however, must be exercised. This examen is not meant to be a rigid self-examination. Instead, the adolescent should be reflecting on both personal, interior dispositions that tell him or her of God's call and personal tendencies that frustrate the realization of this call in his or her life. Discerning reflections and a realization of personal limitation are certainly necessary for true Christian growth, and the adolescent needs a special time to reflect on these limitations. And when this inner examination is conducted in the midst of a conscious realization of God's love, there is a positive opportunity for the adolescent to accept his or her own need for God's forgiveness and grace.

In order to foster this sense of the adolescent's interior movement, it is helpful to provide an appropriate format for the adolescent's reflection. The following four general headings contain some specific questions that adolescents might reflect on daily.

Family   How has God's love been revealed to me today in my family? Specifically, how do I view others in my family? Am I open to them? Do I respect them for who they are in my life? Am I thankful to them? How do I show my thankfulness? What is the quality of my relationships with them? What have I done for them and what am I doing for them? Do I appreciate them or do I take them for granted?

School   To what extent have I given myself to my school work? Do I utilize the talents the Lord has given me? Where do I see my education leading me? In my school experiences, am I growing and caring for others?

Relationships   What has God said to me through my interpersnal relationships? How have these relationships touched my life during this day? How have I responded to those who relate to me?

Are relationships important in my life? Have I used them or taken advantage of them in any way? Are my relationships growing and deepening in an attitude of openness and caring toward my friends?

Self What place has God played in my life today? Have I thanked God in any way today? In what particular experiences of the day has God been present to me? How have I felt God's love today? What response do I make to the Lord for all that He has given me?

After this series of reflections, the adolescent might be moved to a sense of *sorrow*. There can be a few moments of quiet reflection or short personal prayer. Reading a particular scripture text with the adolescent might be helpful here. The adolescent discovers a greater sense of the need for God's grace and love in his or her life. In response to personal inadequacies, the adolescent might ask the Lord for help and support for the next day.

Finally, the adolescent can be asked to make some type of conscious *decision* about how he or she might better live the Gospel message. This decision could involve being aware of something in his or her life that the adolescent can alter or act upon. More positively, it is an attempt to *do something*. This emphasis on action is important for the adolescent because it tends to foster an interior disposition toward Christian service.

During the first examen with the adolescent, encourage him or her to perform an examen daily at a designated time. Periodically, the adolescent can be invited to reflect in dialog on what growth or development is occurring in his or her life, on how he or she is perceiving the Lord's call and on how he or she is responding more and more to this call.

Model 2

For a variety of reasons—age, emotional disposition, current life situation, developmental issues, or the like—many adolescents might find the traditional mode of the examen to be somewhat sophisticated and might therefore profit more from an abbreviated form of examen. With these adolescents—or, for that matter, with the many adults who might also fit this category—a modified form of examen is helpful. One form of examen that might prove helpful is the "thanksgiving examen."[19] This method of examen is limited to the first part of the traditional examen, during which the adolescent spends time in a thankful disposition toward the Lord for what he or she has been given.

In using this form of examen, encourage the adolescent to spend a few moments reflecting on the day's events. The adolescent can reflect on a few categories, such as, for example, the following:

People What individuals—family, friends, or peers—have made a difference in my life today? How have these people touched my life? How have they brought joy and support to me during the day? Am I thankful for these people? How do I show my thankfulness?

Actions What have I experienced today that has made me feel that I am a person who is blessed and happy? How have my actions brought joy to both my life and others' lives? What have I to be thankful for in the actions of this day?

Events What particular event of this day am I most thankful for? Who or what entered my life today? New people? New experiences? What has happened to me today that I did not expect? How have I grown from the events of this day? How have I been thankful to God for these events?

Ask the adolescent to spend some time thanking God for these people, actions, and events in his or her life. If possible, ask the adolescent (a) to notice what feelings emerge when thanking God, and then (b) to reflect on how thankfulness can be shown to God for all that has happened during the day. Again, the importance of Christian service in the adolescent's life should be noted.

Model 3

Some adolescents, particularly older adolescents, might have difficulty expressing any explicit need for relating to God. These adolescents might be reacting to some emotional experience in their lives, or they might be experiencing a type of faith crisis in which there can be an interweaving of developmental, intellectual, and emotional influences. This type of reaction is common in the later years of high school and frequently occurs on college campuses today. For these adolescents, the best strategy is often to encourage some type of interior reflection in which the thrust is toward positive growth and development.

One approach is to suggest that the adolescent use various personal values as a means for self-reflection. This can be done by encouraging and challenging the adolescent to periodically reflect on what he or she *really* values. This model is actually patterned on the Socratic maxim, "Know thyself."

Afterwards the adolescent might be invited to narrow his or her focus to "concrete" behaviors. In other words, ask the adolescent to consider the following questions: How do my behaviors reflect my values? (Do they? Can they? Why? Why not?) These behaviors, like those discussed in Model 2, can then be divided into relationships, actions, and events. The adolescent should be encouraged to (a) note the congruency between personal actions and professed values; (b) reflect on how values have deepened or altered with time; (c) note the influence in his or her life that has led to the acceptance of these values; and (d) consider where these values are leading and the possibility or need to expand or alter present values.

Encourage the adolescent to continually reflect on how he or she is growing and developing various adult commitments as well as what role these values exercise in helping the adolescent to form these initial commitments to adulthood.

Notes to Chapter Five

1. William J. Connolly, S.J., "Contemporary Spiritual Direction: Scope and Principles—An Introductory Essay," *Studies in the Spirituality of Jesuits* 7, June 1975, p. 101.

2. David L. Fleming, S.J., "Models of Spiritual Direction," *Review for Religious* 34, May 1975, 351–357.

3. William J. Connolly, S.J., "Spiritual Direction: It Begins With Experience," *Human Development* 1, Spring 1980, p. 11.

4. For a discussion of the distinction between counseling/psychotherapy and spiritual direction, see Ruth Tiffany Barnhouse, "Spiritual Direction and Psychotherapy," *The Journal of Pastoral Care* 33, September 1979, pp. 149–163; also, Connolly, "Contemporary Spiritual Direction," pp. 119–120.

5. Jean Leplace, S.J., *Preparing for Spiritual Direction*. Chicago: Franciscan Herald Press, 1975, p. 149. This book is an excellent introduction to spiritual direction.

6. Damien Isabell, O.F.M., *The Spiritual Director: A Practical Guide*. Chicago: Franciscan Herald Press, 1976, p. 39. This small book is an excellent practical discussion of spiritual direction.

7. Charles Shelton, S.J., "Some Techniques for Self-Exploration," *The School Counselor* 26, January 1979, pp. 191–192.

8. Eamonn O'Doherty suggests this technique when dealing with adolescent guilt and personal responsibility. *See* O'Doherty's *The Religious Formation of the Adolescent*. New York: Alba House, 1973, pp. 49–52.

9. For an extensive review of role-taking, see: Mark J. Miller, "Role-Playing as a Therapeutic Strategy: A Research Review," *The School Counselor* 27, January 1980, pp. 217–226.

10. Eugene W. Kelly, Jr., and Thomas J. Sweeney, "Typical Faulty Goals of Adolescents: A Base for Counseling," *the School Counselor* 26, March 1979, pp. 236–246.

11. Clifford H. Swensen, "Ego Development and a General Model for Counseling and Psychotherapy," *The Personnel and Guidance Journal* 58, January, 1980, pp. 382–388.

12. Eamonn O'Doherty, *Religious Formation*, p. 15.

13. David R. Leaman, "Confrontation in Counseling," *The Personnel and Guidance Journal* 57, June 1978, pp. 630–633.

14. Evelyn Easton Whitehead and James D. Whitehead, *Christian Life Patterns*. Garden City, NY: Doubleday & Co., 1979, p. 26.

15. For a study of discernment, see: Jacques Guillet, et al., *Discernment of Spirits*. Collegeville, MN: The Liturgical Press, 1970.

16. George A. Aschenbrenner, S.J., "Consciousness Examen," *Review for Religious* 32, January 1972, pp. 14–21.

17. Ibid., p. 15.

18. Merton Strommen, *Five Crises of Youth*. New York: Harper & Row, 1974, pp. 12–32.

19. Louis M. Savary, S.J., "The Thanksgiving Examen," *Review for Religious* 39, March 1980, pp. 238–246.

CHAPTER SIX

Adolescent Morality

*Do not conform yourselves to this age
but be transformed by the renewal of
your mind, so that you may judge what
is God's will, what is good, pleasing,
and perfect.*

Romans 12:2

When we speak of adolescent morality, we do not mean to imply a morality that is unique to adolescents. Rather, by adolescent morality we simply mean to assert that authentic moral decision making by adolescents is often clouded by critical developmental issues that influence and, at times, obfuscate so much of their lives. Adults ministering to youth need to focus on how young people form their own growing, evaluative sense of what they *ought* to do in the context of Jesus' call to "come, follow me."

According to psychologist Ervin Staub, "morality is a set of rules, customs, or principles that regulate people's conduct in relation to other people, conduct that affects human welfare."[1] Morality, therefore, consists of accepting a distinctive scope of behaviors that one believes one ought to adhere to, and that prove to be acceptable in social interactions and interpersonal relations with others. In every culture, these behaviors no doubt have some latitude, and the scope of these behaviors often mirrors the pluralistic make-up of a particular society. Nonetheless, on the one hand, there are behaviors that are encouraged, and on the other hand, there are behaviors that are proscribed, considered unacceptable in the eyes of both the individual and the community. Within Catholic moral thinking, for example, what one *ought* to do has traditionally been labeled *objective morality,* or the *natural-law approach.* Within this framework, through the experience of human reflection, both the individual and the community realize distinct behaviors that foster the common good of the entire human community.[2]

Humans basically come to a moral stance in one or two ways.

First, a person can conform to the external rules and regulations of the group or community of which he or she is a member. This type of morality is called *group* morality because personal standards of behavior are largely determined by forces outside the self. That is to say, personal belief about what is right yields to the group's interpretation of what the right is. On the other hand, a person can internalize a morality that is personal. In this case, a person does not simply take on or conform to the rules and regulations of the group (although certainly individuals must learn from the group). Instead, through a complex process of give-and-take-interaction, a person comes to internalize the values and norms of the community or group and, through reflection and personal evaluation, develops a personal morality, which to some degree is consonant with the group morality or at variance with it.[3] No doubt, for each of us, the internalization of moral principles is a complex interplay of accepting and rejecting group norms that, in turn, fashion a moral stance that each person must then call his or her own.

Currently, there are numerous adult Catholics within the church who have developed (some almost exclusively) an external or group-centered morality that is based on their own religious upbringing. Instead of reflecting on their personal values and considering the various moral choices that foster moral growth, many adult Catholics have accepted the external, group-morality approach. This means that they rely almost exclusively on *authority* as the defining norm in the formation of their moral decisions. In such instances, Catholics appeal to the group—in this case, it is *the church*—to determine what moral behavior is appropriate. Most certainly the church should exert and exercise an integral function in the Catholic's moral decision making. The church's guidance is something every adult Catholic needs to intently listen to as he or she forms personal moral decisions. What is problematic, however, is that such listening can supplant a careful and honest examination of personal values, which actually form the basis for authentic human decision making and personal moral growth.

Conscience and the Adolescent

Catholic theology stresses the important role that conscience exercises in determining right from wrong. In a recent ecclesial document, the Episcopal Conference of Ireland defines conscience in general terms as a "sense of right and wrong and of the fundamental principle that we are to do what is good and avoid what is evil."[4] In a more particular sense, though, conscience can be defined as the attempt "to discern the moral values at stake in particular situations."[5] Conscience, then, is concerned with the ethical guiding of self in concrete human actions. When I answer my conscience, I act freely and responsibly in a manner that professes my values in the concrete existential situation of my life.

Historically, the church has viewed conscience as an essential instrument for ethical decision making.[6] What has developed, however, is a tension between divergent views regarding how we come to make moral decisions. In some circles there has been a concerted emphasis on church law. Yet, on the one hand if church law is overemphasized, an unintentional legalism that can stymie authentic human choosing can appear. On the other hand, some have dismissed the church's guidance while relying almost exclusively on their own opinions and beliefs, and thus have fostered an unreflective moral choice. What emerges, then, from the perspective of human development, is a divergent emphasis. Catholic adults often ask themselves, How can I follow my conscience when my own views might contradict the church? Adolescents, however, generally assert, "I'm going to follow my conscience"—an assertion that often veils a nongrowthful and, at times, harmful moral choice.

Far more helpful to both groups is an approach that respects authentic human choosing in the midst of the believing faith community. Religious educator Robert Friday has stated that, because of a tendency to overemphasize law, many Catholics are still "children" in their moral decision making. Friday believes that "what is needed now is a presentation of the Gospel message in adult terms for individuals whose own lived experience has better prepared them for accepting or rejecting the mature demands of a Christian ethic."[7] The Catholic must be encouraged to accept both the "risk" and the "ambiguity" involved in taking on the personal responsibility of moral decision making. It is true that adult moral decision making means a departure from a secure approach that is regulated by law, but, as Friday concludes, "the risk, the living with ambiguity and limited certainty regarding moral norms, is perhaps the price to be paid for maturity in moral decision making."[8] This emphasis on developing "maturity" in moral decision making is a primary goal for adults who minister to adolescents—those at the high school level and those at the college level.

Three Levels of Conscience

Stressing the importance of conscience in moral decision making can create for many Catholics a dilemma because they sometimes find their own sense of moral right in conflict with what church law has to say about a particular moral problem. What is the Catholic's response in such cases? In an attempt to explore the importance of conscience, to illuminate the dilemmas and conflicts that can arise, and to further enhance the richness of the meaning of conscience, moral theologian Timothy O'Connell has suggested that conscience be viewed in a three-fold dimension.[9]

Conscience 1   The first level of conscience reflects humanity's acceptance of responsibility for what is right and wrong. It is true that there are numerous ideas about what is right, but as humans we are charged to discover, by virtue of our humanity, what is *good* in the concrete reality of our human situation. This first level of conscience is not predisposed to complacency but continually challenges each of us through responsible human actions to search for the *moral good* in every life decision.

Conscience 2   When we then consider the human reasoning that gives meaning to my moral actions, then we are focusing on the second level of conscience. Conscience at this level is the actual understanding I have of various issues and concerns that influence my judgment of a particular act. It is at this level that human beings disagree on what is morally right. During the shrill, convulsive early seventies, for example, I might have believed in all sincerity that voting for George McGovern was unconscionable in view of what I perceived to be his extreme positions on many political and social issues. On the other hand, a friend might have viewed the unlawful activities of the Nixon administration and the revelations of Watergate to be so reprehensible that George McGovern was clearly the only acceptable candidate. Certainly in such a situation both my friend and I are acting morally, because we both perceive what is the rightful good and follow our conscience in the carrying out of our civic duty. Nonetheless, we disagree on what we must do.

This type of disagreement spills over into religious issues, and it is at this level, Conscience 2, that the individual Catholic and the church encounter disagreement. Examples of these conflicts could be social policies (foreign policy decisions such as military aid to certain governments, positions on capital punishment, a constitutional amendment on abortion) or personal issues (pre-marital sexuality, for example, or birth control, or abortion). O'Connell wisely labels conscience at this level a "fragile reality," one that is in need of the insights and advice of others to help correct false assumptions and all-too-fallible reasoning. For a great variety of reasons, Conscience 2 is capable of mistakes, distortions, and false reasoning. In helping to form this conscience, the church, as the community of the Spirit, represents a fundamental source of guidance and truth. Yet it is at this level that the developmental issues of adolescence impinge on the young person's evaluative sense of right and wrong. Various life issues can distort the adolescent's growing moral sense and lead to decisions that are based on developmental needs rather than on a clear sense of what is morally right.

Conscience 3   It is at the third level of conscience, however, that I encounter conscience as an infallible guide. Conscience 3 simply cannot be disobeyed. It is at this level that I commit myself to what I genuinely and honestly understand to be the right course of action. In effect, I am saying, "I must do this, because I *believe* it is the right thing to do." Consequently, I might actually do something that is wrong, but experience no sinfulness. My reasoning from Conscience 2 might be false, but if conscience at this level judges my action to be morally right, then in the concrete reality of this situation, I must obey my conscience, that is, Conscience 3. Quoting moral theologian Bernard Häring, O'Connell explains that "everyone, of course, must ultimately follow his conscience; this means he must do right as he sees the right [Conscience 3] with desire and effort to find and do what is right [Conscience 2]."[10]

Hence, adolescent utterances and actions regarding various social behaviors, attitudes toward sexuality, and rebellion against rules and authority often characterize the reasoning of Conscience 2, which is objectively questionable or even harmful to both moral and psychological growth. Yet, from an evaluative standpoint, the adolescent accepts this reasoning and sincerely believes his or her action to be morally acceptable.

The formation of adolescent conscience opens up three vital areas that need to be discussed. First, we need to examine what we mean by a *mature* conscience. Second, we need to explore the various *developmental issues*, which the adolescent faces in the high school and college years, that influence conscience formation. Third, we need to provide some *reflective instrument* that will aid the adolescent's own self-reflection on his or her personal moral life and, in turn, will provide the opportunity for deepening moral growth.

The Mature Conscience   It is not a simple process to develop maturity in one's conscience. Rather, it is a lifelong task of ongoing openness and critical self-reflection, a process of actualizing personal moral commitments, and the continually searching for deeper truths and meanings based on the experiences of life. Certainly, then, the forming of a conscience is intimately tied to the New Testament teaching that proclaims the response to Jesus' call is never a decisive "Yes," but a gradual process of continual conversion.[11]

Ewert Cousins has characterized the mature conscience as having three essential characteristics.[12] First, the mature conscience grasps with greater clarity its own *ambiguity* and *limitation*. In this regard, the mature person comes to acknowledge human limitations, the actual existence of evil, and what can and cannot be done in any concrete human situation. But the limits that Christians acknowledge are not sources for despair; rather, the presence of Christ and the Spirit are an essential source of strength and the underpinning for the work and action that Christians perform in the world, as well as for our own commitment to true Christian discipleship.

Second, the mature conscience is capable of understanding that growth in the spiritual life involves *suffering* in this world. The mature Christian conscience adds to this awareness of suffering an appreciation of the death and resurrection of Jesus Christ. As a consequence, growth in the Christian life is not a simple, idealistic adventure of variegated experiences. It entails the call to discipleship—a call that makes demands and exacts sacrifices.

Third, the mature conscience implies an acceptance of *responsibility* for our life and actions. As we grow older, it also incorporates responsibility toward others and various commitments to communal and social undertakings outside the family. And the focus of this responsibility has currently extended beyond the confines of our own society and culture to include other cultures and peoples. This responsibility includes an awareness of how our present life behaviors will shape and influence life for future generations.

Conscience and the Church

In helping the adolescent to form his or her conscience, the church needs to proclaim the deepest values and meanings that will enlighten the young person about "the way, and the truth, and the life" (John 14:6). Adults who minister to adolescents need to give particular attention to aiding them, as they form their consciences, in the assimilation of the church's guiding message. Ultimately, adolescents need to see the importance of the church community as they form their moral decisions (1 Cor 12:12–14).

As we have seen, the importance of the church's influence is sometimes difficult for adolescents to comprehend. Adolescents are often so engulfed in various developmental issues, peer group influences, and re-evaluations of their own lives that they tend to disregard the church's message. Timothy O'Connell advances three reasons why the church must be given special consideration in the area of moral decision making.[13] First, our complex and searching world needs the *moral leadership* that the church can provide. Second, the church presents a unique international flavor that encompasses a *cumulative wisdom* —a wisdom that allows her to speak with an authentic voice that is beyond other institutions or groups of peoples. Third, the church is *imbued with the Spirit,* and is guided by it. This does not mean that every decision of the church is infallible; the church rarely makes solemn declarations of an infallible nature. Yet, the presence of the Spirit gives great merit and persuasion to the church's pronouncements. It is important, therefore, to stress the role of the church in coming to authentic moral decisions.

Likewise, theologian Charles Curran has commented on the place of the conscience in Christian life.[14] The notion of conscience has previously been weighed down, Curran says, by an overemphasis on law. We need to lessen the emphasis on law and place greater importance on personal responsibility and relationships. Moreover, the human person as the agent of a moral act needs greater emphasis. In addition, the understanding of conscience usually has unduly stressed the cognitive element while paying little attention to the affective dimension of conscience. Finally, more emphasis needs to be given to how the Christian actually comes to a decision. We must very carefully ask how a person actually makes decisions in his or her life. Curran's points are particularly appropriate for the adolescent years. Adolescents need to center their concerns on responsibility, relationships, affective responses, and personal decision making. Each of these factors is a critical influence in the young person's life and each helps the adolescent to deepen his or her quest for maturity.

In other writings, Curran remarks that two important characteristics for the Christian conscience must be the stress on *communal relationships* and the *development of creativity*.[15] In terms of relational understandings, the person needs to realize his or her relational commitment to both God and neighbor. We view here the socio-personal nature of the human conscience. In terms of creativity, the Christian increasingly moves away from legalistic tendencies and, under the guidance of the Spirit, is led to create unique and personal ways to labor in God's Kingdom.

Toward an Adult Conscience

During the adolescent years, ethical decision making takes on a more adult form. Irene Josselyn notes that, through this process of growth, two dynamic processes are very much part of the adolescent's experience. First, in the adolescent's world there is a parental "symbolization" as conscience. In other words, the adolescent's parents may actually take on the role of conscience. An ambivalent rebellion often flows out of this situation. Thus, at some times the adolescent desires the parent's guidance and control, but at other times the adolescent seeks his or her freedom and rejects any type of parental influence. Second, there emerges the peer group, which has an integral role in helping the adolescent define his or her values and provides him or her with security. In this peer interaction, the adolescent group is often seen devising its own specific rules and behavior, both of which weigh heavily on the adolescent's own personal decision making.

In attempting to minister to adolescents, particularly in the area of mature, ethical decision making, we often find a tension between the adolescent's decision and the views of the teaching church's magisterium. Although we acknowledge the gratuitous and free nature of grace in faith and the Vatican Council II's proclamation on religious liberty, we also find a strong tendency to uphold the magisterium on all counts. Analyzing the official catechetical documents, Thomas Sullivan has concluded that the emphasis is heavily weighted toward endorsement of the church's magisterial teaching.[16] He quotes the statement, *Sharing the Light of Faith:* "When faced with questions which pertain to dissent from noninfallible teaching of the Church, it is important for catechists to keep in mind that the presumption is always in favor of the magisterium."[17]

Still, even though the formulation presents the notion in "muted" and "timid" form, Sullivan concludes that this call for "presumption" recognizes the possibility of respectful dissent from nonbinding church teachings. Sullivan observes that for a catechetical program to be successful, there must be the "freedom" for the person to reflectively evaluate what is right and wrong. This position, of course, parallels the statement of Vatican Council II in which we find the assertion that "young people have a right to be encouraged to weigh moral values with an upright conscience, and to embrace them by personal choice."[18]

Again, of course, the instruction of youth must pay particular attention to the cumulative wisdom of church teaching as an authentic, viable force in personal decision making.

Toward a Christian Adult Conscience

Particularly in adolescence, the threshold for Christian adulthood, ministry to youth must seriously consider the issues that are central in the formation of the *Christian* adult conscience. Several important points need exploring before ministers can help adolescents effectively deal with the formation of their conscience.

First, the adolescent quest for deeper relational experiences blends well with the current theological emphasis on the Christian life as a *relational* encounter with God through Jesus Christ. Conscience formation among adolescents needs to accentuate the adolescent's personal relationship with Jesus Christ along with the commitment and obligations that flow out of this relationship. The relational emphasis also receives support from the current emphasis on sin as a relational phenomenon. The real essence of sin, advises Robert Friday, is "breaking or rupturing the loving personal relationship between the human person and God, a relationship initiated by God and accepted in Christian baptism."[19] This relational understanding of sin complements moral theology's current focus on a fundamental life choice that reflects one's deepest life stance toward God. We call the rupturing of this fundamental relationship "serious sin"; traditional theology has called this rupturing "mortal sin."

From this perspective, the serious disruption of a personal relationship with God, although certainly possible, is likely to be infrequent. With adolescents, this fundamental break in one's relationship with God is quite uncommon but *still possible*. This does not mean, of course, that adolescents are immune from culpability in their moral action. Sin is most certainly part of all human existence and certainly occurs in the adolescent's life. It is extremely important that adults who minister to youth not minimize an adolescent's capacity to commit sin. Although such an attitude is well intentioned, this perspective actually shortchanges youth. If we take away adolescents' capacity to commit sin, we take away their capacity to need the redemptive experience of Jesus Christ. Thus, along with the numerous psychological factors and developmental issues that often cloud the responsibility that adolescents take for their actions, adults need to be aware of and be capable of discussing with youth their own dispositions, tendencies, and habits that predispose them to commit sinful actions.

The growing into Christian adulthood is just that—a process of *growth* that includes advancement, setbacks, retreats, successes, and disappointments. Adolescents, too, need to be viewed in this growth perspective because it accentuates the strengthening of their own relational bond with God through Jesus Christ. Perhaps Richard McCormick best summarized this notion when he remarked that "the moral-spiritual life is a gradual unfolding (or drying up) of our personal beings as Christians."[20] Clearly, in our ministry to adolescents, this emphasis on growth and on the personal, deepening relationship with Jesus deserves primary weight.

The Christian life is, after all, the deepening of our relationship with God as we experienced it in our personal relationship with Jesus Christ. More than anything, the conscience formation of adolescents must speak to the growing adolescent relationship to Jesus. It is Jesus who strengthens, who supports, who sustains, who challenges, and who forgives the adolescent when he or she does not answer His call to "come, follow me." It is the graced encounter of this ever deepening relationship that touches the adolescent and

213

leads him or her to understand the call of discipleship and respond to it more fully.

When we focus on this personal relationship with Jesus, it is important for us to stress that this relational commitment should be lived in a believing community of faith, where the person lives in relation to others, called first in baptism, and then nourished and sustained by the Bread of Life, the Eucharist. As the adolescent grows in maturity, his or her moral stance becomes increasingly tied to friendship with Jesus (John 15:15), so that, in future years, the maturing adolescent might echo St. Paul and come to say with him, "The life I live now is not my own; Christ is living in me" (Gal 2:20). Furthermore, in moral choices, the adolescent increasingly realizes that his or her selections involve the call to *real discipleship*. Through the personal, relational experience of Jesus as a friend, the adolescent grows to truly understand that suffering, disappointment, and hardship are part of his or her response to Jesus' invitation, "come, follow me."

Second, moral growth in adolescence must also take into account the central features of the *identity acquisition* that preoccupies so much of the adolescent's experience. The adolescent develops a greater sense of self which comes increasingly to act both freely and responsibly in making personal moral decisions. This process is a gradual one, however, and is sometimes painful. Making decisions regarding relationships, work, college, career choices, sexuality, values, and a philosophy of life help to shape this unfolding sense of self during the adolescent years. And the growing acquisition of personal selfhood allows the adolescent to more freely make moral decisions. Thus, as the adult helps the adolescent to greater moral growth through conscience formation, emphasis must be given to fostering these various facets of the adolescent's life and integrating these experiences with the developing self. Authentic moral decisions for adolescents flow from this integration of self and experience.

Third, conscience formation in the adolescent years must place increasing stress on fostering Christian values. It may well be that insisting that the adolescent conform to rules and regulations and assimilate those behaviors that are socially acceptable will produce desirable behaviors in the adolescent, but such approaches hardly allow the adolescent the freedom to make an authentic response to Jesus' invitation. We need to encourage deeper Christian values:

"love, joy, peace patient endurance, kindness, generosity, faith, mildness and chastity" (Gal 5:22). Likewise, we need to ask whether the environment in which we interact with the adolescent mirrors these values.

Adolescent conscience formation must seek to answer not only the question, Who I am?, but also the equally important question, What am I about? It is in answering this second question that the adolescent's life is consciously affected by values that reflect who he or she really is. It is in the adolescent's deepening concern for values that he or she really comes to realize the call of Jesus and respond to it.

Finally, conscience formation in the adolescent years must not be isolated from the larger issue of the lived faith of the *community*. Particularly during the adolescent years, youth need the ratifying experience of a vibrant community that nourishes and sustains the adolescent's forming of values and commitments. The church must provide the environment for "moral discourse"[21] in which adolescents can reflect on, inquire into, and challenge their own moral stances and others in order to foster and deepen their own evaluative responses. It would be unreasonable to expect adolescents to arrive at mature ethical decisions without the experience of the nurturing and sustaining church community that speaks to their developmental needs. For this reason, then, ever greater attention should be given to youth retreats, youth ministry, and campus ministry programs that help to foster this experience of community.

The strategies, techniques, and questions interspersed throughout chapters 3, 4, and 5 are offered as suggestions to help enhance the adolescent's moral growth. It is hoped that through the adult-adolescent interaction, the adolescent can come to a deepening evaluative response that will indicate this growing commitment to Christian values.

Developmental Issues

As in other areas of the adolescent's life, we are struck by the importance of developmental issues that influence conscience formation. The developmental aspects of adolescence, particularly the emotional and cognitive changes that adolescents undergo, deeply influence both their relationship to Jesus and their attempts at living a life of true Christian commitment. Consequently, the formation of

the adolescent's conscience is intimately related to the central maturation issues that are so commonplace during these adolescent
years. As young persons progress through the secondary and college years toward adulthood, they experience an increase of freedom and the accompanying need to use this newly found freedom
in responsible, Christian ways. As we have seen, for early adolescents, the separation from parents and the formation of peer group
support exert a profound influence on moral decision making. In
middle adolescence, concern with identity needs and the demands
of initial, possibly intense relational encounters with peers can
sometimes unduly influence the adolescent's life. Finally, in late
adolescence, the growing solidification of personal identity and the
ever widening demands for intimacy combine with an expanding
outward attention to studies, career choices, and a developing philosophy of life. Taken together, these factors sometimes confuse—
and can actually sway—the adolescent's deepening evaluative
stance. For the experiences of these developmental years soon bring
adolescents to realize that previous answers and values will no
longer suffice. As the adolescent more and more confronts the complexity, ambiguity, and uncertainty of the world, the cumulative
wisdom that has been gathered during these developmental years
should lead the adolescent to reflect a value system that is personally meaningful and coincides with the values that (a) find Jesus
more and more at the center (Col 1:15–19), and (b) are lived in a
faith community that proclaims and nutures such values.

Yet developmental issues often sway the adolescent to foresake
the call of Jesus. Religious educator James DiGiacomo notes that
adolescents tend to champion ideals and religious values on a theoretical plane, but in the practical order, they display a remarkable
"realism."[22] In other words, adolescents gravitate toward the material aspects of our secular culture, just as their elders do, and are—
rather predictably—like everyone else. They give notional assent to
the importance of the Christian ideal, yet they are moved by the
stark reality of cultural influences to accept compromises as well as a
secular culture that prizes advancement, power, and material gain.

In the same vein, psychologist John Mitchell has captured the
"hypocritical" nature of the adolescent experience, which results in
"their desire for social acceptance, their need to explore forbidden
pleasures, and their preoccupation with the present [which]

216

incline[s] them toward social pragmatism and self-centered expedience—the nuclear ingredients of all hypocrisy."[23] Thus, the adolescent's developmental needs, which thread themselves throughout the high school and college years, allow for the possibility of hypocritical behavior. Ironically, adolescents can readily discern hypocrisy in adults, but are often blinded to the same behavior in themselves. Mitchell writes that this adolescent "hypocrisy" results from several new experiences. For one, adolescents are forced into many situations (family, school) in which they are expected to show satisfaction and contentment when, in reality, they feel uneasy and dissatisfied. Likewise, they are often expected to deny, or at least not indicate, various inner feelings in certain social situations. Furthermore, in their need for social acceptance, adolescents are sometimes prone to subject other peers to embarrassment in order to enhance their own prestige. Eventually, according to Mitchell, this hypocritical behavior must be confronted. "Thus, a natural consequence of adolescent social interaction is a crisis in moral viewpoint, usually occurring during the late adolescent years after the turmoil of early adolescence has taken its toll."[24]

Mitchell's notion of the "hypocritical" adolescent parallels James Fowler's assertion that adolescents express a synthetic-conventional stage of faith development. As we have discussed in chapter 3, Fowler observes that adolescents often exhibit a compartmentalization of their behaviors. This compartmentalizing behavior leads the adolescent to display different behaviors, depending on the group with which he or she is interacting, e.g., peers, family, sports team, etc. This diversity (and contradiction) in the adolescent's behavior reflect the young person's attempts to deal with the complexities arising from the growing demands of adulthood.

Similarly, we have noted that adolescents tend to rely on significant others, particularly their own peers, as guides for their moral reasoning. Once adolescents arrive at the threshold of making deeper commitments, they often resort to a morality that is individualistic ("I can do what I want") before they arrive at a stance in which personal commitment and respect for others are determining factors in their moral reasoning.

The phrase "follow your conscience," therefore, takes on special significance during the adolescent years. Ideally, as we have said, this phrase represents an authentic moral stance that has been arrived at from openness, prayer, and deeper reflection; in the adolescent years, however, as a result of the developmental urgencies that accompany this period, this utterance is all too often a license to do whatever the adolescent desires.[25]

In conclusion, the adolescent conscience cannot be discussed without attending to the vast array of influences and developmental issues that preoccupy so much of the adolescent experience. When ministering to adolescents, then, adults need to discern these various developmental factors in the adolescent's struggle to achieve a personally meaningful value system that reflects a maturing evaluative stance.

The Decalog for Adolescent Self-Reflection

Having examined the place and function of conscience, it is important to move toward an actual content for Christian decision making, for Christian decision making needs clear, substantive values, and must give witness to an authentic Christian commitment. Adolescents are particularly receptive to the use of an instrument that can aid interior self-reflection and responsible moral decision making. There is, however, the matter of what criteria or guidelines can be used for developing Christian decision making and reflectively growing in it. *Sharing the Light of Faith*, the National Catechetical Directory, has noted that, in moral matters, the Ten Commandments, the Sermon on the Mount (especially the Beatitudes), and Jesus' discourse at the Last Supper, as well as personal prayer, catechetical instruction, and sacramental participation are sound bases for growth in conscience and moral development.[26]

To further deepen the adolescent's basis for Christian decision making we turn to a recurrent theme throughout this book, the call of Jesus. In Mark's Gospel (10:17–21), a young man asks Jesus about eternal life. Jesus responds that in order to obtain this life, the man must follow the Commandments. The young man replies that he has done this. Thereupon, Jesus says, "There is one thing more you must do. Go and sell what you have and give to the poor; you will then have treasure in heaven. After that, come, follow me." The Gospel relates that the young man, for whom riches were important, was "sad" and went away. Might we not glean from this story something much more profound than the contrast between riches and poverty? Jesus was saying that His invitation must touch the person at the deepest level. In following Jesus, the deepest part of the self is affirmed. Jesus' call is about life—the total commitment to the Gospel message to which each Christian is called—to live life fully in service to Him. The call of Jesus beckons us to constant growth and conversion through the affirming of our own lives. The question for the Christian, then, is, How do my actions and behaviors affirm the deepest part of my own self—my life lived fully and totally in service of Him?

The Ten Commandments can provide such guidelines; the Decalog can truly be a strategy for affirming life. In the scene from Mark's Gospel, the deeper question asked is: What is real life? What is the good to which we are all called? Jesus beckons the young man not to fulfill numerous regulations and rules, not to go off and simply do what he desires, but rather, to follow Him, to look to Jesus as his source of strength, to find in Jesus' life the real presence of God and what this means for his own life. The Decalog, then, can be a way for us to be personally responsible for our lives.[27] As such, at the deepest core of ourselves, we take responsibility for who and what we are, for what we value, and for what we do. In this way, we affirm not only our very selves, but also Jesus' invitation to "come, follow me."

Recall that in the first chapter we viewed adolescence as a distinctive time that is echoed in the words of Ecclesiastes 3. It is a time for searching, questioning, and deciding. It is a time when moral decision making is increasingly interwoven in the context of developmental issues; it is a search for values, and a desire for deeper responses to life and its demands. Like the young man, the adolescent is invited to respond to Jesus' call, but as the adolescent approaches young adulthood, he or she experiences this call in a much deeper and more profound way.

Historically, the Commandments were a way for Israel to celebrate, ratify, and embrace the community's faithfulness toward God. In our time, too, the Decalog can be a means for ratifying what is deepest in life. The Commandments can be a road map, a strategy for the adolescent's journeying on the road to Jesus' call. The Commandments can speak of what is good, of what is of value, of what life at its deepest meaning really and truly is. The Decalog is especially helpful to adolescents for the following reasons:

219

1   The Decalog affirms life and points up constant growthful, life-enhancing behaviors. Adolescents need this growth in personal moral decision making, which in turn mirrors the continual growth that is taking place within them.

2   The Decalog offers adolescents a valid instrument for interior self-reflection. Given the increased cognitive and affective capacities of adolescents, they must now undertake interior reflection on personal moral decisions and their implications.

3   The Decalog speaks to specific values that challenge adolescents to conversion and greater growth.

4   The Decalog encourages responsible behavior and invites adolescents to accept responsibility for themselves in relation to both God and their neighbor.

The Decalog is presented here as an instrument for adolescent self-reflection. Each Commandment is cited and briefly explained; this is followed by a number of self-reflecting questions to aid adolescents in their own reflection. The questions can be used in personal dialog, small group discussions, classroom presentations, lectures, retreats, or personal counseling.

1 *I, the Lord, am your God, who brought you out of the land of Egypt, that place of slavery. You shall not have other gods beside me.* (Ex 20:1–3)

Explanation   The first commandment proclaims the origin of life itself. It speaks of God's presence, of the Transcendent bursting forth within the human community. Just as God has arisen in the human community, so, too, must the human person emerge as a free, responsible member of a community—a community whose life mirrors God's presence and whose presence is life-giving to others. This God beckons each of us to an exclusive relationship, a relational existence that is demanding, all-encompassing, and unique.

Questions   The first commandment poses several questions for adolescents:

How do I live my life in thankfulness to God for all that He has done? How do my actions and behaviors show this thankfulness? What actions and behaviors fail to show my thankfulness to God? What are my talents and resources? List these talents. How do I give them back to God? Are there ways I can make better use of these talents?

Are there moments in my life when this presence of God is experienced (in prayer, for example, or in relational encounters)? Do I find time for prayer to acknowledge God's presence? Do life experiences such as disappointments, crises, and unexpected happenings, draw me closer to God? Can I find God's presence in these experiences? Can I talk about a recent hurt or disappointment and how I have grown from this experience?

Have I noticed growth in my relationship with God from these ever expanding experiences?

How do my future life work, plans, college choices, career, and personal relationships give me a truer vision of God (Mt 6:24)?

Do I experience Jesus as the source of my life (1 Cor 8:4–6)?

What place do money, comforts, power, control, pride, greed, and jealousy have in my life, and how do they influence various aspects of my work, relationships, and future plans? What are these "false gods" that occupy my life? Can I list them? How do I deal with these "false gods?"

2 *You shall not take the name of the Lord, your God, in vain.* (Ex 20:7)

Explanation   One of the most individual characteristics of a person is his or her name. A name gives a person meaning and defines the person in relation to others. In uttering God's name, I refer to my relationship with Him. Using His name demonstrates His presence in our lives as well as the need we have to be attentive to His name by showing both respect and homage. God's name embraces what is prayerful, contentful, strong, and dignified. This God whose name we utter has a profound impact on our life story. His relationship with us challenges us in our everyday actions.

Questions   We must seriously consider whether we respond to this name in gratitude or attempt to control both God and our neighbor as a way to mask our insecurities and selfish desires. We must ask ourselves the following questions:

How is my gratitude to God realized in my life? In my family? In my work? In my school? In play?

Am I watchful and reverent when using God's name in public utterances, oaths, and everyday conversation? Do I show proper humililty and reverence for God's name?

In what ways has my knowing God made a difference in my life here and now? Make a list.

Do I dwell on my own desires and wishes rather than acknowledge my need for God's presence?

3 *Remember to keep holy the sabbath day.* (Ex 20:8)

Explanation   This third commandment points to the celebration of life. This commandment reminds us that life needs strengthening and renewal. This commandment challenges us to view life as a celebration. We must concentrate on the extent to which our personal lives are a source of renewal and celebration of God's life in us. We must try to create an atmosphere for others in which life is celebrative and freeing for them. Our behaviors, attitudes, and thoughts must show continual renewal and growth in God's presence.

Questions   When reflecting with adolescents, we might inquire about the following:

How do our behaviors, actions, and words help us to celebrate and renew life? Are we joyful in living life? Does our presence give joy to others? Do we find time to thank God for this gift of life that He has given us? Do we utilize all our talents and resources to grow and renew both ourselves and others?

Can others see the presence of Jesus in our lives (Gal 2:20)?

Do we set aside time to celebrate God's gift of life to us in the church community? In the Eucharist? In prayer?

Do new experiences, people, and events challenge us to grow more deeply in God's love? How is this done?

How do patience, tolerance, and openness reflect our own vision of life?

Do we encourage others to celebrate life and realize their gifts?

Can we view our lives as a source of constant renewal? That is, can present insecurities, joys, disappointments, and fears, as well as the burdens and joys of past experiences be accepted and constitute part of our renewal of life? In turn, can we find deeper meanings from these events and find them as celebrations of our own growth?

Is prayer part of the renewal of our lives? How do we pray?

4 *Honor your father and your mother, that you may have a long life in the land which the Lord, your God, is giving you.* (Ex 20:12)

Explanation   The fourth commandment deals with the respect

and obedience we owe our parents. Yet we can view this commandment in a much wider perspective. To respect life goes beyond parental support. It constitutes the recognition that our lives have been
influenced by past generations, traditions, and our own life history
up to the present moment. As a human community, we need the
guidance and cumulative wisdom of past generations. In light of our
past and its influence upon us, this commandment challenges us to
take responsibility for life, here and now. It calls us to be responsible
for our own actions. At the same time, we are called to a life stance
that includes open communication with others (authorities, traditions, customs, and the social milieu) so that we can discover those
behaviors that are most life-enhancing. Through the exercise of responsible behavior, we discover what is truly meant by sharing life
with others.

Questions   We might suggest the following questions to
adolescents:

Do we admit the need to listen to the advice of authorities and
accept counsel from them? How well do we listen?

Is our criticism of others, especially those in authority, both
honest and respectful?

When we challenge authority, can we honestly ask why we are
making this challenge? As a result of this challenge, are we really
more loving? More caring? More responsible?

As we have matured, do we use our greater experience of freedom in caring and loving ways?

In what ways are we respectful of our family? Parents? Brothers
and sisters?

Do our reactions toward authority avoid both blind obedience
and unfounded criticism?

Have we profited from the experiences of our lives and grown
in responsible behaviors? In what ways do we still need to grow in
our responsibility?

5 *You shall not kill* (Ex 20: 13)

Explanation   The fifth commandment reflects society's concern for human life. For contemporary Christians, this concern for
life extends to the human community. We are called to a universal
concern for our brothers and sisters—a concern that takes an ex-

panding view of life. This commandment is both personal and communal, for we not only grow interiorly, but we also call others to personal growth and affirmation. Thus, we encourage and challenge others to be responsible for their own lives.

Questions   We might suggest that adolescents ask themselves the following questions:

How do we show support and respect for ourselves as persons?

Do we engage in behaviors (drugs, habits, compulsions, and narrow attitudes) that are not life-enhancing, that prevent either our own growth or another's growth? Reflect on society's laws and institutions to see how they affirm life and also how they might be unfair and actually limit life.

Do we have personal life stances on various life issues such as abortion, euthanasia, war, self-defense, and capital punishment? Or are we attempting to formulate positions on these issues? Do we understand these issues? Why do we hold certain positions on any of these issues? What are the Christian values underlying our position? Do we understand the complexity of these issues? Can we understand opinions on these issues that differ from our own? When dealing with these issues, no matter how complex the situation, do we attempt to affirm life in whatever way is possible?

In what ways are we angry toward others? Can we acknowledge these feelings? How do we deal with them? Can we forgive others? In what ways do we each need forgiveness? Do we harbor ill will toward others? If so, can we understand why?

Do we harbor resentments of others? Do we brood over happenings and relationships in unhealthy, ungrowthful ways?

6 You shall not commit adultery (Ex 20:14)
(From a theological perspective, the ninth commandment, Ex 2:17,
can be subsumed under the sixth commandment.)

Explanation   Christians today have come to see the sixth commandment as protecting life through the covenant of the marriage bond. Likewise, this commandment leads us to a theological understanding of the forming of life itself. Life is a process of God's continuous, creative endeavors carried on through our own Christian service and ministry toward others. We proclaim life lived-in-relation-to-God by challenging ourselves, our relationships, and our society to fuller and more responsible humanity.

Questions   We might discuss together with adolescents the following questions:

Do our relationships, friendships, and experiences with others lead us to true growth in the Lord? In what ways do they not lead to this growth?

Do our commitments to others evince commitment to both human growth and our love for God?

Do our relationships foster faithfulness and fidelity toward others?

Do we help others "create" their own selves through care, support, and acceptance of them?

Are we aware of our limitations in relationships—the way we manifest selfishness and insecurities in our relationships? What are these ways? How might we control others?

How do we view our own sexuality? What role does Jesus exercise in our deepening understanding of our own sexual self?

Do we use our sexuality as a sign of God's love and a realization of faithfulness and true commitment?

Do we lust? Do we control others through the use of our sexuality?

Do we stereotype members of the other sex?

Are we faithful and life-enhancing to friends, family, and others in our lives?

Do we view ourselves as instruments of God's love in relationships?

7 You shall not steal (Ex 20:15)
(From a theological perspective, the tenth commandment, Ex 20:17,
can be subsumed under the seventh commandment.)

Explanation   The seventh commandment can be viewed in light of our personal need for the freedom to create a community that is nurturing and life-enhancing. As Christians, we are co-creators with God, helping to create His Kingdom in our own communities. We are free, responsible human beings who deserve personal space and basic necessities to make our own contribution to the human community. We contribute to society through both who we are and what we have to offer to others. At the same time, we are aware that we must recognize others' freedom to possess their own goods and personal space, too. By developing our own talents, by partaking in the workings of society, by accepting the challenge to transform the world to build a new human community, we become a co-creator with God. Our personal activities enhance life, for we are the means through which God's creating presence fills the world. Therefore, we must ask whether we use our talents in an honest and creative way to enhance life for all peoples.

Questions   We might suggest that adolescents ask themselves the following questions:

Do we make a positive contribution to our own growth and the growth of others through honest work, study, and other life-enhancing activities?

Do we respect both the rights and property of others?

Do we have an attitude of humility whereby our endeavors work to realize and broaden the development of others and do not just proclaim our own accomplishments? In what ways is this done or not done?

Can we learn from others?

Do we compliment and encourage others to use their gifts and talents?

Are we envious of others' gifts and talents?

8 You shall not bear false witness against your neighbor (Ex 20:16)

Explanation   The eighth commandment seeks to protect the reputation of the person. It is not possible for life to be enhanced if personal integrity is denied. The critical issue in this commandment is a person's right to fuller self-expression. Do our actions create an atmosphere in which we might express ourselves and, in turn, allow others to express themselves in an honest and forthright manner. Does such discourse allow for the fullest expression of human growth in both ourselves and others.

Questions   We can ask adolescents the following questions:

Do we speak about others in accurate and responsible ways?

Do we "build others up" in our communication with them?

If there is misunderstanding between ourselves and another, can we give the other the benefit of the doubt? Can we forgive others?

Do we respect the privacy of others?

Do we respect the confidences of those who confide in us?

Do we maintain stereotypes and prejudices of other groups of peoples?

Are we open toward others? Do we attempt to get to know others?

Do we act in a hypocritical manner? That is, do we act in certain ways with one group of friends and in different ways with others? What particular behaviors reflect this two-sidedness in us? How might we alter this behavior?

Do our actions and behaviors really express our inner feelings and attitudes?

The Sacrament of Reconciliation: Some Reflections

Pastorally speaking, one of the most difficult areas for dialoging with the adolescent focuses on his or her participation in the Sacrament of Reconciliation. Especially as young persons progress through adolescence, they show increasing disinclination toward the Sacrament of Reconciliation. This sacrament, says theologian Jared Wicks, "is both a sacrament of reconciliation and healing. Its reconciliation heals the fractured relationships with God's people and with God himself. The healing grace it confers transforms hearts for living a reconciled life."[28] This sacrament proclaims the mission of Jesus who, in His own ministry, healed sinners and forgave their sins (Mk 2:5; Luke 7:48). The need for this sacrament is universal; everyone needs this sacrament, for "we are all sinners, not just those seriously estranged from God and the Church, and we all find here an opportunity to confront our sinfulness, acknowledge our need for conversion, seek pardon and peace, and celebrate our union with the healing, merciful Christ and His Church."[29]

Nonetheless, adolescents often distance themselves from this sacrament. This developmental period of adolescence, encompassing a ten-year span, is a time of change. Indeed, sometimes everything seems tentative for the adolescent. It is a time of re-evaluation, a time of questions, a time during which the pursuit of truth and values readily comes to the forefront. When "sin" is experienced during adolescence, it is often the result of the characteristic adolescent retreat into the self or the adolescent response to the familiar admonition to "do your own thing." The searching and re-evaluation of adolescence might also lead young persons to take refuge in the safety of the peer group and relinquish their personally held beliefs, which are now abandoned for the solace of peer morality.[30] Thus, the Sacrament of Reconciliation must speak to these experiences in the adolescent's life in order to foster both growth and healing.

Several suggestions can be made for using this sacrament with adolescents.

1 Because the "group" is a pivotal influence in the adolescent years, it is often advantageous to present this sacrament in a group setting. For example, the sacrament might be adminstered within the setting of an athletic team, a school class, a retreat group, a social club, or a dormitory floor. This approach is often a supportive experience.

2 Because relationships are a major concern for adolescents, discussions of this sacrament should be placed in the context of the young person's relationship with God and neighbor. Focus on sin as relational and stress this aspect in all discussions of this sacrament.

3 When adolescents do realize personal transgressions, stress the healing and forgiving aspects of the sacrament. At the same time, however, the significance of this sacrament should not be limited to this healing and forgiving experience. Rather, discuss the sacrament in terms of where this experience now leads the adolescent. What conversion might follow from this experience? What growth might take place? How does this sacramental reception aid the adolescent on the road to Christian maturity? The thrust of this sacrament must have a definite future orientation.

4 Discuss this sacrament in the context of the values it represents. We have already stressed the fundamental importance of values in the adolescent's moral growth. Explore the adolescent's own experiences of forgiveness and healing. How important are these events in the adolescent's life? Likewise, how does the adolescent show forgiveness and healing to others? Does he or she place any priority on showing forgiveness and healing to others?

5 Discuss together with the adolescent and reflect on the deep bond between this sacrament and the life of Jesus. Because relational demands and needs are so strong in adolescence, they emphasize Jesus as healer, friend, and reconciler.[31] It is essential that adolescents experience this sacrament as a personal call from

Jesus to share His life, despite our own personal weaknesses (2 Cor 12:10).

6 Regardless of what dialog might take place, adolescents will often exhibit alienation from this sacrament. In a pastoral context, it is best to minister to the individual needs of the adolescent. In dialog with each adolescent, we must emphasize our own acceptance of the adolescent and help him or her to grow in personal reflection and self-insight.

Notes to Chapter Six

1. Ervin Staub, *Positive Social Behavior and Morality: Social and Personal Influences*, vol. 1. New York: Academic Press, 1978, p. 10.

2. For a deeper understanding of the natural law tradition, see Timothy E. O'Connell, *Principles for a Catholic Morality*. New York: The Seabury Press, A Crossroad Book, 1978, pp. 117–198; and Charles E. Curran, *Themes in Fundamental Moral Theology*. Notre Dame, IN: University of Notre Dame Press, 1977, pp. 27–80.

3. For a brief but excellent description of morality, see Ervin Staub, *Positive Social Behavior and Morality*, pp. 10–11.

4. Irish Episcopal Conference, *Conscience and Morality*. Dublin: Irish Messenger Publications, 1980, p. 4.

5. Ibid.

6. Vatican Council II's document, *Declaration on Religious Freedom*, says, for example: "On his part, man perceives and acknowledges the imperatives of the divine law through the mediation of conscience. In all his activity a man is bound to follow his conscience faithfully, in order that he may come to God, for whom he was created. It follows that he is not to be forced to act in a manner contrary to his conscience. Nor, on the other hand, is he to be restrained from acting in accordance with his conscience, especially in matters religious" (p. 681). See Walter M. Abbott, S.J., *The Documents of Vatican II*. New York: The America Press, 1966. The essential dignity of the human person lends itself to fostering this freedom. Since conscience must seek the truth, however, a constitutive element in following one's conscience is seeking this truth, which consists in an openness to important experiences and life issues as well as reflection on them. Of course, this openness in turn takes into account the wisdom and thought of others, most notably the church.

7. Robert M. Friday, *Adults Making Responsible Moral Decisions*. Washington, DC: National Conference of Diocesean Directors of Religious Education, USCC, 1979, p. iii.

8. Ibid., p. 14.

9. Based on O'Connell, *Principles for a Catholic Morality*, pp. 88–93.

10. Ibid., p. 92.

11. See Karl Rahner, S.J., "Reflections on the Problem of the Gradual Ascent to Christian Perfection," *Theological Investigations*, vol. 3. New York: The Seabury Press, A Crossroad Book, 1974, pp. 4–5.

12. Ewert H. Cousins, "The Mature Christian Conscience." In *Conscience: Theological and Psychological Perspectives*, edited by C. Ellis Nelson. New York: Newman Press, 1973, pp. 150–152.

13. Based on O'Connell, *Principles for a Catholic Morality*, pp. 93–95.

14. Curran, *Themes in Fundamental Moral Theology*, pp. 203–214.

15. Charles E. Curran, "The Christian Conscience Today." In *Conscience*, edited by C. Ellis Nelson, pp. 138–139.

16. Thomas F. Sullivan, "Evaluative Knowledge and Moral Catechesis," *Chicago Studies* 19, Fall 1980, pp. 250–253.

17. Ibid., p. 253. See also *Sharing the Light of Faith: The National Catechetical Directory*, Washington, DC: USCC, 1979, 190, p. 114.

18. Abbott, *The Documents of Vatican II*, pp. 639–640.

19. Friday, *Adults Making Responsible Moral Decisions*, p. 14.

20. Richard A. McCormick, S.J., "Personal Conscience," *Chicago Studies* 13, Fall 1974, p. 250. For an understanding of the current emphasis in Catholic theology on sin, see McCormick, "Personal Conscience," pp. 241–252; O'Connell, *Principles for a Catholic Morality*, pp. 67–82; Curran, *Themes in Fundamental Moral Theology*, pp. 145–164; and Friday, *Adults Making Responsible Moral Decisions*, pp. 17–20.

21. For a discussion of the church as a place for ethical reflection and moral growth, see James M. Gustafson's "The Church: A Community of Moral Discourse," *The Church As Moral Decision Maker*. Philadelphia: Pilgrim Press, 1970, pp. 83–95.

22. James J. DiGiacomo, S.J., "Socialization for Secularization," *New Catholic World* 223, March/April 1980, p. 62.

23. John Mitchell, "Adolescent Hypocrisy," *Adolescence* 15, Fall 1980, p. 731.

24. Ibid., p. 734.

25. Ironically, it is adults who sometimes contribute to this nongrowthful subjectivism of the adolescent. James DiGiacomo notes with insight that many adults who have now reached Fowler's four stages of faith development (individuative-reflective faith) will brush aside the more positive aspects of stage three faith, such as obedience, loyalty, and stability. Thus, adults can unfairly give the wrong interpretation to adolescent demands for freedom by seeing it in a far too positive light. Adults therefore are not inclined to establish regulations or demand any type of conforming behavior. Hence, adults, too, must examine their own perspective on moral growth in light of their own level of moral-faith development. See James J. DiGiacomo, S.J., "Follow Your Conscience," *Catholic Mind* 77, March 1979, pp. 49–50.

26. *Sharing the Light of Faith*, the National Catechetical Directory, 101–105, 190, pp. 57–61.

27. The author is indebted to Philip Schmitz, S.J., Adjunct Professor of Pastoral Theology, The Jesuit School of Theology, Berkeley, CA, for his insights and thoughtful comments on the Decalog as an instrument for Christian self-reflection.

28. Jared Wicks, S.J., "Sacraments," *Chicago Studies* 12, Fall 1973, p. 334.

29. *Sharing the Light of Faith, 125, p. 73.*

30. Megan McKenna and Bernarda Sharkey, "The Adolescent and the Sacrament of Reconciliation." In *The Rite of Penance: Commentaries Implementing the Rite,* edited by Elizabeth McMahon Jeep, vol. 2, pp. 61–76. Washington, DC: The Liturgical Conference, 1976. For a sensitive treatment of reconciliation in the adolescent years, see Brian McClorry, S.J., "Reconciliation in Matryona's Church," *The Month* 241, October 1980, pp. 342–346.

31. For an excellent work dealing with hurt and healing, see Dennis Linn, S.J. and Matthew Linn, S.J., *Healing of Memories.* New York: Paulist Press, 1974.

CHAPTER SEVEN

Adolescence, Sexuality, and Spiritual Growth

Throughout these chapters, we have referred to the call of Jesus. In discussing adolescent spirituality, we have reflected on youth's response to this call in the context of their own life experiences. One life experience that adolescents often find perplexing is the growing awareness of themselves as sexual persons. Flowing from this maturation process is the need for a spirituality that situates adolescent sexuality in a developmental context and invites the adolescent to respond more freely and deeply to Jesus' beckoning to "come, follow me."

We have noted that some adolescent experiences foster spiritual development. We have seen that the need for friendship, a sense of belonging to a community, and a deepening reflective capacity all lend depth to the adolescent encounter with Jesus Christ and the demands of the Gospel.

At the same time, however, given the developmental issues that arise in adolescence, there are experiences that perplex, frustrate, and create difficulties in youth's quest to answer Jesus' call. When dialoging with adolescents at the secondary school or college undergraduate level, the self-discovering experiences of sexual feelings, thoughts, and relationships can contribute to confusion, negative attitudes toward religion, and an estrangement from the institutional church. Pointing to this phenomenon in his research findings, Catholic University sociologist Dean Hoge remarks that youth's demands for "personal freedom" have increased since the 1950s. He observes that "it will be harder and harder for young people to find authentic Catholic faith while at the same time accepting the church's moral teachings, especially in the whole area of sexuality."[1]

Sexual urges and feelings, the experience of one's self in relation to others, the psychological needs of adolescence, and the cultural lifestyle and environment within which the adolescent interacts—all these elements can, for many adolescents, lead to a distancing from traditional religious beliefs and practices. The adolescent experiences a contradiction between what the self actually *feels* and what the self has been socialized to feel by home, religion, school, and adult influences. Thus, adolescent spirituality must address the sexual development of adolescents and provide a context for integrating their sexuality into their response to the call of Jesus.

The Adolescent Experience of Sexuality

The adolescent's growing realization of a sexual self parallels his or her growing cognitive capacity for symbolization, logical reasoning, and abstract thought (see the discussion of Piaget in chapter 3). Flowing from this parallel development are two of the central tasks of the adolescent years: the deepening of reflective thought and the mastery of the sexual self. Sexual maturation entails (1) that adolescents come to understand that their own sexual values, attitudes, and interests are distinct from those of others, and (2) that they come to assume responsibility for their own sexual self and realize, at the same time, that their peers are achieving this same sexual self-understanding in similar and dissimilar ways. Adolescents' deepening realization of their own sexuality parallels their cognitive growth whereby they leave behind their egocentric thinking and the "imaginary audience" that their thinking has constructed. Thus, just as adolescents must cognitively shed this "imaginary audience," so, too, must they rid themselves of the idea that others are always interested in focusing on their sexual growth. Gradually, the adolescent becomes aware that his or her own sexual feelings are distinct and separate from the feelings of others, and that others are not all that preoccupied with his or her personal sexual maturation.[2]

Similarly, the adolescent's new-found formal thinking is involved in the construction of a "personal fable" that permits the adolescent to assume that he or she is personally immune from the consequences of irresponsible or unthinking sexual behavior (e.g., broken commitments, dishonesty in relationships, or unwanted pregnancy). Many adolescents come to believe that the consequences of sexual behavior can happen to others but not to them.[3]

Survey of Adolescent Sexual Behavior

In light of the importance of sexuality during the adolescent years, it is helpful to briefly survey adolescent sexual behavior. Surprisingly, even with all the media attention and talk about adolescent sexuality, much research in this area is still needed. In a recent overview of adolescent sexuality, psychologist Carol Wagner has noted that "adolescent sexuality has been relegated to a minor role in the developmental research and literature on adolescence."[4]

One stark realization for any adult who ministers to young people is the focus that sexuality often occupies in an adolescent's life. The physiological changes that adolescents undergo combine with their burgeoning psychological needs and cultural-environmental influences to bring about the experience of newly found sexual feelings and impulses, which can be emotionally charged and disturbing.[5]

Research evidence tends to indicate a profound increase in the level of sexual activity as the adolescent proceeds through secondary school and into the college undergraduate years. Survey results not only note increased sexual involvement among adolescents, but also reveal that sexual behavior among adolescents is occurring at increasingly earlier ages. Another striking trend is growing sexual activity among female adolescents, although the extent of this sexual behavior is still not as great as that of male adolescents. Additionally, there has been a change in adolescent attitudes toward premarital sexuality; more and more adolescents view such activity as morally acceptable. Adolescent attitudes about sexual morality are currently guided less by rules and regulations, and more by the personal commitment and affection that two people are experiencing.[6]

Alongside an examination of the sexual behavior of adolescents, it is important to identify reasons *why* adolescents express themselves sexually. Adults who are ministering to adolescents must comprehend the dynamics beneath the sexual behavior of high school and college youth. Failure to recognize the motives that underlie adolescent sexual behavior can result in (a) a limiting of the adult's capacity to form an evaluative response to the adolescent's behavior, (b) a circumscribing of the adult's perspective with which he or she hopes to encourage future growth and development for the adolescent, and (c) a restricting of the adult's understanding of the developmental dynamics that relate to the total experience of this young person.

During our examination of the psychological basis for adolescent sexual behavior, we will be guided by psychologist Sidney Callahan's observation that, because of the numerous theories and diverse, often questionable, scientific findings, "psychology can at times provide only insights rather than proofs for consideration in pastoral decision making."[7] Furthermore, we must remember that, although human psychology does not provide the moral foundation for evaluating adolescent sexual expression, yet an understanding of the psychological factors operative in adolescent sexuality is nevertheless important in our pastoral ministry to an individual adolescent.

Psychological Factors for Adolescent Sexual Behavior

Psychologist John Mitchell has cited numerous "psychological factors" for adolescent sexual behavior.[8] These factors include the following:

1 *The need for intimacy*   The late adolescent years are a time when the need for intimacy becomes acute. The adolescent desires to trust and care for another and, at the same time, share with the other his or her own deepening feelings and concerns. New-found thoughts and feelings need expression in bonds with others. Physical interactions, such as embracing, kissing, petting, and sexual intercourse, become manifestations of these needs. Mitchell has pointed out that "for adolescents with minimal meaningful involvement elsewhere, sexual behavior is a basic avenue for creating bonds of psychological intimacy."[9]

2 *The need for belonging*   The need to belong is a vital force in human interaction. For adolescents, this need to belong leads to associations and interactions with peers. Although adolescents do not relate with peers, at least initially, for sexual reasons, daily interactions, which foster a growing sense of security, can quite naturally lead to subsequent sexual involvement. This social interaction is a crucial variable for adolescent development because it is through social interaction that the adolescent gains the competencies and social skills that are required by the adult world.

3 *The notion of dominance*   The notion of dominance reflects the adolescent's capacity to exert some type of control in a sexual

relationship. For male adolescents, this contol is often more direct and can take on aggressive characteristics. By achieving a sense of dominance in sexual relationships during the adolescent years, adolescents compensate for feelings of inferiority. Some adolescents, no doubt, act out their personal inadequacy in sexual behaviors.

4 *The desire for submissiveness*   Submissiveness occurs when the adolescent allows the self to be controlled by another. An interesting type of submissiveness is that of "idolatrous love." In this form of relating, the adolescent's attempt at consolidating his or her identity leads the adolescent to lose his or her self through idolizing the other. The intensity of this experience tends toward disappointment, because the adolescent eventually finds fault in the other, who inevitably fails to live up to the inordinate expectations placed on him or her.

5 *The motives of curiosity and competence*   The motives of curiosity and competence involve the basic inquiring about and experiencing of one's own sexuality. Sexual behavior for adolescents is sometimes an attempt to understand and experience a part of the self that is new, exciting, and intense. This underlies the obvious fact that in order to achieve some type of competence in sexual matters, the adolescent must simply experience his or her sexuality, inasmuch as there is no other way to gain this adequate mastery and competence. It is interesting to note, however, that many adolescents often stipulate certain conditions, such as some level of commitment in their relationship, before any type of physical expression occurs.

6 *The desire for passion and intensity*   Because emotions are felt at deep and intense levels during adolescence, passion and intensity are ways for adolescents to both admit and acknowledge their inner, subjective feelings. Passionate sexuality in the adolescent years enables youth (a) to experience the self in an intense way, (b) to experience another person in an equally intense way, and (c) to have another person acknowledge one's own intense feelings. Mitchell notes that in adolescence "passion is especially important as a source of psychological rejuvenation, serving to uplift the person, giving a sense of validation, and reinforcing the sense of personal identity."[10]

7 *The need for identification and imitation*   The environmental factors that surround the adolescent cannot help but be a factor in

adolescent sexuality because with maturity comes an increasing awareness of environmental surroundings. Sexuality receives prominent display through our culture's stress on visual arts, language, and reading materials. As a consequence, many adolescents develop a sense of "incompleteness" in their own selves. This sense that something is missing in their lives and that they must experience what others do can help contribute to the adolescent's sexual behavior.

   8   Rebelliousness and negative identity.   For some adolescents, negative feelings toward the family or society can lead to sexual activity (see the discussion of Erikson, chapter 3). Because parental and adult norms point to behaviors that constrict or oppose adolescent sexual expression, it is thus reasonable to conclude that for some adolescents sexual activity is used as a way to express negative feelings toward parents and other adult authorities.

   In *Sexual Counseling,* psychologist Eugene Kennedy contributes to our understanding of the dynamics that underlie adolescent sexual behavior. Kennedy notes that sexual behavior is tied to Erikson's concept of identity: "Sexuality for many young people is a vehicle for generating and maintaining self-esteem, a phenomenon that is used instrumentally in the search of the young for a firm identity."[11] The adolescent is increasingly engaged in the developmental agenda of self-discovery—finding out who he or she really is. Integral to this discovery process is the adolescent's attempt to both express himself or herself as a sexual person and relate to others in intimate, loving, and caring ways. Thus, sexuality in the adolescent years is, in many ways, tied to the young person's efforts at identity consolidation.

   As adolescents gradually acquire a sense of personal identity, they develop a capacity for a deepening sharing of self in personal relationships that reflect their growing need for intimacy. As the adolescent proceeds through high school and the college years, there is a growing desire for commitment or more developed human relationships that engage the adolescent in deeper and more intense emotional expressions. This capacity to relate intimately to another person varies among adolescents, and no doubt some adolescents find such attempts at relating to be both difficult and anxiety provoking.

   Summarizing a discussion by psychiatrists Michael W. Cohen and Stanford B. Friedman, Kennedy has explored other reasons for the adolescent engagement in sexual activity (see *Medical Aspects of Human Sexuality,* September 1975). These reasons include the following:

Peer approval   Society has developed an adolescent culture in which peer influence is profound. In this culture, the importance of peer acceptance cannot be overestimated. For some adolescents, sexuality can be a means for achieving this needed peer approval. By successfully relating in a sexual way, an adolescent can gain peer esteem and acceptance. Conversely, when there is no satisfaction in sexual activity the adolescent's self-esteem is threatened and the adolescent is placed in a vulnerable situation that, in turn, leads to continued or more pronounced difficulties. According to Kennedy, "the use of sex to solve personal problems is not limited to adolescents, of course, but it is important to understand how much weight this activity bears in the adolescent's world."[12]

Rebellion   The religious values and views of parents can exercise a crucial influence in the adolescent's sexual life. Because parents overwhelmingly disapprove of their children's sexual activity, adolescent sexual expression can be a way of rejecting parental rules in order to act out adolescent rebellion, and thereby achieve some measure of independence from parental control.

Hostility   When feelings toward parents are intensely negative, sexuality can become a channel for displaying hostility. Sex can be an ideal way of hurting parents.

Escape   Because adolescence is often a time of turbulence and discomfort for the young person, it is no wonder that sexual behavior is sometimes used as a form of escape from problems at home, at school, or in a personal relationship itself. Studies have shown that teen-age pregnancies among adolescent girls often are the result of attempts to escape from problems or difficulties.

A cry for help   Sometimes sexual activity among adolescents, especially extended periods of overt sexual activity, is indicative of the need for help. The adolescent's use of sexuality might be a signal that some type of intervention is both appropriate and necessary.

In addition to the reasons explored by Kennedy, my own pastoral work leads me to believe that there are three more reasons why adolescents often engage in sexual behavior.

Fear of intimacy   Just as adolescents can engage in sexual behavior to show intimacy, so, too, adolescent sexual behavior can

239

sometimes be a subterfuge to avoid intimacy. Adolescents who fear the self-disclosure, the sharing of feelings, and the personal risk taking that are involved in opening oneself can mistakenly convince themselves that because they are engaged in intimate physical expressions they are involved in intimate sharing in a relationship. In actuality, these adolescents are engaged in a coping strategy that effectively allows them to avoid the experience of intimate self-disclosure. These adolescents often find difficulty maintaining relationships in which a true mutuality of the selves can exist in a healthy, growthful way.

Pleasure   An often overlooked fact in explaining adolescent sexual behavior is the simple fact that sex is pleasurable. The enjoyment of pleasure in one's sexual behavior is often combined with newly found interest in one's own sexual self, thus leading to a mutually reinforcing tendency to engage in sexual behavior.

Love   When we discuss adolescent sexuality, we need to give more attention to the actual experience of love that can certainly be part of the late adolescent's sexual experience. For some adolescents, who have attained a stable sense of identity and the desire for mature intimacy, the experience of sexuality can be, to a significant degree, a truly selfless sharing and giving to another. These feelings for another person can be grounded in true caring and nurturing, based on a desire for the good of the other as experienced in this deepest sharing of the self. No doubt an initial experience of love is often intense, passionate, and narrowing for the adolescent. Yet, for some adolescents, sexual expression can certainly in part be based on a desire to share with another through total, selfless giving.

For almost all adolescents, a mature adult Christian sense of love in relation to another is yet to be realized. Of course, this is, unfortunately, the case among many adult Christians, both married or unmarried. For the Christian, love has several distinctive features.[13] First, and primarily, love in relation to another reflects the Christian's own personal desire to grow and live in relationship with Jesus Christ. The Christian, in relation to another, is asking a two-fold question: How does my love reflect the love of Jesus? and How can this relationship grow more in the love of Jesus Christ? The Christian's relationship with Jesus is the cornerstone of his or her relationships with others and is a conscious reality in those relationships.

Furthermore, the Christian's love of another is characterized by the desire to forget the self and to discover and make evident the good of the other. Jesus' own life of self-emptying (Phil 2:7) is the model for the Christian's relationship with another. This Christian love of the other is distinguished by an honest openness that invites genuine communication, self-disclosure, and the mutual risking of selves through deep trust. Such vulnerability leaves the Christian open to failure and hurt, ever present dangers that are accentuated by the Christian's realization of the imperfect nature of his or her relationship. Sin touches every human relationship, and so, there is a need for God's sustaining presence, which is realized through His redemptive presence of forgiveness. The Christian realizes that the commitment involved in this relationship entails the continual striving to grow in love in the midst of imperfect love, the need to forgive the other just as he or she finds forgiveness, and the commitment to hope in a trusted fidelity just as his or her life has been touched by a graced faithfulness that knows no end.

A final factor in any discussion of Christian love is the presence of community. Christian love is never simply a personal experience. It encompasses an ongoing dynamic whereby the individual Christian's love is nourished and sustained by the community's presence while, at the same time, the individual gives and shares with the community so as to build up the body of Christ.

In reality, adolescent sexual expression is a combination of many of the factors that have been briefly discussed here. Even when there is mature adult Christian love in an adolescent relationship, that relationship is nevertheless interspersed with many of the psychological needs of this developmental stage. Thus, we see that youth's sexual behavior is both complex and inextricably tied to the developmental issues and needs of these growing years. It is incumbent on adults who minister to adolescents to have an understanding of the dynamics of adolescent sexuality so that they can minister adequately to young people. Additionally, of course, these complex adolescent motivations exercise a fundamental role in any moral evaluation of adolescent sexual behavior.

Moral Factors in Adolescent Sexual Behavior

Just as developmental research in the sexuality of adolescents has been limited, so, too, theological and moral reflection concerning adolescent sexuality has received far too little attention in theological circles. Yet, because sexuality is an important developmental issue during the adolescent years, and because spirituality must speak to the total human experience, it is vital that we discuss the role that sexuality exercises in adolescent spiritual growth. No reflection on the spiritual life of the adolescent is complete without attention to this critical area.

Adults who minister to youth today pinpoint three specific areas of adolescent sexual behavior that require special attention—masturbation, petting experiences, and premarital sexual activity. Before we discuss these specific adolescent sexual behaviors, it would be helpful to briefly shift our focus to an overview of recent moral thinking concerning sexuality. After this examination, we will present a pastoral approach for ministering to adolescents called *developmental limitedness*. This pastoral approach shows sensitivity to the adolescent's experience of sexuality but also challenges the adolescent to future spiritual growth.

Historical perspective   Traditional Catholic moral thinking, at least prior to Vatican Council II, has often been labeled a "manual" approach. In this perspective, objectified moral rules were enunciated and human behavior was expected to conform to these moral norms. These norms became the guides for one's personal actions. Unfortunately, the result of such thinking often was a legalism that admitted to few, if any, exceptions—particularly in the area of sexuality. All too often, the point of interest was simply how well the person conformed to the moral norm.[14]

In regards to sexuality, traditional Catholic thinking pinpointed the following themes:

1   Traditional Catholic moral thinking tended to emphasize *the external act* (an incident of masturbation, for example, or a premarital sexual encounter) to the exclusion of all other considerations. In this perspective, when the external act is isolated, far too little attention is given to the developmental level of the person who engages in the act (that is, for our purposes, the adolescent). It is especially pertinent to understand this perspective when considering adolescents because developmental issues, as we have seen, thread themselves through much of adolescent sexual behavior.

2   Arising from a natural law viewpoint, traditional Catholic moral thinking emphasized *the end of the act itself*. Sexual activity, for example, is ordered toward an end—procreation—that is only hu-

manly realized in the marriage of a man and a woman. Thus, sexual activity would preclude acts that lack either the procreative capacity, such as masturbation,[15] or the commitment to marriage, such as premarital sexuality. This way of thinking, however, gives undue attention to the physical aspect of sexuality (procreation) and very little attention to the other dimensions of human relating, such as authenticity and growth, which are strong developmental needs both in the adolescent years and in human living, as well.

3 Traditional Catholic morality tended toward *legalism*. Moral law was often viewed as absolute, and few, if any, exceptions were permitted. This rigidity of thinking does not mesh with the adolescent experience, which increasingly encounters relativity, diversity, and complexity in human experience (see the discussion of Perry, chapter 3). This widening perspective, coupled with the developmental demands of identity and intimacy, and the need for separation from parents and distancing from adult rules, leads many adolescents to forsake this legalistic interpretation of sexuality in their own relationships.

4 Traditional Catholic moral thinking subsumed sexual activity under the general category of *serious sin*. In traditional thinking, the ability to admit degrees of evil in one's actions is known as "gravity of matter." Yet Catholic thinking tended to see human sexual acts as having no degree of sinfulness. In effect, all suspect sexual activity was viewed as serious sin. In all other areas of the moral life, however, human actions are subject to degrees of sinfulness. We can be upset with someone, for example, or be angry with someone, or actually hate a person, or even commit murder; each of these behaviors portrays a different degree of sinfulness. Regarding sexuality, it is quite possible to assert that there are distinctions to be made in the sinfulness of such sexual behaviors as masturbatory practices, petting experiences, chance or isolated instances of premarital activity and sexual intercourse between a couple who are engaged and have publicly stated their commitment to marry. These distinctions in sexual behaviors and relationships mirror the adolescent's own experience, which seeks deepening levels of meaning through self-understanding and relationship with another.

A discussion of the church's perspective on sexuality does not in any way mitigate the valuable place church teaching gives to human sexuality. The Catholic perspective of human sexuality has always honored the exclusivity and permanence of the sacramental commitment wherein sexuality finds its most authentic expression. Church teaching has laudably highlighted the generative nature of sexuality, a value that is all too easily disposed of in today's pleasure-oriented and consumer needy society.

Current moral theology   Recent trends in Catholic theology have attempted to deepen our understanding of human sexuality and, through this reflection, forge a theology of sexuality that not only is grounded in Gospel teaching and the person of Jesus Christ, but also remains fundamentally true to the nature of human experiencing. The *Declaration On Certain Questions Concerning Sexual Ethics*[16] was issued in 1976. This document accepts the more traditional approach of Catholic moral thinking (as indicated in the preceding section) regarding sexuality. At the same time, however, this study did reflect more contemporary thinking and pastoral insights regarding such issues as masturbation and homosexuality. Although this document has been questioned and severely criticized in some theological circles, not enough credit is given to the distinctive pastoral emphasis that permeates it.[17] Nevertheless, the publication of this document has failed to stem the growing debate in Catholic theology concerning the morality of various sexual behaviors.

More recent theological thinking has proposed a broadened view of human sexuality. Among suggestions and approaches that have arisen in recent theological writings are the following: (1) an acceptance of a "degree" of moral seriousness in sexual behavior; (2) an increasing emphasis on the "developmental level" of the person; (3) a tendency to consider the "growth" that is taking place in the person and the effect that human actions have on this growth toward maturity; (4) a stress on "love"; (5) an emphasis on the "consequences" of actions; (6) an increasing attention to the "situational" variables present in sexual encounters (e.g., social pressures, or geographic and cultural tendencies); and (7) a priority on the "integrative" nature of one's life, that is, how does this action allow for integration and growth of the total self.

In the late 1970s *Human Sexuality: New Directions in American Catholic Thought* appeared. Like the earlier Vatican document, this report has also received mixed reviews in theological circles.[18] Catholic theologians who contributed to this book attempted to use recent insights in theology and the social sciences to present a broadening view of human sexuality. In this context, the study noted "wholesome sexuality is that which fosters creative growth towards integration."[19]

Questions and issues regarding morality and sexuality have, of course, led to discussion, confusion, and controversy in adult circles. Adults are aware that many adolescents react negatively toward traditional Catholic moral teaching. Questions and statements such as, Why is it sinful? There is nothing wrong with it; we love each other, and Everyone does it, challenge any adult who ministers to high school or college youth today. This questioning attitude—combined with the actual behavior of adolescents, the complex reasons and motivations for adolescent sexuality, and the insights of contemporary moral thinking—make it particularly important to address the moral dimension of the adolescent's sexual behavior. It is certainly true that sexual morality requires more than simplistic answers to questions about what is right or wrong; yet the concrete moral dilemmas reflected in their questions and statements are often what adolescents really experience. These adolescent questions regarding sexuality need the focus and attention of adults who minister to today's youth.

When we discuss the morality of adolescent sexuality, an antecedent question arises concerning the distinction between moral norms and the pastoral application of these norms. All too often in the moral life, a moral principle is enunciated in such a way that too little attention and sensitivity are accorded the concrete human experience in which the person finds himself or herself. Although this emphasis on the importance of the moral principle is well intentioned, it can attentuate the significance and complexity of the personal, human response of the individual in the concrete situation of his or her own experience.

Moral theologian Bernard Häring captures the essence of the critical distinction between enunciating a "moral principle" and understanding, in a "pastoral couneeling" situation, the *actual lived experience* of the person. Moral theology, says Häring, deals with a level of ethical discourse at which "questions are raised about general rules or considerations that would justify a particular moral judgment."[20] In other words, the language of moral theology pertains to ethical reflections, on a more principled level, that must then be applied to concrete human situations. Hence, in addition to the ethical imperatives of moral theology, there is a level of discourse that is applicable to the human, concrete situation—"the level of pastoral counseling."[21] When we engage in pastoral counseling, we attempt to discern the lived experience of the person, at a particular point in time, at that person's concrete developmental level.

Pastoral counseling, then, is concerned with "the art of the possible." Pastoral counseling asks the following questions: What is the level of moral growth possible in this person? and What response on the counselor's part will offer the greatest opportunity for this growth to occur? Pastoral counseling attempts to take into account the emotional, intellectual, economic, motivational, and physical aspects of the person's developmental experience and personal concrete situation in an attempt to lead the person to greater Christian maturity. From this perspective, it must not be concluded that pastoral counseling is an abdication of moral principles. Rather, as Häring concludes, "the whole of moral life is characterized by the 'law of growth' by the need for constant but gradual conversion."[22]

Häring's distinction presents pastoral counselors who minister to youth a delicate tightrope, which must be walked. As the result of either an adult desire to appear understanding, or an adolescent misperception of the adult's position, adolescents far too often mistakenly conclude that the adult minister has "no problem" with the sexual behavior under discussion or "does not care" about what the adolescents do or thinks it is "no big deal." It is often difficult for adolescents to comprehend the distinction between the adult's attempt to accept and understand the adolescent and, at the same time, the adult's personal reservations about the adolescent's behavior. Such discussions between an adult and an adolescent demand honest communication, openness, and a willingness to listen to and appreciate what the other is saying. The following is one way for adults in such situations: When appropriate, can the adult offer the adolescent a gentle challenge to continue growing in his or her moral life? An inviting challenge to continued growth is one of the best gifts an adult can offer an adolescent as he or she aids youth in confronting the issues that crop up during youth's quest for Christian adulthood.

Developmental Limitedness

To aid the adult who, in ministering to adolescents at the high school and college age level, must deal with the experience of adolescent sexuality, the following pastoral approach, called "developmental limitedness," is proposed. This approach attempts to incorporate both traditional Catholic thinking about sexuality and recent insights from theology and psychology. Such an approach is ideally suited to ministering to adolescents because it is pastoral (dealing with the actual experience of adolescents at their developmental level in the context of the present moment) and, at the same time, challenges toward growth (concentrating on the present experience of the young person and calling for deeper levels of reflection, conversion, and commitment concerning the adolescent's attempt to heed Jesus' call to "come, follow me"). Thus, developmental limitedness attempts to situate the adolescent experience of sexuality under the Gospel's call to follow Jesus.

How can this approach be used in ministering to the adolescent's sexual behavior? Before answering this question, three points must be discussed. First, the traditional Christian notion that sexuality is fully realized and made meaningful in the sacramental commitment of marriage must be confirmed. In the marital relationship, a man and a woman personally and publicly proclaim the commitment they have made to one another and the faith community. Sexuality represents total self-giving in a covenant relationship that proclaims Paul's description of Jesus' intimate union with His church (Eph 5:25–33). Likewise, the physical union of husband and wife in marriage provides a nurturing and trusting environment of permanence and exclusivity in which children can be nourished and raised. In supporting this view, Charles Curran affirms that "in a sexual encounter one accepts responsibility for another; to accept full responsibility means that the persons are totally committed to one another."[23] Philip Keane asserts that "only in the context of marital fidelity can genital sexual acts have the possibility of accomplishing all the goodness for which such acts are apt."[24] Summing up the Christian view of sexuality, Catholic ethician Lisa Sowle Cahill states: "It is a familiar teaching of Christianity that sexual activity belongs in marriage, where the complete commitment of the partners provides an appropriate context for its physical consummation and for the nurturing of children. Any sexual relations which digress from this pattern are serious moral matters."[25]

Secondly, the adult who ministers to adolescents must not lose sight of this Christian view of sexuality. In an attempt to be pastorally sensitive, especially with youth, pastoral counselors might be tempted to downplay this commitment as "too difficult" or "unrealizable" in the adolescent's life. Although cultural standards and peer pressures may make adolescents "feel ashamed if they are not involved in sex," religious educator Dick Reichert observes that "we do have a clear and defensible moral position on premarital sexual intercourse."[26] The diminution of the Christian understanding of sexuality and its relationship to marital commitment is particularly regrettable in the context of the adolescent experience. Above all, adolescents need adults who are honest and forthright in their own commitment to Christian values and to the need for fidelity and commitment in the area of one's sexual life. An adult who refrains from expressing this need for commitment deprives the adolescent of a valued source for reflecting on Christian values.

Third, in light of the two principles already enunciated, consideration must be given to the possibility that certain admittedly rare situations exist wherein exceptions might be morally tolerated, even though the sexual act suffers, in these situations, from incompleteness or lack. In our complex society, and in light of the demands of developing human relationships as they are experienced in concrete situations, there can exist, for example, exceptional instances of sexual expression that compel a broader understanding of the Christian ideal of sexuality. In such situations, which again, are rare, the norm fails to provide for the total expression of the growth and depth of the relationship between a particular man and woman. In the complex area of sexuality and human relationships, we may encounter as we minister to adolescents a situation in which the norm is inadequate to fully appreciate the experience of a given adolescent in relation to another. When making this point, we take into account the insightful comment of Richard McCormick concerning the "tentativeness of moral formulations."[27] Moral utterances are rooted in historical consciousness and must be examined and reflectively attended to over time. These formulations, then, are assertions of far deeper, more substantive truths that must not be lost. At the same time, however, in light of cultural influences and human knowledge, the formulation of these utterances must be subjected to the expanding critical insights of successive generations. Thus, the level of commitment portrayed by the Christian value of sexuality must not be diminished, but the deeper understanding of what this commitment means in light of the complexity of human life situations demands both accountability over time and rigorous examination.[28]

The Pastoral Approach of Developmental Limitedness

Before we consider actual pastoral situations with adolescents, it is important that the pastoral approach of developmental limitedness be delineated. Developmental limitedness places sexuality in the context of an expanded or broadening view of sexuality. This notion affirms that sexuality is, simply, how one experiences one's own self as male or female. It encompasses both the way we *are* and the way we *relate* to the world. Hence, sexuality is more than the self—it is the self in relation to others. We can agree, then, with Donald Goergen who makes the point that "sexuality is not primarily procreative as much as it is celebrative, expressive, eschatological, and unitive."[29] Developmental limitedness beckons each person to constant growth and completion both in one's personal life and in one's life lived in relationship with others. In the adolescent's life, developmental limitedness situates sexuality as a fundamental human experience in both being and growing, calling the young person forth to a deeper awareness, a deeper understanding of, and a more wholesome acceptance of his or her sexual self. Additionally, the adolescent is challenged to integrative growth that entails deeper awareness and commitment to others, in both human friendship and genital expression, which is realized in the marriage commitment.

Developmental limitedness touches the adolescent's life in several ways. First, the very notion *developmental* is a key term. Of primary importance in ministering to the sexual experience of adolescents is the emphasis placed on the developmental level and needs of the adolescent experience. Of course, this does not deny that attention must be given to the act itself as well as the situation in which the act occurs—what moral theology labels the "total context" of a moral action. Any pastoral ministry to adolescents must take these factors into account. Nonetheless, during the adolescent years, when sexual identity is so crucial, and the demands for an understanding and experiencing of sexuality are so great, pastoral

249

sensitivity reiterates the central role played by this developmental focus.[30]

Moral theologian William Cosgrave conveys a sensitive appreciation of how adolescence is intimately linked, often in an acutely felt way, to the process of human growth. Writing about adolescent sexual behavior, Cosgrave observes: "Adolescence in particular is a time of great sexual growth; it is during this period that the young person learns what it is to be a sexual person, to establish and maintain relationships of sexual love with members of the opposite sex and to lay the foundation for adult sexual loving. It will be important to keep this fact of growth in mind, above all in assessing the moral quality of sexual activities, especially those of adolescents."[31]

On what grounds can we make this concentration on the developmental perspective for moral evaluation? We can provide two reasons for our assertion: First, adolescence is the primary developmental stage for the person's experiencing of the self in preparation for adulthood. The degree to which the adolescent's identity (included here are motivations, emotional needs, self-discovery behaviors, psychological needs—in this sense, "identity" means one's total self) is freely involved in the sexual behavior that is taking place is closely related to the adolescent's consolidation of personal identity issues. In other words, full and free participation in moral actions involves the self as a mature moral agent. Nonetheless, during the adolescent years, and particularly with regard to sexual behavior, this identity consolidation, which allows free participation, is often a process that is yet to be realized. Quite often the adolescent's sexual behavior is the experience of a self in transition—the adolescent is attempting to grow in personal selfhood. To divorce this identity issue from a discussion of adolescent sexuality is to construct an adolescent self that has little credence in the actual lived experience of youth. Hence, above all, developmental limitedness asks the following questions regarding adolescent sexual behavior: At what level is this adolescent freely and maturely investing himself or herself in this sexual behavior, at this moment in time, and, furthermore what level of spiritual growth is possible, given this particular level of the adolescent's development? Without this developmental awareness as the central factor, the richness and complexity of the true adolescent self is narrowed and results in a circumscribed pastoral awareness of the adolescent.

Secondly, because adolescence is a stage of becoming, of growing, this developmental perspective helps adolescents to appreciate their present life experience in the context of the future spiritual growth to which they are called, Unless a developmental process is taken seriously, the adolescent self is relegated to a stationary existence that completely contradicts the true adolescent experience. Through this developmental perspective, then, adolescents can gain, by means of dialogs with adult youth ministers as well as personal reflection, a perspective of their own growth (where they have come from) and accept the challenge of needed, future spiritual growth as they journey toward Christian adulthood.

In addition to this developmental aspect, a second dimension of developmental limitedness aids adolescents in their growing need to *integrate* the various facets of their lives. Developmental limitedness seeks to help adolescents understand, in a more deeply Christian context, what growth in sexuality really is; at the same time, developmental limitedness strives to integrate sexuality into the affective, intellectual, moral, and faith dimensions of the adolescent life. In this way, again, the adolescent can more fully realize and understand what it means to respond to Jesus' invitation to "come, follow me."

A third dimension of developmental limitedness emphasizes adolescent growth in *self-awareness*. This perspective seeks to offer adolescents a growing insight into their own sexual self. From these insights, adolescents emerge with a greater self-understanding of who they really are. In addition, they often grow in accepting the self as more fully responsible and become more capable of understanding their own sexual person.

From this self-awareness arises a fourth dimension of developmental limitedness. This perspective provides the *motivational* context in which adolescents seek to grow in the integrative aspects of sexuality and, during these developental years, ally this deepening understanding with Jesus' call.

Finally, developmental limitedness encourages adolescents to grow into a life-giving stance that is increasingly realized in caring and sharing—*commitment*. In this sense, the growth of the adolescent takes root specifically in caring attentiveness toward others, deepening friendships, and the eventual sacramental commitment of marriage.

Limitedness, like developmental, implies several dimensions.

251

First, human sexuality is limiting in that it fails to ever concretely and fully appropriate the law of love demanded by the Gospel challenge. Sin is an ever present reality in the Christian life (Rom 3:22). As Charles Curran remarks, "The Christian view of sin reminds us that sin affects all human reality."[32] As such, then, when developmental limitedness is applied to human sexuality, and specifically to adolescent sexuality, it tries to help adolescents realize the imperfect nature of their attempt to share, to love, and to care for another. Adolescent relationships are tinged with the presence of selfishness, which exists to some degree in all human relationships, as well as all the developmental insecurities, defenses, and possessiveness that are so much a part of this developmental age. Thus, this particular pastoral approach seeks not only to foster the loving commitment and growth that are so necessary for Christian love, but also to aid adolescents in realizing the unloving aspects and tendencies of their relationships as well as the continual need for conversion.

Limitedness focuses, secondly, on the *lived experiences* of the adolescent—here and now. This approach hopes to aid adolescents in realizing that they—indeed, all of us—are limited in the concrete, existential situation in which we all exist. Given our own life situations, we are never as loving or caring as we wish; yet, this limitedness is made enriching and empowering when it is united to the saving power that is Jesus Christ. Developmental limitedness poses the following question: What does this presence of Jesus Christ do, and how does His presence influence my relationships here and now?

Finally, this approach attempts to expand the limiting character of adolescent immediacy and self-absorption by fostering a *widening context* for adolescent relationships that are balanced, integrative, maturing, and other-centered. Thus, adolescents view and experience their sexuality not so much inwardly, but in an altruistic sense of being in relation to others.

In summary, then, developmental limitedness seeks to minister to the actual, lived experience of adolescents. It attempts to understand adolescents in the limiting nature of their personal experience and, at the same time, encourages them to realize the growing need for commitment to Jesus' invitation to "come, follow me."

In light of this definition of developmental limitedness, the following questions are offered as guidelines to aid adults who are attempting to give some moral interpretation to adolescent sexual behavior.

1   What are the developmental issues that underlie this adolescent's sexual behavior or relationship? Or, what are the motivational reasons for this adolescent's sexual behavior?

2   In what ways is this sexual behavior leading to growth and integration in the adolescent's own emotional and spiritual life? How much awareness does the adolescent have of the growth that is taking place within himself or herself?

3   To what extent is the adolescent obtaining a deepening level of awareness of and insight into both his or her own self and his or her relationships with others?

4   Does this relationship lead the adolescent to seek more growth in his or her relationships—a growth that is characterized by the deepening desire to accept responsibility and commitment in his or her relationships with others?

5   What is the conscious level of commitment that is expressed in this relationship? Can the adolescent reflect on and talk about this commitment?

6   To what extent can this adolescent admit to and discuss unloving aspects of this relationship, that is, selfishness, possessiveness, jealousy, dishonesty, or defensiveness? How capable is the adolescent of facing these limits in the relationship and how is he or she attempting to grow in facing these limits? Does this adolescent desire to deal with these limits and grow from them?

7   Does the adolescent have a realistic assessment of his or her relationship with the other?

8   What role does Jesus Christ exercise in this adolescent's life? How does Jesus touch and influence this adolescent's relationships? In other words, does the presence of Jesus make a difference in this relationship for this adolescent?

9   How does this adolescent's experience of sexuality allow him or her to more fully relate to others and be aware of them and their needs? Does this relationship help the adolescent to overcome tendencies toward self-absorption and eventually lead the adolescent to more fully care for others and share with them? Does this growing sense of others deepen as this adolescent's relationship is deepening?

Specific Sexual Behaviors

Having examined the pastoral approach of developmental limitedness, we now consider three specific sexual behaviors: masturbation, petting, and premarital sexual intercourse. We will first discuss the sexual behavior in the context of Catholic moral thinking and then seek to integrate this thinking with the perspective of developmental limitedness.

Masturbation

Masturbatory behavior is a common occurrence in the sexual development of the human person. Likewise, studies have indicated a high degree of masturbatory activity in the general adolescent population.[33]

In regard to the morality of masturbatory acts, the Vatican declaration speaks of masturbation in terms of an "intrinsically and seriously disordered act." At the same time, however, the document notes that, in the area of moral responsibility, "the immaturity of adolescence" diminishes the moral culpability to the extent that there "may not always be a serious fault." The document also cautions against presuming this as a general practice. But we should note that, by lessening the culpability of adolescents, the document has made a highly significant statement. We must keep this in mind as we attempt a moral evaluation of masturbation.

Many contemporary theologians have taken an understanding, yet challenging perspective toward masturbatory behavior in adolescence. Charles Curran, for example, states that masturbation reflects an inadequate "integration of sexuality" and a "less than ideal" form of sexual expression. Curran notes, however, that "in the developing adolescent, individual acts of masturbation are definitely not that important at all provided the individual is trying to develop his personality and enter into healthy relationships with others."[34] Curran sees adolescent masturbation as not especially significant. At the same time, though, he cautions against conveying to the adolescent the attitude that there is nothing wrong with masturbation. Because sexuality should be viewed in relationship to others, the adolescent needs encouragement in order to view sexuality as other-centered and in order to enjoy personal growth in his or her relationships.

Likewise, Bernard Häring maintains that the main point in deal-

254

ing with adolescent masturbation must be to develop an altruistic orientation in the adolescent's life.[35]

Philip Keane employs contemporary psychological thinking to determine that, to a large extent, "masturbation, especially among adolescents, can be interpreted as part of a normal human growth pattern."[36] Masturbation is a "phase" that an individual passes through in order to achieve a more mature, integrated sexuality that normally leads to marriage. At the same time, though, masturbation can be symptomatic of other, deeper personal problems. In this sense, any attempts to evaluate the person's emotional maturity cannot dismiss masturbation as unimportant. Keane situates masturbatory behavior in adolescence in terms of "ontic" evil that is not necessarily moral evil. Ontic evil describes actions that "for one reason or another significantly fail to reach the full potential of human goodness and possibility."[37] This ontic evil is present in all human reality and constitutes part of our human condition. Regarding masturbatory behavior in adolescence, Keane maintains that "adolescent masturbation should be seen as a somewhat morally significant (but still not all that weighty) ontic evil. Adolescents should be mature enough to be aware that they ought to transcend masturbation and grow toward a higher expression of their sexuality; on the other hand, adolescents are adolescents and the fact that they have not yet moved to higher sexual maturity should not be given undue moral significance."[38]

The authors of *Human Sexuality* reflect the views of Curran, Häring, and Keane. The study notes that the process of "self-discovery" in adolescence leads the young person to close in on the self. According to the authors, adolescents need support and encouragement to direct their attention outward and develop healthy and growthful human relationships. The study advises that "as the adolescent reaches out to others and progresses in personal development, the masturbation in most instances will gradually disappear."[39]

Psychologist Eugene Kennedy claims that there are numerous reasons for masturbatory behavior and that masturbation can be indicative of growth, or used as a way to deal with lack of self-esteem, or associated with human stress. Kennedy warns that it is often difficult to unravel the true meaning of masturbatory activity.[40] He notes with insight: "Perhaps the greatest current temptation is to quickly reassure persons with masturbation conflicts without hearing them out, without giving them the opportunity to express themselves or explore their feelings deeply. Neither is it wise to give symbolic absolution to adolescents on the subject of masturbation. They are not seeking permission so much as understanding; they deserve the help that will assist them to make the move toward more adult sexuality. Providing them with excuses for not working through the larger issues of their identity—letting them indulge their narcissism instead of breaking through it—is not helpful."[41]

The pastoral approach of developmental limitedness concurs with the recent pastoral insights regarding masturbation. This orientation tends to focus on what the adolescent is *experiencing* in his or her own development and how this development more and more reflects an *other-centeredness* that reaches out toward others in caring, growthful, and more committed ways. Concomitantly, this approach attempts to appreciate the deeper dimensions of sexuality, including the *limited* nature of the adolescent's present behavior and the importance of *outward-reaching* behavior that reflects this commitment and sharing. Pastoral concern for the adolescent includes (a) support for the development of positive, growth-filled relationships, (b) aid in discovering deeper *self-insight* (such as "who I am" and "what I am about"), and (c) encouragement to both realize the *inadequacy* of this form of sexual expression and develop expanding and widening adolescent behaviors that reflect commitment toward others in sharing and caring forms of expression. Specific suggestions for helping adolescents grow in their sexuality are provided at the end of this chapter.

Finally, the perspective of developmental limitedness admits that an evaluation of the moral nature of masturbation in adolescence does not preclude sin. It would be naive to believe that masturbation could not be motivated by self-seeking or lustful desires. Certainly the disposition and tendency of the human condition can twist and violate the goodness of human sexual expression, even regarding adolescent masturbation. Yet the overall dynamics of adolescent growth lead us generally to view masturbatory activity as indicative of the normal adolescent growth process of self-discovery, which, although inadequate, leads eventually to mutually fulfilling relationships of human friendship and marital commitment.

In summary, we need to encourage the adolescent to grow outwardly towards others in nourishing and enriching relationships. The noted psychologist William Kraft who has written extensively on spiritual topics, in a sensitive treatment of this issue, captures this view well when he notes

> The folly of masturbation is that we silence the Spirit urging us to love. We abort an opportunity for growth and end up being more empty and lonely. Although masturbation can to some extent satisfy our yearning for intimacy and transcendence, its satisfaction is momentary and not growth oriented. Masturbation turns our spirit inward and we become intimate with ourselves while impeding what we really want—authentic intimacy with another.*

As adults we need to show compassionate understanding towards the adolescent and at the same time encourage the development of growthful intimacy with others.

Petting

Like masturbation, petting experiences are common in the American population.[42] These experiences become increasingly common during the adolescent years and are a usual part of the adolescent experience. Although "petting" is a somewhat nebulous term that actually encompasses many behaviors, we can define this behavior as intense physical expression that does not lead to sexual intercourse. On the one hand, somewhat less intense physical expressions are usually called "necking," and, on the other hand, extremely intense expressions that lead to intercourse are properly called "sexual foreplay."

When adults attempt a pastoral discussion of the adolescent petting experience during high school and college years, two cautions are warranted: First, eschew any attempt to derive a "moral calculus" when you are discussing adolescent petting experiences. That is to say, it is unwise and pastorally unsound to define an exacting set of behaviors that are applicable to each and every adolescent in each and every situation. This type of moral evaluation, although it may be well-intentioned, is incapable of appreciating the depth and complexity of each adolescent either in his or her own developmental situation or in personal relationship with another.

---

*William Kraft, "A Psychospiritual View of Masturbation," *Human Development*, Summer 1982, pp. 41–42.

The complexity and level of the adolescent's personal moral response and his or her response in relationship to another cannot be subsumed under such tightly knit categories. Also, such guidelines all too often lead to a subtle form of legalism that becomes unanswerable in the concrete human experience of the adolescent. This aspect is equally detrimental.

Secondly, and equally important, the pastoral sensitivity that adults bring to a dialog with an adolescent regarding petting experiences must avoid the view that petting is an innocuous experience and devoid of implications for both emotional and spiritual growth. This nonchalant attitude is a disservice to the adolescent because the depth and mystery of human sexuality are realized in commitment and in the way one shares with and treats another. Likewise, the psychological consequences of the petting experience can mask underlying issues in the adolescent's life, such as security needs, defensiveness, fears of emotional intimacy, self-discovery needs, and the like, that are important factors in the adolescent's own emotional growth. Thus, from both a spiritual and a psychological perspective, one must conclude that petting experiences during the adolescent years take on meaning and significance that are related to the adolescent's own maturing sense of self and growth toward Christian adulthood.

Psychologist John Mitchell views petting as paralleling the adolescent's growth in the emotional expression of intimacy. Mitchell maintains that as the adolescent self becomes deeper, "the impulse for emotional intimacy eventually becomes interwoven with the impulse for sexual expression."[43] He continues: "The body, in the midst of its great sexual unfolding, fills the adolescent with sensations which demand a partner to reach their natural fruition."[44]

Eugene Kennedy notes that the experience of petting in adolescence is closely linked with identity, intimacy, value formation, and the deepening understanding of both the self and others. Kennedy makes two highly significant points regarding the petting experience of adolescent youth. First: "It is clear that a certain amount of physical closeness and physical expression is necessary, but this must be in accord with the level of growth of the individuals involved and also match and reflect a set of ideals about their own dignity and the words of other persons."[45] Second: "The young people in high school and college frequently work out a set of moral judgments

258

themselves which strike older people as strange but which have great significance for them."[46] This attempt at value expression is highly significant. An adolescent's attempt at setting some type of rules or guidelines in sexual behavior allows the young person the opportunity to both confront meaning and value in a very personal way and relate personal values to sexual expression.

Philip Keane points out that the petting experiences of young people might well be an attempt to deal with "sexual tensions." Petting experiences must also be distinguished as those expressions that are experienced for "affection" and those more involved, physical expressions that lead to greater experiences of "sexual arousal." It is important to note, of course, that a particular physical expression by one adolescent might have an entirely different meaning (and effect) for another adolescent. Keane rightly admits that everyone has a human need for affection. Such behavior, when expressed, must take into account the situation, the individual, the partner, and the level of commitment present in the relationship. He wisely concludes that everyone (not just the adolescents) needs other individuals with whom they can consult about the appropriate degree of physical expression that can exist in a particular relationship.

Regarding more involved petting experiences, Keane says that such sexual activity "falls under our basic norm that genital sexual activity is best expressed in marriage."[47] This more intense type of petting expression is an ontic evil (but not always a moral evil), because intense petting experiences are not "a fully satisfactory form of human sexual expression."[48] Keane shows appreciation and sympathy toward those who have a commitment to marry and yet are attempting to delay sexual intercourse until they have actually formalized their marriage commitment. Keane sees vast difference (and so does this author) between premarital sexual petting and premarital sexual intercourse. He also notes the importance of educing the psychological implications of petting, which might exercise a factor in the evaluative determination of this sexual activity.

It is not difficult to understand that the issue of petting in adolescence is both ambiguous and complex for youth today. On the one hand, the process of self-discovery, identity acquisition, and intimacy needs as well as the realization of deeper values and the growing understanding of one's sexual self and the sexuality of another all urge the adolescent to participate in such forms of physical expression. On the other hand, variegated motives, which include possessiveness and the powerful nature of sexuality during the adolescent years, lead the adolescent to a level of sexual expression that is often psychologically and spiritually inadequate as a symbol of authentic Christian commitment.

The author advises that adults who minister to adolescents should not dismiss petting experiences in adolescence as insignificant. At the same time, however, adults must also realize that there is a natural, physical expression that appears normal and important for the developmental experiences of youth. The author therefore offers two points for adults who minister to adolescents in the context of discussing petting experiences. First, the evaluative dimension of petting must be determined in an individual circumstance because behavior signifies and represents different meanings for each adolescent in the context of a particular relationship. Secondly, the more protracted and intense manifestations of petting demand some deeper level of commitment on the part of the adolescent. In other words, petting experiences between a couple who have dated for several years or who are engaged should be evaluated quite differently from the superficial petting experience of the adolescent who has little or no commitment.

From these two statements a third principle emerges. In the concrete situation of a given adolescent relationship, there exists a level of physical expression beyond which moral reservation must be discussed. The presence of moral reservation is essential, since it signifies the *integrity* of the adolescent self and the personal *responsibility* that the adolescent must assume in his or her own personal behavior in relationship to another. In stating the reality of moral reservation that must be accorded to physical manifestations of petting, the author maintains that although instances of petting must be evaluated separately and individually and are thus dependent on the relationship between the two adolescents and the meaning they give their relationship, there does exist, for all practical purposes, a moral norm which can be generalized across the adolescent population. In other words, there does exist in each instance of petting a moral norm beyond which disvalue and sin must be discussed. Of course, in this instance, and in other aspects of adolescent sexuality, adults must be aware of *pastoral realism* in applying these norms. Adults who minister to an adolescent at a particular developmental level must realize what is possible for *this* adolescent and attempt to lovingly challenge him or her to future growth. Here, too, as in other areas of the adolescent's life, utter honesty on the adolescent's part is, of course, needed and should be encouraged.

Developmental limitedness attempts to deal with petting experiences by suggesting the following pastoral practice with adolescents. First, there must be reflection on the reasons for this behavior. What is the real significance that the adolescent attaches to this physical expression? What is the adolescent attempting to say by this behavior? What are the underlying, motivating dynamics that support this type of behavior in this adolescent? Adults should encourage adolescents to assume an honest searching, questioning, reflective stance.

Adults should also note the level of growth that is taking place in the adolescent as a result of this relationship. Is there a growing sense of wholeness, completeness, honesty, or responsibility (to name just a few values) emerging in this adolescent? How is this experience contributing to or inhibiting a growing sense of personal selfhood for this adolescent? Also, how is this adolescent growing in self-awareness and self-insight from this experience? How does this relationship foster self-discovery for this adolescent and how does the adolescent utilize this self-discovery in his or her own life?

Another facet to determine is the significance of this sexual expression in this adolescent's life. In other words, what level of commitment is present? Does this sexual expression truly reflect this commitment? Is there a developing and deepening understanding of what commitment actually entails in this relationship?

Furthermore, it is important that adults reflect with adolescents on the *limiting* nature of this relationship and sexual experience. How capable is the adolescent in expressing the limits and inadequacies of this relationship? In what ways is this sexual expression non-growthful, non-loving, possessive, or jealous? To what degree is this adolescent's sexual expression manifesting these limited forms of human relating? Can this adolescent discuss these personal limitations in his or her own relationship with another?

It is also important that the adolescent reflect on the Christian meaning of this sexual expression. What values are symbolized by this expression for this adolescent? What role does Jesus Christ exercise in this adolescent's relationship with another? A good question for the adolescent quite simply asks, "How is Jesus part of your relationship with . . . ?" Adolescents often need to be challenged in order to reflect on the meaning that Jesus gives to their sexual lives. This is an important focus because quite often adolescents will compartmentalize their Christian commitment. Thus, Jesus is important with family and friends, but in the area of sexuality, adolescents might display a dual stance and be adverse to facing the question of what role Jesus has in their own lives. As the authors of *Human Sexuality* have noted, this type of questioning "may prove frustrating and difficult to apply for those who have not grasped the deeper meaning and purpose of human sexuality."[49] Adolescents, above all, fall into this category. Yet it is this type of pastoral reflection and discussion that truly contributes to the adolescent's growth in honesty, self-awareness, responsibility, and a developing sense of growing Christian adulthood.

In summary, then, if adults are to minister to the sexual behaviors of adolescents, they must focus on aiding adolescents to grow in an understanding of their sexual selves so that these young people might become responsible persons who are committed to the exclusivity and permanence of sexual behavior that is ultimately realized in marital commitment. As a consequence, deeper affective-physical expressions of the adolescent's sexual self should always encourage this reflective inquiry.

Premarital intercourse

Premarital sexual activity has dramatically increased in the adolescent population, at both the secondary and college-undergraduate levels.[50] In his discussion of the changes in moral thinking since Vatican II, Richard McCormick concludes that the church regards premarital sexual activity as "morally wrong—that is something is always missing in such conduct."[51] The Vatican *Declaration* has upheld the traditional teaching of the church, concluding that sexual intercoarse outside the marriage relationship is morally sinful and that, moreover, such sin is serious. The *Declaration* states that "according to Christian tradition and the church's teaching, and as right reason also recognizes, the moral order of sexuality involves such high values of human life that every direct violation of this order is objectively serious."[52] At the same time, however, the document advises the same pastoral approach that it recommended regarding adolescent masturbation. That is to say, the *Declaration* recognizes the need for "prudence" and "caution" in judging the personal level of culpability for those who are involved.

Charles Curran has observed that "Catholic theologians generally uphold the teaching that sexuality outside marriage is wrong."[53] In stating this position, Curran notes that the level of commitment (of which marriage is a fundamental sign), the importance of procreation, and the relational dimension of sexuality all lend support to this position. Curran sees only "quite limited" exceptions to this prohibition.

Philip Keane upholds the traditional Catholic stance and offers positive reflections for this position. Marital sexual love, says Keane, manifests Christ's love for His church and also symbolizes God's covenant love with all humankind. Keane also finds merit in the historical relationship of marriage and sexuality, and the close union among sexuality, marriage, and the family. Moreover, unlike previous times, premarital intercourse in our culture is often experienced with one's fiancé or fiancée. For this reason, according to Keane, we often find a strong emphasis on commitment in sexual expression.[54] Yet we should note, of course, that this level of commitment is rarely part of the adolescent's sexual expression.

Keane delineates several types of premarital intercourse. First, there is *casual intercourse,* in which no commitment exists between the two parties. Intercourse of this sort is without justification from a moral standpoint, and the church's "opposition" to such behavior is sound. Keane remarks: "To put it in another way, the church's traditional opposition to casual premarital intercourse is still quite coherent in our times."[55] Yet here, too, there is also the need for pastoral sensitivity because there are numerous reasons for adolescent sexual behavior.

Another consideration of premarital intercourse involves the *level of commitment* of two people. Keane observes that even when "personal commitment" and "affection" are present, the "Church's basic norm" which views sexual intercourse as "best protected and expressed" in the married state "remains clearly in place." Regarding premarital intercourse, Keane discusses cases in which the intent to marry is present but, because of financial pressures and societal structures—further studies, job qualifications, and so on—the individuals, usually young adults, are not able to marry. It is possible, in some of these cases, that premarital intercourse "may not be wrong." Keane goes on to note, however, that these cases are "rare" and that, when they do occur, they still contain "ontic evil" because these acts do not fully express the goodness and full possibility of the human sexual act that is realized in the marital commitment. Keane also makes the crucially important point that, as soon as exceptions are admitted, it is all too common for the persons involved to view themselves as perfect examples of this exception.[56] This observation is especially pertinent for adolescents who might be contending with strong sexual urges and feelings; they can often be led to believe that their sexual behavior is the result of an authentic commitment and is therefore justified.

It again needs repeating that, for adolescents, situations in which premarital sexual intercourse is without moral wrong are rare. It can plausibly be argued that the very external factors that often prevent a marital commitment at a particular time are the very factors that adolescents should consider when they engage in premarital sexual intercourse. For example, is it reasonable for two young people to assume responsibility for each other if one or both are still in school or lacking a job? Yet it is this very responsibility—the total accepting of the other—that the sexual act symbolizes. Can these two young people actually say at this time in their lives that they totally accept each other and are willing to be totally responsible for each other in the midst of the numerous obligations that their as yet undeclared public commitment (sacramental marriage) entails—that is, financial pressures and obligations, pregnancy, career needs, physical and emotional illnesses, and so forth?

When pastorally ministering to youth, adults should reflect with adolescents on these matters. This reflecting is vital not only because it will aid adolescents in their own growth and reflection toward maturity, but also because quite often the adult youth minister is the only available voice to provide adolescents with this needed reflection and challenge.

Discussions of premarital sexual activity entail many factors. Psychologist Eugene Kennedy notes that such discussions should include an examination of the significance and "meaning" of such behavior for these two young people, the integrative aspects of this sexual behavior, and the place that "Christian values" occupy in this behavior, along with some reflection on evidence in the relationship

264

of such unhealthy aspects of human relating as selfishness and the use of the other.[57]

The authors of *Human Sexuality* conclude that it is difficult to give precise guidelines for what premarital sexual behavior is actually appropriate. They advise that "premarital sexual morality is largely a matter of drawing honest and appropriate lines."[58] In attempting to evaluate premarital sexual activity, the authors offer the following seven values that can be reflected upon.[59]

Self-liberating   The sexual activity contributes to "wholesome" self-interest and fulfillment.

Other-enriching   The sexual activity concerns itself with the care and well-being of the other.

Honest   The sexual relationship reflects, in an open and truthful way, the depth of the relationship between these two individuals.

Faithful   The sexual relationship reflects a trust and commitment to each other that is growing and, at the same time, is enabling each person to continue in a growthful way in other human relationships.

Socially responsible   The sexual relationship must be cognizant of the larger community and not be isolated from the concerns and needs of others.

Life-serving   The sexual relationship is life-enhancing, and this quality usually leads the two individuals to procreation and the development of the family relationship.

Joyous   The sexual relationship is a joyful experience that reflects enjoyment and celebration of the depths of this love relationship.

Pastorally speaking, the author believes that there is a difficulty in attempting to convey the richness and importance of these seven values to adolescents at the secondary and college-undergraduate levels. Quite often, adolescents, because of their own psychological needs, are unappreciative or cannot grasp the depth of these values and the importance of their inclusion in sexual behavior. The suggestions offered toward the end of this chapter attempt to convey the depth of these and other values to adolescents' deepening understanding of sexuality.

It would be helpful in our discussion of premarital sexuality, particularly as it pertains to adolescents, to note four specific points. First, there is a direct link between sexual intercourse and marriage.

The authors of *Human Sexuality* rightly remind: "It bears repeating: there exists an essential relationship between sex and marriage. Even in the wake of a sexual revolution, it can be maintained and substantiated that marriage is the ideal context for the full human realization and self-communication that is involved in the sexual expression of love."[60] This essential relationship needs repeating, and in pastoral work with young people there is an important need to spend time reflecting on this union of sexuality and marriage.

Second, all the authors who have been quoted in this chapter make the point that utter *honesty* is needed in discussing sexuality because sexual intercourse can too often be used for selfish and unchristian motives. In this regard, Curran asks, "Can one be sure one is not taking advantage of another?"[61] Of course, when one considers the powerful effects of adolescent sexual urges, this becomes a critical and important question. Keane observes that premarital sexuality "can cover a fair degree of selfishness and immaturity."[62] Furthermore, the authors of *Human Sexuality* assert that "young people in particular should be challenged to question themselves as to whether they are not simply using each other to prove their respective masculinity, feminity, sexual attractiveness or prowess."[63] Mindful of the developmental needs that adolescents have, it is not unlikely that immature sexual responses and selfishness, which frequently mask a defense of inner insecurity and doubts, are often part of the adolescent sexual experience.

Third, it certainly is true that many adolescent sexual experiences are immature and selfish ways of humanly relating because the adolescents who are involved "often do not feel a sense of responsibility for their partners."[64] Still, there are many examples of adolescent sexual expression that manifest some level of commitment through care and intimacy toward the other. Thus, the *level of commitment* that is operative in an adolescent's relationship with another is an important point of discussion.

Fourth, it is true that the adolescent experience of premarital sexuality can be such that either does not encourage growth or it is clearly harmful. Engaging in sexual intercourse, especially when psychological maturity is still unrealized, can foster in adolescents an illusory sense of commitment. When adolescents experience their sexuality at this most intimate level, an intense attachment, or what might be called "psychic bonding," can occur even though the relationship itself does not evince this depth or intensity. This situation, in turn, is often unfreeing since it leads adolescents to seek more sexual involvement in the relationship, frequently at the expense of greater dialog and understanding, which are, of course, the foundation for any authentic experience of love. Likewise, when there is sexual activity at this deepest of levels, the rupturing or terminating of the relationship (which, of course, is quite common in the adolescent experience) can leave adolescents open to intense hurt. The disappointment and pain that arise from this failed relationship might lead an adolescent to be either wary of future relationships or doubtful of the possibility of a stable, permanent commitment. Adults who have ministered to people in their late twenties and early thirties have frequently been surprised by just how many young adults, who have been rejected and hurt in earlier relationships, have opted to avoid any deep level of commitment to another. It is also possible for the hurt that can arise from premarital sexual behavior to easily lead a person to a negative, exploitative, retaliatory, self-deprecating abuse of sex with future partners, or to a retreat inward that fosters a punitive sense of the self and sows the seeds of insecurity and self-doubt.

Utilizing the perspective of developmental limitedness, the author concurs with the stated opinions of the noted Catholic moralists who have been quoted here. Sexual intercourse is intimately linked to the union of a man and a woman that is realized in the covenant relationship of marriage and proclaimed through sacramental union in the presence of the worshipping community. Bearing this in mind, there is always something *essential* missing in strictly premarital intercourse, which is therefore always morally wrong. The degree of moral wrongfulness, however, in those instances in which such physical expression may occur between adolescents, can be remarkably different. In some cases, even substanially different.

What criteria might serve as the basis for determining this? Four criteria would have to be used in trying to determine the degree of moral wrongfulness in such unfortunate situations when one is confronted with them in a pastoral setting. To be looked for are the following: (1) a distinct level of psychological maturity, that allows for freedom, responsibility, and commitment, that can actually be gendered by each adolescent; (2) a realization that this relationship is an overwhelmingly positive, growthful experience that manifests both human and Christian values; (3) an awareness of Jesus Christ and Christian values in this relationship; and (4) some conscious expression of commitment to marry that realizes the permanency of this physical expression. To expand on these four guidelines the following considerations are offered:

1   In the psychologically mature relationship, there is sufficient level of emotional and psychological maturity to allow these two adolescents to engage freely, responsibly, and honestly in such an act. It is clear that this level of maturity is distinctly beyond adolescents in the secondary school years. Only those adolescents who are in the post-secondary school experience of the working world or undergraduate study could be expected to have acquired the developmental maturity to engage in such sexual activity in a truly free and responsible manner. Futhermore, although this level of psychological maturity is possible in the college undergraduate years, it is questionable whether any significant number of late adolescents have achieved the level of psychological maturity that allows for this type of sexual expression in the context of authentic Christian commitment.[65]

2   In the positive, growthful relationship, two adolescents have developed to the extent that the dominant experience in their relationship is the expression of authentic Christian values. These values include the values expressed by the authors of *Human Sexuality* as well as an evident expression of the Christian values that are mentioned in Gal 5:22–24. Furthermore, there must be the presence and nurturance of human values that are required for positive human growth—values such as empathy, altruism, other-centeredness (increased positive feelings toward family, friends, peers), deepening self-insight, and the motivation for future mature growth.

3   In the third relationship, the experience of Jesus Christ is present as a conscious, validating source of support for the adolescents. That is to say, Jesus exercises a significant role in the adolescent's experience of both his or her personal self and the other's self. In other words, Jesus truly makes a difference for these adolescents. Thus, the adolescents are aware of, committed to, and thankful for Jesus' presence in their relationship with each other.

4   In the fourth relationship, there is a commitment to marriage in the foreseeable future between the two adolescents. "Foreseeable future" is, of course, a relative term that depends on the actual

situation of the young people and is determined, for example, by economic situation, studies, work situation, or other factors.

In addition to the admittedly limited number of adolescents who fit into one or more of these four categories, pastoral consideration must also be given to the vast majority of adolescents, at both the secondary school and the college undergraduate level, who engage in premarital sexual activity within the context of a wide variety of commitments. This variety includes sexual experiences that are devoid of commitment—chance encounters and isolated experiences of intercourse; sexual experiences that have some visible evidence of affection and regard; and sexual experiences in which several levels of commitment are present but, because of personal life situation, psychological factors, lack of maturity, and sinful tendencies, authentic Christian commitment is still impossible. Sexual acts in these circumstances are morally suspect, but pastoral care and solicitousness concerning these young people are nonetheless warranted and should be the norm. In ministering to these adolescents within the framework of developmental limitedness, adults should attempt to follow the guidelines and questions that were mentioned earlier in this chapter and also use the suggestions that can be found in the last section of this chapter.

From an overall perspective, when adults minister to these youth (again, the vast majority of young people who engage in premarital intercourse), they should try to address the following three areas in particular:

Development   What is this adolescent's level of maturity? What issues underlie this adolescent's sexual expression?

Growth   Consider what level of human growth and spiritual growth has taken place and is taking place in this adolescent. How does this adolescent grow? How and to what extent is this adolescent integrating sexuality with other facets of his or her own life (spiritual, emotional, etc.)?

Limitations   At what level is the adolescent's understanding of the inadequacies and limitations of this relationship (insecurities, possessiveness, control, manipulation, use of another)? Does the adolescent have self-insight into these realities? Is he or she capable of gaining greater insight as to the "why" of his or her behavior? How does (or how will) the adolescent deal with these inadequacies?

Finally, it would be a disservice to speak of a pastoral ministry to youth without addressing the use of contraceptive devices. The amount of out-of-wedlock pregnancies is a moral, psychological, and social concern. Any adult who has contact with youth is aware of the huge rise in unwanted teen-age pregnancies and the profound personal, social, and economic dislocation that this experience creates for many adolescents, their families, and, of course, the child who is born. In 1979, the latest year for which statistics are available, "there were an estimated 597,800 out-of-wedlock babies born in America, accounting for an estimated 17 percent of all births."[66] A vast proportion of these unwanted pregnancies involve adolescents who are incapable, both psychologically and economically, to either marry or care for their children. And, of course, there are numerous reasons why adolescents do not take preventive measures when engaging in sexual intercourse.[67]

What is the adult's response, in a pastoral situation, when he or she encounters adolescents who clearly lack the psychological and spiritual maturity—not to mention the financial resources—to be responsible to each other, but nevertheless are engaging in sexual intercourse without attempting any type of precaution (for whatever reasons)? Philip Keane's comments are helpful here. First, Keane states that in those rare instances in which premarital intercourse is not a moral evil, then, the use of contraceptives is also without moral wrong provided the couple is open to having children in later years. He then discusses the vast majority of cases in which premarital intercourse is morally suspect. In these instances, Keane observes, the use of contraceptives lessens the wrong because it is alleviating the possibility of a child for which the couple is incapable of assuming responsibility.[68]

My own belief is that, in light of the magnitude of unwanted pregnancies and the great disinclination among adolescents to use contraceptive devices or take preventive measures regarding their sexual behavior, adolescents who use contraceptive measures might well be growing in maturity and be willing to take at least some responsibility for their behavior. In these instances, I find their behavior to be morally tolerable.[69] By this statement, however, I do not mean to sanction the use of contraceptive devices. I merely maintain that in this complex pastoral situation, in which two adolescents are engaging and will continue to engage in a sexual relationship, regardless of what an adult says, adults have a serious obligation to deal with the adolescents' situation *as it is*. At the same time, of course, adults need to lovingly challenge the adolesents to reflect on their level of commitment, the responsibility that each one is taking for the other, the inadequacies in their relationship, and the ways in which their relationship is still in need of growth.

This complex pastoral situation is often further complicated by the lack of deep reflective capacities on the part of one or both adolescents. In such situations, both adolescents should be encouraged to discuss their feelings and views on various methods of birth control. The use of artificial contraceptives is also complicated by the ages of the two young people. It is one thing for an adolescent boy to use a contraceptive device, and quite another matter for an adolescent girl, especially when the contraceptive device is used internally—birth control pills, for example. The two adolescents must not only honestly air their feelings on these issues, but also actively seek both medical advice and professional opinions about the consequences of using artificial means of contraception. This is especially true for adolescent girls whose developmental-physiological changes might be seriously affected by various contraceptives.

In discussing the use of contraceptives with adolescents, it is important that adults facilitate and encourage honest, candid discussions with the adolescents concerning the use of contraceptives and, most importantly, *who* will be using them. This particular decision should be arrived at freely, after a thorough, frank discussion—a discussion that does not allow the coercing dominance of one adolescent to influence the other. It is important to remember that the use of contraceptive devices always has the potential to be morally wrong when they are used, for example, under the cloud of force, fear, threat, intimidation, or manipulation. Adults can profit pastorally from discussions with adolescents on this topic because the discussion can discover how this couple make decisions, how they relate to each other, and the degree to which they communicate with each other as well as the quality of the communication. It might also be helpful for adults to offer their own reflections to the couple about how these two adolescents make decisions and communicate with each other. Adult reflection on the adolescents' interaction can be a valuable resource for them as they continue to grow in their relationship.

In summary, then, the following maxim can be a guide in discussing this issue with adolescents: If adolescents feel that they must take on the adult behavior of a sexual relationship, then how do they take *responsibility* for the consequences of this relationship? This approach might appear deceptively pragmatic and, therefore, morally questionable, yet it contains the essential element of *pastoral realism*, which is so necessary whenever we call one another to Christian growth through our ministry.

Counseling Suggestions for Adolescent Sexuality

The following suggestions, questions, and techniques incorporate the pastoral approach of developmental limitedness and might prove helpful to adults who minister to adolescents when they must confront the area of adolescent sexuality.

Suggestion 1

Any adult who ministers to adolescents regarding their sexuality must first consider his or her own approach to sexuality. Adults might well ask themselves the following questions as they continue their ministry to youth.

1 How do I personally respond when I am confronted with questions, challenges, or dilemmas regarding sexuality?

2 What is *my* theology of sexuality?

3 Do I (or have I continued to) pray, reflect, and discuss my theology of sexuality with other adults and professionals?

4 What are my personal positions on sexual questions? To what extent have I used the church and theological writing as a source for my position?

5 If and when I discuss questions of sexuality with adolescents, how would I characterize my own manner? Am I open? defensive? competent? frightened? uneasy? challenging? domineering? loving?

6 *Why* do I want to discuss sexual matters with adolescents or counsel them in this area?

7 What *values* do I wish to convey to adolescents about sexuality when I minister to them?

8 Am I mature enough, both spiritually and psychologically, to discuss sexual questions with adolescents?

Suggestion 2

One of the major tasks in ministry to adolscents is helping them grow in the acceptance of their own sexuality. It is to be hoped that adolescents can grow to accept their own sexuality as being far more than mere physical expression. Sexuality is a *way of being;* it is *the* way in which we experience ourselves in relation to the world. Donald Goergen points to this when he states that sexuality has an affective dimension that is distinct from the genital-physical side, the aspect that is the usual center of attention during the adolescent years. Goergen calls this affective dimension "the totality of affection, friendship, and tenderness in life."[70]

Attention to the expanding, deepening dimension of sexuality is important in adolescent development. All too often, the adolescent understanding of sexuality is limited to a genital definition. This perspective deprives adolescents of the rich mystery that sexuality encompasses. Our broadening view of sexuality, for example, incorporates the presence and reality of human friendship. What do adolescents mean when they talk about friendship or a particular friend? How is friendship experienced in an adolescent's life? How have certain friendships deepened with time? It is often good to discuss *specific* friendships in an adolescent's life. Ask, for example, how the adolescent shows affection in these relationships. (See also the strategies presented in the discussion of Erikson in chapter 3 for a further discussion of friendship in adolescence.)

A related question reflects the adolescent's sense of maleness or femaleness. Ask, for example, what being a man or a woman means to this adolescent. Another way to approach this issue is to ask the adolescent—usually middle and late adolescents can best deal with this question—What does it mean for you to be a person? After this reflection, a more specific question might be, What does being a woman (or a man) mean for your definition (or how does it add to your definition? Adolescents can also be invited to share feelings and views on the opposite sex. These responses can often indicate to the adult any gender roles and stereotypes that the adolescent has.

To give Christian values to these questions, the adolescent might further reflect on this dimension of personhood by exploring what is *Christian* about being a person? About being a *sexual* person? This particular reflection often provides insight into the adolescent's values. Again, it is also helpful to spend time with the affective dimension of Scripture, exploring the characters and personalities of individuals such as David and Samuel, or friendships such as those between Ruth and Naomi, Mary and Elizabeth, Jesus and John, Paul and Timothy. What did it mean for these people to be friends? To be truly caring for one another? How did they experience friendship in their lives? This technique is often helpful with younger adolescents who might appreciate such models or are in need of concrete expressions of personhood and friendship. For adolescents of every age, Jesus, Mary, and Paul are valuable expressions of personhood and Christian adulthood. Discuss, for example, how Jesus showed, through His own person and manhood, His love and care for others.

One of the most helpful ways to understand the mystery and depth of human friendship is to examine how the Jesus who emerges from John's Gospel can be viewed as a model of friendship. Through the Last Supper Discourse, Jesus proclaims His own openness (John 14:14), His own intimate union with the Father (John 14:11) and with us (John 15:4), His personal faithfulness (John 14:18), His own commitment to the Father and to us (John 15:9–10), His willingness for self-sacrifice (John 15:13), the need for dependency (John 15:4–5), the inevitability of departure (John 16:5–16), and the promise of eventual return and faithfulness (John 16:16). Jesus' own life is lived in a very real commitment to this friendship. We might reflect with an adolescent on the extent to which these different qualities from Jesus' life are present in the adolescent's friendship with others. Are these qualities important for the adolescent? Does the adolescent view these qualities as growing in himself or herself? Reflection on the human mystery of friendship is invaluable in helping to broaden and expand an adolescent's understanding of his or her own sexuality.

Suggestion 3

Because adolescent maturation involves a growing experience of complexity, it is helpful to examine what roles in an adolescent's life he or she finds nurturing and life-giving. Examine the various roles that the adolescent has taken on—for example, friend, son, daughter, student, close friend. Reflect with the adolescent on the quality of these roles, how comfortable the adolescent is with these roles, and the relational needs inherent in these roles. Again, the focus should be on how these various roles are *life-giving* and *nourishing* for both the adolescent and others. The following questions can help adults aid adolescents in examining their role in relationship: What does the relationship do for you? Are there ways in which this relationship has changed you? How do you give to the other(s) in this relationship? How do you let others give to you in this relationship? How are you growing in this relationship? By linking the relationship to a specific role, adolescents are often more able to consciously reflect on their own life experience. Specifically, regarding the experience of sexuality, ask adolescents to reflect on how their sexuality is part of the relationship, how this might be altering or influencing the relationship.

Because honesty is a critical aspect of sexuality, the authors of *Human Sexuality* suggest that honesty and other Christian values be explored in various roles and relationships in the adolescent's life.[71] This can be an excellent focus for adolescent self-reflection. Adults can concentrate on specific content-filled experiences, roles, and relationships, and reflect with the adolescent on how honesty, caring, and sensitivity are present. Adults might then shift the discussion to see if these same values are present in the adolescent's sexual behavior. Usually by the later years of secondary school, and certainly by the college years, adolescents can make meaningful associations between their own values and behaviors and then reflect on these associations across various areas of their lives. Comparing how values are expressed in a sexual way with how they are expressed in other areas of the adolescent's life can be very enlightening for the adolescent. Adults might also note whether there is any defensiveness in the adolescent response. Can this adolescent actually face the possible "disvalue" in this relationship—the lack of honesty, the lack of care, etc.?

Suggestion 4

The Christian perspective on sexuality has always stressed the nature of responsibility through personal commitment in a relationship. We have already noted that the adolescent passage involves attempts to establish an identity and deal with intimacy needs. As a person's identity and the need for intimacy find increasing expression in commitment to others, it is helpful to spend time reflecting on what commitment means in the adolescent's life. Adults might keep in mind the following questions: What ideas and values most reflect this adolescent as a person? How does the adolescent show commitment in this relationship? How is this commitment deepening? In what ways is sexual expression a part of this commitment?

Adults would do well to note not only the adolescent's ideas on commitment, but also the behavioral characteristics and affective dimension of the adolescent's response. Do the adolescent's behaviors—cognitive (what one thinks of another's actions and one's own actions), affective (how one feels about another's self and one's own self), and behavioral (how one treats and acts toward another)—reflect this commitment? Does the adolescent commit himself or herself in all these areas of his or her life? Adults might then note the following: What is the adolescent's notion of permanency in this relationship? Can the adolescent understand the importance of permanency in sexual expression? The adolescent needs to reflect on what commitment means in the relationship not only for himself or herself, but also for the other—that is, the adolescent must ask how this commitment is part of *our* relationship? In what sense is this relationship viewed by the adolescent as incomplete? Can this adolescent reflect on what might be lacking in this relationship?

Jacqueline Haessly and Daniel DiDomizio note that meaningful commitment incorporates four basic qualities:[72]

Trust   How open can I be with this other person about my own self? Can I share with the other the deepest levels of my self?

Equality   Can I accept this other person for who he or she really is? Do my attitudes toward this other person respect him or her as my equal?

Mutuality   How are my needs in this relationship being met? How are the needs of the other being met? Do I demonstrate a sensitivity toward the other's needs? How do I do this?

Fidelity   Can I allow both myself and the other to grow in this relationship? How do I resolve conflicts and misunderstandings in this relationship? Can I be both present and loyal to this person even when difficulties emerge or in the future?

Reflection on these and other aspects of commitment can be quite helpful to adolescents' growing understanding of what commitment actually entails and how their sexual behavior does and does not meet or express authentic selfless commitment to the other.

Suggestion 5

Because adolescence is a developmental stage in which human growth is intensely experienced, it is important that adults note positive features of growth in adolescents. When an adult ministers to an adolescent, for example, and the focus of their discussion is the adolescent's sexual behavior or a particular relationship, the adult should attempt to discover how the adolescent is actually growing in the relationship. Some of the signs of positive growth that the adult might look for include the following: a more positive self-image, a sense of inner security, an increasing capacity for self-disclosure (which is usually more difficult for males than for females[73]), a greater awareness of the adolescent's own affective life (as well as an awareness of the other in the relationship), a growing sense of self-identity, and an increasingly greater capacity for intimacy. The adult might also note the extent to which this relationship helps the adolescent face personal difficulties and deal with inner insecurities and fears.

Related to this question of positive growth is one of the most difficult pastoral dilemmas facing adults who minister to youth today. What is the adult's pastoral approach to adolescent sexual behavior that lacks mature commitment and quite often exhibits only a limited understanding of what commitment means and entails? Concrete manifestations of such a relationship include the following: no agreement to marry, a limited degree of intimacy (self-disclosure or open communication), a significant lack in the capability for mature love, and a limited perspective and understanding about the future of this relationship. At the same time, however, there exists in the relationship some level of emotional commitment that can be characterized by an affective closeness, a positive liking, a loyalty to the other, and a level of caring that goes beyond the self to an actual desire to aid the other. In such relationships, positive signs of human growth are frequently evidenced in the adolescent; that is, there is a growing comfortableness with self, a greater feeling of security (both emotional and sexual security), a growing desire to care for the other, an increasing degree of sensitivity, and a greater capacity for self-disclosure. In other words, although the sexual behavior of these two adolescents fails to embody the level of commitment that mature human and Christian love would entail, an appreciable growth nevertheless exists for these adolescents as a result of this relationship. This dilemma leaves many adults in a quandary, which is an increasingly common occurrence today. In essence, the adolescents have found in this relationship an experience for both self-discovery and human growth. How should the adult respond in such situations?

First, I believe that this description of youth applies only to late adolescents. Sexual intercourse before this time, that is, prior to a significant level of maturity that is characterized by growing self-identity, is best viewed in terms of the psychological motivations that have been discussed earlier in this chapter as well as the adolescent's own disvalue of sexuality and failure to appreciate the goodness of his or her sexual nature. (Of course, these same factors are also part of the late adolescent's experience of sexuality.)

Developmental limitedness seeks to both minister to this adolescent in the context of the adolescent's developmental level and, at the same time, address the limiting character of such sexual expression for this adolescent. First, this approach does not dismiss such sexual experiences as harmless or meaningless. Such encounters are indeed limited and lack the total self-expression of commitment that characterizes the Christian view of sexuality. Yet the adult must take into account both the real possibilities inherent in the actual situation and the current developmental level of the adolescents. And, as a general principle, it is pastorally unsound to demand an abrupt termination of such a relationship. This is especially true if the relationship shows a level of commitment that has developed over time and evinces positive signs of affection and human growth for the adolescents.

Several reasons can be given for not demanding a termination of such a relationship. First, to terminate such a relationship might leave the adolescent with intense pain and isolation. We need only recall the importance that relationships exercise during the adolescent years to understand the psychic investment that is so often involved in adolescent relationships. Second, insisting that such relationships be terminated might well create a bitterness and anger that would foreclose the possibility of continued growth for these adolescents. Finally, the adult with whom these adolescents share such personal experiences might well be the only source of deepening self-insight and reflection for these young persons. It is important that such a channel for growth remain open, and the insistence that this relationship be terminated might lead the adolescents to cease their relationship with the adult.

We should again note that we are speaking of those adolescent sexual relationships in which adolescents find personal meaning and attach some positive level of meaning to this relationship; in essence, there is some degree of commitment for the adolescents who are involved. As we have noted, from a pastoral standpoint, the adult faces a difficult situation. A sexual expression that is limited and lacks a deep level of commitment but, at the same time, is growth-producing (and whose termination might be destructive, given the developmental state of the adolescents) poses a distinct challenge for the adult. In such situations, the adult needs to consider several areas: (1) What is the actual level of commitment that is present in this relationship? How is it growing? (2) What is the personal growth that is occurring in the relationship as it presently exists? How does this growth compare to an earlier time? What are the possibilities for future growth? (3) What is the developing meaning that comes to these adolescents from this relationship? That is to say, does this relationship lead to a deepening of these adolescents' expression of positive human and Christian values, other-centered expressions in other relationships, as well as the place of Jesus Christ in their lives?

With these three emphases in mind, a developmental limitedness perspective accepts the adolescent where he or she presently is. A developmental limitedness approach, however, does not sanction such behavior, but rather understands this behavior, in a pastoral way, and adopts a challenging yet understanding stance. That is to say, the adolescent can be led through discussions with the adult to a growing reflection on what this relationship *means* (the meaning the adolescent gives to the relationship), what *insight* this relationship gives the adolescent about himself or herself, how this relationship allows the adolescent to *grow* and *care,* how this relationship is being *honest* (and how this adolescent is growing in honesty with the other), and how *commitment* to Jesus and others is being realized in this relationship. These relationships are often difficult to minister to, yet it is precisely in these very difficult pastoral situations that adolescents most need adult input. The general norm for adults is to accept the adolescent personally, yet challenge the adolescent to further growth and conversion.

279

Suggestion 6

Charles Curran has remarked that one of the false statements that adolescents offer to justify premarital sexual behavior maintains that if they "feel it is all right" they can do it.[74] Such statements often typify the adolescent's withdrawal into self-absorption and his or her failure to face other factors and perspectives regarding the relationship. This type of statement produces a false dualism because it erroneously distinguishes between the soul and body in sexual expression, whereas the Christian perspective places great emphasis on the body and sees the essential unity of the spiritual and the physical selves (1 Cor 6:15–20). One way to approach the unity of soul and body in ministering to an adolescent is to simply ask the young person what his or her body really means or how he or she reflects the Spirit through his or her body. For younger adolescents, who are often concerned with bodily appearances as they begin to experience adolescence, such questioning is inappropriate. For older adolescents, however, the place of the body in one's Christian life is worth serious reflection.

Theologian Bernard Häring has located the importance of the body in the context of the Christian vocation to serve others.[75] It might be helpful to ask the adolescent to determine how his or her body reflects caring, loving, and sensitivity toward others, as well as how it is used for Christian service. As the need for intimacy grows, adolescents so often focus on feelings and affective notions of the self. This, of course, is natural and good; yet for the Christian it is inadequate. It is important that adolescents experience Jesus' call as a total self-giving that includes their own *physical self*. How is this physical self given over to Jesus so that the call to "come, follow me" might be more real in the adolescent's life?

Suggestion 7

Chastity is not a term we hear much about today. Most probably, the term derives a certain onus from the negative reactions that plague the experiences of many adult Christians. With the advent of the sexual revolution, little is said in the adolescent's surroundings about chastity. Adolescents need to realize that these negative reactions have shaped a false stereotype. Chastity means a *completeness*, a wholeness of self that reflects whether a person is married or single as well as the proper use of the person's sexuality in the way he or she relates with others. Theologian William Cosgrave has proposed three essential elements to any understanding of chastity.[76] First, in the experience of sexuality, there is need for *appreciation*. In other words, a person appreciates the "values" and "ideals" that are present in his or her sexual behavior. Foremost among these values are the care and commitment that the person expresses in his or her sexual behavior. The fullest meaning of sexuality implies an understanding of sexuality's deepest truth—the care and commitment that one person gives to another. Second, there is a real need for *integration*. The integrated self is capable of accepting his or her own sexuality, placing it in proper perspective, and experiencing the sexual self in loving and caring ways, whether the person is married or single. Third, we must realize that in sexuality there is a real need for *control* because "one must discipline oneself so as to ensure truly loving sexual behavior in all one's relationships."[77] A person's inability to control himself or herself reflects an inability to take responsibility for this important area of his or her life. Without control, freedom is lost because a person's sexuality is then left to forces and influences that are beyond the true self.

Yet, in a world that is inundated with sexual objects and nuances, control can often be a stumbling block for many adolescents. The environment, the need for self-expression, and the demands of human intimacy make sexual expression for many youth simply an expected part of their lives. In years past, the chaste life was often viewed as a component of the will; will power was the obvious way to control sexual expression. This emphasis—actually an overemphasis—on will is particularly shortsighted when it is applied to the adolescent years. It has already been noted that sexual activity among young people reflects many needs that encompass many motives. It is obvious that adolescent attempts to deal with sexuality are far more than simply a desire for control by the will.

Control of sexuality during the adolescent years is tied to numerous psychological factors including identity consolidation, the meeting of intimacy needs, and the integration of the self, which leads to adult maturity. Likewise, the adolescent's sexual decisions reflect this personal self at a distinct developmental level as the adolescent's situation and actual environment exert pressures and demands. Additionally, the adolescent's own self-image, feelings of self, and personal sense of support that he or she feels all contribute to an ability to control and master the sexual self.[78] Hence, even though the will is an important factor in sexual behavior, to concentrate solely on a personal self-will as the source of personal self-control is counter-productive, potentially self-defeating, and frustrating for the adolescent.

The adolescent's development of a sense of chasteness in sexual decision making must incorporate the multifaceted influences that contribute to the adolescent's overall sense of personal decision making. Adolescents need a warm, supportive environment in which to dialog about sexuality. In personal dialog, this means compassionate understanding for the adolescent, respect for the adolescent as a person, and acceptance of the adolescent at his or her developmental level. From a communal standpoint, this suggests both positive personal relationships with peers and ample opportunities to dialog with others about faith, meaning, and values. Adults should take the lead both by providing adolescents with resources and opportunities through social environments, such as clubs, programs, and youth ministry, and by helping adolescents find in these communal experiences positive, affirming sources of support for the forming of authentic Christian values.

The concept of inner control has received attention in psychological literature. Psychologists describe the "locus of control" as one's feelings of mastery over the events and actions of one's life.[79] If a person possesses a sense of inner control, then that person considers his or her own personal initiatives and efforts to be the determining factor for successes and failures—the outcomes and consequences of his or her actions. On the other hand, if a person views his or her life as somehow predetermined by an outside "agent," then the person will feel that he or she has little control over his or her life and future possibilities. Developing a sense of inner control is essential for healthy human development since "it is understandable that feelings of security, self-confidence, and satisfaction depend to a considerable extent on the belief people can control their environments."[80]

This deepening sense of inner control meshes nicely with, and presents a psychological complement to, moral theology's distinction between absolutes and ideals, that is, the difference between the commands and the counsels of Jesus's teaching. We are admonished, for example, by the command not to kill, yet as Christians we must also pay heed to Jesus' counsel against anger (Mt 5); in other words, we need to control the interior disposition that might lead us to kill and harm others. So, too, must we pay heed to the command against adultery and the counsel to control our own interior dispositions. Sexual desires, fantasies, or placing ourselves in specific situations can often lead us to external acts that violate the virtue (counsel) of chastity. For real growth to occur, the moral life needs the nurturance and care accorded these interior dispositions. A psychological sense of control of one's life—the feeling that *I* can accomplish what I seek and desire—offers the opportunity for real fidelity and growth regarding the virtue of chastity. As a consequence, adolescents can develop with greater self-confidence because they can control *their own* thoughts, feelings, and attractions regarding sexual matters. In other words, a healthy sense of control complements the adolescent's desire for chasteness.

Likewise, a sense of control can greatly contribute to positive feelings of self and enhance a young person's ability to make decisions, including such sexual decisions as whether to have premarital intercourse, how physically involved to become, or whether to consider marriage. The fostering of an inner sense of control is based on many factors, not the least of which is the level of the adolescent's sense of personal identity. The identity factor is acutely important because "adolescents, who are undergoing identity consolidation, are pressured either to assume responsibility for their sexual decision making or to abdicate responsibility."[81] Other factors that also contribute to this sense of control are the quality of the adolescent's family life, the meaning and importance that the adolescent gives to religious values, and the adolescent's actual understanding of what personal decisions reallly mean for his or her life.[82]

Control for the adolescent, therefore, is far more complicated than a simple volitional response. Adults who are ministering to adolescents must not only aid them in identifying and understanding their sexual feelings and impulses, but also mesh these inner experiences with Christian values.

It is important to emphasize values such as life-giving, sharing, caring, and commitment. Helping adolescents to articulate and reflect these values in their relationships is also a vital component of chaste control for the sexual self. Most of all, however, adults must help adolescents to reflect on both the experience of Jesus in their lives and the real consequences of their commitment to Jesus. In stressing the importance of formulating a "more positive theology of sexuality," Cardinal Joseph Bernardin said during a recent Synod of Bishops:

> Before people can fully live by the values Jesus taught us, they must experi-
> ence conversion. They must come to know and love the Lord. They must
> experience Him in their lives; His love, mercy, understanding and compas-
> sion must be real to them. Only then will they be willing to commit them-
> selves to Him and accept the demands that He makes. Only then will they be
> ready to make that surrender which is expected of every Christian.[83]

Above all, adolescents need this experience of Jesus in their lives. They need a personal experience of the Lord that will nourish, sustain, and challenge them to constant growth and conversion. Any adult who ministers to high school and college adolescents must therefore ask the following critical question: *How does knowing me make the presence of Jesus more real for these adolescents?* How do I contribute to the adolescents' experience of Jesus through my discussion, support, acceptance, and challenges?

Suggestion 8

Because sexuality is limiting—indeed, all human activity is limiting—adolescents need to reflect on the limits and inadequacies of their own sexual expressions. Are there developmental factors and interior dispositions that create a desire for control, manipulation, further jealousies, or lustful desires that deny the Christian view of sexuality for these adolescents?

In ministering to older adolescents, the following questions that explore what one expresses by one's behavior are important for young persons to ask themselves: How do I limit myself in my sexual behavior and fall short of what I desire to express? How do I deal with the inadequacies or shortcomings of my own sexual expression? What do my actions say about me? Are there attitudes or actions in my sexual behavior with another that I do not directly intend? Topics that can be explored with adolescents include frustration, guilt, inadequacy, manipulation, jealousy, insecurity, lack of commitment, immaturity, and selfishness. To aid adolescents in discussing these topics, suggest that they talk about how a sexual relationship is loving and how it expresses Christian values. Then, when this discussion has been completed, pose the following question: Tell me, are there ways in which your relationship is not loving and caring? This technique allows adolescents to compare the elements of a relationship that are enriching, growthful, and graced with the elements that are lacking, incomplete, and sinful. This healthy sense of self-discovery can provide adolescents a needed perspective for their relationship *as they are experiencing it.*

It is critically important for adult ministers to dialog with adolescents about the limits of the relationship. Pastorally speaking, it can be said with some assurance that adolescents who either are unable to discuss limiting factors in the relationship they are experiencing, or are overly defensive about such a topic are the ones whose involvement in the relationship is often motivated by psychological needs and developmental insecurities. Such adolescents do not possess the freedom and maturity to honestly look at their own behavior. Adults should note such reluctance and defensiveness. At the same time, adults who pose such questions and are, in effect, challenging a particular adolescent, should exercise both care and compassion toward the young person. Adults should also ask themselves how this challenge will really aid the adolescent and what they, as adults, hope the adolescent will gain from such a challenge. If this kind of questioning is to be growthful for adolescents, adults, too, must come to the dialog with real self-honesty and genuine care for the young persons.

Some Final Observations

Several final observations can be made about pastoral ministry that concerns adolescent sexuality.

First, adults should not be reticent in expressing and proclaiming the Christian value of sexuality and the central role that commitment exercises in the Christian understanding of sexuality. Eugene Kennedy reminds that adults need "to present their own convictions and their own code of sexual morality. Adolescents expect that adults have thought these things through. They want to hear how adults have worked out their own answers to questions that vex them. When we can be honest and open and not just repeat the statements of others we can reach adolescents more genuinely and they may well want to incorporate our answers into their own moral decisions."[84]

285

Second, as we have noted at the beginning of this chapter, sexual behavior is often symbolic of other needs and motivations for adolescents. This fact is especially pertinent when adults encounter adolescents who might be labeled promiscuous. In many instances, sexual activity can be indicative of deeper emotional struggles and feelings. These adolescents often require more professional guidance and counsel than an adult minister can provide. In such cases, adults should seek advice from other professional sources concerning the possibility of referral.[85]

Third, it must be pointed out that this chapter is not meant to provide a format for fostering positive sex education for adolescents. Rather, its intent is to help adults who are engaged in pastoral ministry with youth to clarify the importance and moral significance of various sexual questions that youth must confront. Yet there might well be some positive steps that religious educators, concerned adults, and pastoral ministers might take in helping to promote an authentic Christian sexual response among adolescents. The author suggests that the following avenues need much more emphasis in pastoral ministry to today's youth.

1   A positive notion of the sacrament of marriage as a joyful, celebrative relationship of two human beings who proclaim in their own unique way the beauty of Christian love.

2   Greater reflections with adolescents on what human intimacy really means in their lives. This would include a broadening definition of the meaning of friendships, an examination of how we truly care for one another, and an emphasis on how loving others through and in Jesus Christ is profoundly linked to our relationships.

3   Special reflection with adolescents on the importance of family life and the role of the family in both the church and today's world.

4   More emphasis on what commitment means in adolescent relationships. Above all, this requires that adults share with adolescents the meaning of their own commitments, how they, as adults, experience commitment, and the value of their commitments.

5   Greater acceptance of adolescents as feeling, thinking persons who deserve respect as persons and who should be provided opportunities in their lives to manifest and witness true Christian service toward others.

6   Active encouragement of adolescents to develop a warm,

affective sense of God's personal love in their lives. In this context, the author cannot help noting Andrew Greeley's tantalizing notion that warm religious images of God are related to positive feelings about sexuality, prayer, and Christian commitment.[86]

Finally, theological reflection and scholarship must never lose sight of the need for loving pastoral care. In a recent article discussing the various perspectives and trends that encompass the term *objective morality*, Philip Keane affirms that the aim of theological utterances is "to lead persons to higher degrees of freedom of action"[87] and that a loving challenge is essential for the individual's growth toward this freedom. He also maintains that in pastoral situations humans "need to be shown care and compassion."[88] He concludes by advising: "If these two points—challenging confrontation and caring compassion—can always be present in pastoral situations, I think the needs of all believers can be reasonably well met while the crucial discussion of moral objectivity continues as it must."[89]

More than anything, it is hoped that these essential ingredients of pastoral ministry—growth, challenge, care, compassion—are highlighted in this chapter through the discussion of adolescent development and the pastoral approach of developmental limitedness. It is when pastoral ministry to youth is designed in terms of loving challenge and continual care that we, as ministers, open for adolescents a deeper awareness of Jesus' call to "come, follow me."

Notes to Chapter Seven

1. Dean R. Hoge, "Students Not Returning to '50s' values," *The Criterion*, September 4, 1981, p. 31.

2. For the interplay of cognitive processes and sexual growth in adolescence, see Richard W. Breese, F.S.C., "The Application of Piagetian Theory to Sexuality: A Preliminary Exploration," *Adolescence* 13, Summer 1978, pp. 275–277.

3. Ann McCreary Juhasz and Mary Sonnenshein-Schneider, "Adolescent Sexual Decision Making : Components and Skills," *Adolescence* 15, Winter 1980, pp. 743–746.

4. Carol A. Wagner, "Sexuality of American Adolescents," *Adolescence* 15, Fall 1980, p. 567.

5. Although the adult need not be an authority on the psychosexual development of the human person, it is important that the adult have an overview of the basic developmental aspects of adolescent sexuality. Recommended reading includes Herant A. Katchadourian and Donald T. Lunde, *Fundamentals of Human Sexuality*, New York: Holt, Rinehart, and Winston, 1975, pp. 1–320; and Janet Shibley Hyde, *Understanding Human Sexuality*, New York: McGraw Hill, 1979, pp. 29–88, 231–255. The importance of the adult's knowledge is reinforced by adolescents' lack of knowledge or misinformation on many aspects of human sexuality.

6. For an overview of adolescent sexual behavior, see Katchadourian and Lunde, *Fundamentals of Human Sexuality*, pp. 221–225; Hyde, *Understanding Human Sexuality*, pp. 240–252; "The Games Teenagers Play," *Newsweek* 96, September 1, 1980, pp. 48–53; and Wagner, "Sexuality of American Adolescents," pp. 567–577.

7. Sidney Callahan, "Personal Growth and Sexuality: Adolescent and Adult Developmental Stages," *Catholic Mind* 80, January 1982, p. 43.

8. John J. Mitchell, "Some Psychological Dimensions of Adolescent Sexuality," *Adolescence* 8, Winter 1972, pp. 447–458.

9. Ibid., p. 449.

10. Ibid., p. 456.

11. Eugene Kennedy, *Sexual Counseling*. New York: The Seabury Press, A Crossroad Book, 1977, p. 106. This book provides an extensive treatment of sexual counseling. Adolescent sexuality is discussed on pp. 105–121.

12. Ibid., p. 108.

13. Of the numerous solid books on the meaning of Christian love, the author has found the following three works quite helpful in his pastoral reflections: John Powell, S.J., *Why Am I Afraid to Tell You Who I Am?* Chicago: Argus Communications Co., 1969; idem, *Why Am I Afraid to Love?* Chicago: Argus Communications Co., 1972; Peter A. Bertocci, *Sex, Love, and the Person*, New York: Sheed and Ward, 1967.

14. For an overview of Catholic moral thinking, the reader should examine Charles E. Curran, *Themes in Fundamental Moral Theology,* Notre Dame, IN, University of Notre Dame Press, 1977; and Timothy E. O'Connell, *Principles for a Catholic Morality,* New York: The Seabury Press, A Crossroad Book, 1978; *Chicago Studies* 13, Fall 1974 (this entire issue is devoted to current thinking in moral theology regarding human life issues. For an extensive theological discussion of Catholic moral thinking regarding sexuality, see Philip Keane, S.S., *Sexual Morality: A Catholic Perspective,* New York: Paulist Press, 1977; and Anthony Kosnik et al., *Human Sexuality: New Directions in American Catholic Thought,* Garden City, NJ, 1979.

15. In traditional thinking, masturbation is viewed as unnatural because the normal physiological process of sexuality (i.e., the insertion of the penis into the vagina) fails to occur. The difficulty with this physiological approach is that even some natural cases of sexual intercourse can fulfill the physiological processes, yet still be unnatural from a human standpoint—rape, for example, sexual abuse or manipulation of another, etc.

16. See the Vatican *Declaration on Certain Questions Concerning Sexual Ethics, Origins* 5, January 22, 1976.

17. For comments on the Vatican Declaration, see Keane, *Sexual Morality,* pp. 184–191; James McManus, C.Ss.R., "Moral Theology Forum: The 'Declaration on Certain Questions Concerning Sexual Ethics': A Discussion," *Clergy Review* 61, June 1976, pp. 231–237; and Charles E. Curran, *Issues in Sexual and Medical Ethics,* Notre Dame, IN, University of Notre Dame Press, 1978, pp. 30–52.

18. For a critique of *Human Sexuality,* see Ralph McInerny, "Do Moral Theologians Corrupt Youth?" *Catholic Mind* 78, April 1980, pp. 33–39. *Human Sexuality* was published too late for Keane to incorporate it into his book, *Sexual Morality,* but it is treated in a footnote at the end of the text; see footnote 22, chapter 9, pp. 227–228. For pastoral reflections and general comments on *Human Sexuality,* see Gregory Kenny, C.M.F., "A New Approach to Sexual Morality," *U.S. Catholic* 43, February 1978, pp. 17–23.

19. *Human Sexuality,* p. 106.

20. Bernard Häring, *Medical Ethics.* Notre Dame, IN, Fides Publishing, 1973, p. 112.

21. For Häring's sensitive treatment of this issue, see *Medical Ethics,* pp. 112–115.

22. Ibid., p. 112.

23. Curran, *Themes in Fundamental Moral Theology,* p. 183.

24. Keane, *Sexual Morality,* p. 93.

25. Lisa Sowle Cahill, "Should I Welcome My Daughter and Her Live-in Mate as Houseguests?" *St. Anthony Messenger* 88, March 1981, p. 30.

26. Dick Reichert, "The Adolescent and Premarital Sex: Moral Pastoral Considerations," *Catholic Charismatic* 5, June/July, 1981, p. 12.

27. Richard A. McCormick, S.J., "Moral Theology Since Vatican II," *Cross Currents* 29, Spring 1979, p. 22.

28. For reflections on the interplay and tension between moral norms and concrete human situations see O'Connell, *Principles for a Catholic Morality,* pp. 155–164; Karl Rahner, S.J., "Morality Without Moralizing," in *The Shape of the Church to Come,* trans. Edward Quinn, London: SPCK, 1974, pp. 64–70; and Charles E. Curran and Richard A. McCormick, S.J., eds., *Readings in Moral Theology No. 1,* New York: Paulist Press, 1979 (see especially Joseph Fuchs, S.J., "The Absoluteness of Moral Norms," pp. 94–137).

29. Donald Goergen, *The Sexual Celibate.* New York: The Seabury Press, A Crossroad Book, 1974, p. 43.

30. This focus on the crucial role exercised by the self in determining the morality of an action highlights current theological reflection by noted Catholic scholars on the role of the self in determining objective morality. See Philip S. Keane, S.S., "The Objective Moral Order: Reflections on Recent Research," *Theological Studies* 43, June 1982, pp. 262–265. Keane brings this issue to the forefront and poses a question of great interest to pastoral ministers of youth when he asks: "Is not our knowledge of the growth traumas undergone by teenagers an objective knowledge which might legitimately be included in a description of the objective moral actions in which they engage?" (p. 264).

31. William Cosgrave, "A Christian Understanding of Sexuality," *Catholic Mind* 78, May 1980, p. 31.

32. Curran, *Themes in Fundamental Moral Theology,* p. 100.

33. For a discussion of masturbatory behavior in adolescence, see Wagner, "Sexuality of American Adolescents," pp. 571–572; Katchadourian and Lunde, *Fundamentals of Human Sexuality,* pp. 274–277; and Hyde, *Understanding Human Sexuality,* 240–241. For a moral treatment of masturbation, see Kosnik et al., *Human Sexuality,* pp. 244–254; Keane, *Sexual Morality,* 57–70; Curran, *Themes in Fundamental Moral Theology,* pp. 180–181; and the Vatican *Declaration, Origins,* pp. 489–490. For some psychological reflections, see Kennedy, *Sexual Counseling,* pp. 122–129.

34. Curran, *Themes in Fundamental Moral Theology,* p. 181.

35. Bernard Häring, "Human Sexuality," *Chicago Studies* 13, Fall 1974, p. 311.

36. Keane, *Sexual Morality,* p. 63.

37. Ibid., p. 47.

38. Ibid., p. 67.

39. Kosnik et al., *Human Sexuality,* p. 251.

40. Kennedy, *Sexual Counseling,* pp. 122–129.

41. Ibid., p. 128.

42. For a discussion of petting behavior during the adolescent years, see Katchadourian and Lunde, *Fundamentals of Human Sexuality*, pp. 224–225. For theological reflection, see Eugene Kennedy, *What a Modern Catholic Believes about Sex*, Chicago: The Thomas More Press, 1971, pp. 60–65; and Keane, *Sexual Morality*, pp. 110–113.

43. John J. Mitchell, "Adolescent Intimacy," *Adolescence* 11, Summer 1976, p. 276.

44. Ibid. [The same page as the preceding note.]

45. Kennedy, *What a Modern Catholic Believes about Sex*, p. 65.

46. Ibid., p. 62.

47. Keane, *Sexual Morality*, p. 112.

48. Ibid.

49. Kosnik et al., *Human Sexuality*, p. 198.

50. For a discussion of premarital sexual behavior during the adolescent years, see Wagner, "Sexuality of American Adolescents," pp. 573–576; Katchadourian and Lunde, *Fundamentals of Human Sexuality*, pp. 312–315; and Hyde, *Understanding Human Sexuality*, p. 242–249. For a theological discussion, see Curran, *Themes in Fundamental Moral Theology*, pp. 182–185; Kennedy, *What a Modern Catholic Believes about Sex*, pp. 65–68; Kosnik et al., *Human Sexuality*, pp. 174–193; and the Vatican *Declaration, Origins*, pp. 491–492.

51. McCormick, "Moral Theology Since Vatican II," p. 24.

52. The Vatican *Declaration, Origins*, p. 491.

53. Curran, *Themes in Fundamental Moral Theology*, p. 183.

54. Keane, *Sexual Morality*, pp. 92–102. Regarding adolescents, Keane says that "we must be pastorally sensitive in dealing with young people who are having casual premarital sexual intercourse" (p. 103). He goes on to say "In no way, however, should our pastoral sensitivity lead us to give the impression that there is any moral justification for casual premarital intercourse" (p. 104).

55. Ibid., p. 103.

56. Ibid., pp. 103–109.

57. Kennedy, *What a Modern Catholic Believes abou Sex*, pp. 66–67.

58. Kosnik et al., *Human Sexuality*, p. 191.

59. Ibid., pp. 112–115. For some pastoral reflections on these values, see Kenny, "A New Approach to Sexual Morality," p. 21.

60. Kosnik et al., *Human Sexuality*, p. 192.

61. Curran, *Themes in Fundamental Moral Theology*, p. 184.

62. Keane, *Sexual Morality*, 105.

63. Kosnik et al., *Human Sexuality*, p. 191.

64. John A. Clippinger, "Adolescent Sexuality and Love," *Journal of Religion and Health* 18, October 1979, p. 277.

65. It is very difficult, of course, to determine how many late adolescents might actually fit this category. My own pastoral work with college undergraduates leads me to concur with Keane's statement that instances of premarital sexual intercourse that are without moral evil are *rare*. There is no doubt, however, that with increasing age and the progression into young adulthood (the twenties), the number of instances does increase, although it is difficult to determine how many people might fit this category. Of course, like all human acts, premarital sexual activity creates its own unique situations. An increasing phenomenon during these years is the number of young adults and even late adolescents who are cohabiting. The pastoral approach to such situations is similar to the emphasis on *commitment* that is suggested toward the end of this chapter. For an interesting perspective on this pastoral situation, see Robert L. Randall, "What Do You Say After They Say, 'We're Living Together'? Suggestions for Beginning Premarital Counseling," *The Journal of Pastoral Care* 33, March 1979, pp. 51–59. In such situations, I believe that the underlying issue is still the level of commitment that is expressed. No matter what is said or discussed, the fundamental fact remains that individuals who are cohabiting are involved in a commitment that is limited, incomplete, and easily terminated—a commitment that falls short of the exclusivity and permanence that exists in the sacramental bond of marriage. At the same time, however, pastoral sensitivity is important in such situations, and adult ministers should convey an understanding of the adolescents' situation, reflect with the adolescents on possibilities for deepening growth and conversion, and gently challenge the adolescents to the possibilities for deepening commitment.

Like cohabiting situations, the issue of homosexuality in adolescence is complex. Suggested reading in this area include the following: Wagner, "Sexuality of American Adolescents," pp. 572–573; Keane, *Sexual Morality*, pp. 71–91; Curran, *Themes in Fundamental Moral Theology*, pp. 181–182; Kosnik et al., *Human Sexuality*, pp. 210–244; the Vatican *Declaration, Origins*, p. 489; and Kennedy, *Sexual Counseling*, pp. 137–147. For an excellent treatment of the morality of homosexuality, see Lisa Sowle Cahill, "Moral Methodology: A Case Study," *Chicago Studies* 19, Summer 1980, pp. 171–181.

66. "Big Rise in Births Out of Wedlock," *San Francisco Chronicle*, October 26, 1981, p. 4.

67. Clippinger, "Adolescent Sexuality and Love," pp. 280–281.

68. Keane, *Sexual Morality*, p. 109.

69. Some Catholic moralists distinguish various types of contraceptives. Some contraceptives, for example, are abortificient, e.g., the I.U.D. and various morning after pills. As we note later in our discussion, all contra-

ceptives have the potential for being morally wrong when used under the cloud of fear, force, threat, and so forth.

70. Goergen, *Sexual Celibate*, p. 57.

71. Kosnik et al., *Human Sexuality*, p. 192.

72. Jacqueline Haessly and Daniel DiDomizio, "Sexuality and Intimacy." In *Young Adult Living*, New York: Paulist Press, 1980, pp. 42–43.

73. Lynda A. Haynes and Arthur W. Avery, "Training Adolescents in Self-Disclosure and Empathy Skills," *Journal of Counseling Psychology* 26, November 1979, p. 529.

74. Curran, *Themes in Fundamental Moral Theology*, p. 184.

75. Häring, *Medical Ethics*, pp. 65–75.

76. Cosgrave, "Christian Understanding of Sexuality," pp. 39–40.

77. Ibid., p. 39.

78. For a discussion of sexual decision making in adolescence, the reader is encouraged to read the following two articles: Juhasz and Sonnen-shein-Schneider, "Adolescent Sexual Decision Making," pp. 743–749; and Juhasz and Sonnenshein-Schneider, "Responsibility and Control: The Basis of Sexual Decision Making," *The Personnal and Guidance Journal* 58, November 1979, 181–185.

79. For a discussion of control, see Sean G. Connolly, "Changing Expectancies: A Counseling Model Based on Locus of Control," *The Personnel and Guidance Journal* 59, November 1980, pp. 176–180; and Juhasz and Sonnenshein-Schneider, "Responsibility and Control."

80. Connolly, "Changing Expectancies," p. 177.

81. Juhasz and Sonnenshein-Schneider, "Responsibility and Control," p. 182.

82. Ibid., pp. 184–185.

83. Joseph L. Bernardin, "The Need for a More Positive Theology of Sexuality," *Catholic Mind* 79, February 1981, pp. 39–40.

84. Kennedy, *Sexual Counseling*, p. 117.

85. See Adele D. Hofmann, "Adolescent Promiscuity," *Medical Aspects of Human Sexuality*, May, 1974, pp. 63–64.

86. Andrew M. Greeley, *The Young Catholic Family*. Chicago: The Thomas More Press, 1980.

87. Keane, "The Objective Moral Order," p. 277.

88. Ibid., p. 278.

89. Ibid. [The same page as the preceding note.]

CHAPTER EIGHT

Adolescent Social Consciousness: Limits and Possibilities

A comparison of the contemporary Christian perspective of the world with the Christian perspective of the late fifties or early sixties reveals a striking difference: the current focus is on developing a social consciousness perspective. For the Christian today, living the Gospel demands this social commitment.[1] Moral theologian Richard McCormick points to this phenomenon in his discussion of the great changes that have taken place in the post-Vatican II era regarding moral thinking. He concludes that contemporary moral thinking demands some type of "social character."[2] Likewise, theologian John Wright captures the same theme when he notes that "believers cannot accept their brothers and sisters as children of God, those for whom Christ died, called to be members of His body and temples of the Holy Spirit, and casually observe them exploited, deprived of human dignity, ground to poverty and despair by economic and social institutions geared primarily to benefit the wealthy and the powerful."[3]

We have situated adolescent spiritually in youth's response to Jesus' call. For the adolescent of the eighties and beyond, this response is now lived out in an awareness of, a sensitivity to, and a motivational response toward those who are less fortunate—namely, the hungry, the powerless, and the suffering. Spiritual writer William Byron correctly observes that "the fullness of Christian spirituality is social, of course, centered in the charity which embraces the proper love of self, the total love of God, and the dedicated love of neighbor."[4] Adolescent spirituality sees as one of its main goals, then, the fostering within youth of a deepening, caring response toward those who are hurting, suffering, and exploited.

The church has recognized the importance of the dimension of social justice and in numerous statements has counseled educators and those who minister to youth to make this focus a priority for the adolescent's faith experience.[5] And in stressing this dimension for adolescents, an awareness of their developmental level is essential. Adults who minister to adolescents at either the high school or college level find that getting young people to internalize social justice is not an easy undertaking. Many educators have become frustrated in their attempts to either influence student attitudes or to discover in adolescents behaviors that mirror a social consciousness perspective. Thus, adults must ask themselves the following important question: How can I present the Gospel to youth in a way that calls forth in them the deepening social commitment that is so necessary for mature adult Christian living? This question becomes especially critical because today's secondary school and college youth are the decision makers of tomorrow.

Adolescent Social Consciousness: The Difficulties

Before answering the question of how adults might foster among youth a developing commitment to social justice, it would be helpful to examine the reasons for these difficulties during the high school and college years.

A primary reason for difficulty in the internalization of social justice among adolescents arises from attempts to give an acceptable definition of social justice. Definitions of social justice are elusive, difficult, and sometimes nebulous in their specific application to social problems. For example, the U.S. Catholic Conference defines social justice in the National Catechetical Directory, *Sharing the Light of Faith*, as "the concept by which one evaluates the organization and functioning of the political, economic, social, and cultural life of society. Positively, the church's social teaching seeks to apply the Gospel command of love to and within social systems, structures, and institutions."[6]

This definition demonstrates the difficulty inherent in any attempt to define social justice. First, applying the "Gospel command of love" is extremely difficult in working with complex social groupings, whether they are "social systems," "structures," or "institutions." An adolescent who makes a personal moral decision, for example, can readily determine whether he or she should steal and clearly understand the rightness or wrongness of such an act. It is a huge jump, however, from this personal, concrete moral decision to the decisions that are made in the complex world of domestic politics, foreign policy, and economics—areas that make up much of a social justice perspective. Another example might be helpful in understanding this difficulty: Christians recognize the right of a human being to a decent standard of living. This statement could be readily subsumed under the mantle of social justice. In the United States, a common public policy that attempts to apply this principle is the minimum wage law. Unemployment in America, however, has traditionally been highest among minorities—most notably minority youth—and this situation has become a national scandal.

To remedy high unemployment among minority youth, some economists have argued that a dual minimum wage is appropriate because it allows businesses to hire youth who presently are economically unattractive, that is, youth whose work is judged inadequate for the investment (wage) that is involved. Such a solution, however, is bound to have rather diverse consequences. A scheming employer, for example, might take advantage of such a law to increase profits, or specific economic and geographic factors might keep unemployment high in certain regions regardless of the law. And, too, youth who are currently employed and benefit from the present minimum wage law might suffer a decline in wages and consequently lose the benefits they now enjoy.

This example is instructive for adolescents, yet it is nevertheless ambiguous. An adolescent who must respond to such a dilemma encounters a situation that is far more complex than the personal decision about whether to steal. Among the several complex realities in the example of the minimum wage dilemma are the various consequences of the action, the complexity of economic and social variables, the possibility of hurting others regardless of the method that is chosen, and the ambiguity of both options in light of the possible benefit involved. Many other examples could be given that attempt to apply the Gospel to such areas as inflation, nuclear arms policy, social welfare programs that are often plagued by limited financial resources, and foreign policy decisions that are often plagued by unclear and at times perilous options.[7] Thus, very difficult questions surface when discussions move from personal moral decision making to the complex decision making in the world of politics, economics, and large-scale social interactions. The difficulty of applying principles of social justice to complex social phenomena quite likely attenuates the adolescent's response to specific social justice concerns.

Adolescents' responses to social justice is likewise weakened by the myriad opinions and responses of the persons who constitute youth's significant relationships. Certainly peers, parents, friends, and teachers might all disagree on what course of action should be taken for a particular social problem simply because of the problem's complexity. It is ironic, yet all too commonplace, that everyone supports justice, peace, and equality, but in outlining how to achieve such ends, opinions are often multitudinous if not contradictory. Significant individuals in an adolescent's life might have opposing views of political candidates, for example, or foreign policy decisions or budgetary expenditures, yet all might claim to represent a social justice perspective. Might not such contradictory influences cloud an adolescent's understanding of social justice? At the same time, adults who are attempting to influence an adolescent's understanding must be aware of the many forces that are competing for that young person's attention. Certainly the family, peer groups, the media, and even the present political and economic situation vie for the adolescent's attention, and, in turn, influence youth's internalizing of a social justice perspective.

In addition, there are developmental reasons that make the internalizing of a social justice perspective during the adolescent years difficult. In chapter 3, the growing cognitive complexity of adolescent thinking was discussed, and it became clear that adolescents can begin thinking of more abstract ideas, such as equality, peace, justice—all central qualities of a social consciousness perspective. The notional understanding of these concepts requires a capacity for abstraction, deductive thinking, and reflective thought that only begins to emerge during the adolescent years. Yet this cognitive capacity is not always present in many adolescents to a degree that would allow a deep comprehension of social justice principles.[8] It might actually happen, then, especially during the secondary school years, that many adolescents would lack the cognitive capacity to grasp and understand the deepening demands of social justice when these are presented in a reflective and abstract way.

Additionally, we cannot ignore the relationship of formal thinking to moral reasoning or the consequences of this bond to a social
justice orientation. As youth proceed through adolescence, they develop the capacity for advanced moral reasoning, a stage of moral
reasoning that allows them to experience the true meaning of the
universal need for justice, peace, and equality, and also realize the
evils of social injustices. Several cautions are warranted, however, in
discussing this advanced level of moral reasoning. First, the lack of
formal, operational thinking in many adolescents undermines their
movement to a postconventional level of moral reasoning that is
most consonant with the internalization of social justice principles.
Recall from chapter 3 that Kohlberg maintains that formal thinking is
necessary for principled reasoning. Without this deeper understanding and commitment to justice, adolescents are limited in their internalization of authentic concern for social justice principles. Second,
because most adolescents operate at a conventional level of moral
reasoning, it is difficult for them to understand the need for the
universal moral principles that form an integral part of any reflection
on social justice. Third, even if some level of principled reasoning is
present, there is no guarantee this reasoning will translate into personal action that reflects a social justice commitment.

Furthermore, a social justice orientation requires an advanced
level of identity formation, which, as Erikson notes, is the primary
task of the adolescent years. Adolescents gradually acquire a growing sense of self by separating from parents, realizing vocational
aspirations, forming a philosophy and ideology of life, and developing deepening relations with peers. Yet this development is a time
consuming process that can often last till the end of the college years
or even beyond before a true identity achievement actually occurs.
In terms of the internalization of social justice principles, this prolonged acquisition of an identity is a crucial factor for social justice
education. Both the questioning and formulating of a value system
that incorporates social justice principles and the actual working to
achieve social justice might prove difficult without a profound experience of one's own identity, including personally reflected and
thought out values and social attitudes. It might only be after the
end of adolescence or during the early years of young adulthood
that many young people develop a true attitudinal and value system
that both indicates a solid identity and reflects social justice princi-

ples, or at least reflects a coherent philosophical-ideological value system of which some social justice principles are a part.

Finally, James Fowler has observed that most adolescents either are in the synthetic-conventional stage of faith development or are slowly making the transition to stage 4. A common characteristic of this stage 3 faith is the tendency to view other social groups in stereotypical and prejudicial ways. Only after time, reflection, and experience can adolescents hope to acquire the openness and commitment of the stage 4 faith experience, which reflects a deeper commitment to the demands of social justice.

Besides these developmental factors, there are internal psychological states that can create resistances for adolescents. Adolescence is a time for gradually achieving independence from the family. An adolescent's task, as we have already noted, involves the forming of an identity, that is, developing a stable sense of self that is capable of relating and interacting in an adult world. Yet forming this identity through the gradual process of separation from parents can pose problems. It is important to note the carry-over from this internal struggle to the acquisition of social justice principles during the adolescent years. If an adolescent's parents do not support Catholic social teaching, then any stress given to social justice principles in the classroom, on a retreat, or in a private conversation might possible confuse the adolescent's own struggles for independence because the adolescent must internally mediate loyalty to parents, moral-social imperatives, and the need for psychic separation. Some adolescents, in order to ease their own separation struggles, might unconsciously, but nevertheless wholeheartedly adopt social justice values and thus establish a fundamental difference with their parents and, in turn, facilitate their emotional separation. In effect, some adolescents might adopt a social justice perspective not so much because they believe in these values and principles, but because they can psychically establish their identity and ease their separation from parental attitudes and influences. For other adolescents, their separation strategy might involve experiencing or "trying out" various attitudes and values that are experientially new and thus make the adolescent "different" from his or her previous self. On the other hand, some adolescents might resist internalizing a social justice perspective in order to assuage separation fears and remain close to their parents. Still other adolescents for a variety of reasons might be indifferent to social justice principles or might even oppose social justice principles on philosophical or ideological grounds. It is important, then, for adults who minister to adolescents to discern the particular reason or reasons why a particular adolescent might or might not be open to social justice education.

In summary, it is highly plausible that psychological processes underlie much of the adolescent's perception and internalization of social justice principles. Adolescence is a distinct developmental period during which social attitudes are formed, but adolescents often resist or struggle with these attitudes. At the same time, the young person's cognitive structure grows increasingly complex so that personal perceptions of the outside world tend to reflect this growing internal complexity. In addition, the internalization of social justice principles must compete with many other important influences in the young person's life—not the least of which are the struggles for freedom and independence that many adolescents undergo. Finally, adolescents nascently encounter the world at a more advanced developmental level while they begin to develop skills in order to deal with an uncertain future. This venturing outward enhances defensive outlooks that aid adolescents in making sense out of an ambiguous and, at times, threatening future.

Social Justice, Spirituality, and the Adolescent

The goal of any pastoral ministry to youth is helping them to integrate a social justice perspective with spiritual growth.[9] How can this social consciousness be realized in a spirituality that speaks to young people? Priest-sociologist John Coleman quotes George Gallup who has observed that "numerous surveys we have conducted clearly indicate a powerful surge of spirituality among young people, as well as a strong interest in service to society. It therefore behooves the churches to bring these two strong impulses together. The evidence would seem to indicate clearly that young people would be responsive to various and new kinds of lay ministry."[10] Certainly part of the church's mission is to tap this caring concern of adolescents by providing ministerial opportunities for young people in the secondary school, college, and youth ministry programs so that real Christian service might be fostered. But what is the underlying focus and foundation for this Christian service?

In addressing this question, the spirituality of St. Ignatius proves helpful. Ignatian spirituality centers on the retreatant's personal relationship with Jesus Christ. The *Spiritual Exercises,* as they were originally written, were not meant to be a full experience or an elaboration of a developed social consciousness. Given the 16th century culture in which Ignatius lived and the purposes for which he wrote, he focused on the person's growing relationship with Jesus as it was made evident in a growing awareness of affective interior movements during the retreat experience.[11]

Nevertheless, several meditations in the *Spiritual Exercises* allow the possibility of developing a social consciousness for our own day. Ignatius presents in the *Exercises* a meditation on the Kingdom—the call of Christ the King—in which a person is asked to focus on the personal call of Jesus. Ignatius says: "I ask the Lord that I might be able to hear His call, and that I might be ready and willing to do what He wants." The call of the King attempts to place Jesus here and now in one's concrete life situation. Ignatius asks us to contemplate Christ the King in order to hear His message; he envisions a response to this call that is lived out in active Christian service. We are to embark, with Jesus, on the road of discipleship to spread the Kingdom.

Ignatius believed that service to the Lord and His Kingdom required that Jesus personally touch one's life. Although Jesus calls each of us "in a particular way," the result of this call is similar for all. It is "to win over the whole world, to conquer sin, hatred, and death—all the enemies between mankind and God." In following Jesus and His Kingdom, we find ourselves serving Him through suffering so that we might follow Him in glory.

This meditation on the Kingdom calls for labors to overcome injustice. For the 1980s and beyond, the call of Jesus has an essential social dimension that leads the Christian to strive to overcome injustice, hatred, and discrimination. Thomas Clarke states that "the Ignatian apostle will set before himself or herself precisely the dream of a better *world,* in which grace and truth, freedom and peace, are verified not only in human hearts and relationship, but in structures, institutions, and the whole climate of human existence. This contribution of societal consciousness is congruous with the symbol of the Kingdom, in the sense that this symbol transcends the purely private dimension of human life."[12]

301

In another meditation entitled "The Two Standards," Ignatius identifies two opposing forces in the world—the Standard of Christ and the Standard of Satan. The standard of Satan leads a person to desire riches, honors, and enslavement of the things of this world. Karl Rahner points out that in the Standard of Satan "the desire to be somebody leads ultimately to the desire to exist absolutely for self, and to the attempt to assert oneself unconditionally through an existential identification of self with one's possessions and capabilities."[13] In reality, the Standard of Satan leads to a loss of personal identity and the gradual identification of the self with power, honor, and things. Under this standard, persons are no longer defined by who they are but only by what they have become, what they have achieved, or what they have acquired.

The strategy of Jesus is diametrically opposed to Satan's strategy. Under Christ's banner, a person is willing to accept poverty, humility, and powerlessness. Ignatius says that 'if I have nothing, my only possession is Christ and this is to be really true to myself—the humility of a person whose whole reality lies in being created and redeemed in Christ."

The social import of Ignatian spirituality can help adolescents formulate a sensitivity to the realities of social injustice. The central aspect of an Ignatian adolescent spirituality is the deepening relationship that has been developed with Jesus, for "I wish to know Christ" (Phil 3:10). As noted in chapter 4, fostering this growing sense of self-identity allows adolescents to increasingly realize this personal relationship with Jesus. Adolescents' developing capacities for deeper relationships nurture not only a personal commitment to Jesus, but also an acceptance of laboring for Jesus in the Kingdom in the specific context of spirituality that mirrors social justice. Summing up this adolescent identification with Jesus in the context of social justice, Jesuit educator Robert Starratt advises that "we need to root our work for justice in Jesus Christ, who points to a good life, what He called the Kingdom, based on selfless love, compassion, and the sharing of life."[14]

With Jesus as the foundation, adolescents can begin to reflect on their personal attitudes and positions on social problems. This requires that adolescents honestly examine what they *really* believe and admit that they have much to learn. The goal of this reflection is to help adolescents construct personal positions on both public policies and social issues that reflect an increasing Christ-consciousness. Adolescents gradually come to rely on a personal experience of Jesus that reflects an understanding and commitment to His message. Of course, this does not mean that the Gospel can simply be translated into ready-made answers for developing adolescents. World hunger, nuclear war, and political oppression are complex social realities that require thorough reflection and discussion. Moreover, because adolescents are growing in cognitive capacities and social awareness, they need time and adequate reflection in order to formulate a personally meaningful perspective on social issues and problems. Nevertheless, adults can be a critical source of encouragement by helping adolescents reflect on that translation of the Gospel that speaks to the complex social realities that the adolescent is now experiencing. Adults must accept each adolescent at his or her own particular developmental level and, at the same time, foster a climate that will challenge and encourage the adolescent to both reflection and Christian service.

In addition to the deepening Christ focus, an adolescent's internalization of a social consciousness perspective must include other characteristics. An adolescent's growing development, for example, allows for acceptance of suffering and self-denial. John Yoder points out that the call of Jesus means a deepening experience of the cross, as Christians attempt to transform social and political realities to reflect increasing concern and care for the suffering, the exploited, and the oppressed.[15] An adolescent's increasing intellectual capacity and his or her growing sense of identity through the secondary and undergraduate college years can contribute to a deeper sense of this commitment and self-sacrifice. What is more, an adolescent's developmental level encourages personal transformation through Jesus so that greater social sensitivity is accorded to the suffering, the hurting, and the exploited. An adolescent then begins to respond with a growing intellectual awareness of society—its functions and workings, and how a transformation in terms of the Gospel and the church's social teaching might take place.

Concurrent with this growing intellectual stance, there also develops a growing affective sense of others. Adolescents can be aroused affectively through a growing sense of concern for those in need, that is, the hurts and pains of others can become an adolescent's own hurts and pains. This empathy is not isolated, however, but rather is subsumed under the Gospel command to love others (Jn 15:17).

Finally, an adolescent's internalization of social justice principles carries the notion of communal activity and praxis. Working for social justice is not only a personal commitment, but the willingness to labor together with others. In chapter 6, we noted that an adolescent's growing moral sense of self could not be isolated from the need for communal and group support. Likewise, although a personal commitment to social justice is important, by itself it is inadequate in developing an adolescent social consciousness, because Christians must labor communally to bring about social change.

A central component of an adolescent social consciousness, then, is the experience of this communal commitment. Related to this commitment are an adequate mastery of basic competencies, such as critical analytic skills and decision making capabilities, and adequate human relation skills that facilitate interaction with the adult world. The development of these competencies allows adolescents to acquire a gradual mastery of self while they also venture outward into the adult world. This is especially important because social psychological research supports the critical role that these competencies exercise in leading one to behave in sensitive and caring ways toward others.[16] The more an adolescent possesses the ability to interact with others and acquire feelings of personal adequacy that go with such interaction, the more likely this adolescent will be oriented outward in caring ways toward others. Hence, a critical factor in the development of adolescent social consciousness is not only a focus on the Gospel, but a much wider perspective that encompasses both a positive sense of self-worth and adequate personal skills that enhance entrance into the adult world.

In summary, then, a social justice perspective arises for adolescents when Jesus Christ develops as a conscious, mediating force for adolescents. Ideally, an adolescent's response to Jesus mirrors the Gospel's concern for the poor and suffering (Mt 25). They reflect and develop strategies to be used in alleviating suffering or injustice, strategies that reflect the Gospel's command to love. In experiencing this developing social consciousness, the adolescent grows more aware of Jesus' personal call and the responsibility toward the poor and suffering that this call entails. On a communal level, adolescents realize the personal responsibility that the community must take in the fostering of social justice. Additionally, adolescents increasingly realize that a social justice commitment means the call to discipleship. They grow in their understanding of the place of self-denial—whether this denial involves material goods, time, or energy in laboring for social justice—and become more service-oriented, recognizing and accepting personal inconveniences as they perform Christian service.

Social Justice and the Adolescent Experiences

Many limiting influences exist in aiding the adolescent's acquisition of a social justice perspective. Yet the adolescent years remain a critical time for the early formation of a maturing social consciousness. What is needed is a *holistic* look at the adolescent's internalization of social justice principles. Far too often, education in social justice principles is mistakenly portrayed as a simple communicative process between adults and adolescents that implies a cause-effect relationship, that is, the adults always transmit social justice values and attitudes to the students. What actually transpires, however, is a complex process whereby an adolescent's growing social consciousness interacts with cognitive, affective, sociopolitical influences, and with environmental factors. It is this complex interaction of numerous influences that shape youth's response and growing identification with Jesus Christ in the context of social justice.

Cognitive influences

At the cognitive level, adolescents are now capable of thinking in more abstract and complex ways about ethical issues, social problems, and social injustices. From the earlier discussion of Piaget, Kohlberg, and Perry (chapter 3), it is clear that adolescents increasingly understand and cope with a complex world; the rather simplistic answers of childhood no longer suffice. Likewise, as adolescent development progresses, there arises the possibility of both greater awareness and a far deeper expression of Jesus as an evaluative foundation for social consciousness. This growing relationship with and laboring for Jesus eventually melds with the adolescent's growing cognitive capacity and engages his or her thinking of the wider dimensions of culture and society. The adolescent increasingly realizes that Jesus is the evaluating force that judges society's commitment to social justice. As the adolescent develops this critical evaluative stance toward society, it is important that he or she be able to distinguish between a personal commitment to social justice and a personal ideological and political stance (although the adolescent might certainly show political and ideological learnings). The basis for this critical reflection is formed by a deepening awareness and understanding of Jesus that is based on a personal relationship with Him. This deepening relationship with Jesus allows for more awareness and sensitivity to society's mistaken values, the shortcomings of institutions and structures, and the cultural enslavement that exists on both personal and societal levels. This critical reflection is the result of a growing cognitive capacity that allows a deeper understanding of poverty, injustice, and conflict.

Equally important, however, is the need to direct the thrust of the adolescent's growing critical stance into more positive directions that stress possible solutions, alternatives, and choices that have the potential of altering the inequalities and injustices that do exist in our world. Emphasizing the consequences of Christian reflection is critical to the development of an adolescent social consciousness. Far too often, education in social justice principles places excessive emphasis on injustices and society's inadequacies and never offers enough time to explore solutions, possible choices, and the possibility for human betterment. If we simply help adolescents foster a stance toward society that is reflective, critical, and based on both Gospel values and a personal relationship with Jesus, then we have inadequately addressed the problems of social justice. What must arise from this relationship with Jesus are positive, constructive, and operative strategies that adolescents might pursue to remedy social injustice. A spirituality for youth must especially encourage adolescents to champion possible solutions and strategies that are consonant with the Gospel. Failing to encourage this positive reflection narrows an adolescent's own understandings of social justice and can wed him or her to an unhealthy negativity during these developmental years.

In the secondary school years, adolescents begin to develop both a deepening understanding of political realities and the capacity to think critically about social realities. In the early high school years, these evaluations are elementary and simplistic. Through the later high school years and during the undergraduate years of college, however, adolescents are capable of developing a rudimentary ideology and philosophy of life that aids them as they evaluate political and social institutions. Particularly during the college experience, this growing critical reflection combines with expanding knowledge, a unique learning environment, and the growing personal development of an adolescent's value system to allow more reflective and critical stances toward political and social phenomena. It is during these college years that the late adolescent might experience a crisis of political commitment that might necessitate a reexamination and deeper reflection on social and political views.

Affective influences

Adolescent social consciousness involves more than a cognitive stance toward public and social issues. To internalize a social justice perspective, adolescents need to be interiorly moved at the affective level. This affective dimension of social justice is most clearly demonstrated in the adolescent's growing capacity for empathic responses to the hurts, the plight, and the concerns of others in need.

Psychologist Kenneth Clark defines empathy as "the capacity of an individual to feel the needs, the aspirations, the frustrations, the joy, the sorrows, the anxieties, the hurt, ideed the hunger of others as if they were his or her own."[17] During the adolescent years, this growing empathic state is closely linked to youth's increasing cognitive capacity because the development of empathy is tied to cognitive growth. Psychologist Martin Hoffman has offered one of the most extensive theories of empathic development and its effects on the individual's capacity to care for others.[18] According to Hoffman, empathic development nurtures a growing understanding of a personal self that is distinct from others. As the child continually develops, a sense of the plight and distress of others merges with a cognitive understanding and affective response to their suffering. By the time the child reaches adolescence, this response to the misfortune of others includes care and concern not only for another individual, but for wider social groupings such as races or classes of people.[19]

The arousal of an empathic response is crucial for youth's internalization of social justice principles because the experience of empathy can be a motivating factor in fostering helping and caring behavior during the adolescent years.[20] An adolescent who does volunteer work in a poor neighborhood, for example, can experience a cognitive and affective sense of what others experience in their everyday lives. This cognitive understanding of the plight of these people coupled with empathic feelings toward them, often stimulates adolescents to behave in caring and loving ways. An empathic response, combined with the growing capacity to take the perspective of another (see Selman's description of role taking in chapter 3), are critical factors in an adolescent's commitment to deepening levels of Christian service. With the acquisition of these capabilities, adolescents not only realize more fully from a cognitive standpoint the difficulties that others experience, but also are aroused to feel deeply others' powerlessness, suffering, and hurt. It is this developing internal capacity for empathy that helps nourish the desire for true Christian ministry.

Sociopolitical influences

Besides a growing critical, evaluative stance and a deepening affective sense of others, a particularly important requirement for the development of adolescent social consciousness is youth's growing sense of a political self. Quite often, it appears that education for social justice is simply an understanding and presentation of moral principles that are then applied to social and political issues. The development of an adolescent social consciousness perspective is, however, not quite that simple. On the contrary, as we have already noted, social justice is tied to the complex workings of social and political phenomena; consequently, the world of politics, decision making, and power relationships cannot be divorced from a social justice perspective. Instead, these political and social realities must be understood and treated in the context of Gospel values.

It is often overlooked that children and future adolescents do not simply have political attitudes, party identifications, and ideological interests. Rather, the acquisition of a political sense of one's self is the result of a complex weaving of various influences and factors.[21] During this ten-year span from early to late adolescence, youth come to develop a sophisticated understanding of political reality. Commenting on the adolescent stage, psychologist Norman Feather notes that "it is only with increasing maturity that the adolescent becomes able to form generalized concepts, to understand the role of history and the impact of the present on the future, to get some feeling for social change and the possibility that men and social institutions may alter and be altered, to weigh up the wider costs and benefits of actions and decisions, and to develop principles and frameworks for judging particular events."[22] This focus on political reality weighs heavily on the internalization of social justice principles because political phenomena are closely linked to complexity and ambiguity.

Psychologist Joseph Adelson has extensively studied the adolescent development of a political self. Adelson observes that when we discuss politics, we are concerned with "the relation of variable means to variable ends; the relation of uncertain means to uncertain ends; the relations between short and long-term ends; the relation between individualistic and collective good; the distinction between particularistic and universalistic orientations; the collisions between values, and also the collision between interests, and between interests and values."[23] Adelson's point is well taken when describing the adolescent conception of a political self. His comments point to the complexity of developing a social justice perspective that must confront the real world of complex political decision making. Social justice principles encompass a vast array of complex issues, moral dilemmas, and ambiguous positions that the adolescent must initially make sense of and conceptualize according to the Gospel's command to love one another (Jn 15:12).

In addition to this personal understanding of the political world, the adolescent's internal sense of his or her political self is complex. The development of a political self is influenced by numerous factors that include family, peers, schooling, communication media, and current political events.[24] Furthermore, internal psychological states can influence how the adolescent reasons politically and also affect the adolescent's openness to the ideas and concerns of others in various political and social settings.[25] Thus the adolescent's growing political self incorporates a variety of external factors as well as personal dispositions that are capable of either fostering or inhibiting a developing social consciousness.

Environmental factors

Finally, the development of social consciousness during adolescence is also influenced by environmental factors. In chapter 3, we noted Lawrence Kohlberg's assertion that the environmental surroundings influence the development of moral reasoning. Likewise, these same surroundings provide a strong influence for the development of an adolescent's social consciousness perspective. Social psychologist Ervin Staub has identified numerous factors, many of them environmental, that influence one's capacity to care for others. Among the factors that contribute toward this caring behavior are: the degree of personal responsibility one has been given in the environment, personal self-esteem, the perception one has of others' needs, personal feelings of competence, modeling influences in the environment, the environmental situation itself, the affective nurturing that the environment provides, and knowledge of and identification with others within one's environment.[26]

Personally, I believe that it is the *combination* of these environmental influences, in conjunction with *internal states* such as empathic arousal, that most orient the adolescent toward helping and caring behaviors. When these influences and internal feelings mesh with a cognitive grasp of the particular issue and/or situation, particularly in the context of political and social reality, when they focus on suffering, injustice, and the plight of those in need, and when they are evaluated in the context of Gospel values, then the basis for a social justice perspective develops.

The foregoing discussion of social justice presents a picture that is far more involved and complex than most discussions of the subject. In ministering to adolescents, then, several points need mentioning.

1 The foundation of a social justice commitment in adolescence is only made possible by and through a commitment to Jesus and Gospel values. Christ is the central evaluative component for any social justice perspective. The realization of social justice is ratified by a study of social justice themes that are manifested in Scripture as well as a study and understanding of the church's social teaching.

2 An adolescent's deepening awareness and relationship with Jesus are partly a result of the young person's own developmental and motivational response. That is to say, the cognitive development allows (1) a clear distinction of self from others and (2) the reflective capacity both to understand rules, values, and ideas, and to form deeper evaluative responses. The affective development of the adolescent creates the opportunity for deepening an interpersonal relationship with Jesus that is based on a greater sense of self-identity and the growing demands of intimacy. In addition, the

development of empathy, based on maturing cognitive and affective responses, aids an adolescent in personally experiencing the plight and misfortune of others.

3   When linked to Gospel values, this cognitive growth fosters the possibility of a critical social justice stance toward society. As such, an adolescent's critical reflection on society must be explored in light of these Gospel values to determine the extent to which it is actually based on values that are consonant with Gospel teaching.

4   The development of social consciousness is a multifaceted dynamic that incorporates adolescent developmental needs along with complex social issues. To divorce these two factors is unwarranted and ultimately self-defeating.

Fostering Social Justice in Adolescents

Adolescent spirituality seeks to tie a developing social consciousness to adolescent spiritual growth. When spirituality, social justice themes, and developmental theory are combined, several suggestions can be made for ministry to adolescents. These suggestions are both general and flexible and are applicable to private conversations, group work, retreats, and classroom settings. Adults are encouraged to find still other ways to adapt these suggestions to the particular situation of ministry.

Suggestion 1

As we have already suggested, there is within the social justice perspective a focus on a *deepening relationship with Jesus*. Adults can suggest particular Scripture passages, such as Mt 25, that speaks of Jesus' concern for the poor. Utilizing the prayer format found in chapter 4, adolescents can experience the personal call of Jesus to aid those who are suffering. Adults might pay particular attention to *how* an adolescent affectively experiences in the presence of Jesus. In Jesus' presence, does this adolescent show real concern and desire to help those in need? Adults might follow up such concerns by suggesting ways for the adolescent to demonstrate this care and concern for others. It is important that adolescents explore ways to care for others because they need to realize the connection between feeling distress over another's plight and needing to develop actual caring and helping behaviors for the persons who are in need.

311

Some passages from Scripture that can be used in reflecting and praying with adolescents are suggested. These passages are specifically oriented to social justice themes. If the prayer format found in chapter 4 is used, these passages provide a rich opportunity for integrating social justice, Scripture, and an adolescent's own internalization of a social justice perspective.[27]

Old Testament

Isaiah 3:13–15 (taking advantage of the poor); Micah 2 (evils against the people); Amos 5:7–17 (seek justice); and Sirach 4:1–10 (help those in need).

New Testament

Matthew 5:3–12 (beatitudes); Matthew 5:43–48 (love your enemies); Matthew 6:19–25 (true riches); Matthew 8:18–22 (following Jesus); Matthew 16:24–26 (taking up Jesus' cross); Matthew 19:16–22 (selling riches); Matthew 25:31–46 (the final judgment); Mark 3:1–6 (Jesus heals); Mark 6:34–44 (Jesus feeds the crowd); Mark 10:17–27 (warning against riches); Mark 12:41–44 (true sharing of wealth); Luke 5:17–26 (curing the paralytic); Luke 7:36–50 (Jesus forgives sins); Luke 10:25–36 (the Good Samaritan); Luke 11:37–54 (woe to hypocrisy); Luke 15:11–32 (the Prodigal Son); Luke 16:19–31 (Lazarus and the rich man); John 13:1–17 (the washing of feet); John 15:9–17 (the command to love); Acts 2:42–47 (community life in the early church); Acts 4:32–36 (sharing in the early church); 1 Cor 13 (the nature of love); 2 Cor 8:1–15 (sharing wealth); Phil 2:1–11 (self-emptying of Christ); 1 Thes 5:12–22 (the norms for community living); Gal 5:22–23 (fruits of the Spirit); 1 Tim 6:7–10 (being poor); James 2 (practicing Christian behavior); and 1 John 4:19–21 (if we love God, we love our neighbor).

Suggestion 2

The acquisition of formal, operational thinking allows adolescents to begin *reasoning deductively* about social problems. Adolescents can talk of a value such as love or freedom, for example, and then they can mention an injustice and then apply the value to a current social problem. The use of this deductive approach is sometimes ineffective, however, because many youth have a limited capacity for formal thinking. A more profitable strategy, at least initially, might be the use of an inductive approach, which is a common method employed in the physical sciences.

Instead of expressing a universal Gospel norm such as love and then applying this norm to a particular social situation, it might be more profitable to focus on concrete examples of injustice, especially those with which an adolescent is familiar—the neighborhood, for example, or the city, or a current popular problem. Identify the particular injustice that is involved, such as poverty, and then reflect with the adolescent on both Gospel values and passages from Scripture that relate to this social injustice. In this way, adolescents cognitively and affectively experience the social injustice while, at the same time, they make a personal response to the injustice through study and reflection. This inductive approach makes the presentation of the Gospel message more meaningful. Explore with adolescents various positive and productive ways in which they might respond to this social problem.

Suggestion 3

Research demonstrates the importance of *empathy* in forming behaviors that help others. Also, the empathic capacity that grows during adolescence allows young persons to relate affectively in much deeper ways to another's pain and hurt. A fruitful strategy in this regard is to encourage adolescents to participate in volunteer work, social service projects, and various experiences that will expose them to the experience of social injustice and human suffering. It is important that such experiences for young persons be accompanied by questions and discussions that (a) *identify* specific feelings and understandings that have surfaced during these experiences; (b) *relate* these insights and understandings to church social teaching and the Gospel, thereby tying the adolescent experience to the history and beliefs of the faith community; (c) *discuss* ways in which the adolescents might immediately respond to these sufferings and injustices, as well as ways in which future endeavors might contribute to alleviating these sufferings.

Suggestion 4

Another adolescent experience that might foster social justice consciousness is *role taking*. The experience of role taking is linked to

313

an increase of caring and helping behaviors toward others.[28] An excellent use of role taking in a group setting is the creation of an atmosphere in which an adolescent takes on the role of someone who is actually suffering injustice. In creating this situation, adults should pay particular attention to (a) stressing the *reality* of the situation, (b) focusing on what *feelings and insights* the adolescent gathers from this role taking experience, and (c) exploring with the adolescent productive *strategies for responding* to this experience. Adults might also suggest some particular passages from Scripture and have adolescents take on the role of a particular character in the passage. Try to determine whether these experiences influence the adolescent's response.

Suggestion 5

Because research has documented the powerful impact of *affective responses* on the development of an orientation that is favorably disposed to helping others, it is important that adults relate to adolescents in ways that tell them that they are accepted and appreciated, and that respect is given to their views on social issues and current public problems. Adults might pose "inquiry" questions that allow the adolescents to reflect more deeply on personally held views and beliefs. If an adolescent develops a strategy that might help alleviate the problem of world hunger, for example, the adult could seriously explore this plan with the adolescent. Inquire about how this plan actually helps those who are suffering, what difficulties are inherent in the plan, what are the limits of the plan, and what are the negative consequences that might follow from the plan if it is implemented. This reflection will help adolescents to recognize not only the complexity and ambiguity of many social problems, but also the limits of political and social policies. Furthermore, this reflection aids adolescents in developing life strategies that actually mirror the real world of decision making, which is often complex and ambiguous.

Suggestion 6

As we have already seen, developmental psychology stresses the importance of *peer relations* in the adolescent years. The interaction among adolescents in peer relationships might well be a crucial determinant in obtaining both their regard for disadvantaged groups and their interest in broader issues such as Third World concerns. Personal relationships, a sense of belonging, and identification with others in a communal setting might well influence the social values of adolescents. Adolescents personally profit by experiencing both the reciprocal rights and responsibilities that are so necessary in personal relationships and the caring and empathic concerns that are nourished through personal friendships. The benefits of these relationships might allow adolescents to appreciate more easily the hurts and needs of broader social groupings, such as other races, different social classes, or Third World countries. And because caring behavior is closely associated with empathy and experiencing another's perspective, social justice education should encourage the active development and fostering of positive personal relationships in the lives of adolescents. From this vantage point, having experienced empathy, insight, and satisfaction through personal relationships, adolescents might more easily be receptive to the plight and injustice experienced by others.

Suggestion 7

The climate or *communal environment* that adolescents experience can also have an important effect on their values and attitudes. Adults must ask whether the school, agency, organization, or ministry program—or even their own personal lives—are witnesses to true Christian values. We cannot afford to dismiss the modeling influences present in adult relationships with high school or college adolescents.[29]

Suggestion 8

In recent research, Andrew Greeley points out that Catholic adolescents whose personal experience of God (their "God story") is loving and tender are inclined toward a social justice orientation and show concern for social problems and racial injustice.[30] This finding renders the *religious experience* of adolescents an important variable in social justice education. In light of this fact, adults might wish to explore with adolescents what the young persons's story of God really is and how this story is experienced in their lives. To what extent, for example, can the adolescent's experience of God be described as warm, loving, and tender? It is also important to reflect with adolescents on how these experiences are carried over into their

315

lives. Are personal relationships, for example, caring and loving? Do these experiences of caring and loving extend beyond this immediate relationship to other peoples and groups, and also include various social concerns? (See also chapters 3 and 5 for additional questions and strategies that focus on the God-image relationship.)

Suggestion 9

Because adolescents will enter the adult world and someday be *decision makers*, it is helpful at both the high school and college level to explore with them the values present in their own vocational choice (see also the discussion of Super in chapter 3). In discussing a vocational choice with an adolescent, it is helpful to examine the adolescent's personal values and goals in the vocation. Has he or she considered whether there is a place for Christian service in a future vocation?

Notes to Chapter Eight

1. Two books that trace the historical claims of social justice are L. John Topel, S.J., *The Way to Peace*, Maryknoll, NY: Orbis Books, 1979; and David Hollenbach, S.J., *Claims in Conflict: Retrieving and Renewing the Catholic Human Rights Tradition*, New York: Paulist Press, 1979. The best survey of Catholic teaching on social justice can be found in David J. O'Brien and Thomas A. Shannon, eds., *Renewing the Earth: Catholic Documents on Peace, Justice, and Liberation*, Garden City, NY: Image Books, 1977.

2. Richard A. McCormick, S.J., "Moral Theology Since Vatican II: Clarity or Chaos," *Cross Currents* 29, Spring 1979, p. 19.

3. John H. Wright, S.J., "Catholic Faith," *Theological Studies* 39, December 1978, p. 717.

4. William Byron, S.J., "Social Consciousness in the Ignatian Exercises," *Review for Religious* 32, November 1973, p. 1365.

5. See National Conference of Catholic Bishops, *To Teach as Jesus Did: A Pastoral Message on Catholic Education*, Washington, DC: USCC, 1973; and United States Catholic Conference, *Sharing the Light of Faith: The National Catechetical Directory*, Washington, DC: USCC, 1979, chap. 7, 149–171, pp. 85–97.

6. *Sharing the Light of Faith*, 165, p. 93.

7. For a discussion of the complexity of nuclear arms policy and the Catholic position, see George S. Weigel, Jr., "The Catholics and the Arms Race: A Primer for the Perplexed," *Chicago Studies* 18, Summer 1979, pp. 169–196.

8. See footnote 14, chapter 3.

9. The development of spirituality, social justice, and the adolescent experience is the result of the author's own reflection and the following four sources: Byron, "Social Consciousness in the Ignatian Exercises," pp. 1365–1378; Edward van Merrienboer, O.P., "Toward a Social Spirituality," *Spirituality Today* 31, March 1979, pp. 36–43; Max Oliva, S.J., "An Apostolic Spirituality for the Ministry of Social Justice," *Review for Religious* 36, September 1977, pp. 687–694; Thomas E. Clarke, S.J., "Ignatian Spirituality and Societal Consciousness," *Studies in the Spirituality of Jesuits* 7, September 1975, pp. 127–150.

10. John A. Coleman, S.J., "The Future of Ministry," *America* 144, March 28, 1981, p. 248.

11. Byron, "Social Consciousness in the Ignatian Exercises," p. 1365. Byron goes on to say, however, that a "social content" is given to he *Exercises* through "suggested Scripture texts, from the recommended reading, from the faith experience and world view of the director, and, last but by no means least, from divine activity in the soul of the retreatant" (p. 1376).

12. Clarke, "Ignatian Spirituality and Societal Consciousness," p. 139.

13. Karl Rahner, S.J., *Spiritual Exercises*. New York: Herder and Herder, 1965, p. 175, as quoted in Byron, "Social Consciousness in the Ignatian Exercises," p. 1371.

14. Robert J. Starratt, S.J., *Sowing the Seeds of Faith and Justice*, Jesuit Secondary Education Association, Washington, DC., 1981, p. 11.

15. John H. Yoder, *The Politics of Jesus*. Grand Rapids, MI: William B. Eerdmans Publishing Co., 1972.

16. For a discussion of the influences that affect how we help and care for others, see Ervin Staub, *Positive Social Behavior and Morality: Social and Personal Influences*, vol. 1, New York: Academic Press, 1978.

17. Kenneth B. Clark, "Empathy: A Neglected Topic in Psychological Research," *American Psychologist* 35, February 1980, p. 188.

18. Martin L. Hoffman, "Development of Moral Thought, Feeling, and Behavior," *American Psychologist* 34, October 1979, pp. 958–966; and "Moral Development in Adolescence," in *Handbook of Adolescent Psychology*, edited by Joseph Adelson. New York: John Wiley & Sons, 1980, pp. 307–320.

19. Hoffman, "Development of Moral Thought, Feeling, and Behavior," pp. 962–963.

20. Nancy Eisenberg-Berg and Paul Mussen, "Empathy and Moral Development in Adolescence," *Developmental Psychology* 14, March 1978, pp. 185–186.

21. For an overview of the adolescent's growth of a political self, see Joseph Adelson, "The Development of Ideology in Adolescence," in *Adolescence in the Life Cycle*, edited by Sigmund E. Dragastin and Glen H. Elder, Jr. New York: John Wiley & Sons, 1975, pp. 63–78; M. Kent Jennings and Richard G. Niemi, *The Political Character of Adolelscence*, Princeton, NJ: Princeton University Press, 1974; Judith Gallatin, "Political Thinking in Adolescence," in Adelson, ed., *Handbook of Adolescent Psychology*, pp. 344–382.

22. Norman T . Feather, "Values in Adolescence," in Adelson, ed., *Handbook of Adolescent Psychology*, p. 281.

23. Adelson, "The Development of Ideology in Adolescence," in Dragastin and Elder, eds., *Adolescence in the Life Cycle*, p. 76.

24. See Jennings and Niemi, *The Political Character of Adolescence*, for an extensive treatment of this issue.

25. Richard M. Merelman, *Political Reasoning in Adolescence: Some Bridging Themes*, Sage Professional Papers in Political Science, Series Number 04-026.

26. See Staub, *Positive Social Behavior and Morality*, vol. 1; and *Positive Social Behavior and Morality: Socialization and Development*, vol. 2, New York: Academic Press, 1979.

27. These passages arise from the author's own research, study, and reflection on Scripture. For an excellent scriptural approach to social justice, see Topel, *The Way to Peace.*

28. Ibid., vol. 1, p. 263.

29. Cheryl Hollman Keen, "In Search of Responsible Attachment to Global Issues: The Influence of College on Students' Sense of Responsibility," unpublished paper, Harvard University, February 1980. I am indebted to Ms. Keen for references to several quotes and for her insightful comments regarding the college environment's effects on late adolescents.

30. Andrew M. Greeley, "A Post-Vatican II New Breed? A Report on Contemporary Catholic Teen-Agers," *America* 142, June 28, 1980, pp. 534–537.

CHAPTER NINE

The Adolescent Quest:
Toward Christian Maturity

"Ah, Lord God!" I said, "I know not how to speak:
I am too young." But the Lord answered me,
Say not, "I am too young." To whomever I send you,
you shall go; whatever I command you, you shall speak.

Jeremiah 1:6–7

Ministry to adolescents should always have as its primary goal the development of youth into mature adult Christians. This ministry involves dealing with adolescents where they are, in the immediacy of their own experiences. At the same time, however, there is always the need to challenge them to true Christian growth. What we lack, though, is a perspective for Christian growth during the adolescent years. In other words, we do not exactly know the ostensible signs of Christian adulthood that we should look for in order to help guide adolescents on the road to mature Christian adulthood. Priest-psychiatrist James Gill addresses this issue when he notes that, at present, "countless opportunities are being lost because there is no campus-wide understanding of what the developing, truly Christian adolescent or young adult should look like; what special contributions each adult employed on campus could make by nurturing specific qualities of character in the students."[1]

In this final chapter, we shall attempt to set forth a theory of Christian adult maturity that is specifically oriented to the adolescent years. A discussion of various criteria will provide adults genuine qualities to look for as they help encourage high school and college youth toward Christian maturity.

In order to provide an adequate view of Christian maturity during the adolescent years, we should look for the fulfillment of three particular perspectives. First, we want to find the *spiritual* sources for a theory of Christian maturity. For this we will look to the writings of St. Paul and St. Ignatius to delineate what Christian maturity might be. Second, we need to examine what *psychological theory* has

320

to say about the development of the mature person so that we might learn about the basic characteristics of maturity. Third, we need to find out what the *research evidence* actually says about maturity during the adolescent years. This third perspective is particularly crucial. All too often, when we discuss maturity, we talk about an ideal without applying this ideal to the actual lived experience of adolescents. Our theological supposition has been that grace works through the developing nature of the adolescent. We must therefore pay attention to this developing nature, for without it we are left with a theory that has very little significance for what adolescents actually experience. After examining these three perspectives, we shall then suggest specific criteria that adults can use in their ministry to developing adolescents.

Spiritual Sources

St. Paul on Maturity   For Paul, the first and foremost characteristic of any mature person is a growing and developing relationship with Jesus Christ.[2] Paul proclaims: "I wish to know Christ and the power flowing from His resurrection, likewise, to know how to share in His suffering by being formed into the pattern of His death" (Phil 3:10). Christ, in Paul's writings, is the center of life and the fullness of God (Col 1:19). For Christians, then, there must be life in the Lord because we must all "live in Christ Jesus the Lord" (Col 2:6); and this life in Him means life in the Spirit (Rom 8:9–11). Paul himself tells of his deep desire to know Christ through his work in the Corinthian community, "for while I was with you I would speak of nothing but Jesus Christ and Him crucified" (1 Cor 2:2).

From Paul we can see that the primary identifying mark of mature Christians is a growing realization and deepening presence of Jesus Christ. Mature Christians increasingly realize the Lord's call to imitate Him (1 Thes 1:6), and Paul's first letter to the Corinthians contains an entreaty that the community imitate Paul, who had fashioned his own life on Christ's life: "Imitate me as I imitate Christ" (1 Cor 10:33). This call of the Lord is a call to perfection (1 Thes 5:23–25). Christians, then, are truly "chosen" ones (Rom 8:33), who do God's work and live lives "worthy of the God who calls [them] to His kingship and glory" (1 Thes 2:12). We see in Paul a conscious

"Christ-focusing," that is, a deepening awareness of the centrality that Jesus exercises in the personal experience of Christians. This developing relationship with Jesus is intimately related to the growing sense of maturity that Christians experience. In Ephesians, the Pauline writer speaks of true Christian growth and points out the gifts that have been given by the Lord to the saints (Christians). These gifts are not to lie idle, but must be used "in roles of service for the faithful to build up the body of Christ, till we become one in faith and in the knowledge of God's Son, and form that perfect man who is Christ come to full stature" (Eph 4:12–13).

The Pauline notion of *growth in maturity* comes alive in Ephesians 4:14–16: "Let us, then, be children no longer, tossed here and there, carried about by every wind of doctrine that originates in human trickery and skill in proposing error. Rather, let us profess the truth in love and grow to the full maturity of Christ the head. Through Him the whole body grows, and with the proper functioning of the members joined firmly together by each supporting ligament, builds itself up in love."

This passage is instructive in several ways. First, we note the overwhelming importance given to the union of Christians with Christ; we must be tied to Christ who is the important focus of all human endeavors. Second, an individual's talents are not meant to be privatized; rather, they are meant to be used for the sake of the community, for others. Third, the movement of the community is toward union—the harmony of all working together for growth and the building of the community in love.

Paul's understanding of maturity is outlined in his first letter to the Corinthian community. The Corinthians were mistaken in their notion of what maturity really meant. As a result, they developed what might be called a presumptive attitude toward their own salvation. Because they had been baptized, they mistakenly assumed that they had therefore gained salvation, and so they began to grow lax in their own behavior. Their distorted notion of salvation led them to erroneously conclude that they possessed wisdom, and then spurred them to engage in illicit sexual behaviors and gluttonous practices. Disputing among themselves, they divided into factions, each championing its own leader (1 Cor 1:10–12).

Paul admonished them about such thoughts and behaviors: "Brothers, the trouble was that I could not talk to you as spiritual men but only as men of flesh, as infants in Christ. I fed you with milk, and did not give you solid food because you were not ready for it. You are not ready for it even now, being still very much in a natural condition" (1 Cor 3:1–2). The Corinthian community was not ready for Paul's message; they had developed a false wisdom that led them to deviate from true Christian behavior. As a result, their belief in their own personal salvation fostered a deadly complacency that rendered them immature. They were incapable of taking the "solid food" that was meant for mature Christians. This is why Paul treated them as infants who were still very much "in a natural condition."

The Corinthians who took their salvation for granted were simply immature. The truly "wise" (mature) persons were led by the Spirit, for "the Spirit we have received is not the world's spirit but God's Spirit, helping us to recognize the gifts He has given us. We speak of these, not in words of human wisdom but in words taught by the Spirit, thus interpreting spiritual things in spiritual terms" (1 Cor 2:12–13). The Spirit lead the Christian to recognize that true wisdom resides in folly, for "we are fools on Christ's account" (1 Cor 4:10). And this insight is limited to those who are mature, since "there is, to be sure, a certain wisdom which we express among the spiritually mature" (1 Cor 2:6). Christians must be prepared, then, to be considered foolish and weak, and to suffer for Christ. Furthermore, mature Christians must show an awareness of the needs of others within the community. In this way, the Christian response *builds up* others and attends to their needs. And this care and concern for one another is, according to Paul, the true test of a mature Christian life.

Two examples in 1 Corinthians points to the emphasis that Paul placed on the Corinthians' need to care for one another, which, in turn, would strengthen the Christian community. In 1 Cor 8, Paul writes of the discord prevalent in the Corinthian community over the eating of meat that had been offered to idols. Some Christians had perceived no problem in eating this food, whereas others found these practices to be immoral, based largely on their pre-conversion upbringing, and were scandalized by those Christians who were eating such meat.

What would the mature Christian response be in such a case? Paul saw nothing inherently wrong for the believing Christian to eat idolatrous food (1 Cor 8:9). On the other hand, if eating this food caused a scandal among other Christians in the community, then the mature Christian was obliged to forego eating this food. "Therefore, if food causes my brother to sin, I will never eat meat again, so that I may not be an occasion of sin to him" (1 Cor 8:13). For Paul, then, the needs and concerns of one's fellow Christians take priority over one's own desire and preferences. In this way, the "folly" of the cross is made real when Christians surrender personal desires for the good of the community. Many would judge this surrender of personal desire to be foolish, but mature Christians realize the importance of this action for the well-being of the total community.

Paul restates his theme of "building up" in 1 Cor 14 when he discusses the place of 'tongues" in the Corinthian church. Members of the Corinthian community had the gift of tongues and were flaunting this gift at the expense of other gifts. In fact, it appears that the entire community was guilty of placing far too much emphasis on the gift of tongues. Paul remonstrated against this inordinate emphasis on one particular gift: "Brothers, do not be childish in your outlook. Be like children as far as evil is concerned, but in mind be mature" (1 Cor 14:20).

Paul advised the Corinthians to keep in mind the desires and needs of the entire community. A person's gifts must be seen in light of the needs of others. True maturity, then, is making one's own needs secondary to the good of the community. Paul responds to this Corinthian situation by saying that all things must be done "with a constructive purpose" (1 Cor 14:26). We see again that Paul's attention is not on the privatized good of any one person, but rather on the good of the entire community, which is paramount for Paul.

Paul saw that true maturity depended on the care and concern that Christians have for one another. Paul considers this care and concern for others to be indispensable if one is to "lead a life worthy of the Lord" (Col 1:10). Yet there is one more important aspect of Christian maturity; mature Christians recognize personal weakness and realize that constant perseverance is necessary in the Christian life. Strength for this patient persistence comes through Christ, who strengthens "to the end" (1 Cor 1:8). No greater example of this Christian stamina is given than Paul's eloquent statement to the Phillipian community (Phil 3:8–14). Paul considers "all as loss in the light of the surpassing knowledge of my Lord Jesus Christ," and longs for the "prize," which is "life on high in Christ Jesus." Yet he is content to wait in patient endurance until he is "grasped by Christ Jesus." He concludes by noting that "all of us who are spiritually mature must have this attitude" (Phil 3:15).

For Paul, the Christian experience of maturity is a realization of one's own weakness and fraility, of the need to rely always on the Lord. Historian William J. Bouwsma calls this Christian need for vigilance a paradox.[3] The goal of the Christian life is identification and union with Christ; yet, this goal can never be realized during earthly existence. Christians must constantly, vigilantly strive to achieve this goal.

In conclusion, Paul sees the fundamental test of maturity to be a growing identification in Jesus Christ. Mature Christians are, then, "ambassadors for Christ" (2 Cor 5:20), and their witness is lived out in the everyday building up of the community, that is, through care and concern for others. For many people, this behavior appears to be folly, but for Christians, such behavior leads to true life (2 Cor 4:10–15). Yet, Christians also realize that the example of Christ is a prize that they can never fully realize, for Christians are engaged in a constant striving for the "finish line," which is "life on high in Christ Jesus" (Phil 3:14).

St. Ignatius on Maturity   St. Ignatius did not write specifically on the meaning of Christian maturity, yet his writings, particularly the *Spiritual Exercises*, detail the importance of discernment in a person's life. It was said that everything Ignatius did in his later years was done with a discerning vision.[4] Christian maturity from an Ignatian perspective, then, is a growing sensitivity to the beckoning of the Lord in the interior movements of the self.

In a fascinating article entitled "Christian Maturity and Spiritual Discernment," David Asselin captures what it really means to be a mature Christian in the context of this discerning spirit.[5] Asselin quotes Heb 5:14 in which the "mature" are described as "those who have their faculties trained by practice to distinguish good from evil." As we grow in Christian maturity, we develop a deepening ability to sort out and sift through these movements of good and evil.

On a personal level, maturity includes several qualities. The first characteristic of a mature Christian is that he or she *listens*. Christians are increasingly sensitive to the movements of God in their lives. Combined with this listening to the Lord is the second quality—a growing capacity for *reflection*. For Christians, the interior life is increasingly characterized by the capacity to reflect on life, that is, Christians can determine where they are and where they are going. They are disposed to both sort out movements, impulses, and inclinations, and, at the same time, grow in identifying those that come from the Lord. Third, says Asselin, there is a personal *response* to these movements. After they have identified what is truly a movement from the Lord, Christians then respond willingly to the Lord's call. Growth in the Lord thus becomes an extension of Ignatius' First Principle and Foundation, an insight that determines that the first obligation of one's life is to praise, reverence, and serve God. This obligation is fostered, in turn, through an increasing receptivity to the Lord and the discovery of His will in one's life. As Evelyn and James Whitehead have remarked, religious growth is "growth in one's ability to discern patterns of God's presence within human life and to respond in an increasingly open way to this presence."[6]

Another important factor in Christian growth is the unique personal encounter with Jesus. Asselin says the personal experience of Jesus "must lie within the capacities of ordinary Christian faith-maturity."[7] Mature Christians not only clearly demonstrate inward growth and the sorting out of their inner experiences, but also experience, in a unique and personal way, the Lord calling them.

The Ignatian perspective on Christian maturity parallels the Pauline notion of maturity; both maintain that discerning Christians are always in need of growth. Paul reminds the people of Corinth that they must remain vigilant and not be foolish in thinking that they possess all wisdom. In discernment, Christians have a responsibility to reflect on their lives in ever deeper ways so that they can become more sensitive to the Lord's call. This reflection is never a complete task, for one is always encountering new experiences that present a challenge in following the Lord's call. The view of maturity from a discerning perspective involves an ever deepening realization of Jesus' call as well as a response to this call that is mediated through one's lived experience.

By combining the notions of Paul and Ignatius, several distinct characteristics emerge that help us to distinguish the mature Christian. Above all, Christ is the key figure in life. In our relationship with the Lord, it is vital that we grow increasingly sensitive to the direction in which Jesus' call is leading. We must respond to this call through our helping and sustaining responses to others. As maturing Christians, we are thereby caught up in a distinct dynamic: there is a growing interiority, reflection, and experiencing of Jesus' call; at the same time, this relationship with Jesus is lived outwardly through actions that proclaim our love and care for others. With time, we realize that this call is ever deepening, always challenging us to deeper levels of growth and commitment. In summing up this definition of the mature Christian, we can be guided by Evelyn and James Whitehead's remark that "religious growth will be charted in terms of an adult's maturing sense of identity (discipleship), the ability to love and give of oneself (charity), and the capacity for responsible care (stewardship)."[8]

In order to foster Christian maturity among adolescents, adults must concentrate on the presence of Jesus in their lives. Similarly, adults must look for a growing realization among adolescents of the Lord's movements within them, and their living of Jesus' call in personal actions that witness to Christian love. Before we attempt to define these qualities in the lives of adolescents, however, we must review what the psychological literature says about maturity and about how this maturity is experienced during the adolescent years.

Psychological Theories

Increasingly, adults who minister to adolescents look for guidelines to identify what it really means to be mature. Several psychologists have spoken of maturity as the stage of being competent, effective, functioning adults. Before we explore what Christian maturity in adolescence entails, however, it would be helpful to examine what psychologists have said about the mature self.

In their overview of the literature, psychiatrists Daniel Offer and Melvin Sabshin submit that "a mature and normal person is one who successfully overcomes the obstacles in each and every stage of his development."[9] For adolescents, of course, this includes meeting identity and intimacy needs and accepting growing independence as exhibited in responsible behavior toward others.

Psychologist Carl Rogers has used the phrase "fully functioning persons" to describe persons who have undergone therapy.[10] Rogers notes that this person exhibits three distinct characteristics:

An Increasing Openness to Experience   This person does not erect defenses against new things, feelings, or people but remains open to them. He or she develops a greater capacity for dealing with feelings such as fear, pain, tenderness, and awe that he or she has not previously experienced or recognized.

Increasingly Existential Living   This characteristic allows the individual to experience, at the present moment, the richness of life in real openness. This person neither shows rigidity nor attempts to control his or her environment. Instead, a freer flow of self emerges from this new experience.

Trust of Self   The fully functioning person is one who really *trusts* himself or herself and increasingly goes with what he or she feels is the best response. The individual grows in the capacity to trust his or her own instincts, feelings, and sense of what is right.

Rogers places great emphasis on an individual's capacity to listen to and trust his or her own self. What is the difference, then, between this interior trust of self and the Ignatian experience of discernment? When spiritual writer William Johnston addressed this very question, he found that a discerning vision, which relied solely on feelings, to be inadequate.[11] We must not be content to concentrate exclusively on our feelings; we must seek to discover the *source* of our feelings. Are they motivated by what is good, or is there an element of self-deception involved in this inner experience? We must also look at the end or goal of interior experiences. Are these interior movements ordered toward obtaining what is good or what is evil? We cannot concentrate solely on the inner self. In the context of faith, we must attempt to discover the motivations that underlie our inner experiences, as well as the direction in which these interior movements are leading us.

Adolescents have a real need to examine their interior experiences and reflect on them, to ask themselves what role Jesus exercises in their values, goals, personal feelings. They need to ask how Jesus touches and influences their lives here and now. Adults must help adolescents realize both the underlying motivations for their actions, as well as where those actions are leading.

Psychologist Gordon Allport has attributed six characteristics to the mature personality:[12]

Extension of the Sense of Self.   The mature person is capable of going beyond his or her own self. Maturity is seen as investing oneself in activities that point one beyond the present. A person is not wedded to self-absorption, but rather, participates and shares in human interactions. This person makes commitments to others in the area of religion, politics, work, family, and relationships.

Warm Relating of Self to Others.   The mature person's extension of self provides for the development of deep and personal human relationships. The demands of intimacy take hold of this person and a compassionate awareness of another's needs emerges. This person's attention tends to be devoted to the *bestowing* of love, whereas the immature person is more concerned with the *receiving* of love from others.

Self-acceptance.   The mature person tends to be realistic in his or her own life situation. This person responds to inner needs in a realistic fashion. He or she exhibits control over impulses and is capable of withstanding frustration, disappointments, and ambiguity. Along with this self-acceptance are values to guide their lives.

Realistic Perception, Skills, and Assignments.   The mature person has a realistic notion of his or her capabilities. Attitudes and skills are derived from personal interactions in the world. This person is capable of taking on various life tasks and seeing them through. There is a healthy sense of being involved and accepting the responsibility that goes with this involvement. A related aspect is the fact that the mature person possesses a realistic understanding of the economic facts of life. Given today's economic insecurities, this understanding is becoming increasingly important.

Self-Objectification: Insight and Humor.   The mature person has insight into self that is based on a genuine understanding of who he or she really is. This understanding in turn enhances his interactions with others and with the world. In addition, such a person possesses a sense of humor that allows him or her to accept personal shortcomings and disappointments. Humor and insight go together, because as the mature person confronts many of life's situations, he or she realizes the inadequacy of personal self-knowledge in dealing with the many demands and situations that are part of human living.

The Unifying Philosophy of Life.   The mature person has developed a philosophy of life that incorporates values, goals, and a

329

purpose that give his or her life a sense of direction. This person's religious preference and faith response form part of this purposeful direction.

Priest-psychologist George Croft sees a distinct similarity between Allport's six characteristics and the theological virtues of faith, hope, and love.[13] This comparison lends support to some psychological validation for a Christian adulthood. Faith, hope, and love steer a person to an openness to life, an awareness and conviction of self, a sense of purpose, and a commitment that goes outward to others.

Psychologist Donald Blocher, who has gathered together what Rogers, Allport and other psychologists have said about maturity, has identified five distinct factors for what he calls "the effective personality."[14] Briefly stated, Blocher's effective personality manifests the following characteristics:

Consistency   The mature person shows consistency in behavior across roles, situations, and time. This is possible because this person has developed a sense of identity that fosters this consistency. As a result, the mature person has a sense of direction and purpose in his or her life.

Commitment   The mature person possesses goals and personal desires that allow for risk and an outward focus to obtain these ends. Likewise, values are an important part of a person's life, and the committed person embraces these values in order to give his or her life meaning.

Control   The mature person is able to experience control over a variety of emotional states in relation to various life situations. This person realizes what is appropriate behavior and what is not. Part of this control is not repressive. "It is rather the result of an inner strength and conviction that one is adequate to meet even the most tragic circumstances of life."[15]

Competence   Another characteristic of the mature person is the capacity to use abilities and talents in his or her personal life. This person can relate effectively in various situations, roles, and relationships.

Creativity   The final characteristic of the mature person is the ability to think in diverse, original ways. The creative person is open to new impulses, ideas, and feelings, and he or she profits from these experiences. Present in this person's relationships are a sensitivity to and an awareness of his or her own personal feelings.

Psychologist Douglas Heath has done the most extensive research on the concept of maturity.[16] He maintains that maturity is important for the adolescent years because "the psychological maturity of an adolescent is one of the most powerful predictors of his adult mental health."[17] Heath's model of maturity has four sectors of personality: cognitive skills, self-concept, values or motives, and personal relations. In order to evaluate the level of maturity for each sector, we must examine the five interdependent developmental dimensions: symbolization, allocentrism, integration, stability, and autonomy. The following diagram shows Heath's model.

DIMENSIONS OF DEVELOPMENT

Personality Sectors	Symbolization	Allocentrism	Integration	Stability	Autonomy
Cognitive					
Self-concept					
Values					
Personal Relations					

MODEL OF MATURING   Reprinted from Douglas H. Heath, "Wanted: A Comprehensive Model of Healthy Development," *The Personnel and Guidance Journal*, 58, January 1980, p. 393. By permission of the American Personnel and Guidance Association.

In order to explain Heath's model, we need to look more closely at the five developmental dimensions.

Symbolization   Symbolization is an individual's capacity to transform his or her experience into a symbolic form. Examples of this would be language, art, music, and words. This person can symbolize within himself or herself the complex outer world that he or she experiences. This representation, in turn, enhances the formation of reflection and an increasing awareness of others. This dimension is reflected in deeper insights and greater sensitivity in interpersonal relationships.

Allocentrism   Heath observes that this developmental dimension is characterized by the movement "from self-centered narcissism to other-centered empathy."[18] This dimension of maturity is characterized by a greater awareness of another's feelings and thoughts as well as a greater concern for another. This person is also the most capable of realizing others' impressions of him or her.

Integration   The mature person shows greater levels of integration. His or her thinking, for example, is more organized, complex, and divergent. Greater levels of integration facilitates a congruence between inner thinking and outer behavior. A growing consistency characterizes the person's behavior, and personal relationships take on more openness, mutuality, and respect.

Stability   The mature person's thinking becomes more stable as time goes on. This person is also capable of thinking about a variety of situations, even if they are complex and stressful.

Autonomy   The mature person has acquired a sense of his or her values and can function in a variety of situations in which he or she must exhibit a commitment to personal value orientation. There is a greater sense of independence, and interpersonal relations become more stable. The mature person is able to act out of inner motives and is less subject to the control of external influences.

Heath says that a relationship exists between the four sectors of personality and the five dimensions of development. A person who expresses a mature value system, for example, will manifest a high degree of symbolization, allocentrism, integration, stability, and autonomy. Similarly, a low self-concept will be reflected in a lower level of these same developmental dimensions.

A central assumption of Heath's model is that growth toward maturity is an "organismic process"—in other words, we tend to experience growth along all sectors of our personality. An overly advanced level of maturity in one sector will level off until other sectors can reach a greater level of growth and catch up. This, says Heath, is one reason why many especially bright students might flee toward nonintellectual pursuits, including those that might be harmful, such as drugs or sex. In effect, these youth are engaged in a delaying action until other areas of growth can emerge.[19] No doubt adolescents might show sophistication in one sector of their lives—they might be highly developed in interpersonal relationships, for example, or in a well-thought-out personal value system—and yet still need more development in other sectors. The increasing maturity of adolescents will manifest greater growth in these other sectors of their lives.

Other research on maturity notes that it is related to a selfless interest in others and a growing awareness of another's perspective. Similarly, adults whose cognitive thinking demonstrates a high degree of maturity also tend to prize values that reflect Erikson's and Kohlberg's higher stages. Individuals who are judged to be mature also tend to favor activities and services that typify a caring concern for others.[20]

Research Evidence

Having examined the theological and psychological dimensions of maturity, we now turn to the actual lived experience of adolescents. We must ask what it means for adolescents in the high school and college years to be mature.

Psychologist Ellen Greenberger and her associates have developed a concept of maturity that stresses three dimensions: (1) the capacity to function adequately on their own; (2) the capacity to interact adequately with others; and (3) the capacity to contribute to social cohesion.[21] The attributes that combine to allow a person to function adequately on his or her own are self-reliance, a developing sense of one's identity (Erikson), and the capacity to work.

The attributes that define interpersonal adequacy include the capacity to communicate with others (this includes an empathic sense of others), the capacity to trust (this includes the willingness to depend on others, the realization of the complexity of the human person, and the recognition of various situations that might limit the ability to trust), and the ability to take on and act out appropriate behaviors for various roles.

The main attributes that contribute to social cohesion include social commitment (developing the sense of community, working for goals, forming alliances with others), openness to sociopolitical change (an awareness of both the positive and the negative aspects of the status quo as well as various alternatives), and tolerance for differences in others (accepting people for who and what they are and being sensitive to these differences).

Along with psychologists Ruthellen Josselson and David Mc-Conochie, Ellen Greenberger has detailed the actual behavior of maturing adolescents at the secondary school level.[22] Their research documents the difference between high- and low-maturing adolescents of both sexes.

Among the boys, the researchers discovered that those who were low in maturity exhibited a lack of self-reflection and a low level of self-awareness. These adolescents are concerned more with the present than with the future and what it might hold, and they demonstrate a great reliance on external factors. In other words, outside influences, rather than a reliance on internal resources, determine much of the lives of adolescent boys. Moreover, these boys exhibit close dependency ties with their parents, problems with aggressive impulses, and difficulty in making friends and entering into more intimate relationships with others. Among these adolescents, friends are valued for what they can do for you.

In contrast to these low-maturing males, adolescent boys who are high on maturity scales tend to place less emphasis on material goods and place greater value on school, hobbies, and religious practices. But it is more difficult to describe the high-maturing adolescent boy than the low-maturing male. High-maturing adolescent males are more diversified in interests and activities and are more active; at the same time, they depend less on others' impressions of them. They tend to focus on their own future and what it holds for them. They have periods of self-doubt, but they can live with this ambiguity. They are enhanced by their own personal sense of individuality. Moreover, they demonstrate particular control of their impulses and great concentration on personal goals.

In summary, when high-maturing adolescent males are compared with the low-maturing males, high-maturing males are characterized by a sense of personal adequacy. This phenomenon allows these adolescents to draw upon their own inner resources as they strive for future personal goals.

In describing low-maturing girls, two characteristics appeared. Low maturers had the desire both to have fun and to possess material goods. Two groups of low-maturing girls appeared in the data. The first group reflected the popular stereotype: they were attractive, interacted socially, and concentrated on and reflected the views and behaviors of their own adolescent culture. These girls appeared to lack complexity and ambiguity, but, at the same time, tended to be nonreflective and to manifest a basic self-centeredness. Friendship did not appear to be overly important to them. Like the low-maturing boys, these girls depended on external restraints to guide their lives and impulses. The second group of low-maturing girls was characterized as having little fun in their lives. These girls were often caught in a difficult situation in their home environment; they suffered from both low self-esteem and feelings of inferiority; and they desired the fun-loving, carefree life of the first group of low-maturing girls. All in all, low-maturing girls demonstrated little sense of self-awareness and were dominated by their need for external controls.

In contrast to the low-maturing girls, the high maturers reflected both complexity and multidimensional aspects. High-maturing girls placed less emphasis on material things and pleasures. They took themselves seriously and thought reflectively on themselves, their own actions, and their own sense of future commitment. Unlike their low-maturing peers, these girls were more resistant to the demands of peer pressure. Their relationships were characterized by mutual give-and-take and an empathic sense of others. Moreover, the high maturers were also capable of working through conflicts in their own personal lives, valued their independence, and were aware of the larger dimensions of life beyond their own environment.

For late adolescence, that is, those in their undergraduate college years, the most extensive study of maturity has been done by Douglas Heath. After examining the definitions of maturity that have been advanced by both experts in psychology and non-experts—undergraduate college students—Heath noted that the two groups were remarkably similar in their definitions of what constituted a mature person.

> In either case," writes Heath, "the mature person emerges as a judiciously realistic individual with a reflective sense of values and an underlying meaning to his life which he maintains with integrity. However, he is not closed to new experience, but is open to continued growth. Such a person can adapt to others, can tolerate and control most of the tensions of living. He has a basic human warmth or compassion and respect for his fellow man.[23]

Heath has studied the late adolescent's maturity in college and found, during his interviews with freshmen and seniors, the following characteristics to be some of the more prominent features.

Heath discovered that the students tended to mature through the college years. He found that students grew in their intellectual skills and in their self-concept or awareness of themselves. Relationships were regarded as a primary factor in their own growth in self-awareness. There was also a growth in allocentric development, although seniors showed some mixed results in this area. There were increased feelings for others and the development of closer personal friendships. Heath reports that an allocentric perspective increased when students realized that they needed others.

Seniors were understandably more integrated than freshmen, especially in the areas of cognitive and intellectual skills. During their college years, students also showed a more developed and integrated self-concept and value system, both of which tended to foster a sense of meaning and purpose in their lives. As undergraduates matured, they tended to have a greater understanding of themselves and their own interests. Seniors were also more capable of controlling their impulses and were more accepting of their weaknesses.

Also, an increasing stability about their own cognitive skills emerged among college students, and they were increasingly capable of handling emotionally upsetting situations that normally might have impinged on their intellectual efforts. During these college years, students' beliefs and values also appeared to be increasingly stable. Furthermore, seniors thought that their own sense of self had become more consistent since their freshman year.

Finally, seniors appeared to be more autonomous than freshmen. In keeping with the seniors' growing sense of autonomy, their values and beliefs were more distinctive than the values and beliefs of freshmen. Heath concludes that "the process of maturing in college involves primarily a progressive integration, an expanding capacity for symbolization, particularly of oneself, and a developing allocentrism."[24]

The Maturing Adolescent Christian

The journey we have traveled is now almost complete. As we have traversed the various aspects of adolescent spirituality, we have always been cognizant of both the adolescent experience and the developmental influences that are part of these growing years. One question still remains, however: What are the signs of growing Christian maturity during these developing years? Having examined the literature on maturity from both a spiritual perspective and a psychological perspective, and having now looked at the characteristics of maturity that are actually displayed during this developmental period, we can now point to distinguishable characteristics that are signs of true Christian growth during the high school and college years. The characteristics that are listed are healthy, positive signs of a growing Christian maturity in youth during the high school and college years.

We should note one caution, however, in discussing the maturing Christian qualities of the adolescent. Any adolescent may show more maturity in some areas than in others. It is nonetheless our thesis that growth in one area usually signals growth in other areas. To state this another way, it is unlikely that an adolescent would be quite advanced in some characteristics and quite low in others. On the other hand, it is no doubt true that adolescents are uneven in expressing various characteristics that are part of their own maturity. The emotional disposition, the personal life situation, and the environmental influences combine to signal ambiguous or even erratic expressions of maturity. As time passes, however, the adolescent self will experience a growing stability in the expression of these maturing qualities.

We now turn to the ostensible signs of Christian adulthood as they are experienced during the adolescent years. They include the following:

Christ-centeredness   The central characteristics of adolescent maturity is a developing and deepening relationship with Jesus Christ. During early years of adolescence, this is characterized by accepting Jesus as someone I can talk to about the growing questions of self. During the middle and late adolescent years, this relationship takes on a more profound expression that is manifested through a deepening level of commitment, an affective experience of the Lord, and an evaluative stance in which the person of Jesus becomes the guiding principle for the adolescent's moral decisions and choices. As the adolescent matures, his or her choices are experienced with even greater complexity and ambiguity; yet, interiorly the adolescent is capable of approaching these life situations with greater clarity of what Jesus' call really is.

The process of selecting from among various choices, whether the choices involve careers, relationships, or personal beliefs, is an experience that will enable the adolescent to personally understand what it means to be with Jesus and what life with Jesus really calls him or her to.

As we have seen, the personal journey with Jesus will involve many adolescents in periods of questioning, self-doubt, or even distancing from God. These turbulent periods can nevertheless be times in which adolescents find meaning and a growing commitment to a personally significant value system.

Ultimately, the central question for the adolescent is: How does the person of Jesus Christ make a difference in my life, and what does this difference mean to me in my life and in my relationships with others? Above all, as adolescents grow in maturity, they are able to respond to this question; they experience Jesus as a person who comforts, supports, and challenges them to Christian commitment.

Christian commitment   The experience of Jesus is not without substance. Flowing from the adolescent's relationship with Jesus is a commitment to Christian values, which realizes a deepening understanding of the Gospel message. This commitment fosters in the adolescent both a deeper appreciation of his or her role as a member of the believing community, that which sustains and supports these Christian values, and a growing acceptance of others for who and what they are. Christian commitment involves the adolescent's growing realization and acceptance of self-sacrifice and personal giving to others. For the adolescent, commitment to Christian values is the growing experience of *direction* in his or her life. The fact that meaning and purpose exist in an adolescent's life gives witnesses to this expression that is manifested in growing Christian commitment.

During the early adolescent years, these values are often understood only in rudimentary fashion or are echoes of lingering expressions from childhood years. As adolescents proceed through the high school and college years, however, their curiosity is aroused and they ask questions. This process leads, in turn, to a greater understanding of Christian values in terms of both what they mean and what they call adolescents to. Adolescents who accept Christian values indicate that they are growing to call these values *their own*.

As adolescents become more mature, they come more and more to *define* a personal commitment to Jesus and His message. During the adolescent years, these values are no doubt often realized and expressed in a seesaw fashion. At times, the values surface, but at other times they disappear. The ebb and flow of the adolescent search for identity throughout the secondary and undergraduate years makes the integration and acceptance of these values a slow, uneven experience. In specific situations, adolescents may profess Christian values, but the slow process of identity formation—the process of establishing *who I am* and *what I believe*—makes it unlikely that they will fully evolve during these developmental years. Yet maturing adolescents gradually experience a deepening commitment regarding what they believe and what is important in their lives. These growing, but often tentative assertions and reflections become the seeds from which maturing commitments are harvested in the later years of Christian adulthood.

In addition, adolescents slowly realize the need for personal responsibility for their actions and, through their growing cognitive and reflective capacities, come to understand that what they *believe* is intimately tied to what they *do*. Accompanying adolescent growth, then, is both a deepening understanding of what these values mean and a greater consistency between these values and personal behaviors. Adolescents grow in a reflective understanding of these values and the relation of these values to their own personal moral decisions.

As we have already noted, these values are often expressed only after adolescents have adopted a searching and questioning stance that provides periods of doubt, questioning, self-absorption, or even the jettisoning of Christian values. This retreat into the self often manifests the adolescent attempt to shed the ways of childhood and move to an as yet unrealized commitment. During this time, which, for some adolescents, can last for several years, adolescents engage in a give-and-take battle that gradually develops into a personal value system of meaning in which Jesus Christ and the believing community exercise a pivotal role. For adolescents, the critical challenge during this period is to come to accept the demands of Christian commitment.

Prayerfulness   Adolescent maturity, which is founded on a personal experience of Jesus and the commitment to Christian values, is supported and nourished in the adolescent's growing experience of prayer. Adolescents find more and more meaning in Jesus' presence. During the early adolescent years, this is often characterized by the security Jesus provides and the ensuing confidence that a relationship with Him instills in the adolescent. This experience of Jesus remarkably parallels the function of personal friendship that is expressed in need and security during the early adolescent years. During this period, Jesus is experienced as someone who can help the adolescent. As time passes, however, this relationship with Jesus matures through prayer. Adolescents then grow in the experience of honesty and openness in their life with Jesus. They develop the capacity to share with Jesus the deepest joys and sorrows of their hearts. This, too, parallels the growing adolescent identity that seeks greater integrity through closeness and intimacy with others. And, something else begins to happen for maturing adolescents— they not only share with Jesus, they also begin to *listen* to Him. As these developmental years pass, adolescents develop a receptive stance toward Jesus and actually ponder *what* Jesus is saying to them, *where* He is leading them. More and more, this listening stance provides a foundation for adolescents to commit themselves to Christian values and behavior that truly portrays these values.

Similarly, adolescents grow to realize that the prayer of the Christian is not only personal, but communal; as Christians, we live as social beings in need of one another. A relationship with Jesus is also a relationship with others, for to be with Jesus means to be one with "His body" and "His people."[25] Thus, adolescent prayer is not only personal, but communal. Adolescent growth toward this communal orientation is sometimes tempered by a reaction against the more institutional aspects of communal worship and the need for time to personally reexamine the self. Both of these conditions can lead to a period of disengagement from the Eucharist and the other sacraments. This behavior is understandable and quite common among youth; yet, adolescents need to be challenged to realize that their support and sustenance can truly be found either through prayer or with others in community.

Other-centeredness   The adolescent's growing experience of Jesus, the formation of Christian values, and the experience of personal prayer combine with developmental needs during these years to point to an increasing outward focus. Adolescents come to more and more see that discipleship is the lived experience of Jesus' message. Adolescents grow personally in realizing the need to share and care for others, even if this means self-sacrifice. During the early adolescent years, this outward thrust is limited to family, friends, and individuals who touch adolescents in an immediate way. As development continues, however, this other-centered interest deepens into a greater personal commitment to valued friendships with both sexes, and widens to include individuals and groups of people beyond an adolescent's immediate experience. Likewise, this growing other-centeredness eases the shedding of stereotypes and prejudices toward other groups and people.

Openness Maturing Christian adolescents are also characterized by a growing sense of openness. Adolescents increasingly trust the self, and this allows a venturing outward to encounters with new people and new experiences. Other people, new ideas, and new questions gradually emerge to allow adolescents to think, reflect, and understand in deeper ways. Adolescents then increasingly open themselves to other people and come to experience others as sources of greater self-understanding and personal growth.

Maturing adolescents not only encounter these new experiences, but also gradually begin to reflect on these experiences say *to adolescents*. Especially in this area, adults can exercise a pivotal role in helping adolescents realize deeper meanings. And this increased self-knowledge, which derives from experience, leads adolescents to ask more questions and to think more critically of themselves, of others, and of society. It encourages adolescents to personally assess where they are going with their lives.

Acceptance Maturing adolescents also grow in deeper self-acceptance. During the early adolescent years, a sense of awkwardness develops that leads to a growing wondering about the self. Self-acceptance during these years is often limited. But, as time passes and adolescents have the growing, affirming encounters of inter-personal relationships, adolescents come to face and accept the mystery of their own self. This process includes the experience of reflecting on and coming to understand the sexual self, as well as the growing future sense of the self as an adult.

Accompanying this growing self-acceptance is a corresponding sense of realism in which adolescents come to realize and accept their own limits and how their future life choices in careers, relationships, and personal self-expression actually match their own understanding of their talents, limits, intelligence, and temperament. Finally, the adolescent experience of self-acceptance allows for a growing sense of personal weakness and acceptance of personal faults. Adolescents grow in their understanding of the need for conversion, reconciliation, and personal growth. Maturing Christian

341

adolescents come to understand that spiritual growth, as well as emotional and intellectual growth, is a life-long process that demands honesty and humility with the self, as well as the guidance and advice of others.

Giftedness   As adolescents develop, an experience of self increasingly emerges as a gift. As they become mature, adolescents grow to realize that God's love is a gift that underlies their lives. Slowly, adolescents begin to see that their talents and their personal relationships are gifts—indeed, that their very lives are gifted events. Yet this gift is not kept in isolation; as a gift from the Lord, it makes *demands* on a person. Adolescents must ask themselves, in the words of St. Ignatius, "In the past, what responses have I made to Christ?" and "How do I respond to Christ now?"

During early adolescence, this emphasis on gift is limited to the young person's experience of a talent, a friend, or a special event that brings personal joy and happiness. In time, adolescents gradually discover that God's grace touches them in a very personal, unique way. There is the growing realization that the experiences of life, whether joyful or sorrowful, whether exciting or mundane, are gifted encounters in which the Lord speaks in a special way to each person. A person's experience of the Lord is a special call that beckons him to serve the Lord and His Kingdom. Adolescents experience this call as something special, something unique that leads them to a future life of Christian service.

Our journey with adolescents is now complete. Through our travels with adolescents, we have come to see that their own discovery of Jesus' call is grounded in their own experience, as it is influenced by developmental issues that are threaded throughout these developing years. We have also seen adults exercise a pivotal role in the adolescent experience, for it is through adult-adolescent relationships that young persons can capture in a fuller and richer sense what it means to "come, follow me" down the road toward Christian adulthood.

Notes to Chapter Nine

1. James J. Gill, S.J., "The Development of Persons," *Human Development* 2, Spring 1981, p. 31.

2. For an understanding of Paul's thought on maturity, the author relied on George T. Montague, S.M., *Maturing in Christ*, Milwaukee: The Bruce Publishing Co., 1964; Victor Paul Furnish, *Theology and Ethics in Paul*, New York: Abingdon Press, 1968, 207–241; Rudolf Schnackenburg, *Christian Existence in the New Testament*, vol. 2, Notre Dame, IN: University of Notre Dame Press, 1969, pp. 54–84 (originally published as "Christian Adulthood According to the Apostle Paul," *Catholic Biblical Quarterly* 25, July 1963, pp. 354–370).

3. William J. Bouwsma, "Christian Adulthood," *Daedalus* 105, Spring 1976, p. 81.

4. George Aschenbrenner, S.J., "Consciousness Examen," *Review for Religious* 31, January 1972, p. 21. St. Ignatius' own experience of discernment is contained in his autobiography; see *The Autobiography of St. Ignatius Loyola*, San Francisco: Harper Torchbooks, 1974, pp. 21–26.

5. David Asselin, S.J., "Christian Maturity and Spiritual Discernment," *Review for Religious* 27, July 1968, pp. 581–595.

6. Evelyn E. Whitehead and James D. Whitehead, *Christian Life Patterns*, Garden City, NY: Doubleday & Co., 1979, p. 36.

7. Asselin, "Christian Maturity and Spiritual Discernment," p. 587.

8. Whitehead and Whitehead, *Christian Life Patterns*, p. 21.

9. Daniel Offer and Melvin Sabshin, *Normality*, New York: Basic Books, 1974, p. 36.

10. Carl R. Rogers, *On Becoming a Person*, Boston: Houghton Mifflin Co., 1961, pp. 187–192.

11. William Johnston, S.J., *The Inner Eye of Love*, New York: Harper & Row, 1978, pp. 156–158.

12. Gordon Allport, *Pattern and Growth in Personality*, New York: Holt, Rinehart, and Winston, 1961, pp. 275–307.

13. George Croft, S.J., "Psychological Maturity in Christian Perspective," *Supplement to the Way* 8, November 1968, 221–232.

14. Donald Blocher, *Developmental Counseling*, New York: The Ronald Press, 1974, pp. 97–100.

15. Ibid., p. 99.

16. For an elaboration of Heath's theory, see Douglas H. Heath, "Wanted: A Comprehensive Model of Healthy Development," *The Personnel and Guidance Journal* 58, January 1980, pp. 391–399; "Educating for Maturity," *College & University Journal* 13, March 1974, 15–16, 21–22; "Adolescent

and Adult Predictors of Vocational Adaptation," *Journal of Vocational Behavior* 9, August 1976, pp. 1–19; *Growing Up in College,* San Francisco: Jossey-Bass Inc., 1968; and *Explorations of Maturity,* New York: Appleton-Century Crofts, 1965.

17. Heath, "Wanted: A Comprehensive Model of Healthy Development," p. 391.

18. Heath, "Educating for Maturity," p. 15.

19. Ibid. [The same page as the preceding note.]

20. David McClelland et al., "What Are the Qualities of Maturity?" *Psychology Today* 12, June 1978, p. 50.

21. See Ellen Greenberger and Aago B. Sorenson, "Toward a Conept of Psychosocial Maturity," *Journal of Youth and Adolescence* 3, December 1974, pp. 329–358; and Ellen Greenberger et al., "The Measurement and Structure of Psychosocial Maturity," *Journal of Youth and Adolescence* 4, June 1975, pp. 127–143.

22. Ruthellen Josselson, Ellen Greenberger, and Daniel McConochie, "Phenomenological Aspects of Psychosocial Maturity in Adolescence: Part 1, Boys," *Journal of Youth and Adolescence* 6, March 1977, pp. 25–55; and "Phenomenological Aspects of Psychosocial Maturity in Adolescence: Part 2, Girls," *Journal of Youth and Adolescence* 6, June 1977, pp. 145–167.

23. Heath, *Explorations of Maturity,* p. 7.

24. Heath, *Growing Up in College,* p. 157.

25. Richard A. McCormick, S.J., *How Brave A New World?,* Garden City, NY: Doubleday & Co., 1981, p. 12. Pages 10–17 are an excellent summary of the foundation for a Judeo-Christian ethic.

Bibliography

Joseph Adelson, "Adolescence and the Generalization Gap." *Psychology To-day Magazine*, February 1979. © 1979, Ziff Davis Publishing Co. Re-printed with permission.

Joseph Adelson, "The Development of Ideology in Adolescence." In *Adolescence in the Life Cycle*, edited by Sigmund E. Dragastin and Glen H. Elder, Jr. John Wiley & Sons, 1975. Reprinted with permission.

American Psychiatric Association, *A Psychiatric Glossary*, 4th ed., Washington, DC, APA, 1975. Reprinted with permission.

George A. Aschenbrenner, S.J., "Consciousness Examen," *Review for Religious*, January 1972. Reprinted with permission.

David Asselin, S.J., "Christian Maturity and Spiritual Discernment," *Review for Religious*, July 1968. Reprinted with permission.

Jerald G. Bachman and Lloyd D. Johnston, "The Freshman, 1979," *Psychology Today* Magazine, September 1979. © 1979, Ziff Davis Publishing Co. Reprinted with permission.

Robert M. Baird, "The Creative Role of Doubt in Religion," *Journal of Religion and Health*, Fall 1980. Reprinted with permission.

"Big Rise in Births Out of Wedlock," *San Francisco Chronicle*, October 26, 1981. Reprinted with permission of the Associated Press.

Donald Blocher, *Developmental Counseling*, The Ronald Press, 1974. John Wiley & Sons, Inc. Reprinted with permission.

Anthony Bloom, *Beginning to Pray*, Paulist Press, 1970. Reprinted with permission.

William J. Bouwsma, "Christian Adulthood," *Daedalus*, Journal of the American Academy of Arts and Sciences, 105, Spring 1976. Reprinted with permission.

Richard W. Breese, F.S.C., "The Application of Piagetian Theory to Sexuality: A Preliminary Exploration," *Adolescence*, Summer 1978. Adapted with permission of Libra Publishers, Inc.

Raymond E. Brown, S.S., *Jesus: God and Man*. Copyright © 1967 by Raymond E. Brown, S.S. Glencoe Publishing Co., Inc. Reprinted with permission.

William Byron, S.J., "Social Consciousness in the Ignatian Exercises," *Review for Religious*, November 1973. Reprinted with permission.

Lisa Sowle Cahill, "Should I Welcome My Daughter and Her Live-in Mate as Houseguests?" *St. Anthony Messenger*, March 1981. Reprinted with permission.

Sidney Callahan, "The Challenge of Living With Adolescents," *New Catholic World*, Nov/Dec 1979. Reprinted with permission of Paulist Press.

Sidney Callahan, "Personal Growth and Sexuality: Adolescent and Adult Developmental Stages," *Catholic Mind*, January 1983. Reprinted with permission of *Chicago Studies*.

Carlo Carreto, *Letters from the Desert*, Orbis Books, 1972. Reprinted with permission.

Gary Chamberlain, "Faith Development and Campus Ministry," *Religious Education* 74, May/June 1979. Reprinted with permission.

Kenneth B. Clark, "Empathy: A Neglected Topic in Psychological Research," *American Psychologist*, February 1980. Reprinted with permission of the American Psychological Association.

Thomas E. Clarke, S.J., "Ignatian Spirituality and Social Consciousness," *Studies in the Spirituality of Jesuits*, September 1975. Reprinted with permission of the American Assistancy Seminar on Jesuit Spirituality.

John A. Clippinger, "Adolescent Sexuality and Love," *Journal of Religion and Health*, October 1979. Reprinted with permission.

John A. Coleman, S.J., "The Future of Ministry," *America*. March 28, 1981. Reprinted with permission of America Press, Inc., 106 West 56th Street, New York, NY 10019. © 1981. All rights reserved.

John Janeway Conger, *Adolescence and Youth: Psychological Development in a Changing World*, 2nd ed., Harper & Row Publishers, Inc., 1977. Reprinted with permission.

John J. Conger, *Current Issues in Adolescent Development*, JSAS Document, American Psychological Association. Reprinted with permission of the American Psychological Association.

Sean G. Connolly, "Changing Expectancies: A Counseling Model Based on Locus of Control," *The Personnel and Guidance Journal*, November 1980. Reprinted with permission of the American Personnel and Guidance Association.

William J. Connolly, S.J., "Contemporary Spiritual Direction: Scope and Principles—An Introductory Essay," *Studies in the Spirituality of Jesuits*, June 1975. Reprinted with permission of the American Assistancy Seminar on Jesuit Spirituality.

William J. Connolly, S.J., "Exploring Relational Prayer," *Human Development*, Winter 1981. Reprinted with permission.

William J. Connolly, S.J., "Spiritual Direction: It Begins with Experience," *Human Development*, Spring 1980. Reprinted with permission.

Fredrick Coons, "The Developmental Tasks of the College Student," in *Adolescent Psychiatry Developmental and Clinical Studies*, vol. 1, edited by

Sherman C. Feinstein and Peter L. Giovacchini, Basic Books, Inc., 1971. Reprinted with permission.

William Cosgrave, "A Christian Understanding of Sexuality," *The Furrow*, Vol. 30, No. 6, June 1979. Reprinted with permission.

Ewert H. Cousins, "The Mature Christian Conscience," *Conscience Theological and Psychological Perspectives*, edited by C. Ellis Nelson. Newman Press, 1973. Reprinted with permission of Paulist Press.

George Croft, S.J., "Psychological Maturity in Christian Perspective," published in *Supplement to the Way*, No. 8, Nov. 1968. Reprinted with permission.

John Devolder et al., "Religious Values and Practice of the College Freshman," *Counseling and Values*, April 1979. Reprinted with permission of the American Personnel and Guidance Association.

James J. DiGiacomo, S.J., "Evangelizing the Young," *America*, October 13, 1979. Reprinted with permission of America Press, Inc., 106 West 56th St., New York, NY 10019. © 1979. All rights reserved.

James J. DiGiacomo, S.J., "Socialization for Secularization," *New Catholic World*, March/April, 1980. Reprinted with permission of Paulist Press.

James J. DiGiacomo, S. J. "Teaching the Next New Breed," *America*, June 27, 1981. Reprinted with permission of America Press, Inc., 106 West 56th Street, New York, NY 10019. © 1981. All rights reserved.

Documents of Vatican II, Abbott-Gallagher edition. Excerpts reprinted with permission of America Press, Inc., 106 West 56 Street, New York, NY 10019. © 1966. All rights reserved.

R. S. Downie et al., *Education and Personal Relationships: A Philosophical Study*, Methuen & Co., Ltd. 1974. Reprinted with permission.

Ronald Duska and Mariellen Whelan, *Moral Development: A Guide to Piaget and Kohlberg*, Paulist Press, 1975. Reprinted with permission.

David Elkind, "Child Development and Counseling," *The Personnel and Guidance Journal*, January 1980. Reprinted with permission of the American Personnel and Guidance Association.

Erik Erikson, *Identity, Youth, and Crisis*, W. W. Norton, 1968. Reprinted with permission.

Norman T. Feather, "Values in Adolescence," in *Handbook of Adolescent Psychology*, edited by Joseph Adelson. John Wiley & Sons, 1980. Reprinted with permission.

"Fewer Liberals, More Moderates among this Year's Freshman," *The Chronicle of Higher Education*, February 1981. Reprinted with permission.

David L. Fleming, S.J., "Models of Spiritual Direction," *Review for Religious*, May 1975. Reprinted with permission.

Forms of Intellectual and Ethical Development in the College Years: A Scheme, by William G. Perry, Jr. Copyright © 1968, 1970 by Holt, Rinehart and Winston, Inc. Reprinted with permission of Holt, Rinehart and Winston, CBS College Publishing.

James W. Fowler, "Faith Development Theory and the Aims of Religious

Socialization," in *Emerging Issues in Religious Education*, edited by Gloria Durka and Joanmarie Smith, Paulist Press, 1976. Reprinted with permission.

James W. Fowler and Sam Keen, *Life Maps: Conversations on the Journey of Faith*, Word Books, 1978. Reprinted with permission.

James W. Fowler, "Stages in Faith: The Structural-Developmental Approach," in *Values and Moral Development*, edited by Thomas Hennessey, S.J., Paulist Press, 1976. Reprinted with permission.

James W. Fowler, *Stages of Faith*, Harper & Row, Publishers, Inc., 1981. Reprinted with permission.

Matthew Fox, *On Becoming a Musical, Mystical Bear*, Paulist Press, 1976. Reprinted with permission.

Robert M. Friday, *Adults Making Responsible Moral Decisions*, 1979. Reprinted with permission of the United States Catholic Conference.

Victor Paul Furnish, *Theology and Ethics in Paul*, Abingdon Press, 1968. Adapted with permission.

Judith Gallatin, "Political Thinking in Adolescence," in *Handbook of Adolescent Psychology*, edited by Joseph Adelson, John Wiley & Sons, 1980. Reprinted with permission.

George Gallup, Jr. "The Family and Evangelization," *Catholic Mind*, October 1979. Reproduced with permission of George Gallup, Jr.

Donald L. Gelpi, S.J., *Experiencing God*, Paulist Press, 1978. Adapted with permission.

"General Instructions of the Liturgy of the Hours," excerpted with permission of the Confraternity of Christian Doctrine, Washington, DC. All rights reserved.

James J. Gill, S.J., "The Development of Persons," *Human Development*, Spring 1981. Reprinted with permission.

James J. Gill, S.J., "Indispensable Self-Esteem," *Human Development*, Fall 1980. Reprinted with permission.

Donald Goergen, *The Sexual Celibate*, The Seabury Press, 1974. Reprinted with permission.

Andrew M. Greeley, "A Post-Vatican II New Breed? A Report on Contemporary Catholic Teenagers," *America*, June 28, 1980. Reprinted with permission of America Press, Inc., 106 West 56th St., New York, NY 10019. © 1980. All rights reserved.

Thomas H. Groome, *Christian Religious Education: Sharing Our Story and Vision*, Harper & Row Publishers, Inc., 1980. Reprinted with permission.

Group for the Advancement of Psychiatry, *Normal Adolescence: Its Dynamics and Impact*. Copyright © 1968, Group for the Advancement of Psychiatry (New York: Charles Scribner's Sons, 1968).

Adolf Guggenbuhl-Craig, *Power in the Helping Professions*, Spring Publications, 1971. Reprinted with permission.

Jacqueline Haessly and Daniel DiDomizio, "Sexuality and Intimacy, in *Young Adult Living*, Paulist Press, 1980. Reprinted with permission.

Bernard Häring, *Medical Ethics*, Fides Publishing, 1973. Reprinted with permission.

Douglas H. Heath, "Educating for Maturity," *College and University Journal*, 1974. Reprinted with permission of the Council for Advancement and Support of Education.

Douglas H. Heath, *Explorations of Maturity*, Appleton-Century-Crofts, 1965. Reprinted with permission.

Douglas H. Heath, "Wanted: A Comprehensive Model of Healthy Development," *The Personnel and Guidance Journal*, January 1980. Reprinted with permission of the American Personnel and Guidance Association.

Martin L. Hoffman, "Development of Moral Thought, Feeling, and Behavior," *American Psychologist*, October 1979. Adapted with permission of the American Psychological Association.

Martin L. Hoffman, "Moral Development in Adolescence," *Handbook of Adolescent Psychology*, John Wiley & Sons, 1980. Reprinted with permission.

Dean R. Hoge, "Social Factors Influencing Youth Ministry in the 1980s," in *Hope for the Decade: A Look at the Issues Facing Catholic Youth Ministry*, United States Catholic Conference, 1980. Reprinted with permission.

Dean R. Hoge, "Students Not Returning to '50s' Values," *National Catholic News Service*. Reprinted with permission of the United States Catholic Conference.

The Individual and His Religion, by Gordon Allport. Copyright © 1950 by Macmillan Publishing Co., Inc., renewed 1978 by Robert B. Allport. Reprinted with permission.

Irish Episcopal Conference, *Conscience and Morality*, Irish Messenger Publications, 1980. Reprinted with permission.

Damien Isabell, O.F.M., *The Spiritual Director: A Practical Guide*, Fransciscan Herald Press, 1976. Reprinted with permission.

William Johnston, S.J., *The Inner Eye of Love: Mysticism and Religion*, Harper & Row Publishers, Inc., 1978. With permission.

Ruthellen Josselson, "Ego Development in Adolescence," in *Handbook of Adolescent Psychology*, edited by Joseph Adelson. John Wiley & Sons, Inc., 1980. Reprinted with permission.

Ruthellen Josselson et al., "Phenomenological Aspects of Psychosocial Maturity in Adolescence: Part 1, Boys," March 1977; and "Phenomenological Aspects of Psychosocial Maturity in Adolescence: Part 2, Girls," *Journal of Youth and Adolescence*, June 1977. Both adapted with permission of Plenum Publishing Corp.

Philip S. Keane, S.S. "The Objective Moral Order: Reflections on Recent Research," *Theological Studies*, June 1982. Reprinted with permission.

Phillip S. Keane, S.S., *Sexual Morality: A Catholic Perspective*, Paulist Press, 1977. Reprinted with permission.

Eugene W. Kelly, Jr. and Thomas J. Sweeney, "Typical Faulty Goals of Adolescents: A Base for Counseling," *The School Counselor*, March 1979. Reprinted with permission of the American Personnel and Guidance Association.

349

Eugene Kennedy, *Sexual Counseling*, The Seabury Press, 1977. Reprinted with permission of The Crossroad Publishing Co.

Eugene Kennedy, *What A Modern Catholic Believes About Sex*, The Thomas More Press, 1971. Reprinted with permission.

Robert Knopp, "Not Just Experiences—Relationship Experiences," *The Living Light*, Spring 1980. Reprinted with permission of William H. Sadlier, Inc.

Lawrence Kohlberg and Carol Gilligan, "The Adolescent as a Philosopher: The Discovery of Self in a Postconventional World," *Daedalus*, Journal of the American Academy of Arts and Sciences, 100, Fall 1971, Boston, MA. Reprinted with permission.

Lawrence Kohlberg and Elsa R. Wasserman, "The Cognitive-Developmental Approach and the Practicing Counselor: An Opportunity for Counselors to Rethink Their Roles," *The Personnel and Guidance Journal*, May 1980. Reprinted with permission of the American Personnel and Guidance Association.

Lawrence Kohlberg, "The Cognitive-Developmental Approach to Moral Education," *Phi Delta Kappan*, June 1975. Reprinted with permission.

Lawrence Kohlberg, "Education, Moral Development, and Faith," *The Journal of Moral Education*, October 1974. Reprinted with permission of the NFER-Nelson Publishing Co., Ltd.

Lawrence Kohlberg, "Moral Development," *International Encyclopedia of the Social Sciences*, David L. Sills, ed., Vol. 10, pp. 483-494. Copyright © 1968 by Crowell Collier & Macmillan, Inc. Adapted with permission.

Anthony Kosnik et al., *Human Sexuality: New Directions in American Catholic Thought*, Doubleday, 1979. Reprinted with permission.

William Kraft, "A Psychospiritual View of Masturbation," *Human Development*, Summer 1982. Reprinted with permission.

Jean LaPlace, S.J., *Preparing for Spiritual Direction*, Franciscan Herald Press, 1975. Reprinted with permission.

Thomas N. Lay, S.J., "Symbols to Grow On," *Journal of Religion and Health*, Fall 1980. Reprinted with permission.

Daniel J. Levinson et al., *The Seasons of a Man's Life*. Alfred A. Knopf, Inc., 1978. Reprinted with permission.

Richard Logan, "Identity Diffusion and Psycho-Social Defense Mechanisms," *Adolescence*, Fall 1978. Reprinted with permission of Libra Publishers, Inc.

Nicholas Lohkamp, O.F.M., "Communing with the Spirit," *Religion Teacher's Journal*, April 1980. Reprinted with permission of Twenty-Third Publications.

John Lynch, "Sacraments: Key to Evangelization," *America*, October 13, 1979. Reprinted with permission of American Press, Inc., 106 West 56th Street, New York, NY 10019 © 1979. All rights reserved.

James E. Marcia, "Development and Validation of Ego Identity Status," *Journal of Personality and Social Psychology*, May 1966. Reprinted with permission of the American Psychological Association.

James E. Marcia, "Identity in Adolescence," in *Handbook of Adolescent Psychology*, edited by Joseph Adelson. John Wiley & Sons, 1980. Reprinted with permission.

Richard McBrien, "Church," *Chicago Studies*, Fall 1975. Reprinted with permission.

Richard A McCormick, S.J., "Moral Thology Since Vatican II: Clarity or Chaos," *Cross Currents*, Spring 1979. Reprinted with permission.

Richard A. McCormick, S.J., "Personal Conscience," *Chicago Studies*, Fall 1974. Reprinted with permission.

Ann McCreary Juhasz and Mary Sonnenshein-Schneider, "Adolescent Sexual Decision Making: Components and Skills," *Adolescence*, Winter 1980. Reprinted with permission of Libra Publishers, Inc.

Ann McCreary Juhasz and Mary Sonnenshein-Schneider, "Responsibility and Control: The Basis of Sexual Decision Making," *The Personnel and Guidance Journal*, November 1979. Reprinted with permission of the American Personnel and Guidance Association.

Edwin J. McDermott, S.J., Book Review, *Human Development*, Winter 1981. Reprinted with permission.

Kenneth McGuire, C.S.P., "A Spirituality for Searching People," *New Catholic World*, September-October, 1979. Reprinted with permission of Paulist Press.

Megan McKenna and Bernarda Sharkey, "The Adolescent and the Sacrament of Reconciliation," *The Rite of Penance Commentaries: Implementing the Rite*, II. © The Liturgical Conference, 810 Rhode Island Avenue, N.E., Washington, DC 20018. All rights reserved. Used with permission.

Bruno Manno, "Distancing One's Self Religiously," *New Catholic World*, Sept/Oct. 1979. Reprinted with permission of Paulist Press.

John J. Mitchell, "Adolescent Hypocrisy," *Adolescence*, Fall 1980. Reprinted with permission of Plenum Publishing Corp.

John J. Mitchell, "Adolescent Intimacy," *Adolescence*, Summer 1976. Reprinted with permission of Libra Publishers, Inc.

John J. Mitchell, "Some Psychological Dimensions of Adolescent Sexuality," *Adolescence*, Winter 1972. Reprinted with permission of Libra Publishers, Inc.

John M. Murphy and Carol Gilligan, "Moral Development in Late Adolescence and Adulthood: A Critique and Reconstruction of Kohlberg's Theory," *Human Development*, no. 2, 1980. Adapted with permission of S. Karger, AG Basel.

Howard Muson, "Moral Thinking: Can It Be Taught?" *Psychology Today*, February 1979. Adapted with permission of Ziff Davis Publishing Co.

Maturing in Christ by George T. Montague, S.M. Copyright © 1964 by Macmillan Publishing Co., Inc. Adapted with permission.

Rolf E. Muuss, *Theories of Adolescence*, Random House, 1975. Reprinted with permission.

Henri Nouwen, "The Faces of Community," *The Catholic Worker*, March-April, 1978. Reprinted with permission.

Robert Ochs, S.J., *God Is More Present Than You Think*, Paulist Press, 1970. Reprinted with permission.

Laurence J. O'Connell, "God's Call to Humankind: Towards a Theology of Vocation," *Chicago Studies*, Summer 1979. Reprinted with permission.

Timothy E. O'Connell, based on *Principles for a Catholic Morality*, The Seabury Press, 1978. Reprinted with permission of the Seabury Press.

Eamonn O'Doherty, *The Religious Formation of the Adolescent*, Alba House, 1973. Reprinted with permission.

Daniel Offer and Melvin Sabshin, *Normality*, Basic Books, Inc., 1974. Reprinted with permission.

Max Oliva, S.J., "An Apostolic Spirituality for the Ministry of Social Justice," *Review for Religious*, September 1977. Adapted with permission.

Patrick O'Neill, "Ministry with Single Young Adults," *New Catholic World*, September-October 1979. Reprinted with permission of Paulist Press.

Eric Ostrov and Daniel Offer, "Loneliness and the Adolescent," in *Adolescent Psychiatry: Developmental and Clinical Studies*, Vol. 6, edited by Sherman C. Feinstein and Peter L. Giovacchini. Reprinted with permission of The University of Chicago Press. © 1978.

Excerpted from *Out of Solitude* by Henri J. M. Nouwen. Copyright © 1974 by Ave Maria Press, Notre Dame, IN 46556. Used with permission of publisher.

Gordon W. Allport, *Pattern and Growth in Personality*, copyright 1937, © 1961 by Holt, Rhinehart and Winston, Inc. and renewed © 1965 by Gordon W. Allport. Reprinted with permission of Holt, Rhinehart and Winston, CBS College Publishing.

John J. Phillips, *The Origins of Intellect: Piaget's Theory*, W. H. Freeman, 1975. Adapted with permission.

Jean Piaget and Barbel Inhelder, *The Growth of Logical Thinking from Childhood to Adolescence*, Basic Books, Inc., 1958. Reprinted with permission.

Jean Piaget, *The Origins of Intelligence in Children*, W. W. Norton & Co., 1963. Adapted with permission.

Jean Piaget, *Six Psychological Studies*, translated by David Elkind and Anita Tenzer, Random House, 1968. Reprinted with permission.

Michael D. Place, "Philosophical Foundations for Value Transmission: Part 1," *Chicago Studies*, Fall 1980. Reprinted with permission.

Joseph Powers, S.J., "Faith, Mortality, Creativity: Toward the Art of Believing," *Theological Studies*, December 1978. Reprinted with permission.

Dennis Raphael and Helga G. Xelowski, "Identity Status in High School Students: Critique and a Revised Paradigm," *Journal of Youth and Adolescence*, October 1980. Reprinted with permission of Plenum Publishing Corp.

Dick Reichert, "The Adolescent and Premarital Sex: Moral Pastoral Considerations," *Catholic Charismatic*, June/July, 1981. Reprinted with permission of Paulist Press.

Carl Rogers, adapted from *On Becoming A Person,* © 1961 by Houghton Mifflin Company. Reprinted with permission.

Milton Rokeach and John F. Regan, "The Role of Values in the Counseling Situation," *The Personnel and Guidance Journal,* May 1980. Reprinted with permission of the American Personnel and Guidance Association.

Louis M. Savary, S.J. "The Thanksgiving Examen," *Review for Religious,* March 1980. Reprinted with permission.

J. Peter Schineller, S.J., "The New Approaches to Christology and Their Use in the Spiritual Exercises," *Studies in the Spirituality of Jesuits,* September-November, 1980. Reprinted with permission of the American Assistancy Seminar on Jesuit Spirituality.

Robert L. Schmitt, S.J., "The Christ-Experiences and Relationship Fostered in the Spiritual Exercises of St. Ignatius of Loyola," *Studies in the Spirituality of Jesuits,* October 1974. Reprinted with permission of the American Assistancy Seminar on Jesuit Spirituality.

Rudolf Schnackenburg, "Christian Adulthood According to the Apostle Paul," *Catholic Biblical Quarterly,* July 1963. Adapted with permission.

Scripture texts used in this work are taken from the *New American Bible.* Copyright © 1970, by the Confraternity of Christian Doctrine, Washington, DC, and are used by permission of copyright owner. All rights reserved.

Robert L. Selman and Ellen Ward Cooney, "Children's Use of Social Conceptions: Towards a Dynamic Model of Social Cognition," *The Personnel and Guidance Journal,* January 1980. Reprinted with permission of the American Personnel and Guidance Association.

Robert L. Selman, "The Development of Socio-Cognitive Understandings: A Guide to Educational and Clinical Practice," in *Moral Development and Behavior: Theory, Research, and Social Issue,* edited by Thomas Lickona. Copyright © 1976 by Holt, Rinehart and Winston. Reprinted with permission of Holt, Rinehart and Winston, CBS College Publishing.

Robert L. Selman, *The Growth of Interpersonal Understanding,* Academic Press, 1980. Adapted with permission.

Excerpts from *Sharing the Light of Faith: The National Catechetical Directory for Catholics of the United States.* Copyright © 1979, by the United States Catholic Conference, Department of Education, Washington, DC, are used by permission of copyright owner. All rights reserved.

John Shea, *Stories of God,* © The Thomas More Press, 1978. Reprinted with permission.

Charles M. Shelton, S.J., "Some Techniques for Self-Exploration," *The School Counselor,* January 1979. Reprinted with permission of the American Personnel and Guidance Association.

Milton F. Shore, "Youth and Jobs: Educational, Occupational, and Mental Health Aspects," *Journal of Youth and Adolescence,* December 1972. Reprinted with permission of Plenum Publishing Corp.

The author wishes to thank the following editors for their permission to expand and adapt previously published articles for incorporation into this book.

Charles M. Shelton, S.J., "Spirituality and College Youth," *Process*, III, Winter 1977, pp. 22–24.

Charles M. Shelton, S.J., "Psychological Dynamics in Adolescent Spiritual Direction," *Pastoral Life*, XXVIII, April 1979, pp. 27–32.

Charles M. Shelton, S.J., "The Adolescent, Social Justice, and the Catholic School: A Psychological Perspective," *The Living Light*, 17, Fall 1980, pp. 223–233.

Also, to Rev. George Ganss, S.J. for permission to quote freely from

David L. Fleming, S.J., *The Spiritual Exercises: A Literal Translation and a Contemporary Reading*, The Institute of Jesuit Sources, St. Louis, 1978.

Index